Contributors

Dr Sally Bell MB, BS, FRACP, MD
Consultant Gastroenterologist, St Vincent's Hospital, Melbourne, Australia

Mr Gordon Buchanan MSc, FRCS
Surgical Research Fellow, St Mark's Hospital, North West London Hospitals NHS Trust

Mr Mark Cheetham MB, BS, BSc, FRCS
Specialist Registrar in General Surgery, North West Thames

Ms Sonya Chelvanayagam MSc, RN, RMN
Senior Lecturer in Mental Health Nursing, University of Hertfordshire

Dr Graham Clayden MD, FRCP, FRCPCH
Reader in Paediatrics at the Guy's, King's & St Thomas' School of Medicine, King's College, London
Honorary Consultant Paediatrician, Guy's & St Thomas' Hospital NHS Trust, London

Mr C. Richard G. Cohen MD, FRCS
Consultant Surgeon, St Mark's Hospital, North West London Hospitals NHS Trust

Dr Anton Emmanuel BSc, MD, MRCP
Senior Lecturer and Honorary Consultant Gastroenterologist, St Mark's Hospital, North West London Hospitals NHS Trust

Dr Danielle Harari FRCP
Senior Lecturer and Consultant in Geriatric Medicine, St Thomas' Hospital, King's College, London

Ms Gillian Hollins RGN
Paediatric Bowel Motility Nurse, Guy's & St Thomas' Hospital NHS Trust, London

Ms Nicky Horton RGN
Nurse Practitioner in Polyposis, St Mark's Hospital, North West London Hospitals NHS Trust

Mr Nicholas J. Kenefick MA, MB, BChir, MRCS
Specialist Registrar in Coloproctology, South West Deanery
Formerly Research Fellow, St Mark's Hospital, North West London Hospitals NHS Trust

Mr Andrew Malouf FRACS
Colorectal Surgeon, Illawarra Area Health Service, NSW, Australia

Dr Tanya Nicholls BSc, PhD
Senior Clinical Scientist, St Mark's Hospital, North West London Hospitals Trust

Prof Christine Norton PhD, MA, RN
Nurse Consultant (Bowel Control), St Mark's Hospital, North West London Hospitals NHS Trust
Honorary Professor of Nursing, Florence Nightingale School of Nursing, King's College, London

Ms Linda Smith MA, MSc
Consultant Clinical Psychologist, Northgate & Prudhoe NHS Trust

Dr Paul Smith MA, MSc, PhD
Consultant Clinical Psychologist, County Durham & Darlington Priority Services NHS Trust
Honorary Lecturer in Clinical Psychology, University of Newcastle

Ms Maggie Vance, MSc, RGN
Nurse Consultant (Gastroenterology), Endoscopy Unit, St Mark's Hospital, North West London Hospitals NHS Trust

Ms Helen White RGN, RHV
Former Director, PromoCon, Manchester

Dr Paul Wiesel MD
FMH Specialist in Gastroenterology, University Hospital – CHUV Lausanne

Mr Andrew Williams MSc, FRCS
Consultant Colorectal and General Surgeon, Guy's & St Thomas' Hospital NHS Trust, London

Ms Julia Williams MSc, RGN
Lecturer in Colorectal Nursing, City University, London

Ms Solveig Wilson CSS
Medical Social Worker / Counsellor, St Mark's Hospital, North West London Hospitals NHS Trust

Bowel Continence Nursing

Editors

Christine Norton
PhD, MA, RN

Nurse Consultant (Bowel Control), St Mark's Hospital
North West London Hospitals NHS Trust
Honorary Professor of Nursing, Florence Nightingale School of Nursing
King's College, London

Sonya Chelvanayagam
MSc, RN, RMN

Senior Lecturer in Mental Health Nursing
University of Hertfordshire

BEACONSFIELD PUBLISHERS LTD
Beaconsfield, Bucks, UK

First published in 2004

Email: books@beaconsfield-publishers.co.uk
Website: www.beaconsfield-publishers.co.uk

British Library Cataloguing in Publication Data
Bowel continence nursing
1. Fecal incontinence – Nursing 2. Intestines – Diseases – Nursing
I. Norton, C. S. II. Chelvanayagam, S.

ISBN 0-906584-52-3

Illustrations and cover design by Nigel Webb, DipAD, SCD, MIMI, RMIP
Typeset by Gem Graphics, Trenance, Cornwall in 9.5 on 12 point Times
Printed and bound in Great Britain at The Alden Press, Oxford

Preface

Patients with a bowel disorder frequently report difficulty in expressing their symptoms, and as a result can feel that they are not being fully understood by the professionals who are responsible for their treatment. When we first ran a module at St Mark's Hospital on 'Bowel Continence Nursing', in conjunction with City University, we were unable to find any existing teaching material that met our needs or answered all of our students' questions. In conjunction with our fellow contributors we have therefore written this book for nurses and other health care professionals who encounter patients with faecal incontinence.

Much has now been written about urinary incontinence – far less about faecal incontinence. It was hard to find an evidence base from which to teach and on which to plan care, and the little evidence that was available was spread over a wide variety of sources and not easily accessible. Working mostly with the lecturers from our course, with a few invited guests, we have attempted to put together a body of knowledge in a practical format. Much work remains to be done, and in many areas there has been little or no research to date. However, we have been heartened to find just how much is already known about this often-neglected subject.

Our thanks are due to the many people who have helped us. These include colleagues at St Mark's Hospital and those who have attended the bowel continence module over the past few years. Our contributing authors have provided us with excellent reviews of their subjects. We are grateful to Dr Mikel Gray and Marlene Powell for advice at the initial planning stage and to Dr Anton Emmanuel, Mandy Fader, Sue Ryder and Liz Symons, each of whom worked through the detail of a late draft, and whose comprehensive comments we were very pleased to be able to take into account when preparing the final version for publication. Professor Michael Kamm has been a very supportive head of department, and Dr Anton Emmanuel has been very helpful throughout in providing clarification on much of the investigative and medical management of bowel disorders. John Churchill of Beaconsfield Publishers guided us through the process with meticulous attention to detail and wonderful support for a topic that many publishers would avoid. We would also like to express our appreciation to Nigel Webb, a creative illustrator who much improved on our original ideas.

We would like to thank our families for their unending support and encouragement: Charlotte and Luke Norton, Gavey Chelvanayagam, and Michael and Catharina Josephina Wood. Finally, we must thank our patients who encouraged and inspired us to take our ideas forward in the hope of reducing the stigma of faecal incontinence. We are of course responsible for any faults in the final product.

Christine Norton and Sonya Chelvanayagam

Contents

Chapter 1

The Development of Bowel Control

Christine Norton

Normal bowel control

The bowel and its contents remain a taboo topic in western societies. Most people acquire bowel control in the second to third year of life, by a combination of physical maturation and social conditioning, learning that there are 'right' and 'wrong' places for defaecation and that to pass faeces in the wrong place is considered unacceptable. By adulthood the whole process has usually become a subconscious, although still largely voluntary, function. Defaecation is a private and seldom-mentioned bodily function, which people prefer to take for granted and seldom consider. It forms part of the background working of the 'absent' body (Leder, 1990), unless it fails to function as expected. Adults who are unable to control their bowel function are faced with coping not only with physical symptoms, but also with the threat of embarrassment, shame and stigma should others become aware of the problem.

Bowel control is a complex, and as yet poorly understood, skill and most adults have great difficulty in describing what they actually do to defer the urge to defaecate until a socially convenient time and place is reached. Most people learn bowel control at an age too young to remember in adult life. Few adults have a memory for events which occurred before they were four years old. The body tends to disappear from consciousness when it is functioning normally, and many complex voluntary skills, once learned and truly 'incorporated', become inaccessible to, indeed interrupted by, conscious effort (Leder, 1990). Bowel control is one of many bodily functions which, while not reflex processes, are difficult for the individual to describe; one knows 'how' to do it, but cannot necessarily access the individual components of the activity. When a habit is acquired the body harmoniously 'understands' what needs to be done, without conscious effort (Merleau-Ponty, 1962).

However, bowel control is not just a physiological skill. Learning bowel control is one of the first socialisations in childhood. We are taught that passing stool into our underwear is naughty and socially unacceptable. Later, we learn to control flatus or to say 'pardon' (Salter, 1997). Those who lose this control suffer a loss of former identity and with it the ability to see themselves as a competent / continent adult.

Psychoanalytic theorists from Freud onwards have suggested that part of a child's development of a sense of self and the boundaries between 'me' and 'not me' involves learning that faeces are not-self. Psychoanalysts have developed complex theories about our childhood relationship with defaecation. For Freud, control of defaecation was an important part of ego development, and 'anal retentive' has passed into common parlance for a person who seems overly self-controlled and obsessive (Freud, 1908; Heimann, 1962).

The child must recognise that it is not threatening to have this apparent part of oneself leave the body and be lost forever down the toilet (Weiss, 1999). Attitudes to defaecation are inherently ambivalent. Our initial sensations are of pleasure and relief associated with elimination and are thought to be experienced as a gift to the mother figure, often producing maternal praise in the early phases of toilet training. The diarist Samuel Johnson is quoted as saying 'Much has been written about the pleasures of sexual intercourse; as for me, give me a solid movement of the bowel' (quoted in Knapp,

1967). This pleasure must be re-interpreted as guilt and disgust once the social connotations of bodily products are assimilated (Knapp, 1967). Elimination is often used as an expression of hostility or aggression, both verbally and physically.

There have been few detailed studies on how it feels to lose bowel control, although intuitively it would seem to be a nightmare scenario. Werner-Beland gives a personal account of her experience as a nurse who became paraplegic: 'Do you know what it feels like to lose control over one of the first functions over which one gains mastery in life? … The very act of messing the sheets because of involuntary bowel activity, or, its reverse of having to have one enema after another to be rid of the stuff was almost more than I could cope with. Nurses would say things like, 'I don't know why you are so upset. It's just an enema.' I wanted to scream: I have crapped on my own for 36 years! You just don't understand! I am dead!' (Werner-Beland, 1980, p. 11). People with ulcerative colitis have been described as choosing major surgery (formation of an ileoanal pouch, which often involves three major abdominal procedures) because of a desire for control of bodily functions and freedom from urgency and the risk of faecal incontinence (Beitz, 1999).

Civilisation has developed patterns of beliefs, norms and values related to body products. 'As far as one can tell there are no human societies where the act of excretion and its products are not subject to public and private arrangements, to expectations involving time and space, regularity and appropriateness' (Loudon, 1977, p. 168). Throughout time, human dwellings have had demarcations for excretion. Maybe the smell of faeces has been an important consideration in this. It seems that in Europe from about the 16th century defaecation gradually became privatised (Elias, 1978). 'Manners' gradually work their way downwards in a society, often starting as the upper classes attempt to differentiate themselves by behaviour from the masses, but gradually generalising until almost all members of a society accept the rules and take them for granted. This is true for table manners as well as dealing with excreta (spitting, nose-blowing, urination and defaecation). Erasmus advised young noblemen 'It is impolite to greet someone who is urinating or defaecating … If it is possible to withdraw (to pass wind), it should be done alone. But if not … let a cough hide the sound … be careful not to fart explosively in the holy place … press your buttocks together … replace farts with coughs …' But this was not universally recommended – 'Fools who value civility more than health repress natural sounds.' (quoted in Elias, 1978, p. 130).

This frank discussion gradually disappeared from discussions on etiquette, and shame crept in. From a time when you could hold up a stool found in the street for your companion to comment on the smell (Elias, 1978, p. 131), there came a time when even the words for bodily functions caused embarrassment and shame. From then on these natural body functions became subject to modesty. These attitudes were strengthened when the link between excreta and disease was later demonstrated by Chadwick in the Victorian era and defaecation was subject to a precisely regulated social ritual (Ross et al., 1968). All natural functions were eventually removed from the sight of other people, including excretion, blowing the nose and sex. This could only happen because engineering kept pace with manners, Victorian plumbing making it possible to defaecate in private.

By the 20th century taboos were so far consolidated that they were taken for granted, and taught by the family to all children, who learn and internalise in the space of a few years customs and manners that have taken centuries to evolve. 'Civilisation' implies, in its modern usage, the privatisation of bodily functions and excreta (Ross et al., 1968) and has become synonymous with the adoption of certain manners. Culture has rendered the body private and unspeakable, invisible (Lawler, 1997a, p. 32). Sociogenic shame and embarrassment about bowel function inevitably has a major impact on those who cannot comply with society's rules. People with faecal incontinence must cope not only with the health and self-care aspects of their symptom, but also with its effects on their own self image and the potential attitudes of others in society, should they become aware of the problem.

Each culture has its own notions of dirt and defilement (Douglas, 1966). All societies have demarcated rules for defaecation (Loudon, 1977). Rituals of purity are central to many religions, and dirt is relative. For example, menstrual blood is seen as innocuous or lethal, depending on cultural beliefs. Excreta may be seen as either dangerous, or as a joke. In many cultures the rituals are shared between religion, aesthetics and hygiene, but not all societies have developed identical rules (Douglas, 1966). Members of each society exhort each other to uphold their common moral code. Today we rationalise our dirt rituals by arguments about hygiene and disease, but they are all arbitrary. We thought faeces dirty long before we knew about micro-organisms and infection. Different cultures have different traditions and arbitrary rules as to what is considered polite or acceptable behaviour. For example, in China no sign of bodily functions should be displayed in front of parents; filial respect precludes a sneeze, cough, belch or yawn (Goffman, 1959, p. 61). In our society, passing flatus is considered 'rude' under most circumstances, but hiccups are not. In India, those from the lowest class and 'untouchable' clean the toilets. In many Muslim societies menstruating women are ritually excluded from religious activity, and lactating women must observe certain rules in some cultures. The need for ritual cleansing before Islamic prayer five times per day can make life very difficult for people with incontinence or a stoma.

Goffman has defined 'an individual who is disqualified from full social acceptance' as experiencing a stigma (Goffman, 1963). If there is something unusual or bad about the body, a deeply discrediting attribute incongruous with our stereotype of what that individual should be, this has implications for the moral status of the individual within society. An individual is capable of being discredited (i.e. is 'discreditable') if others don't know but could potentially find out.

'Civilisation' has become partly defined by control, regulation, lack of dirt and smells and limitations on nature. While earlier generations could not avoid the inevitable stench consequent upon urbanisation proceeding faster than the engineering capability to cope with excreta, Western societies today place a high value on cleanliness and odour-free hygiene, which is associated with virtue and dignity. Our society is bombarded with messages about cleanliness and the necessity of hiding undesirable odours. Western society has negative attitudes to those who smell: 'When I smelled an odour on the bus or subway before the colostomy I used to feel very annoyed. I'd think that people were awful, that they didn't take a bath or that they should have gone to the bathroom before travelling ... to me it seemed they were filthy, dirty. I used to change my seat. ... I believe that young people feel the same way about me if I smell.' (a person with a colostomy quoted in Goffman, 1963, p. 48). Hopefully, stomas are now better managed, but the stigma remains.

Early in life an infant learns that excretion is one of the ways in which he can exert some influence over other people. Once sphincter control is learned, withholding faeces is a potentially powerful weapon which can be used to inflict pain on those closest to him (Loudon, 1977, p. 161). 'A strong case can be made for them (faeces) as playing a much more important part than is generally granted in human social interaction' (Loudon, 1977, p. 162). Faeces may be seen as the prototype of impurity, and the genital region as the frontier *par excellence* of the self: what comes out of the urethra and anus both is, and is not, part of the self. Virtually all bowel metaphors are negative.

The lower, more 'animal' centres are linked with the sense of smell. Certain smells may be a warning sign of danger to animals. Nausea, if not actual retching, may be the reaction to disgust in humans. This may be a biochemical or socio-psychological reaction. Certainly man can learn to repress this disgust at excreta, as evidenced by workers in certain professions (e.g. sewerage workers and nurses). It may be that this is context-specific, with arbitrary features of the situation determining our response. We can mostly cope with the stools of infants, and those we expect to cope with in the course of our jobs, but the same person can still be disgusted at faeces out of these contexts.

Turner has proposed a differentiation in perception between a biologically determined disease (to which no social blame can attach) and illness which is atypical social functioning (Turner, 1984). Illness communicates something about a person, it has social connotations (Sontag, 1977). The sick are often self-stigmatised, sickness devalues the individual and produces an alienation from self and the environment. Once we internalise negative labels, we are stigmatised, and lack a positive self-image. Faecal incontinence is one of the most stigmatising health problems in the context of a modern Western society and its attitudes.

Nursing and bowel care

Bowel care is one of the 'basics' of nursing care. However, there is a very limited research knowledge base from which to plan effective nursing interventions. Even prominent nursing texts which devote a whole chapter to elimination, give no guidance as to nursing care for someone with faecal incontinence other than the practicalities of changing the incontinent person (Roper et al., 1996, p. 218). While these authors encourage a positive attitude ('...faecal incontinence should be seen as a preventable and curable problem. It must not be accepted as inevitable'), they offer no clues as to how this might be done.

'Basic' nursing care has come to have a low status in a technological era, and this, together with an ambivalence to body care (Lawler, 1991, p. 32), has often meant that bowel care is the preserve of the most junior nurses. Clearing up incontinence has always been seen as an inevitable part of nursing that few nurses question. Many assume that common sense alone will suffice to cope (Reid, 1974). Because of society's taboos on excreta it is almost inevitable that many will feel repulsion when dealing with faeces; but as nurses they are expected to repress these feelings and it has been suggested that some nurses may derive satisfaction from the care involved in transforming a soiled patient into a sanitary condition (Reid, 1974).

Perhaps the fact that nurses must break society's rules and become involved with the excreta of others, has meant that nurses in turn have developed their own rituals to detach themselves from their emotions on the subject, such that they can deal with incontinence without having to think about it too much. This has been labelled 'mutual pretence' in relation to urinary incontinence, with both nurses and patients reluctant to initiate a discussion about the topic (Schwartz, 1977). Care for incontinence is seen as a job to be hurried and finished so as to get on to the more pleasant aspects of nursing. Both nurse and patient see the other as unconcerned by incontinence (Schwartz, 1977). It may be that dealing with bowels in a highly ritualised, routine manner may help to manage the nurse's own distaste and embarrassment, but this will militate against individualised patient-centred care and exploring the issue in any depth.

Because some aspects of bodily care are normally considered private and unspeakable (Lawler, 1991) it has often been difficult to articulate nursing's knowledge about the body and how to care for it, with both a lack of vocabulary and a failure to describe processes which are so fundamental to basic nursing. Faecal incontinence is a topic that is likely to make many people (both nurses and their patients) feel uncomfortable, and so it is often easier for the problem to be ignored or managed symptomatically rather than confronted and tackled. Nurses find faeces (and sputum) difficult, but are not allowed professionally to display any discomfort (Lawler, 1991, pp. 173–4).

Nurses have a special relationship with the bodies of their patients. We are allowed, indeed expected, to know things and to do things to the bodies of others that are normally considered taboo in our society. This 'dirty work' (Lawler, 1991) tends to make others feel socially uncomfortable. The body has been 'privatised' in our social life (Lawler, 1991, p. 22). Nurses have privileged access to the bodies of others and can discuss matters normally hidden because of taboos. The body and its functions are a fundamental determinant of how we organise and live our social lives. Given that faecal incontinence is a physical and social malfunction, involving the body as a social as well as a biological entity, nursing is ideally placed to assist patients with this problem.

Nurse specialists and continence care

Specialist continence nurses first emerged in the UK over twenty years ago (Norton, 1984; Roe, 1993; Rhodes and Parker, 1995). Since then, a body of nursing knowledge has been developed and evaluated (Norton, 1996). The Department of Health has given strong support to nursing leadership of continence services in the UK (Department of Health, 2000). It has been found in a controlled trial that specialist nursing intervention for urinary incontinence in primary care cures or improves symptoms in over two-thirds of patients (O'Brien et al., 1991), and that this benefit is largely maintained in the long term (O'Brien and Long, 1995). Even a small reduction in symptoms of urinary incontinence in response to nursing interventions has been shown to have a significant impact on a patient's quality of life, activities, feelings and relationships (Williams et al., 2000).

Shaw and colleagues, in qualitative interviews with recipients of specialist nursing continence advice, have found that the main themes that emerged were the interpersonal and technical skills of the nurse, which together led to effective treatment (Shaw et al., 2000). An informal friendly approach by nurses with good communication skills relieved patients' embarrassment and anxiety, giving them confidence and trust in the nurse, thus facilitating information exchange and the effectiveness of care. Communication was not too technical, but not patronising. A friendly rapport was felt to promote compliance, without which treatments cannot be effective. Appendix I, page 276, shows Shaw et al.'s conceptualisation of the effects of interpersonal, technical and communication skills of the nurse on the effectiveness of continence treatment. This model would seem to be equally applicable to other areas of nursing.

Although nurses have often taken a lead on continence care, faecal incontinence has remained a largely neglected component of this. Even amongst the emerging specialist knowledge of Continence Advisers, faecal incontinence is a 'Cinderella' area, with most courses and texts devoting limited space to the topic (for example, one chapter of sixteen in one textbook on continence care: Norton, 1996). Many continence services developed from a urology or gynaecology base and focus almost exclusively on bladder care. Other nurses from the colorectal or gastroenterology field have not filled the gap, and in general other health professionals often take little interest in faecal incontinence, so at present there is often no health professional taking a special interest in faecal incontinence within a geographical area.

Definitions of faecal incontinence

Faecal incontinence has been variously defined. The Royal College of Physicians has proposed 'the involuntary or inappropriate passage of faeces' (Royal College of Physicians, 1995). An international panel of experts has defined 'functional faecal incontinence' as 'recurrent uncontrolled passage of faecal material for at least one month, in an individual with a developmental age of at least four years …' (Whitehead et al., 1999, p. 1155). Some authors also include the inability to control the passage of flatus, or an arbitrary frequency with which symptoms must occur, to be included. The term 'anal incontinence' is usually used to denote any involuntary leakage, whether of solid, liquid or gas. For the purposes of this discussion the definition developed by the World Health Organisation Consultation on Incontinence will be adopted: 'Anal incontinence is the involuntary loss of flatus, liquid or solid stool that is a social or hygienic problem' (Norton et al., 2001). This definition takes cognisance of the fact that people react very differently to the same objective situation. For example, loss of flatus which is hardly noticed by one person is experienced as socially incapacitating by another.

The need for research

Until the natural history of the symptom of faecal incontinence has been defined in longitudinal studies, it will be difficult to judge the outcome of any intervention for this problem. It may be necessary to go one stage further back to find out what really bothers people with faecal incontinence and what they consider as a successful, or at least an acceptable, outcome from treatment. Until there are standardised and widely-accepted definitions and internationally validated patient-based outcome measures, it will remain difficult to judge whether any intervention is useful and impossible to compare outcomes between studies.

There is a pitifully small literature on bowel care for older and disabled people. Comparison of different treatment modalities for faecal incontinence in similar patient populations has very rarely been undertaken.

Nursing and research on the effectiveness of nursing does not always fit well with the 'medical' model. Some nurses have suggested that science is not able to explain all of nursing and its effects (Taylor, 1994). The nursing process has had a tendency to reduce the patient to a set of problems to be solved with defined interventions. With increasing sophistication in nursing research methodology, more exploratory work is both feasible and needed on the complexities of the whole content and context of care, rather than concentrating on single 'interventions'.

To build up a body of expert experiential knowledge, nurses must systematically record what they learn from their own experience in order to pass this on (Benner, 1984, p. 11). Nurses need to practise nursing and reflect on it to progress knowledge. The positivistic methods of biomedical sciences are relatively helpful for answering some questions in nursing, but it is not possible to completely 'objectify' a science of caring. Much of what we know comes from being a nurse and doing nursing (Lawler, 1997a, p. 32). Nursing cannot be reduced to a series of defined interventions, it is more than just the sum of what is done: sometimes the best thing is to do nothing, to watch and wait for the patient to find their own way (Lawler, 1997a, p. 47). If care is the essence of nursing (Taylor, 1994) it may be the nature of the therapeutic relationship (Peplau, 1988) that is the most important. An in-depth qualitative study of patients' perspectives on outcomes and what is felt to change is needed to explore this.

More generally, there is a need for much more work on nursing patients with bowel problems. We need more knowledge on health-seeking behaviours, on the refinement of assessment techniques to aid selection of the most appropriate treatment, and on the effectiveness of the full range of therapeutic options. There is also a need to develop, describe and then evaluate completely new modalities of care.

References

Beitz, J.M. (1999) The lived experience of having an ileoanal reservoir: a phenomenologic study. *Journal of Wound, Ostomy and Continence Nursing* **26**, 185–200.

Benner, P. (1984) *From novice to expert: uncovering the knowledge embedded in clinical practice.* California: Addison-Wesley.

Department of Health (2000) *Good practice in continence services.* PL/CMO/2000/2. London: NHS Executive.

Douglas, M. (1966) *Purity and danger: an analysis of concepts of pollution and taboo.* London: Routledge & Kegan Paul.

Elias, N. (1978) *The history of manners: the civilizing process.* New York: Pantheon Books.

Freud, S. (1908) Character and anal eroticism. *Collected Papers, Hogarth, London* **9**, 172.

Goffman, E. (1959) *The presentation of self in everyday life.* New York: Penguin Books.

Goffman, E. (1963) *Stigma: notes on the management of spoiled identity.* Englewood Cliffs: Prentice-Hall.

Heimann, P. (1962) Notes on the anal stage. *International Journal of Psychoanalysis* **43**, 406–414.

Johanson, J.F. and Lafferty, J. (1996) Epidemiology

of fecal incontinence: the silent affliction. *American Journal of Gastroenterology.* **91**, 33–36.

Knapp, P.H. (1967) Some riddles of riddance. *Archives of General Psychiatry* **16**, 586–602.

Lawler, J. (1991) *Behind the screens: nursing, somology and the problem of the body*. Melbourne: Churchill Livingstone.

Lawler, J. (1997a) Knowing the body and embodiment: methodologies, discourses and nursing. In: Lawler, J. (ed.) *The body in nursing*. pp. 31–51. Melbourne: Churchill Livingstone.

Lawler, J. (1997b) *The body in nursing*. Melbourne: Churchill Livingstone.

Leder, D. (1990) *The absent body.* Chicago: University of Chicago Press.

Leigh, R.J. and Turnberg, L.A. (1982) Faecal incontinence: the unvoiced symptom. *Lancet* **1**, 1349–1351.

Loudon, J.B. (1977) On body products. In: Blacking, J. (ed.) *The anthropology of the body*, pp. 161–178. London: Academic Press.

Merleau-Ponty, M. (1962) *Phenomenology of perception.* New York: Routledge & Kegan-Paul.

Norton, C. (1984) Challenging specialty. *Nursing Mirror* **159**, xiv–xvii.

Norton, C. (1996) *Nursing for continence* (2nd edn) Beaconsfield: Beaconsfield Publishers.

Norton, C. and Kamm, M.A. (1999) *Bowel control – information and practical advice.* Beaconsfield: Beaconsfield Publishers.

Norton, C., Christiansen, J., Butler, U., Harari, D., Nelson, R., Pemberton, J.H., Rovner, E.S. and Sultan, A.H. (2002) Anal incontinence. In: Abrams, P., Khoury, S.E. and Cardozo, L. (eds) *Incontinence.* Plymouth: Health Books.

O'Brien, J. and Long, H. (1995) Urinary incontinence: long term effectiveness of nursing intervention in primary care. *British Medical Journal* **311**, 1208.

O'Brien, J., Austin, M. and Sethi, P. (1991) Urinary incontinence: prevalence, need for treatment and effectiveness of intervention by a nurse. *British Medical Journal* **303**, 1308–1312.

Peplau, H.E. (1988) *Interpersonal relations in nursing.* London: Macmillan.

Reid, E. (1974) Incontinence and nursing practice: an investigation of the nursing management of soiling in non-bedfast patients. Unpublished MPhil thesis: University of Edinburgh.

Rhodes, P. and Parker, G. (1995) The role of the continence adviser in England and Wales. *International Journal of Nursing Studies* **32**, 423–433.

Roe, B. (1993) Promoting continence in Denmark and UK. *Nursing Standard* **7**, 28–30.

Roper, N., Logan, W.W. and Tierney, A.J. (1996) *The elements of nursing* (4th edn). Edinburgh: Churchill Livingstone.

Ross, W.D., Hirt, M. and Kurtz, R. (1968) The fantasy of dirt and attitudes toward body products. *Journal of Nervous and Mental Disease* **146**, 303–309.

Royal College of Physicians (1995) Incontinence. Causes, management and provision of services. A Working Party of the Royal College of Physicians. *Journal of the Royal College of Physicians of London* **29**, 272–274.

Salter, M. (1997) *Altered body image* (2nd edn). London: Ballière Tindall.

Schwartz, D.R. (1977) Personal point of view – a report of seventeen elderly patients with a persistent problem of urinary incontinence. *Health Bulletin* **35**, 197–204.

Shaw, C., Williams, K.S. and Assassa, R.P. (2000) Patients' views of a new nurse-led continence service. *Journal of Clinical Nursing* **9**, 574–584.

Sontag, S. (1977) *Illness as metaphor.* New York: Farrar, Straus and Giroux.

Taylor, B.J. (1994) *Being human: ordinariness in nursing*. Melbourne: Churchill Livingstone.

Turner, B.S. (1984) *The body and society.* Oxford: Basil Blackwell.

Weiss, G. (1999) *Body images*. London: Routledge.

Werner-Beland, J.A. (1980) *Grief responses to long-term illness and disability.* Reston, Virginia: Reston Publishing Company.

Whitehead, W.E., Wald, A., Diamant, N.E., Enck, P., Pemberton, J.H. and Rao, S.S.C. (1999) Functional disorders of the anus and rectum. *Gut* **45**, 1155–1159.

Williams, K.S., Assassa, R.P., Smith, N., Jagger, C., Perry, S., Shaw, C., Dallosso, H., McGrother, C., Clarke, M., Brittain, K.R., Castleden, C.M. and Mayne, C. (2000) Development, implementation and evaluation of a new nurse-led continence service: a pilot study. *Journal of Clinical Nursing* **9**, 566–573.

Chapter 2

The Physiology of Defaecation and Continence

Anton Emmanuel

Introduction

The anal sphincter is a relatively simple structure that performs an extraordinarily complex function. Not only do the anal sphincters regulate faecal continence, but they are also increasingly recognised as controlling defaecation. Understanding the physiology of defaecation and continence depends on understanding the interplay between the anal sphincter, rectum and pelvic floor. The motor component of the mechanism involves both involuntary and voluntary muscle, and the sensory component is modulated by pelvic nerves which also have a somatic (voluntary nerve) function. Throughout this brief review, the pathophysiology of ano-rectal function in the spinally injured patient will be highlighted. This is because an understanding of the changes in the spinal patient helps shed light on 'normal' physiology, and also because such patients have a large burden of symptoms with regard to continence and bowel function.

Colonic motility

The colon comprises two layers of muscle underlying the colonic mucosa, namely the inner circular and outer longitudinal layers. Co-ordination of contraction of these muscles occurs through the local 'enteric' nervous system. Contraction of the circular muscle results primarily in mixing ('ring contractions') of faecal matter, whilst contraction of the longitudinal muscle ('sleeve contractions') results in propagated peristaltic movement of that faecal matter. The right colon primarily serves a reservoir and mixing function, helping to make the faecal content more solid by allowing time for water re-absorption. In the transverse and descending colon, contractions are mostly peristaltic in the form of episodic 'mass movements'. This activity delivers the relatively solid faecal matter into the sigmoid colon and rectum, which act as a further reservoir. When there is filling of the rectum and sigmoid to a critical level, the urge to defaecate is initiated.

Anatomy (Figure 2.1)

The rectum

The two layers of colonic muscle are smooth muscle structures with no external somatic (voluntary) nerve input. The muscle of the rectum is thus not under voluntary control. Extrinsic autonomic nerves act upon the intrinsic ('enteric') nerves at submucosal plexuses to innervate the rectum. The combined effect of these nerves is to allow the rectal muscle to relax and gradually accommodate increasing content as faecal material enters the rectal ampulla. This phenomenon is known as rectal compliance and is dependent upon the function of rectal muscle and its nerve supply. Spinally injured patients have normal rectal compliance. This is in contrast to the loss of bladder tone that is seen in patients with a chronic spinal injury.

Traditionally ano-rectal pressures are expressed in centimetres of water (cm H_2O); 1 cm H_2O is approximately equal to 0.75 mm mercury (Hg). Resting pressure in the rectum is low, between 5 and 20 cm H_2O, and does not increase appreciably with increasing rectal content.

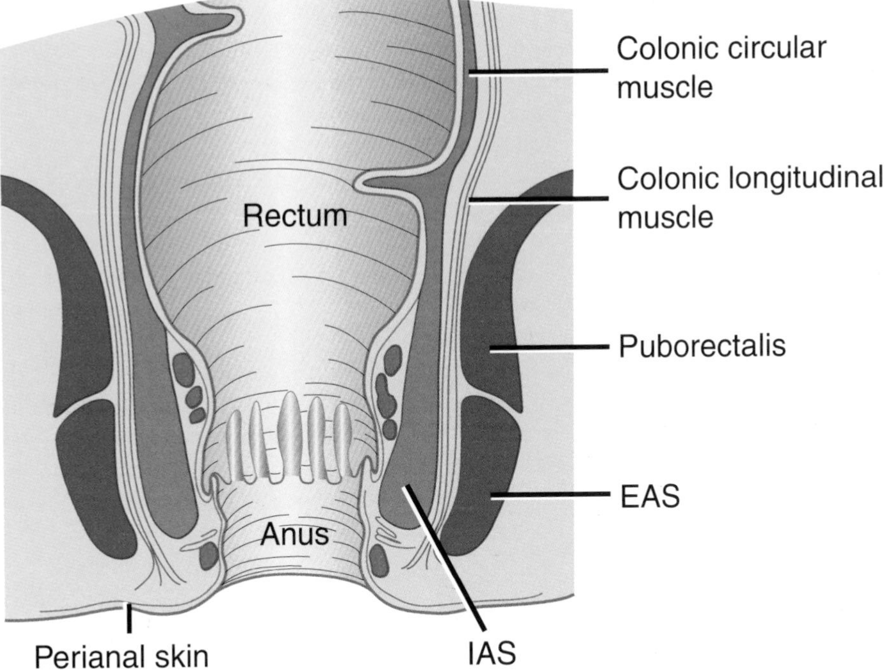

Figure 2.1 *A diagrammatic representation of the structures involved in the mechanisms of defaecation and continence. IAS = internal anal sphincter (smooth muscle); EAS = external anal sphincter (striated muscle).*

The internal anal sphincter

The inner layer of rectal smooth muscle, namely the circular muscle layer, becomes about three times thicker at the distal end of the rectum. This condensation of muscle is the internal anal sphincter. It is approximately 3 cm long and 3 mm wide, being slightly longer in men and getting thicker with age. It does not extend downwards as far as the skin of the anal verge, ending some 10 mm above it. Like all smooth muscle sphincters, the internal anal sphincter is able to maintain tonic contraction for long periods of time.

The internal sphincter has an intrinsic, sinusoidal 'slow wave' activity with a frequency of 20–40 cycles per minute. The continuous activity of the sphincter is primarily responsible for the resting tone of the anus. The internal sphincter contributes about 85% of the resting anal sphincter pressure, which is measured at between 60–110 cm H_2O in health. Weakness or disruption of the internal anal sphincter results in the passive leakage of faecal contents and incontinence of flatus. The resting tone is greatest in the lower internal sphincter, and the importance of this in ano-rectal 'sampling' is discussed below.

Distension of the rectum results in a reflex relaxation of the internal anal sphincter (the recto-anal inhibitory reflex). This reflex is mediated at spinal level. The extent of the relaxation depends on the degree of distension – with large volume rectal distension the internal sphincter relaxation can be prolonged, and with slight distension only partial sphincter relaxation occurs (see ano-rectal sampling below).

The external anal sphincter

The external anal sphincter is a striated muscle and as such is under voluntary control, its nerve supply being provided by the pudendal nerve. It surrounds the internal anal sphincter and extends down to the skin at the anal verge. Unlike the internal sphincter, it is a fatigable muscle. The external anal sphincter is composed of both tonically contracting 'slow twitch' fibres and phasically contracting 'fast twitch' fibres.

The external sphincter contributes only around 15% towards resting anal tone. It is primarily responsible for the voluntary contraction of the sphincter. Pressures of between 60 and 250 cm H_2O are generated during a voluntary anal squeeze in normal subjects.

Rectal distension results initially in a progressive increase in external anal sphincter activity, which temporally precedes the relaxation of the internal sphincter. However, when a critical volume of distension is reached (usually above 200 ml) the external sphincter activity then disappears, resulting in loss of pressure in both anal internal and external sphincters. This too is a reflex mediated at spinal level, and is therefore present in spinally injured patients.

There is one further important aspect of external sphincter contraction to consider. When traction is applied to the external sphincter (by pulling gently but firmly away from the anus with a gloved finger at the anal verge) there is an initial increase in contraction which is then exaggerated when the traction is released. This is termed the 'closing reflex' and is the basis on which the anal sphincter snaps shut at the end of rectal evacuation. In patients with spinal injury traction results in external sphincter relaxation, and this is the basis of some spinal patients employing digital anal stimulation to achieve evacuation (see Chapter 17). The difference in this reflex in spinal patients illustrates that there is a descending cortical influence upon it.

The pelvic diaphragm (pelvic floor)

This is a striated muscular layer, with a central ligament that surrounds the rectum, the vagina in women, and the urethra. This 'pelvic diaphragm' is composed of a number of muscles, all of which can be considered as acting in concert. The puborectalis muscle component of the diaphragm, in particular, contributes to maintenance of the ano-rectal angle which is believed to be important in preserving continence (Figure 2.2). Although there are known to be certain changes in the pelvic diaphragm during straining in the laboratory setting, the correlation with events during normal defaecation is uncertain. However, it seems clear that the whole pelvic diaphragm mechanism works in tandem with the external anal sphincter during defaecation.

Nerve supply of the rectum and anus

The rectum and internal anal sphincter receive an extrinsic autonomic innervation from lumbar (sympathetic) and sacral (parasympathetic) nerve roots. This innervation conveys information in each direction between the hindgut (lower bowel) and the brain. There is also a dense network of 'local' enteric neurones in the gut wall which mediate the fine processing of information from brain to rectum and anus. This enteric nervous system (ENS) comprises a dense network of neurones connected to each other by a series of plexuses within the gut wall. The ENS is second only to the central nervous system in complexity and quantity of nerve tissue. The ENS is the only region of the peripheral nervous system which is capable of mediating reflex activity without input from the central nervous system (CNS). Peristalsis is the result of descending influences from the CNS integrated with local reflexes elicited within the gut wall by luminal content.

The motor supply to the striated (voluntary) muscle of the external anal sphincter is from the second to fourth sacral spinal cord segments via the pudendal nerves. The spinal nuclei for this nerve output are directly influenced by descending input from the higher centres in the brain (see Chapter 17).

Sensory information from the ano-rectum travels in afferent fibres of the pudendal nerve and is handled in two ways – firstly it is relayed to the central nervous system by these extrinsic autonomic nerves and secondly it initiates local reflex arcs. The combination of these two systems results in the potential for both

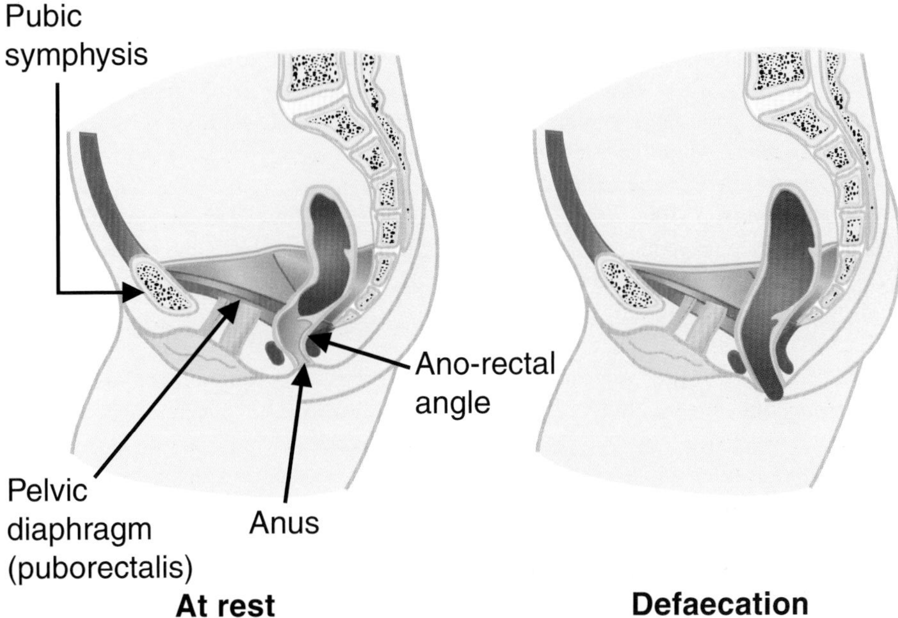

Figure 2.2 *A diagrammatic saggital representation of the pelvic floor at rest and during defaecation. Note that at rest the puborectalis and the rest of the pelvic diaphragm are in tonic contraction to maintain an acute ano-rectal angle, contributing to continence. During defaecation, relaxation of the puborectalis results in straightening out of the angle, to ease rectal evacuation.*

conscious and subconscious processing of gut feelings. This can be demonstrated by balloon distension of the rectum (see Chapter 8 for description of the use of this technique in ano-rectal tests). At low balloon volume mucosal receptors in the rectum are activated, resulting in patients' first perception of rectal sensation ('threshold sensation'). Further distension then stimulates the mechano-receptors (stretch receptors) in the muscular layer of the mucosa, resulting in the sensation of need to defaecate ('urge sensation'), and finally a point is reached with the activation of serosal mechano-receptors and nociceptors (pain receptors) up to the point of discomfort or 'maximum tolerable volume'.

Rectal compliance

The normal rectum is capable of accommodating increases in volume with only minor alterations of pressure. This phenomenon of compliance is most pronounced at lower volumes of rectal filling. As the maximum tolerable volume is approached, even small increments in volume are accompanied by changes in rectal pressure. Thus sensory perception of ano-rectal activity depends on both luminal content and also the state of contractility, or compliance, of the rectum. In conditions where the rectum is inflamed (inflammatory bowel disease, infection, radiation proctitis) there is reduced compliance and an associated increase in sensitivity.

Ano-rectal sampling

It is known that applying local anaesthetic to the anal canal results in a reduced ability to maintain external anal sphincter contraction. This is evidence of the close link between ano-rectal sensation and motor function in the maintenance of continence. This association between sensation and motor function is characterised by the phenomenon of ano-rectal sampling. With progressive rectal filling, reflex relaxation of the upper internal anal sphincter occurs. This happens every eight to ten minutes as rectal contents are presented to the anal sensory mucosa. Since the lower internal sphincter exhibits higher resting pressure, incontinence does not occur. In fact, the slow wave activity in the lower part of the sphincter complex, coupled with contraction of the external anal sphincter and puborectalis, results in the contents being returned to the rectum. Each of these episodes lasts less than ten seconds. The importance of this anal 'sampling' is that it allows the sensory epithelium of the anal canal the opportunity to distinguish solids from liquids and from gas, important in the maintenance of perfect continence.

The dynamics of continence

Normal stool output per day is of the order of 200 gm. The proximal (upper) colon defines the consistency and volume of delivery of contents to the rectum. The rectum has a reservoir function to accommodate this content until such time as defaecation is socially and practically appropriate. As rectal filling gradually proceeds, ano-rectal sampling occurs allowing subconscious perception of the consistency of the content. An intact internal anal sphincter, especially in the lower part, ensures continence; in situations where this has been damaged (typically iatrogenically after anal dilatation or lateral sphincterotomy) passive loss of anal contents may occur.

Ano-rectal sensation of the build up of rectal contents is relayed centrally by autonomic nerves. These afferents result in both conscious perception and activation of local reflexes, such as the recto-anal inhibitory reflex, to begin relaxation of the internal anal sphincter. In health, reflex voluntary external sphincter contraction then maintains continence until voluntary defaecation is possible. By contrast, spinally injured patients who are unable to contract their external anal sphincter experience incontinence when the internal sphincter relaxes. A similar but reflex activation of the external sphincter to maintain continence occurs when there is a rise in abdominal pressure, for example with coughing. Partial external sphincter contraction is also observed during passage of flatus, and coupled with intact ano-rectal sensation this is the mechanism by which faecal continence during passage of gas is maintained. The voluntary passage of flatus depends on reflex relaxation of the internal anal sphincter and partial voluntary relaxation of the external anal sphincter.

Patients in whom there is either a loss of sensation or impaired perception (for example in diabetes, following stroke, or with a rectal prolapse) may become incontinent due to the loss of recognition of 'normal' ano-rectal sensation and its relationship to continence. Thus the preservation of continence depends on the normal functioning of ano-rectal sensation, the appropriate perception of that sensory information, the integrity of local and higher reflex arcs, and the action of the internal and external anal sphincters.

The dynamics of defaecation

Defaecation commences with rectal sensory awareness of a critical level of filling, which is relayed to the cerebral cortex as the perception of the need to evacuate the rectum. The actual volume depends on the nature of the contents (volume, consistency) and the rectum (mucosal inflammation, rectal wall compliance). When the subject is in a socially appropriate context for defaecation, the person adopts a sitting, or squatting, position. The latter position results in straightening of the rectal angle, thereby allowing for a more effective propulsion of contents. The external sphincter and puborectalis relax. The rectal contents provoke reflex relaxation of the internal anal sphincter and the subject then performs a Valsalva manoeuvre (holding the breath and forcibly trying to exhale against a closed glottis, creating a pushing down effect). Abdominal pressure is raised, and the muscles of the anterior abdominal wall tense to funnel the pressure down to the pelvis. The relaxation of the pelvic floor then allows some stool to enter the lower rectum. This in turn tends to initiate a spontaneous giant recto-sigmoid contraction, which pushes stool through the relaxed anal canal. Further large propulsive contractions of the rectum occur until the rectum is empty. A sensory input from the anus maintains this propulsive activity until the rectum is fully voided. This seems to be a reflex mediated at spinal cord level, since even spinally injured patients can void a complete stool from the rectum, once initiated. Such patients tend to use digital rectal stimulation to initiate the propulsive contractions of the recto-sigmoid. As the stool passes through the anal canal it stretches the external anal sphincter creating a traction force upon it. After the last bolus of stool is passed, the 'closing reflex' of the external sphincter is stimulated by the release of traction. In this way anal continence is maintained after the act of defaecation.

The mechanisms of control continence and defaecation are complex. This review has presented a basic overview of the subject, the emphasis being to highlight the synergy of structure to function in these complex processes.

Further reading

Ambroze, W.L., Pemberton, J.H., Bell, A.M., Brown, M.L. and Zinsmeister, A.R. (1991) The effect of stool consistency on rectal and neorectal emptying. *Digestive Diseases and Sciences* **34**,1–7.

Christensen, J. (1987) Motility of the colon. In: Johnson, L.R. (ed.). *Physiology of the gastro-intestinal tract* (2nd edn), pp. 665–688. New York: Raven Press.

Dickinson, V.A. (1978) Maintenance of anal continence: a review of pelvic floor physiology. *Gut* **19**, 1163–1169.

Duthie, H.L. (1982) Defaecation and the anal sphincter. *Clinics in Gastroenterology* **11**, 621–628.

Longo, W.E., Ballantyne, G.H. and Modlin, I.M. (1989) The colon, anorectum and spinal cord patient: a review of the functional alterations of the denervated hindgut. *Diseases of the Colon and Rectum* **32**, 261–267.

Miller, R., Bartolo, D.C.C., Cervero, F. and Mortensen, N.J.M. (1988) Anorectal sampling: a comparison of normal and incontinent patients. *British Journal of Surgery* **75**, 44–47.

Read, N.W., Harford, W.V., Schmulen, A.C., Read, M.G., Santa Ana, C. and Fordtran, J.S. (1979) A clinical study of patients with faecal incontinence and diarrhoea. *Gastroenterology* **76**, 747–751.

Speakman, C.T.M. and Kamm, M.A. (1991) The internal anal sphincter – new insights into faecal incontinence. *Gut* **32**, 345–353.

Sun, W.M., Read, N.W. and Miner, P.B. (1990) Relationship between rectal sensation and anal function in normal subjects and patients with faecal incontinence. *Gut* **31**, 1056–1061.

Swash, M., Snooks, S.J. and Henry, M.M. (1985) Unifying concept of pelvic floor disorders and incontinence. *Journal of the Royal Society of Medicine* **78**, 906–913.

Chapter 3

The Epidemiology of Faecal Incontinence

Nicholas Kenefick

Introduction

The word epidemiology is derived from Greek and literally means studies upon people. Present-day epidemiology is a speciality in its own right and has an essential role to play in modern medicine. It can be defined as the study of how often a disease occurs in different groups of people, and why (Coggon et al., 1997).

Two important epidemiological terms need to be defined. The incidence of a disease is the rate at which new cases occur in a population during a specific period (Farmer, 1977). For example, the annual incidence of faecal incontinence in the general population would be the number of *new cases reported per year* from the general population. The prevalence of a disease is the *proportion* of a population that are cases at a given point in time (Farmer, 1977). So for faecal incontinence this would be the number of individuals in the population at a certain time who suffer from the condition. As faecal incontinence is often a chronic condition, the prevalence will be greater than the incidence.

The definitions of faecal incontinence vary greatly between different studies, ranging from poor control of flatus or occasional soiling of underwear to the uncontrolled passage of formed stool. It is common, but not universal, to define 'anal incontinence' as any loss from the anus (stool or flatus), and 'faecal incontinence' as stool loss only. Some have sub-divided stool incontinence into solid or liquid, but this is inevitably arbitrary. While flatus incontinence is an embarrassing symptom it is usually, but not always, considerably less physically, mentally and socially disabling than full faecal incontinence. Thus depending on the definition, the rates of incidence and prevalence can very greatly. A French population study published in 1992 of approximately 4000 people aged over forty-five showed a prevalence of 15.5% for anal incontinence (including flatus) but of 3.2% for weekly faecal incontinence (Denis et al., 1992). For the purposes of this chapter faecal incontinence is defined as 'the uncontrolled passage of solid or liquid faeces at socially inappropriate times', unless otherwise stated.

Faecal incontinence in the general population

Faecal incontinence in the general population is a common condition that has been largely ignored in the past. It may cause physically, mentally and socially crippling symptoms that can devastate the individual's quality of life. In addition it is well known that only a minority of patients suffering with this condition will report it to a health care professional, either due to social embarrassment and stigmatisation or to a lack of active enquiry by the professional. A large German study (Enck et al., 1991) showed that only 50% of patients with faecal incontinence had reported this to a health care professional and similar findings are reported from England (Tobin, 1992; Tobin and Brocklehurst, 1986) and the USA (Johanson and Lafferty, 1996). There are a number of studies from different countries that have reported the prevalence of faecal incontinence in the general population and the larger studies are summarised in Table 3.1 (overleaf).

The wide range in reported prevalence rates for faecal incontinence is a manifestation, at least in part, of differing definitions used for incontinence as previously discussed, both in the severity and frequency of symptoms. When interpreting these figures it must be remembered that since all popular survey studies tend to underestimate the true prevalence rates due to embarrassment in reporting, the overall prevalence rate for faecal incontinence in the general population as a whole widely accepted as between 2% and 5%.

It is not clear why some studies have found prevalence rates higher in men than in women. Of the associations and risk factors listed in Table 3.1, the link between cause and effect remains to be established. It is known that women with symptoms of the irritable bowel syndrome are more likely to seek healthcare than men (Drossman et al., 1982), and the same may be true of women with faecal incontinence, as most clinical services see many more women than men.

Faecal incontinence in elderly people

The prevalence of faecal incontinence rises sharply in older age groups, particularly in advanced old age. Several studies looking at individuals either over the age of 65 years or individuals resident in long-term care facilities have been performed and show a much higher rate of faecal incontinence than in general population, summarised in Table 3.2 (pages 18–19). Chapter 13 gives more details of faecal incontinence in old age.

It can be seen that there is a wide variation in incontinence rates, probably due to differing study methodologies. However, it is clear that the overall rate of incontinence in the elderly, particularly those living in institutions, is much greater than the general population and is approximately 20% for those in long-term care. The majority of these are retrospective studies but there is one prospective study. Chassagne and colleagues conducted a prospective study of 1186 patients over 60 years of age living in long-term care facilities who did not have faecal incontinence (Chassagne et al., 1999). Over a 10-month period new symptoms of faecal incontinence, defined as the involuntary loss of faeces, occurred in 20%. They also identified five associated risk factors for the development of faecal incontinence:

- A history of urinary incontinence (which is often found in association with faecal incontinence)
- Neurological disease
- Severe cognitive impairment
- Poor mobility
- Age greater than 70 years

In addition, the prognosis of faecally incontinent patients was prospectively assessed by comparing their survival rates with those of continent patients. At 10-months the mortality was 26% for patients with faecal incontinence, as opposed to 6.7% for the continent patients.

Thus incontinence in the elderly is common and may be a symptom indicative of poor and declining overall health in the nursing home context. The high prevalence of approximately 20% of patients in long-term care with faecal incontinence has a major cost implication.

Faecal incontinence after childbirth

There is a connection between faecal incontinence in women who have sustained childbirth injuries to the anal sphincter. A minor degree of perineal damage is common to most vaginal deliveries, but third-degree tears involving a disruption of the vagina and anal canal occur in approximately 1% of all deliveries in the Western world. Faecal incontinence can occur in up to one third of women who sustain a major tear (Bourguignon, Bauer, and Atienza, 1998). If the anal canal is examined with endo-anal ultrasound, minor degrees of structural damage to the anal sphincters can be found in 33% of women after a normal atraumatic delivery of their first baby; however, few of these patients will develop symptomatic incontinence (Bourguignon, Bauer, and Atienza, 1998). The majority of significant injuries occur at the first delivery and up to 20% of primiparous women will develop transient symptoms of faecal incontinence after delivery (Fynes et al., 1999). There are a number of associated risk factors

Table 3.1: Prevalence of faecal incontinence in the general population

Authors, year & country	*Method*	*Study population*	*Definition*	*Associations or risk factors*	*Prevalence*
Perry et al., 2002, UK	Postal survey, 10,116 respondents	Over 40 years old, living at home	Any FI in previous year	FI more prevalent and more severe in older people. Associated with increasing age, long-term illness, problems with mobility and UI. Not associated with gender or ethnicity.	Men: 6.2% Women: 5.7% Disabling FI: 0.7%
Roberts et al., 1999, USA	Postal survey, 1,540 respondents	Over 50 years	Any FI in previous year	51% of men and 60% of women with FI also had UI. FI increased with age in men but not in women. Men with UI more likely to also have FI than women with UI.	Men: 11.1% Women: 15.2%
Giebel et al., 1998, Germany	Questionnaire, 500 people selected to reflect age and sex of general population	Over 18 years. Excluded digestive diseases and abdominal surgery	4 point scale for frequency	Men more soiling than women; women more urgency, symptoms worse with age.	4.8% solid stool; 6.7% liquid; 5.5% no control flatus; 30% some urgency
Johanson and Lafferty, 1996, USA	Interview, 881 people	Over 18 years, consulting GP or gastroenterologist	Any FI	Increased with age. 1.3 times more common in men than women.	18.4% overall; 7.1% < monthly, 4.5% weekly, 2.7% daily. 1.3 times more men than women. Only 1/3 had consulted
Nelson et al., 1995, USA	Telephone survey, 2570 households, 6959 individuals reported on	Living at home	Anal incontinence (stool or flatus) in past year	Associated with female gender, increasing age, physical limitations and poor general health.	2.2% anal incontinence: 0.8% solid stool, 1.2% liquid stool, 1.3% flatus
Drossman et al., 1993, USA	Postal survey, 5430 respondents	Householders	Rome criteria	Increased with age. 13% currently too sick to work.	7.8%: 7.9% men, 7.7% women. Gross FI; 0.5% men, 0.9% women.

Table 3.1: Prevalence of faecal incontinence in the general population (continued)

Authors, year & country	*Method*	*Study population*	*Definition*	*Associations or risk factors*	*Prevalence*
Denis et al., 1992, France	General population: gallup poll 1,100 people over 45 years; 3914 seen by family doctor or gastro-enterologist; 500 patients consultaing for UI; 1,136 neuro-logical patients with bladder problems; 10,157 older people in care homes or hospital	Gallup poll or survey	Anal incontinence (stool or flatus), daily or weekly	Increased with age in those with UI and those in care homes.	11% anal incontinence in general population, FI 6%, daily or weekly FI 2%. GP or gastroenterologist consulters: 15.5% anal, 7.9% FI, 3.2% weekly FI. 33% elderly in homes or hospital
Thomas et al., 1984, UK	Postal survey, 14,844 respondents, total population	Over 15 years	Twice or more in the past month	Very few of those with FI were known to health or social services.	0.43% of total population (under 65: men 0.42%, women 0.17%; over 65: men 1.09%, women 1.33%)

FI = faecal incontinence; UI = urinary incontinence

Table 3.2: Prevalence of faecal incontinence in older people

Authors, year & country	*Method*	*Study population*	*Definition*	*Associations or risk factors*	*Prevalence*
Chassagne et al., 1999, France	Incidence study, 1,186 nursing home residents without FI, over 10 months	Institutionalised, over 60 years	At least one episode FI	Urinary incontinence, neurological disease, poor mobility, severe cognitive decline, age over 70 years. 10 month mortality 26% with FI, 6.7% in non-FI group.	20% incidence of new cases
Brocklehurst et al., 1999, UK	Audit tool: 498 residents in 17 nursing homes and 4 continuing care elderly hospital wards	Nursing home and long-stay hospital residents	Nursing staff evaluation of presence of FI	Immobility; need for assistance in transfer from bed to chair. Prevalence highest in dementia (71% FI), stroke (54% FI). Irritant laxative (danthrin) associated with FI. Enemas and suppositories negatively associated with FI.	48 never FI; 23% less than weekly; 29% weekly or more often. Higher % of men than women. One Home had 95% FI.
Nelson et al., 1998, USA	Survey 35,351 nursing home residents (used statutory Minimum Data Set)	Nursing homes, mean age 84 years	Not complete faecal continence	Associations in order: Urinary incontinence, tube feeding, loss of activities of daily living, diarrhoea, truncal restriants, pressure sores, dementia, impaired vision, faecal impaction, constipation, male gender, age, increasing body mass index.	46–47%
Johanson et al., 1997, USA	388 residents of 5 nursing homes	Nursing homes, questionnaire to residents, or nurses if resident could not complete	Any involuntary leakage of stool or soiling of undergarments	1.5 times more common in males and those younger than 65 years. Diarrhoea, dementia, immobility and male gender associated with FI. Constipation not associated with FI.	46% FI. Over 60% men, over 40% women.
Lopes, 1997, Portugal	146	Age over 75 years, community dwelling			10.9%

Table 3.2: Prevalence of faecal incontinence in older people (continued)

Authors, year & country	*Method*	*Study population*	*Definition*	*Associations or risk factors*	*Prevalence*
Peet et al., 1995, UK	Census, 5758 residents	Long-term care, over 65 years	Weekly or more often	Physical dependency	3.1% FI alone; 17.7% double incontinence
Borrie et al., 1992 Canada	435 patients, rated by nurse manager.	Mean age 73 years, long-term hospital patients	Less than weekly or more than weekly	Immobility (67% FI), severe mental impairment (83% FI), dementia (66% FI).	46 % FI; 62% UI; 44% double incontinence. Annual cost per patient calculated as $9771 (Canadian) per patient
Talley, 1992, USA	Startified random sample, postal questionnaire, 328 respondents	Community dwelling, aged 65–93	More than weekly or need to wear a pad	42% chronic diarrhoes; 21% chronic constipation; 42% neither constipation nor diarrhoea.	3.7% more than weekly FI: 3.1% women, 4.5% men 6.1% wear pad for FI
Kok et al., 1992, Netherlands	Postal survey, 719 respondents	Community-dwelling women over 60 years	Occasional involuntary loss	60–84 years: poor mobility. Over 85 years: no predictors of FI found.	60–84 years: 4.2%; Over 85 years: 16.9%
Thomas et al., 1987, UK	370 residents, interview patient, or staff if patient unable	8 residential homes	Involuntary leakage of faeces twice or more per month	Wheelchair users, dementia passage or	16% men, 17% women (of these 92% men and 73% women doubly incontinent)

FI = faecal incontinence; UI = urinary incontinence

Table 3.3: Faecal incontinence rates after common colorectal surgery

Operation	*Faecal incontinence rate*	*References*
Haemorrhoidectomy	1–5%	Hardy et al., 1975; Read et al., 1982.
Anal dilatation	2–10%	Hardy et al., 1975.
Lateral sphincterotomy	1–5%	Nyam and Pemberton, 1999.
Anal fistula surgery	1–12%	Cox et al., 1977; Saino, 1985; Saino and Hosa, 1985.

that increase the likelihood of developing faecal or anal incontinence:

- forceps delivery
- a large baby (especially over 4 kg birth weight)
- abnormal presentation, particularly occipito-posterior presentation
- a prolonged second stage of labour.

The incidence of faecal incontinence in women after childbirth is higher than the general population and may reach 20% in the immediate post-natal period. It is not clear from available studies what proportion remit spontaneously and who will have persistent symptoms.

Faecal incontinence after colorectal surgery

After childbirth, surgery to the anal area is probably the second commonest cause of faecal incontinence in younger adults. Procedures where the sphincter muscles are damaged inadvertently (e.g. haemorrhoidectomy) and those where the sphincters are cut for a purpose as part of the procedure (e.g. to allow drainage of a perianal fistula or during a lateral sphincterotomy to allow a chronic anal fissure to heal) may damage the sphincter continence mechanism. There are differing rates of incontinence quoted after each operation, depending on the definition used and the length of follow-up. For example, a study published in 1999 of the incontinence rates after lateral sphincterotomy for anal fissure showed an initial rate of 45% of some level of incontinence but at five years this had dropped to only 1% (Nyam and Pemberton, 1999). The rates of post-operative incontinence for the commonly performed procedures are summarised in Table 3.3. The rates after surgery for rectal prolapse surgery reflect some pre-existing incontinence which was associated with the prolapse and has not resolved.

Faecal incontinence in childhood

Faecal incontinence in children is covered in more detail in Chapter 19. It is defined by the same criteria as in adults but the child must have a mental age of at least four years as defined by the Rome II criteria (Whitehead et al., 1999). The majority of children are continent to stool by the age of four, but between 1–2% of seven-year-old children will remain faecally incontinent (Morgan, 1984). Chapter 18 addresses the subject of children with learning disabilities. Many of these children will have a considerable behavioural or psychological element to their symptoms, and their treatment needs to be directed to behavioural re-education and bowel training. Most incontinent children soil due to faecal impaction secondary to constipation, which normally resolves once the bowel is emptied. There is however a prevalence of approximately 1–4% of children in the general population that remain faecally incontinent and suffer with similar physical and social problems to the adult population (Whitehead, 1996).

Conclusions

Faecal incontinence is a physically and socially disabling condition with an overall prevalence of between 2% and 5% in the general population. This is higher in certain specific populations, namely the institutionalised elderly, post-partum women, and in people after surgery to the anal canal. At present the majority of those affected neither seek nor receive health care for their symptoms.

References

Borrie, M.J., Bawden, M.E., Kartha, A.S. and Kerr, P.S. (1992) A nurse/physician continence clinic triage approach for urinary incontinence: a 25 week randomised trial. *Neurourology and Urodynamics* **11**, 364–365.

Bourguignon, J., Bauer, P. and Atienza, P. (1998) Effect of delivery on the anal sphincter. *Presse Medicale*, **27**, 33, 1702–1706. [In French].

Brocklehurst, J.C., Dickinson, E. and Windsor, J. (1999) Laxatives and faecal incontinence in long-term care. *Nursing Standard* **13**, 32–36.

Chassagne, P., Landrin, I., Neveu, C., Czernichow, P., Bouaniche, M., Doucet, J., Denis, P. and Bercoff, E. (1999) Fecal incontinence in the institutionalised elderly: incidence, risk factors, and prognosis. *American Journal of Medicine* **106**, 2, 185–190.

Coggon, D., Rose, G. and Barker, D.J.P. (1997) *Epidemiology for the Uninitiated* (4th edn). London: BMJ Publishers.

Cox, S.W., Senagore, A.J., Luchtefeld, M.A. and Mazier, W.P. (1997) Outcome after incision and drainage with fistulotomy for ischiorectal abscess. *American Surgeon* **63**, 8, 686–689.

Denis, P., Bercoff, E., Bizien, M.F., Brocker, P., Chassagne, P., Lamouliatte, H., Leroi, A.M., Perrigot, M. and Weber, J. (1992). Prevalence of anal incontinence in adults [In French]. **16**, 4, 344–350.

Drossman, D.A., Sandler, R.S., McKee, D.C. and Lovitz, A.J. (1982) Bowel patterns among subjects not seeking healthcare: Use of questionnaire to identify a population with bowel dysfunction. *Gastroenterology* **83,** 529–534.

Drossman, D.A., Li, Z., Andruzzi, E., Temple, R.D., Talley, N.J. and Thompson, W.G. (1993) U.S. householder survey of functional gastrointestinal disorders. *Digestive Diseases and Sciences* **38**, 1569–1580.

Drossman, D.A., Sandler, R.S., Mckee, D.C., and Lovitz, A.J. (1982) Bowel Patterns Among Subjects Not Seeking Healthcare: Use of a Questionnaire to Identify a Population With Bowel Dysfunction. *Gastroenteology* **83**, 529–534.

Enck, P., Gabor, S., von Ferber, L., Rathmann, W. and Erckenbrecht, J.F. (1991) Prevalence of fecal incontinence and degree of information possessed by family physicians and health insurance *Zeitschrift fur Gastroenterologie* **29**, 10, 538–540. [In German]

Farmer, R. (1996) *Lecture notes on epidemiology and public health medicine* (4th edn). Oxford: Blackwell Science.

Fynes, M., Donnelly, V., Behan, M., O'Connell, P.R. and O'Herlihy, C. (1999) Effect of second vaginal delivery on anorectal physiology and faecal continence: a prospective study. *Lancet* **354**, 9183, 983–986.

Giebel, G.D., Lefering, R., Troidl, H. & Blochl, H. (1998) Prevalence of fecal incontinence: what can be expected? *International Journal of Colorectal Disease.* **13**, 2, 73–77.

Hardy, K.J., Wheatley, I.C. and Heffernan, E.B. (1975) Anal dilatation and haemorrhoidectomy. A prospective study. *Medical Journal of Australia* **2**, 3, 88–91.

Johanson, J.F. and Lafferty, J. (1996) Epidemiology of fecal incontinence: the silent affliction. *American Journal of Gastroenterology* **91**, 1, 33–36.

Johanson, J.F., Irizarry, F. and Doughty, A. (1997) Risk factors for fecal incontinence in a nursing home population. *Journal of Clinical Gastroenterology* **24**, 156–160.

Kok, A.L.M., Voorhorst, F.J., Burger, C.W., van Houten, P., Kenemans, P. and Janssens, J. (1992) Urinary and faecal incontinence in community-residing elderly women. *Age and Ageing* **21**, 211–215.

Lopes, M.C., Teixeira, M.G., Jacob, F.W., Carvalho Filho, E.T., Habr-Gama, A. and Pinotti, H.W. (1997) Prevalence of anal incontinence in the elderly population: an epidemiological study of the elderly population served at the geriatric ambulatory service of the Hospital das Clinicas da Faculdade de Medicina da Universidade de Sao Paulo. *Revista do Hospital das Clinicas; Faculdade de Medicina da Universidade de Sao Paulo* **52**, 1, 1–12.

Morgan, R. (1984) *Childhood incontinence*. London: Heinemann Medical Books. [In Portuguese]

Nelson, R., Norton, N., Cautley, E. and Furner, S. (1995) Community-based prevalence of anal incontinence. *Journal of the American Medical Association* **274**, 7, 559–561.

Nelson, R., Furner, S. and Jesudason, V. (1998) Fecal incontinence in Wisconsin nursing homes: prevalence and associations. *Diseases of the Colon and Rectum* **41**, 1226–1229.

Nyam, D.C. and Pemberton, J.H. (1999) Long-term results of lateral internal sphincterotomy for chronic anal fissure with particular reference to incidence of fecal incontinence. *Diseases of the*

Colon and Rectum **42**, 10, 1306–1310.

Peet, S.M., Castleden, C.M. and McGrother, C.W. (1995) Prevalence of urinary and faecal incontinence in hospitals and residential and nursing homes for older people. *British Medical Journal* **311**, 1063–1064.

Perry, S., Shaw, C., McGrother, C., Matthews, R.J., Assassa, R.P., Dallosso, H., Williams, K., Brittain, K.R., Azam, U., Clarke, M., Jagger, C., Mayne, C. and Castleden, C.M. (2002) Prevalence of faecal incontinence in adults aged 40 years or more living in the community. *Gut* **50**, 4, 480–484.

Read, M.G., Read, N.W., Haynes, W.G., Donnelly, T.C. and Johnson, A.G. (1982) A prospective study of the effect of haemorrhoidectomy on sphincter function and faecal continence. *British Journal of Surgery* **69**, 7, 396–398.

Roberts, R.O., Jacobsen, S.J., Reilly, W.T., Pemberton, J.H., Lieber, M.M. and Talley, N.J. (1999) Prevalence of combined fecal and urinary incontinence: a community-based study. *Journal of the American Geriatrics Society* **47**, 7, 837–841.

Sainio, P. (1985) A manometric study of anorectal function after surgery for anal fistula, with special reference to incontinence. *Acta Chirurgica Scandinavica* **151**, 8, 695–700.

Sainio, P. and Husa, A. (1985) Fistula-in-ano. Clinical features and long-term results of surgery in 199 adults. *Acta Chirurgica Scandinavica* **151**, 2, 169–176.

Talley, N.J., O'Keefe, E.A., Zinsmeister, A.R. and Melton, L.J. (1992) Prevalence of gastrointestinal symptoms in the elderly: a population-based study. *Gastroenterology* **102**, 895–901.

Teunissen, T.A. and Lagro-Janssen, A.L. (2000) Fecal incontinence: prevalence and role of rupture of the anal sphincter during delivery; literature analysis. *Nederlands Tijdschrift voor Geneeskunde* **144**, 27, 1318–1323.

Thomas, T.M., Egan, M., Walgrove, A. and Meade, T.W. (1984) The prevalence of faecal and double incontinence. *Community Medicine* **6**, 3, 216–220.

Thomas, T.M., Ruff, C., Karran, O., Mellows, S. and Meade, T.W. (1987) Study of the prevalence and management of patients with faecal incontinence in old people's homes. *Community Medicine* **9**, 232–237.

Tobin, G.W. (1992) Incontinence in the elderly. *West of England Medical Journal* **107**, 3, 79–81.

Tobin, G.W. and Brocklehurst, J.C. (1986) Faecal incontinence in residential homes for the elderly: prevalence, aetiology and management. *Age and Ageing* **15**, 1, 41–46.

Whitehead, W.E. (1996) Functional anorectal disorders. *Seminars in Gastrointestinal Disease* **7**, 4, 230–236.

Whitehead, W.E., Wald, A., Diamant, N.E., Enck, P., Pemberton, J.H. and Rao, S.S. (1999) Functional disorders of the anus and rectum. *Gut*, **45** (Suppl. II), 55–59.

Chapter 4

Causes of Faecal Incontinence

Christine Norton and Sonya Chelvanayagam

Introduction

For some people there is a single straightforward cause for the symptom of faecal incontinence. For others a number of factors will combine to determine whether continence or incontinence will result. A summary of the most common causes is given in Table 4.1 (overleaf). These causes are by no means mutually exclusive and for many people these conditions co-exist, with the combination precipitating frank faecal incontinence. For example, a woman might sustain some insult to the anal sphincter during childbirth, but be continent until she also develops irritable bowel syndrome, has anal surgery, or passes the menopause. Many other chapters in this book expand on these types of faecal incontinence, and so this chapter is intended as an overview only.

There are several different ways of classifying faecal incontinence, with no universally accepted definitions as yet.

Anal sphincter damage

There are two distinct anal sphincters important in maintaining continence (Figure 4.1). The internal sphincter is a thin (2–3 mm) smooth muscle sphincter, largely responsible for resting tone in the anal canal. An intact internal sphincter should prevent passive seepage of stool. The external sphincter is a voluntary muscle and its main function is to preserve continence during the urge to defaecate and during rises in abdominal pressure (such as exercise). Damage to one or both sphincters is the most common cause of faecal incontinence in younger adults.

Obstetric trauma to the anal sphincters

Sultan et al. (1993) and Zetterstrom et al. (1999) found all the following aspects to be independent risk factors to subsequent anal incontinence (Figure 4.2, overleaf):

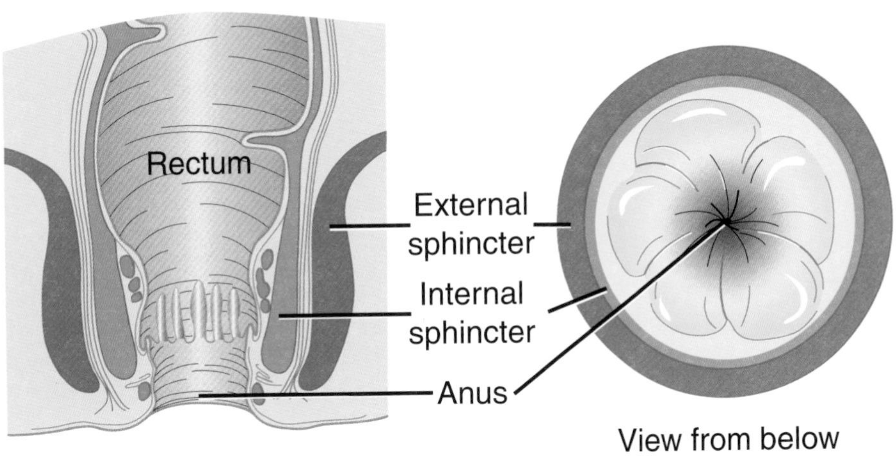

Figure 4.1 *Internal and external anal sphincters.*

Table 4.1: Causes of faecal incontinence in adults

Primary problem	*Common causes*
Anal sphincter or pelvic floor damage	Obstetric trauma
	Iatrogenic (haemorrhoidectomy, anal stretch, lateral sphincterotomy, gynaecological surgery)
	Idiopathic degeneration
	Direct trauma or injury (e.g. impalement)
	Congenital anomaly
Gut motility/stool consistency	Infection
	Inflammatory bowel disease
	Irritable bowel syndrome
	Pelvic irradiation
	Diet
	Psychological state, e.g. anxiety
Ano-rectal pathology	Rectal prolapse
	Anal or recto-vaginal fistula
	Haemorrhoids or skin tags
Neurological disease	Spinal cord injury
	Multiple sclerosis
	Spina bifida / Sacral agenesis (usually secondary to constipation)
Secondary to degenerative neurological disease	Alzheimer's disease
Impaction with overflow 'spurious diarrhoea'	Institutionalised or immobile elderly people
	Severe constipation in children
'Lifestyle' and environmental	Poor toilet facilities
	Inadequate care / non-available assistance
	Drugs with gut side effects
	Frailty and dependence
Idiopathic	Unknown cause

- Vaginal delivery
- Instrumental delivery
- Abnormal presentations
- Prolonged active second stage of labour
- Birthweight over 4 kg
- Higher maternal age
- First baby

Sultan et al. (1993) found evidence of new anal sphincter damage in 35% of women after a first vaginal delivery. Although only 13% had symptoms of urgency or incontinence of flatus six weeks after delivery, and only one was actually incontinent of liquid stool, it is thought that others will present with problems in later life,

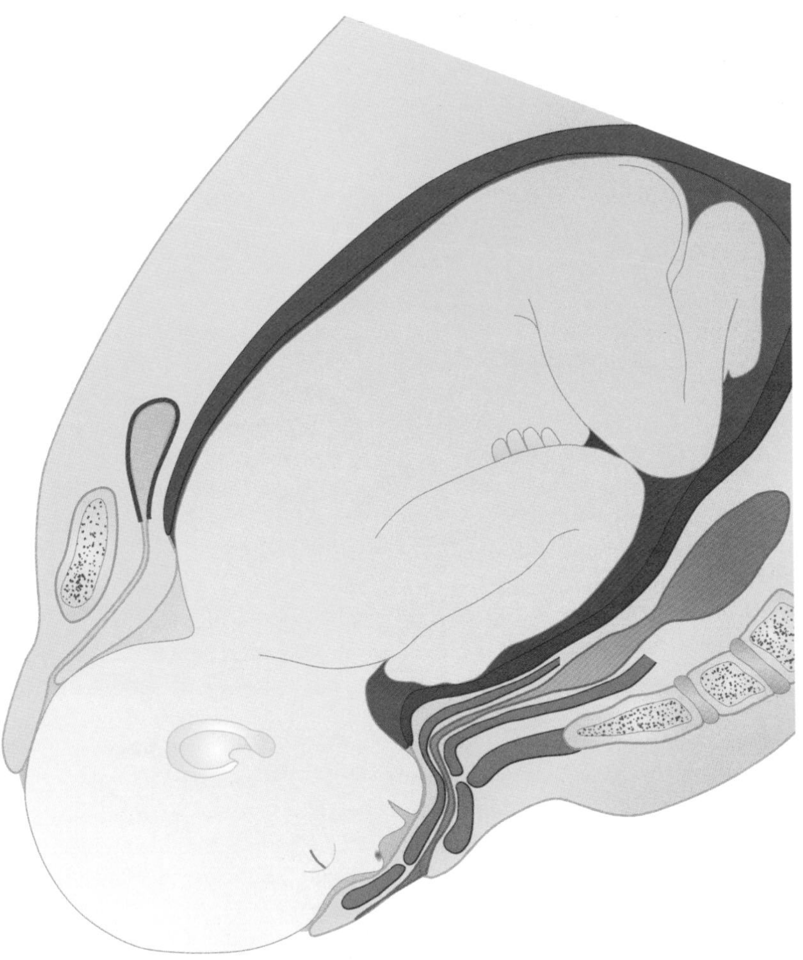

Figure 4.2 *Vaginal delivery can distort or disrupt the anal sphincters.*

particularly around the menopause. Forty per cent of multiparous women had a pre-existing sphincter defect before their second or subsequent delivery and did not tend to develop more damage following the second or subsequent delivery. This, and the finding that no woman having a caesarean section had a new defect after the birth, suggests that the first vaginal delivery is the most likely to cause damage.

If instrumental delivery is required, forceps seem to be more likely to cause damage than vacuum extraction. Sultan (1993) found that eight out of ten women having a forceps-assisted delivery had sphincter damage, compared with none of those having a vacuum extraction (n=5), although other studies have found equivalent rates with both forceps and vacuum delivery (MacArthur et al., 1997). More than three or four births and more than three caesarean deliveries also seem to pose an increased risk, although the mechanism for multiple caesarean deliveries increasing risk is not clear. Elective, but not emergency, caesarean delivery has been found to be protective (MacArthur et al., 1997).

Flatus incontinence is a permanent feature after 1.2% of first births, 1.5% second births and 8.3% third deliveries (Ryhammer et al., 1995). Others have found much higher rates of flatus incontinence (25%), which can be troublesome, although the symptom seems to improve with time (Zetterstrom et al., 1999). Women with pre-existing irritable bowel syndrome are prone to increased urgency of defaecation and flatus incontinence after delivery (Donnelly et al., 1998).

There is also evidence that vaginal delivery may cause damage to the pudendal nerve, and for some time it was thought that this damage was progressive over time and was the major underlying mechanism for post-childbirth faecal incontinence (Snooks et al., 1984). However, more recent research suggests that although women do have evidence of pudendal nerve damage, particularly with a heavier baby or a prolonged second stage of labour, this is poorly associated with bowel symptoms, and there is a tendency for the nerve to recover within six months of delivery (Sultan et al., 1994). There is also some debate about the methodology and validity of pudendal nerve latency measurement as an indicator of pudental neuropathy. Current thought is that mechanical sphincter damage is more important in causation of problems presenting immediately after childbirth, although it is still possible that progressive nerve damage may explain some of the later-onset symptoms (Snooks et al., 1990; Kamm, 1994).

The question of whether an episiotomy is protective or not is, as yet, unanswered. However, if a woman has sustained a third-degree tear during delivery (extending from the vagina through to the anal sphincter), repair at the time is often inadequate, with half experiencing some subsequent incontinence and 85% having a persistent sphincter defect despite repair immediately after delivery (Sultan et al., 1994). It has been suggested that the common obstetric practice of end-to-end repair should be replaced with a colorectal-style overlap sphincter repair, preferably under anaesthetic in an operating theatre (Sultan and Kamm, 1997). Early studies have suggested that the technique of overlap repair is feasible in the immediate post-delivery period and may produce better results (Sultan et al., 1999).

Midline episiotomy is commonly practised in the USA. It has been found to increase the risk of subsequent risk of faecal incontinence three-fold and to double the risk of flatus incontinence, compared to a spontaneous tear. Women with a midline episiotomy are five times more likely to have faecal incontinence than those with an intact perineum at three months post-partum (Signorello et al., 2000). Mediolateral episiotomy (with the incision directed away from the mid line) has not been shown to be so clearly related to subsequent faecal incontinence, but neither has it been shown to be protective and may even weaken the pelvic floor (Sultan and Kamm, 1997). There is a conflict of opinion as to whether routine liberal use of episiotomy is protective (especially if combined with pelvic floor exercises: Taskin et al., 1996) or whether it should be abandoned altogether (Klein et al., 1994).

The active pushing phase of the second stage of labour may be important, with pushing for more than one hour associated with increased risk of neuromuscular injury (Handa et al., 1996). Caesarean delivery does seem to be partly protective against both urinary (Wilson et al., 1996) and faecal incontinence (Sultan et al., 1993), although rates tend to equalise after two caesarean births.

There is debate about how to manage subsequent deliveries in women known to have sustained some anal sphincter damage already. Some would advocate allowing another vaginal delivery, on the basis that the damage has already been done, while others would advocate repair of the sphincter and plan for future caesarean births (Sultan and Kamm, 1997).

Iatrogenic damage to the anal sphincters

Colorectal surgery

Several common ano-rectal procedures are associated with an increased risk of faecal incontinence. Lateral sphincterotomy to relieve a chronic painful anal fissure has been reported to result in minor symptoms of passive soiling (22%) and flatus incontinence (35%) and major faecal incontinence in 5% of cases (Khubchandani and Reed, 1989). Women have a naturally shorter anal canal than men and the anterior ring of sphincter is normally incomplete in the upper anal canal. It is not uncommon for a sphincterotomy to extend for the full length of the internal anal sphincter in women (Sultan et al., 1994).

Surgical haemorrhoidectomy is reported to result in varying rates of faecal incontinence. Given that the reported rates do vary widely, it may be that variations in surgical technique or skill are important. There does seem to be an increased willingness to take these 'minor' procedures more seriously and not leave them to the most inexperienced surgical trainees. Increased use of 'chemical sphincterotomy' (e.g. topical glycerin trinitrate (GTN) or diltiazem), and injection or banding of haemorrhoids, with surgery reserved for the most severe or resistant cases, may lead to fewer future problems. The practice of anal stretch seems to have fallen into disrepute because of subsequent problems with faecal incontinence (Snooks et al., 1984), except in paediatric practice, where presumably the internal sphincter is more elastic and less prone to fragment (see Chapter 19).

There is an increasing tendency to avoid creating a stoma when a patient needs all or part of the large bowel removed. Resection of the rectum for rectal cancer is often preferred by patients as an alternative to living with a colostomy, but those with a low resection may find continence compromised. The mechanism for this may be a combination of reduced capacity, reduced rectal compliance and possibly damage to the sensory and/or motor function of the anus during resection.

Anastomosis of the small bowel to the rectum or anus, or fashioning of an ileoanal internal pouch ('restorative procto-colectomy') usually results in frequent and fairly fluid bowel actions, possibly with urgency; some patients find their ability to control this unreliable. A few also experience passive soiling, especially at night. There is controversy as to whether better continence is achieved with differing surgical techniques, such as stapling or handsewing the anastomosis, or performing removal of the mucosa or not.

Gynaecological surgery

There is some evidence that surgical solutions for one pelvic floor problem may unmask another and cause it to become symptomatic, or even possibly create new problems by distorting the anatomy or disrupting the neurological supply. For example, repairing a vaginal prolapse may unmask a tendency to urinary or faecal incontinence as the prolapse was actually supporting a cystocele or rectocoele. Colposuspension is known to create new symptoms of prolapse in a proportion of patients (Wiskind et al., 1992). Repair of a rectocoele corrects the anatomical defect for three-quarters of women undergoing posterior colporrhaphy, but there is not a clear relationship between anatomical defect and dysfunction. Repair of a rectocoele has been found to create new symptoms of faecal incontinence in 7% in one series, with some patients also reporting new sexual dysfunction (9%), rectal evacuation difficulties (11%) and poor control of flatus (Kahn and Stanton, 1997).

Hysterectomy has been found in retrospective studies to change bowel function (Taylor et al., 1989), with over one third of women reporting newly decreased bowel frequency or increased difficulty with evacuation. It is postulated that the associated factors might include:

- damage to the hypogastric nerve plexus during surgery
- hormonal changes
- common thread of chronic abdominal discomfort
- anxiety in polysymptomatic women.

Only 59% reported normal bowel function prior to hysterectomy (van Dam et al., 1997). It may be that the surgery disrupts the pelvic nerve plexus and structural support to the bladder. However, often the primary reason for hysterectomy is pelvic floor dysfunction and so it may be a symptom rather than a cause of the problem (Bump and Norton, 1998).

Idiopathic degeneration of the anal sphincters

It seems that sometimes the internal anal sphincter may degenerate and become very thin, for reasons as yet unknown (Vaizey et al., 1997). This thin atrophic sphincter often has a low resting closure pressure and the patient complains of passive seepage of stool. It is not known whether degeneration can also affect the external anal sphincter, although clinically it is often reported as appearing atrophic on ultrasound or MRI (see Chapter 9).

Direct trauma or injury to the anal sphincters

Impalement injuries are not common, but can occur following road traffic accidents or climbing over fences. Often the patient will need an emergency colostomy to divert the faecal stream and then a sphincter repair.

There is some debate about the role of sexual use or abuse of the anus as a cause of faecal incontinence. Some evidence suggests that unwanted or forced anal sex can cause direct anal sphincter injury (Engel et al., 1995). Most people may also have some psychosocial issues after such an event, which could contribute to symptoms (Berkelmans et al., 1996). Consensual anal sex does not appear to cause sphincter damage (Chun et al., 1997) or symptoms of faecal incontinence.

Congenital anomaly (see Chapter 19)

Congenital abnormalities of the ano-rectum are relatively common. Most will be spotted in infancy and will need surgical correction. However, continence is not always perfect. A few disorders may not be discovered until a much later date, emphasising the importance of comprehensive assessment.

Gut motility / Stool consistency

Anyone with very frequent or loose bowel motions is more prone to episodes of incontinence than other people. As anyone who has had acute 'holiday tummy' knows, frequency, flatulence and urgency, together with disturbed sensation (which makes distinguishing flatus from faeces difficult), may mean that an occupied toilet spells disaster.

Diarrhoea itself has many possible causes, the more common of which include inflammatory bowel disease (ulcerative colitis and Crohn's disease), irritable bowel syndrome (where it may alternate with bouts of constipation), post-surgery where a substantial amount of large bowel has been removed (e.g. for carcinoma or inflammatory bowel disease), post-radiotherapy for any pelvic tumour, infective gastroenteritis, and as a side effect of some drugs (notably antibiotics). Some people develop diarrhoea in response to intolerance of an element in their diet (e.g. people with coeliac disease in response to gluten). Anxiety leads to frequent loose bowel actions for others. Many people with faecal incontinence clinically present with frequent loose stools. It is often not clear if this is the 'cause' of their problem, or if it is a result of the anxiety created by this condition (see Chapter 5).

If the individual with diarrhoea also has some sphincter damage for any of the reasons outlined above, then control can be very precarious and it may be impossible at times to venture far from a toilet. Chapter 10 covers causes and management of diarrhoea in detail.

Ano-rectal pathology

There are many minor anal conditions, such as haemorrhoids and skin tags, which can make anal cleaning difficult and may lead to passive soiling with stool or mucus. There are also some more major conditions such as rectal prolapse and anal fistula which can impair continence. These conditions are covered in detail in Chapter 11.

Neurological disease

This topic is covered in detail in Chapter 17. Care should be taken when reading the literature on the subject as the term 'neurogenic incontinence' is often used in the specialised colorectal literature to denote faecal incontinence associated with pudendal nerve damage during childbirth, and does not refer to that caused by major neurological disease or injury.

Consequences of degenerative neurological disease

Elderly people with Alzheimer's disease or other dementias have a high prevalence of incontinence. The aetiology of this seems to be a complex interaction of the following:

- neurological impairment causing loss of sensation and ability to control bowel function
- decreased intellectual functioning and social awareness of need for confidence
- medical physical ability to cope with bowel function.

Individuals who are also immobile easily become constipated with faecal impaction (see below). In institutional settings, this may be compounded by staff shortages or lack of individualised care. Chapter 13 considers faecal incontinence in old age and Chapter 18 covers behavioural approaches which can be applied in this group.

Impaction with overflow

There is a well-recognised association between severe constipation with faecal impaction and incontinence, either of solid stool or of liquid stool – often referred to as 'spurious diarrhoea'. The condition is especially prevalent amongst the frail elderly population in institutional care. However, the mechanism for this incontinence remains somewhat obscure. It has often been suggested that impaction of the rectum causes anal relaxation, but anal resting and squeeze pressures have been found to be similar in impacted individuals as to pressures in age-matched non-impacted controls. There is, however a reduction in sensation and in the volume of rectal distension needed to elicit internal sphincter relaxation via the recto-anal inhibitory reflex, and some loss of the ano-rectal angle in incontinent individuals. It is unclear which of these mechanisms is the cause or the effect of impaction or subsequent incontinence. It may be that once impaction is present (possibly caused by a combination of immobility, low fluid and fibre intake, drug side effects, confusion, lack of privacy and many other factors), lack of sensation makes it difficult to contract the external sphincter appropriately to prevent leakage when the internal sphincter relaxes in response to rectal distension (Read and Abouzekry, 1986; Barrett, 1993). The 'impacted' stool may be hard or soft and putty-like in consistency (Barrett, 1993).

Megarectum or megacolon and severe constipation in children are covered in Chapter 19. Bowel care in institutionalised or immobile elderly people is covered in detail in Chapter 13.

Environmental factors

Individuals who have physical or mental impairments may have their ability to maintain continence impaired by an adverse physical or social environment. This is particularly relevant to those in institutional settings. Environmental factors include:

- toilet facilities which are inaccessible or lack privacy so that the person avoids using the toilet
- carers who are not sensitive to the individual's needs and bowel habit
- clothes which are difficult to manipulate in a hurry
- variety of other factors which vary with abilities of the individual.

The toilet itself may be too high, leaving the feet dangling and making abdominal effort to assist defaecation difficult. Or it may be too low, making sitting and rising difficult for those with immobile hips. A social environment in which staff are always overworked and harassed may lead the individual to repeatedly ignore the call to stool, in the hope of finding a quieter time later, and eventually lead to the impaction described above.

'Lifestyle' and other factors

There are several other factors which may contribute to the development of the symptom of faecal incontinence.

There is no evidence about the effect of body mass index (BMI) on faecal incontinence. A BMI of 30 or over is an independent risk factor for urinary incontinence (Brown et al., 1999), but it is not proven that weight loss is protective nor that it alleviates established urinary incontinence, except in the morbidly obese requiring surgery for weight loss. Extra weight may impair the blood flow or nerve function to the pelvic floor and this may be reversible (Bump and Norton, 1998).

Racial origin also seems to be important, with Asian and white races more prone to pelvic floor problems (Handa et al., 1996; Brown et al., 1999) than black women. While this does not give scope for primary prevention, it may enable secondary prevention programmes to be targeted to those most at risk.

It is known that nicotine stimulates distal colonic motility and may therefore exacerbate a tendency to faecal urgency (Rausch et al., 1998). Smoking is a known risk factor for urinary incontinence and prolapse (odds ratio 2.9) (Bump and Norton, 1998), presumably via chronic coughing, but there may be also less general health awareness than in non-smokers. Caffeine stimulates both bladder and bowel as well as acting as a diuretic (Brown et al., 1990).

Athletes who undertake a lot of high-impact exercise are more prone to stress urinary incontinence (Bump and Norton, 1998). Excessive exercise may also be a factor in rectal prolapse. Nurses and others whose jobs involve a lot of heavy lifting are more likely to need vaginal prolapse surgery that the general population (odds ratio 1.6) (Jorgensen et al., 1994).

A common factor in the genesis of pelvic floor problems may be chronic straining with perineal descent from constipation, with subsequent pelvic floor damage (direct or neurological) (Snooks et al., 1985; Lubowski et al., 1988) resulting in prolapse or urinary or faecal incontinence. Straining at stool by young women has been found to be associated with later prolapse and stress urinary incontinence (Spence-Jones et al., 1994).

A vast number of drugs have possible direct or indirect effects on the gastrointestinal system, tending to cause constipation, diarrhoea, or either in different people. The most common are listed in Chapter 10 (for diarrhoea) and Chapter 21 (for constipation), but these are by no means exhaustive, and each person with bowel symptoms should have a careful drug history taken (including all over the counter or 'herbal' preparations) and possible gut effects should be considered. It is beyond the scope of this chapter to review drug effects in detail, and prescribers should be aware of unintended side effects on faecal incontinence.

Frailty and dependence on others will mean that the individual's ability to maintain continence is influenced by the availability and attitudes of carers. These may be conducive to continence, or may make good bowel control very difficult.

It may be that a number of lifestyle modifications, such as regulating bowel habit and avoiding straining, not smoking, regular physical exercise, oestrogen replacement if indicated and weight loss may help to prevent the development of incontinence in at-risk women.

Idiopathic incontinence

Despite all available assessment and investigation methods, there is a group of patients in whom no 'cause' for the symptom of faecal incontinence can be identified. There is undoubtedly much more that we need to learn about the mechanism of bowel control before we fully understand the aetiology of this common problem.

Conclusions

There are many possible causes or contributory factors which may lead to the symptom of faecal incontinence. Chapters 6 to 9 give details of investigation and assessment that can help to determine which cause or causes are relevant to each individual patient.

References

Barrett, J.A. (1993) *Faecal incontinence and related problems in the older adult.* London: Edward Arnold.

Berkelmans, I., Leroi, A.M., Weber, J. and Denis, P. (1996) Faecal incontinence with transitory absence of anal contraction in two sexually or physically abused women. *European Journal of Gastroenterology and Hepatology* **8**, 235–238.

Brown, J.S., Grady, D., Ouslander, J.G., Herzog, A.R., Varner, R.E. and Posner, S.F. (1999) Prevalence of urinary incontinence and associated risk factors in postmenopausal women. Heart & Estrogen/Progestin Replacement Study (HERS) Research Group. *Obstetrics and Gynecology* **94**, 66–70.

Brown, S.R., Cann, P.A. and Read, N.W. (1990) Effect of coffee on distal colon function. Gut **31**, 450–453.

Bump, R.C. and Norton, P.A. (1998) Epidemiology and natural history of pelvic floor dysfunction. *Obstetrics and Gynecology Clinics of North America* **25**, 723–746.

Chun, A.B., Rose, S., Mitrani, C., Silvestre, A.J. and Wald, A. (1997) Anal sphincter structure and function in homosexual males engaging in anoreceptive intercourse. *American Journal of Gastroenterology* **92**, 3, 465–8.

Donnelly, V.S., O'Herlihy, C., Campbell, D.M. and O'Connell, P.R. (1998) Postpartum fecal incontinence is more common in women with irritable bowel syndrome. *Diseases of the Colon and Rectum* **41**, 586–589.

Engel, A.F., Kamm, M.A. and Bartram, C.I. (1995) Unwanted anal penetration as a physical cause of faecal incontinence. *European Journal of Gastroenterology and Hepatology* **7**, 65–67.

Handa, V.L., Harris, T.A. and Ostergard, D.R. (1996) Protecting the pelvic floor: obstetric management to prevent incontinence and pelvic organ prolapse. *Obstetrics and Gynecology* **88**, 470–478.

Jorgensen, S., Hein, H.O. and Gyntelberg, F. (1994) Heavy lifting at work and risk of genital prolapse and herniated lumbar disc in assistant nurses. *Occupational Medicine* **44**, 47–49.

Kahn, M.A. and Stanton, S.L. (1997) Posterior colporrhaphy: its effects on bowel and sexual function. *British Journal of Obstetrics and Gynaecology* **104**, 82–86. [see comments]

Khubchandani, I. and Reed, J.F. (1989) Sequelae of internal sphincterotomy for chronic fissure *in ano*. *British Journal of Surgery* **76**, 431–434.

Klein, M.C., Gauthier, R.J. and Robbins, J.M. (1994) Relationship of episiotomy to perineal trauma and morbidity, sexual dysfunction, and pelvic floor relaxation. *American Journal of Obstetrics and Gynecology* **171**, 591–598.

Lubowski, D.Z., Swash, M. and Nicholls, R.J. (1988) Increases in pudendal nerve terminal motor latency with defaecation straining. *British Journal of Surgery* **75**, 1095–1097.

MacArthur, C., Bick, D.E. and Keighley, M.R.B. (1997) Faecal incontinence after childbirth. *British Journal of Obstetrics and Gynaecology* **104**, 46–50.

Rausch, T., Beglinger, C., Alam, N. and Meier, R. (1998) Effect of transdermal application of nicotine on colonic transit in healthy nonsmoking volunteers. *Neurogastroenterology and Motility* **10**, 263–270.

Read, N.W. and Abouzekry, L. (1986) Why do patients with faecal impaction have faecal incontinence? *Gut* **27**, 283–287.

Ryhammer, A.M., Bek, K.M. and Laurberg, S. (1995) Multiple vaginal deliveries increase the risk of permanent incontinence of flatus and urine in normal premenopausal women. *Diseases of the Colon and Rectum* **38**, 1206–1209.

Signorello, L.B., Harlow, B.L., Chekos, A.K. and Repke, J.T. (2000) Midline episiotomy and anal incontinence: retrospective cohort study. *British Medical Journal* **320**, 86–90.

Snooks, S.J., Henry, M.M. and Swash, M. (1984) Faecal incontinence after anal dilatation. *British Journal of Surgery* **71**, 617–618.

Snooks, S.J., Barnes, P.R.H., Swash, M. and Henry, M.M. (1985) Damage to the innervation of the pelvic floor musculature in chronic constipation. *Gastroenterology* **89**, 977–981.

Spence-Jones, C., Kamm, M.A. and Henry, M.M. (1994) Bowel dysfunction: a pathogenic factor in uterovaginal prolapse and urinary stress incontinence. *British Journal of Obstetrics and Gynaecology* **101**, 147–152.

Sultan, A.H. and Kamm, M.A. (1997) Faecal incontinence after childbirth. *British Journal of Obstetrics & Gynaecology* **104**, 979–982.

Sultan, A.H., Kamm, M.A., Hudson, C.N., Thomas, J.M. and Bartram, C.I. (1993) Anal sphincter disruption during vaginal delivery. *New England Journal of Medicine* **329**, 1905–1911.

Sultan, A.H., Kamm, M.A., Nicholls, R.J. and Bartram, C.I. (1994) Prospective study of the extent of internal sphincter division during lateral sphincterotomy. *Diseases of the Colon and Rectum* **37**, 1031–1033.

Sultan, A.H., Monga, A.K., Kumar, D. and Stanton, S.L. (1999) Primary repair of obstetric anal sphincter rupture using the overlap technique. *British Journal of Obstetrics and Gynaecology* **106**, 318–323.

Taskin, O., Wheeler, J.M. and Yalcinoglu, A.I. (1996) The effects of episiotomy and Kegel exercises on postpartum pelvic relaxation: a prospective controlled study. *Journal of Gynecological Surgery* **12**, 123–127.

Taylor, T., Smith, A.N. and Fulton, P.M. (1989) Effect of hysterectomy on bowel function. *British Medical Journal* **299**, 300–301.

Vaizey, C.J., Kamm, M.A. and Bartram, C.I. (1997) Primary degeneration of the internal anal sphincter as a cause of passive faecal incontinence. *Lancet* **349**, 612–615.

van Dam, J.H., Gosselink, M.J., Drogendijk, A.C., Hop, W.C. and Schouten, W.R. (1997) Changes in bowel function after hysterectomy. *Diseases of the Colon and Rectum* **40**, 1342–1347.

Wilson, P.D., Herbison, R.M. and Herbison, G.P. (1996) Obstetric practice and the prevalence of urinary incontinence three months after delivery. *British Journal of Obstetrics and Gynaecology* **103**, 154–161.

Wiskind, A.K., Creighton, S.M. and Stanton, S.L. (1992) The incidence of genital prolapse after the Burch colposuspension. *American Journal of Obstetrics and Gynecology* **167**, 399–404.

Zetterstrom, J.P., Lopez, A., Anzen, B., Dolk, A., Norman, M. and Mellgren, A. (1999) Anal incontinence after vaginal delivery: a prospective study in primiparous women. *British Journal of Obstetrics and Gynaecology* **106**, 324–330.

Chapter 5

Psychosocial Aspects of Patients with Faecal Incontinence

Sonya Chelvanayagam and Solveig Wilson

'The cure of the part should not be attempted without treatment of the whole. No attempt should be made to cure the body without the soul.'
Plato, *The Republic*, 382 BC

Introduction

Faecal incontinence is a symptom which detrimentally affects psychological, physical, and social functioning (Marcio et al., 1993). Individuals with compromised bowel control report feeling stigmatised and are reluctant to discuss their symptoms even with health professionals (Johanson and Lafferty, 1996). Not surprisingly, urinary incontinence affects people similarly. However, individuals who have both urinary and faecal incontinence report their greatest concern and embarrassment is related to their bowel function (Khullar et al., 1998). It is important to understand where and how these attitudes towards the importance of bowel control developed. Historically, faeces has been regarded as unclean for at least 400,000 years; fossilised stools of that period have been found away from clean designated areas in archaeological remains. Faeces have also been associated with disease. When the London sewage system was improved due to the Public Health Act in 1848, death rates decreased significantly (Smith and Smith, 1987). Elimination has for centuries been regarded as a highly private activity and throughout the world people are socialised into eliminating in private, which therefore inhibits them from discussing this activity (Roper et al., 1985).

Continence was initially defined in relationship to sexual self-control, and treatment remedies for incontinence from 1500 BC onwards all focused on punishment. It was not until the late 20th century that the term incontinence came to have its present meaning, although unfortunately the stigma persists.

This chapter examines the psychological and social aspects relevant to faecal incontinence and the effect of this distressing symptom on individuals.

Developing bowel control

A newborn baby exposed to unpleasant smells such as ammonia or acetic acid is capable of turning his head away from the aversive odour, although at that stage the child has not yet learned that it is offensive. The child becomes aware of a sense of fullness, which precedes defaecation and may communicate this to a carer by pulling at their nappy or taking up a squatting position and using a familiar word. Toddlers learn quickly that defaecating in the wrong place is socially unacceptable and their need to please others, coupled with their fascination of placing something in a container, leads to the acquisition of bowel control. Bowel control is usually achieved before bladder control in a toddler (Schuster and Ashburn, 1980).

Maintaining bowel control

Adults are often unaware of the mechanism that allows deferment of defaecation as this is not an explicitly taught process (see Chapter 3). Therefore, when bowel control is compromised, individuals have difficulty understanding how to manage these symptoms. Also, due to the taboo nature of the subject people are fearful of seeking help (Leigh and Turnberg, 1982). However, most people soon realise what affects their bowel control. They become rapidly aware that certain foods or situations cause loose stools. It only requires 'one near miss' for fear to develop and lead to avoidance of the specific trigger. Increased stress to avoid the perceived trigger occurs, which then increases bowel motility (Almy, 1951). This causes a sense of urgency and a risk of faecal incontinence (Toner, et al., 1998). The unpredictability of the symptoms of incontinence means that the individual feels continually threatened as 'today could be the day'. Therefore a vicious cycle begins (Figure 5.1). Obviously this does not only relate to bowel control. In any situation where an individual feels endangered, a sense of vulnerability arises and normal functioning is threatened. Fortunately, in most situations help can be accessed and support gained. Difficulties arise when the subject is taboo and causes shame to the individual concerned. A reluctance to discuss the problem or seek help occurs and the longer this continues the greater the impact on health and quality of life.

Tom, a 20-year-old student had started to have abdominal pains and diarrhoea prior to his exams. After an initial diagnosis of 'nerves', he was diagnosed with ulcerative colitis some months later. He felt relieved at having a diagnosis but frustrated that the medication did not make him feel better. He suffered continued abdominal pain and became fatigued. He lost his appetite and found it difficult to concentrate. His college work suffered and he felt depressed. Tom stopped going to the bar with the other students. His girlfriend was initially sympathetic, but could not understand why he did not get better. Tom felt angry at his condition and felt it was too embarrassing to discuss any details with his friends. He was too unwell to study for the end of term exams and decided to take time off to see if the lack of pressure made a difference. He was referred for counselling, which enabled him to explore issues in his life that may have contributed to his coping skills. A major issue was 'rage'. A minor argument could become a major incident with furniture broken and doors kicked in. In the safe, non-judgemental environment of the counselling

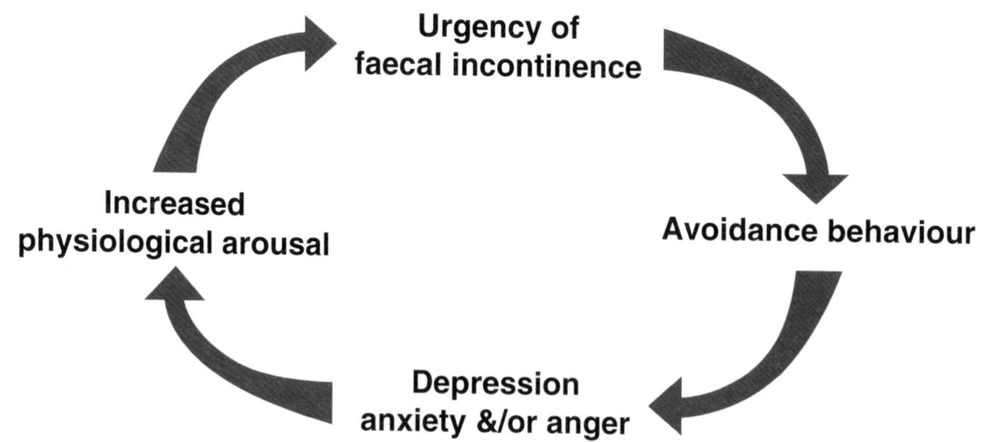

Figure 5.1 *Cycle of incontinence.*

sessions he developed an understanding of himself which enabled him to confront his fears and his aggression. He acknowledged that he suffered from a chronic condition, for which there was no permanent cure except radical surgery and the possibility of a permanent ileostomy. He learnt to recognise potentially stressful situations and adapted to them. He did not seek to avoid stress altogether but became more aware of the physical and emotional impact it would have on him.

Psychosocial impact of faecal incontinence

Coping and control

Bowel continence is essentially a matter of control. When a disease or disability cannot be 'cured', the individual must try to cope with the symptoms and their ramifications. Nurses can help patients to 'reframe' a previously held secret so that the tension and fear of discovery are transformed into the open sharing of a problem (Benner and Wrubel, 1988, p. 168). If people hold a Cartesian (Descartes 1596–1650) view of measuring oneself against an unattainable ideal, they can never measure up. The gap between reality and that ideal creates dissonance. What is often needed is to let go of that ideal, to re-define the situation and develop realistic expectations of function (Benner and Wrubel, 1988, p. 395). Those for whom there is a technological failure to cure symptoms need to learn to cope. By recognising the patient's own expertise about their body – that is, the experiential knowledge gained from living with a chronic condition – people can learn to recognise their own bodily signs and listen to their own body.

When an individual experiences an uncomfortable or stressful event, different types or levels of control may become operant. Increased decision-making has been found to be associated with a reduction in anxiety (Surla, 1984, cited in Lewis, 1987).

Some people exhibit 'learned helplessness' in an environment that is perceived as beyond control (Seligman, 1992). They give up, as there is an expectation that whatever their response to a situation may be, it will have no effect on the event; outcomes are not seen as linked to her/his own behaviour.

Anxiety is caused by unpredictability and uncontrollability. Conversely, those who perceive a link between their actions and the outcome or who can predict events and outcome, experience a sense of control, with higher levels of motivation and lower levels of anxiety and depression. If events are experienced as totally unpredictable, there is a lack of a safety signal to predict unavoidable danger and so the individual never has a sense of being safe (Seligman, 1992).

Psychological aspects of faecal incontinence

There is a strong association between psychological factors and gastrointestinal disorders. Stress affects gastrointestinal function in normal subjects and greatly exacerbates gastrointestinal symptoms in those with pre-existing symptoms. Psychological problems exist more frequently in those individuals with a functional gastrointestinal disorder and affects their illness perception and health-seeking behaviour Drossman, 1999). Individuals who report two or more gastrointestinal symptoms have been Reported to have significantly higher rates of long-term psychiatric disorders, and conversely 'lifetime' gastrointestinal symptoms are seen in subjects with long-term psychiatric disorders (North et al., 1996). Due to the nature of gastrointestinal disorders there will be an impact on an individual's quality of life and psychological state.

Glickman and Kamm (1996) studied bowel dysfunction in spinal-cord injury patients. Those who reported difficulties with bowel function saw it as a major physical and psychological problem. The patients with greatest disability in bowel function scored high levels of anxiety and depression; however, it was not possible to assess whether bowel dysfunction caused psychological distress or whether those with greater anxiety and depression developed worsening bowel function.

There is a dearth of literature examining the psychological impact of faecal incontinence, even though there is a general acknowledgement of the psychological distress seen in this group (Whitehead et al., 1999). The few studies that have been performed are mostly concerned with children or adolescents with faecal incontinence. Ludman et al. (1994) studied the psychological impact of faecal incontinence after surgery for ano-rectal abnormalities. One hundred and sixty children / adolescents and parents were assessed by psychiatric interview, parental assessment and a child self-report depressive scale. The children were also clinically assessed by a surgeon who completed a scoring measure of incontinence. Teachers were asked to complete behavioural questionnaires. The results showed that there was an association between levels of continence and psychological adjustment only in young girls (6–11 years). Teachers and parents reported more behavioural problems in this group. Generally there was a higher prevalence of psychological difficulties such as internalising problems and depression compared to a normal population. There appears to be an increased risk of psychosocial problems, which highlighted the need for early assessment, treatment and appropriate advice for both parents and children.

Cavet (1988) completed an extensive study of teenagers' experiences living with faecal incontinence and the psychosocial effects on their lives and their families. They faced exclusion, humiliation, ignorance, ridicule and embarrassment. Not only were the teenagers dealing with the physical and psychological changes associated with puberty but also with a hidden 'disability'.

Self-confidence and supportive personal relationships are important factors in how the condition is managed. Low self-esteem and the absence of a supportive partner make a difficult condition worse. A young unattached person may find it impossible to contemplate having a colostomy for faecal incontinence for fear of being rejected by a potential partner. A middle-aged person in a stable relationship might be able to accept having a colostomy more readily. However, although a colostomy might offer control and freedom, the psychological impact on body-image might still be hard to overcome.

Sickness and disability also have an effect on income and the kind of work that can be done. The aspirations of a highly motivated graduate may be thwarted by the effects of frequency and urgency in inflammatory bowel disease. Work may have to be suspended for a period of time when there is a relapse. Depending on the employment contract, a person may become dependent on the safety net of a welfare system, and a benefits system can either help or hinder a person's motivation to return to work. If self-confidence is low, a person may not feel able to give up any state benefits in exchange for an uncertain job future. This may involve a change in their quality of life and a lower standard of living, but it may feel safer to live on a lower income than to have a job where there is little understanding of what it is like to suffer from compromised bowel control.

Learnt coping mechanisms influence how an individual lives with compromised bowel control. They may influence how help is sought, if expectations of treatment and cure are realistic and how, ultimately, the condition is to be managed (Drossman et al., 1990). The attitude of professionals, family and friends has a bearing on how an individual copes with what is perceived to be an embarrassing condition. The stigma attached to it and the difficulties in talking about the condition may affect individuals of any age. A student may stop socialising if they feel embarrassed at having to go to the toilet more frequently than others and they may become hyper-aware of insensitive remarks or jokes. A woman may leave a half-filled shopping trolley in a supermarket to rush to the toilet or home if she has soiled herself. Elderly people may suffer loss of dignity and independence if they become incontinent. There may be a period of denial, when it is too hard to accept that they have lost bladder or bowel control. They may believe the consequences of incontinence can be hidden, but often this, in turn, may alienate them from others and cause them to become isolated and lonely.

Faecal incontinence may legitimise the avoidance of situations and actions. It becomes the focal part of a person's life and decision-making. It may distract the person from grieving about other losses. It may not be until the patient is given the opportunity to repeat the illness narrative in a safe yet challenging environment that the personal and social meaning of impaired bowel control can be fully appreciated (Kleinman, 1988).

Quality of life

Health Related Quality of Life is a concept used to quantify the physical, social and psychological functioning which may be impaired by illness or disease (Gill and Feinstein, 1994). The domains typically included in a quality-of-life instrument examine well-being, depression and anxiety, pain and discomfort, body image and sexuality, mobility and the ability to perform activities of daily living, participation in social/recreational activities, ability to attend school/work and personal relationships.

Health Related Quality of Life attempts to measure a condition from the patient's perspective rather than the clinician's. Although objective measures such as blood tests or imaging provide information about a specific condition they do not correspond directly to a patient's functioning. Also patients with the same condition and same extent of disease do not necessarily experience the same impact on their quality of life (Guyatt et al., 1993). Most current clinical research studies on functional disorders incorporate quality of life questionnaires as outcome measures and they are also used in clinical audit and in clinical governance (Higginson and Carr, 2001).

There are three types of Health Related Quality of Life measures: global indices, generic indices and disease-specific instruments. A global index provides an overall assessment of quality of life instead of examining individual domains and therefore is insensitive to modest changes.

Generic instruments are more comprehensive and can compare changes across patient populations but are unable to detect subtle changes within specific conditions.

One of the most widely used generic quality of life measures is the Medical Outcomes Scale Short Form 36 (MOS SF-36), which has been validated across a range of conditions (Stewart et al., 1989). Originally developed as part of a Medical Outcomes Study in the USA, the instrument has also been validated for use in the United Kingdom with some modifications. The questionnaire consists of 36 questions, measuring different dimensions of health-related quality of life and a single question on health transition. The domains are physical functioning, role functioning, social functioning, mental health, health perception and pain. On each scale 100 is judged as maximal or optimal quality of life.

Disease-specific quality of life questionnaires aim to measure functioning within a condition and are not related to the general population. The questionnaire asks about symptoms known to be related to the specific condition and their effect in the relevant quality of life domains. Therefore it measures the impact of a condition on an individual compared to others with the same condition and is useful as an outcome measure for specific treatments (Irvine, 1996).

Ideally, when assessing quality of life in faecal incontinence, it is recommended to use a generic quality of life measure such as the MOS SF-36 with a disease-specific quality of life tool, of which there have been only two produced specifically for faecal incontinence.

Quality of life measures for faecal incontinence

Quality of life measures are frequently used to examine the effect of illnesses which are chronic, debilitating and progressive in nature such as arthritis or diabetes (Fullerton, 1996). Faecal incontinence is not a condition but a symptom. It may occur due to an illness such as inflammatory bowel disease but for many individuals there is no underlying organic illness (see Chapter 4).

The value of a disease-specific instrument

rather than a generic measure is that it tends to be more sensitive to minor changes. This is important when assessing the effect of a treatment or surgery for faecal incontinence, which may not lead to cure but a decrease in the frequency of symptoms. Interestingly, improvement in bowel control does not necessarily correlate with improvement in quality of life (Rockwood, 2000, invited editorial). This needs to be taken into consideration when developing a measure for faecal incontinence, as treatments will need to prove a positive effect on quality of life in addition to a change in bowel symptoms.

Gastrointestinal Quality of Life Index

This questionnaire examines quality of life across a range of gastrointestinal symptoms (Eypasch et al., 1995). The development of this questionnaire began by collating questions and testing these on 70 patients and 56 relatives. The questionnaire enquired about symptoms, and the physical, emotional and social impact of gastrointestinal disease or its treatments. If a symptom or dysfunction was present a patient indicated this on a four-point scale; only those symptoms which were recorded as having a moderate effect on their quality of life and reported by 25% of patients were retained. The questions were modified and then tested on 204 patients and the contents verified by surgeons, gastroenterologists and general practitioners internationally. In its final phase it was tested on 168 normal subjects. It was validated against a global quality of life scale and a questionnaire assessing psychological function.

The questionnaire consists of thirty-six questions with five responses, which are to provide a numerical score. It has four questions related to compromised bowel function, which are excessive flatus, frequent bowel actions, faecal urgency and 'uncontrolled stools' (presumably faecal incontinence). It has been developed for use in clinical practice and research and is available in German and English. It probably has limited use for those individuals with isolated faecal incontinence, but may be more helpful for patients with both irritable bowel syndrome and faecal incontinence where there is a range of symptoms.

The Fecal Incontinence Quality of Life Scale

This scale was developed in America and was the first quality of life measure specifically for faecal incontinence (Rockwood et al., 2000). It consists of twenty-nine items, which form four scales. These are lifestyle, coping/behaviour, depression/self perception and embarrassment. It was compiled by a panel of experts including surgeons and health researchers convening to discuss the relevant quality of life aspects affected by faecal incontinence. Interestingly, the questions included in the questionnaire are generated from experts in the field rather than individuals affected, which is an unusual starting point considering that quality of life attempts to measure the patients' perception of their symptoms. The questionnaire was then tested on two patient groups, one group consisting of individuals with faecal incontinence and the other of patients affected by other gastrointestinal symptoms. This questionnaire has not yet been validated in the UK. Although it does not discriminate between individuals with different degrees of incontinence it can be further developed to become a worthwhile tool for measuring quality of life for individuals with faecal incontinence.

Manchester Health Questionnaire

This was recently developed in England (Bugg et al., 2001). It examines the impact of faecal incontinence on women and was adapted from a validated questionnaire for urinary incontinence. Subjects participated by a postal questionnaire and it was seen to be a reliable and valid instrument. It combines measurement of symptoms (i.e. frequency of incontinence) with effect on quality of life. Interestingly, it was only developed for use with women (which may reflect increased health-seeking behaviour in women with these symptoms). Bugg et al. (2001) are keen that the questionnaire is used as an evaluation tool of bowel function following childbirth.

The effects of faecal incontinence on quality of life

Although quality of life questionnaires have been used to examine the outcome of many surgical procedures for faecal incontinence, there is a paucity of literature examining the direct effect of faecal incontinence on individuals.

Sailer et al. (1998) studied quality of life in 325 patients with ano-rectal disorders at their first visit to the proctology department using the Gastrointestinal Quality of Life Index. Patients were asked to complete the Gastrointestinal Quality of Life Index and the mean score was compared with that of a control group of 150 healthy volunteers. A patient assessment consisting of history, rectal and abdominal examination, proctoscopy and sigmoidoscopy and, dependent on the diagnosis, further investigations such as barium studies, colonoscopy and ano-rectal manometry were performed on all patients but not on control subjects. These patients were classified into nine subgroups with one group consisting of thirty-five patients with faecal incontinence. The results showed that faecal incontinence had a severely detrimental effect on overall quality of life, which was also seen in patients with severe constipation.

Sharpe et al. (1997) reported similar findings with a small study of fifteen patients. They also used the Gastrointestinal Quality of Life Index and the General Health Questionnaire to assess psychological status and recorded incontinence scores. They reported that severity of symptoms did not necessarily correspond with quality of life and that both should be assessed simultaneously.

Patients' quality of life after total colectomy and ileoanal pouch formation was shown to be affected by frequency of bowel actions, nocturnal defaecation and passive soiling. Fujita et al., (1992) investigated eighty patients with either colitis or familial polyposis post-operatively by sending an anxiety measure, and a questionnaire which they had developed examining physical, social and emotional function, attitudes to illness, personality characteristics, relationships, activities of daily living and cost of illness. An increased frequency of bowel symptoms caused restricted social eating in order to avoid defaecation. Increased frequency of bowel actions caused perianal soreness with the need to wash after defaecation and to use ointment. Nocturnal defaecation more than once weekly was associated with loss of energy for activities of daily living. Passive soiling and stool frequency increased with tiredness. Soiling occurred with coitus and also led to a fear of sporting activities. The authors found that improved bowel control increased satisfaction with surgery and that frequent bowel symptoms led to dissatisfaction and deleterious effects on quality of life.

Colorectal dysfunction is prevalent among patients with systemic sclerosis (connective tissue disease). Ninety-six patients with this condition were sent a detailed questionnaire describing a range of bowel disorders and enquiring about quality of life. Thirty-eight per cent reported faecal incontinence with the same figure reporting diarrhoea occurring once or more each month. Fifteen per cent of patients reporting faecal incontinence had some or major restriction on their quality of life (Trezza et al., 1999).

While developing their own quality of life measure, Chelvanayagam and Norton (2000) held focus groups with female participants with longstanding faecal incontinence that had failed to respond to medical or surgical interventions. It was evident that every aspect of the participant's lives was affected by their compromised bowel control. Patients described the location of the toilets being the main focus of their life and governing much of their activities. They were able to give all the locations of toilets to and from hospital and work. As described in Fujita's study, eating and choice of foods were restricted to avoid frequency of bowel actions and soiling, and participants also reported stopping sports activities because they had experienced episodes of incontinence.

Pad wearing was not always an indicator of severity of symptoms. Some reported 'padding up, just in case' but rarely reported episodes of incontinence, whereas others adamantly refused to wear pads as they felt this would detrimentally affect their psychological state by allowing their symptoms to infringe on their lifestyle.

Nursing assessment of psychosocial issues

The nursing assessment (see Chapter 6) ensures that information on patients' physical, psychological and social functioning is gathered. This initial assessment consists of a one-hour session in our practice, and if possible the patient should be unaccompanied. A one-hour session provides the patient with the time to discuss the effect of their symptoms in a relaxed environment, and also helps to develop a therapeutic relationship within which a patient will feel at ease to discuss their situation. Also, if the patient is accompanied by a partner or relative they may not reveal certain details regarding their psychosocial situation. However, this may be inappropriate in certain situations, such as where language interpretation is required or the patient's mental state dictates otherwise.

Mary, aged 47, attended her first session of biofeedback therapy. She asked if her husband could accompany her. She was informed that the preference was that she attend the session alone, which she agreed to. Within the first ten minutes of the session, after having been asked to discuss her symptoms, she informed the therapist that her husband had been having an extramarital affair as a result of her fear of having sex because of her incontinence. She stated she would not have revealed this if her husband had been present. Mary attended for two sessions only. Her symptoms markedly improved after the initial session, which she felt was due to her gaining an understanding of her bowel function and being able to discuss her psychosocial situation openly. Her husband reported a marked improvement in his wife's mental state, which he attributed to the treatment.

The patient should be informed of the duration of the session so that they feel comfortable to discuss their symptoms, knowing that they will not be shown the door within ten minutes! It is also important to ask the patient what they prefer to be called as this helps to develop the therapeutic relationship, since they may not be called by the same name on their medical notes. They should be asked about their symptoms and the effect on their lifestyle, allowing them time to do so as well as an opportunity to express their emotions, which may be anger or tears. Patients are generally keen to discuss their symptoms, as they see this as an opportunity to express all the thoughts and emotions they have not disclosed, many for several years. Many patients benefit from hearing they are not alone, and when discovering the prevalence of faecal incontinence in the general population are frequently both shocked and relieved.

A history of life events and mental illness provides a window on an individual's coping styles and premorbid mental state. It is important to realise that patients with a mental illness may already feel stigmatised and that their symptoms of faecal incontinence therefore cause a double stigma.

Assessment tools such as the Hospital Anxiety and Depression Scale (Zigmond and Snaith, 1983) and a quality of life measure can be given prior to the appointment and will provide an insight into the patient's psychological state. The same measures can be applied at the end of treatment to assess the effect and outcome of the interventions given.

At the end of the assessment the patient should be given the nurse's contact number, providing them with an opportunity to ask any further questions before their next appointment and also to give them a 'lifeline' to discuss their symptoms.

For some patients it is evident that their psychiatric illness prevents them from seeking treatment for their incontinence, because the severity of their symptoms means they may be unable to verbalise their symptoms accurately, and thereby be appropriately referred. They may also have difficulty attending the sessions due to the nature of their psychiatric illness. In these situations the presence of a friend or advocate can be very helpful to ensure that the individual is able to express their symptoms and concerns, and that the appropriate advice is given.

Peter, aged 28, attended his continence assessment with his care worker. Peter had been previously diagnosed with schizophrenia and learning difficulties. His symptoms of schizophrenia were generally well controlled on medication although at times there was evidence of auditory hallucinations. He was employed as a hotel porter. He did have some difficulty with reading and writing and had attended a 'special school'. His symptoms consisted of frequency of bowel actions with loose stool, urgency and urge incontinence. These symptoms usually occurred during his tube journey to work and his anxiety precipitated and maintained them. With his care worker helping to teach him sphincter exercises and his own memory cards he planned his tube journey with toilet stops. Loperamide 2 mg was taken daily to firm his stool and also provide him with confidence as he rapidly began to see an improvement in his symptoms. Gradually he became more confident and began attending the sessions alone. Peter was seen monthly for six months, and although episodes of incontinence still occur these are rare and both he and his care worker are able to manage them.

Changing self-efficacy by building up a patient's confidence and self-worth is one of the most important components of any behavioural healthcare intervention (Crow et al., 1999). Self-efficacy is promoted 'whenever an intervention is designed to provide the patient with the confidence that she / he can cope or behave in such a way the she / he can manage the disease or its treatment' (Crow et al., 1999, p. 11). There are two major components to this: interaction self-efficacy empowers the patient to be more involved in decision-making; management self-efficacy results from the patient acquiring self-management skills, and believing in them. Positive outcome expectancy alone, and information alone, are not as beneficial for health outcomes as when combined with such specific skills; patients need strategies to respond appropriately to information (Crow et al., 1999).

Some individuals will utilise the Continence/Biofeedback sessions purely to discuss their psychological distress, and it may become evident either at the first session or during subsequent treatments that psychological therapy is required. If it is clear that psychological treatment is required, this may be accessed from within the hospital or via the patient's general practitioner. Recognition of psychological problems by the nurse can supportively help the patient to seek treatment. However, it is important the patient can also recognise this and agree that it is the way forward.

Assessment and treatment by psychological services

Once it has been recognised that there are issues in the patient's history which influence how the symptoms are managed, they may then be offered emotional support and the opportunity to explore these issues in some depth. The patient may be best served where there is a multi-disciplinary team providing treatment. At St Mark's Hospital, Harrow (specialist colorectal tertiary referral centre), the nurse specialist presents the case at the weekly psychosocial meeting. The meeting is led by a consultant psychotherapist and is attended by a psychologist, social worker/counsellor, dieticians, nurses and the medical teams. Depending on what has emerged during the nurse specialist's assessment and the multi-disciplinary discussion, recommendations are made regarding psychological treatment. Typically, discussion centres around such questions as: Is it a behavioural issue, where learnt behaviour has not equipped the patient to deal with the problem? Would the patient benefit from Cognitive Behavioural Therapy (CBT) provided by a psychologist? Or is it something in the patient's history which indicates a psychoanalytic approach, where emphasis is on understanding how past experiences may influence present functioning? Or is a person-centred approach or supportive counselling the most appropriate treatment? (Shipton and Smith, 1998).

Much will depend on available resources and how receptive the patient is to psychological therapy. Whatever the approach, the patient may experience the therapeutic effect of being listened to when talking about symptoms that affect all aspects of their everyday life. This experience allows the patient to bring many associated issues to the sessions, such as marital disharmony, loss of perceived good health and feeling stigmatised. They may also ventilate seemingly unrelated issues and come to understand the connection between their physical state and their emotional well-being. This emphasises the importance of the therapeutic relationship between the patient and the therapist in how issues are explored and how change is managed. It requires commitment from both therapist and patient to work through these issues over what may be many months.

The outcome may be enhanced self-esteem and a recognition that the presenting problem can be more effectively managed. In addition, the realisation that expecting a complete cure may be an unrealistic goal allows the patient to move forward and become less preoccupied with their symptoms.

Frances, 35, a married clerk suffered a third-degree tear during the birth of her first child. The wound was sutured by someone she believed was an inexperienced student midwife. The wound did not heal – causing pain and faecal incontinence. After many visits to the GP she was given antibiotics and advised to take salt baths. The wound healed but the incontinence continued. She frequently soiled herself and felt unable to resume sexual relations with her husband. The continued incontinence was initially put down to 'nerves'. She was eventually diagnosed as having a deficient external anal sphincter and a repair was undertaken two years after the birth of her daughter. Unfortunately the sphincter repair wound became infected. Frances became angry and depressed. Her condition increased her isolation, and outings to the shops or the park became fraught with anxiety. Her frequent crying upset her husband, and her baby was frequently looked after by her mother. A second sphincter repair was undertaken with a covering loop colostomy. She felt disfigured by the colostomy and hated her body-image. She became self-conscious and fearful of the odour from the colostomy bag and would not undress in front of her husband. She was unable to let her now 3-year-old daughter climb onto her lap for fear of the bag becoming detached and felt she was not being 'a proper mother'.

After three years the colostomy bag became the symbol of all Frances' losses: loss of bowel control, loss of her 'perfect body', loss of intimacy, loss of the prospect of another baby and the loss of the choice of going back to work. She felt inadequate and resentful of being financially dependent on her husband. A parastomal hernia had developed causing her additional worry and discomfort, and she asked for the colostomy to be reversed. The original tear had healed but the hernia repair and colostomy wound had to be left open. The open wound was dressed by a district nurse and Frances was able to talk openly about her 'embarrassing condition' for the first time. The wound took months to heal leaving an unsightly scar. However, the urge incontinence and soiling returned. Frances felt old, angry, mutilated and full of resentment. She began to resent her husband. She displaced the anger she felt towards the medical profession onto him. Frances felt her husband did not understand the serious impact of the condition on her.

She started biofeedback and counselling. Weekly counselling sessions continued after the biofeedback sessions stopped as Frances reported no improvement and remained incontinent. She was initially sceptical about the value of counselling but began to talk through her symptoms and express anger and sadness – discovering how the meaning of her illness experience was linked to her earlier life experience. Feelings of worthlessness made her feel that her husband would leave her, and she explored how her feelings of anxiety had been reinforced by her mother's anxiety when she was younger. Her learnt coping mechanisms had not prepared her emotionally or physically for this illness experience and she started to recognise that her anger was not just about her bowel control but about other aspects of her life as well. Frances believed that her sense of worthlessness stemmed from the lack of an apology from the maternity hospital where her daughter was born. Frances' hidden agenda was to dispute any improvement in her condition to avoid being denied further psychological or surgical treatment. The therapeutic relationship she developed with her counsellor enabled her to manage her symptoms and improve her quality of life. She felt empowered to become actively involved in seeking employment and enhancing her independence. She recognised how her past experiences had influenced her illness behaviour and took responsibility for making changes.

Conclusions

This chapter highlights the importance of a biopsychosocial assessment to provide patients with the opportunity to talk about the physical, social and emotional effects which compromised bowel control has on the quality of their life. Understanding their symptoms and allowing them to ventilate their anxieties frequently alleviates their fears and reduces the stigmatising effect. Having identified the need for psychological input it is important to develop appropriate resources to provide treatment, ideally within the unit treating their bowel symptoms. Patients find it more acceptable to receive psychological treatment where the physical symptoms are also understood.

References

Almy, T.P. (1951) Experimental studies on the irritable colon. *American Journal of Medicine* **10**, 60–67.

Benner, P. and Wrubel, J. (1988) *The primacy of caring. Stress and coping in health and illness.* Toronto: Addison-Wesley.

Bugg, G.J., Kiff, E.S. and Hosker, G. (2001) A new condition-specific health-related quality of life questionnaire for the assessment of women with anal incontinence. *British Journal of Obstetrics and Gynaecology* **108**, 1057–1067.

Cavet, J. (1998) *People don't understand: children, young people and their families living with a hidden disability.* London: National Children's Bureau.

Chelvanayagam, S. and Norton, C. (2000) Quality of life with faecal continence problems. *Nursing Times Plus* August 3, **96**, 31, 15–17.

Crow, R., Gage, H., Hampson, S., Hart, J., Kimber, A. and Thomas, H. (1999) The role of expectancies in the placebo effect and their use in the delivery of health care: a systematic review. *Health Technology Assessment* **3**, 1–96.

Drossman, D.A. (1999) The functional gastrointestinal disorders and the Rome II process. *Gut* **45** (Suppl. II), 1–5.

Drossman, D.A., Thompson, W.G., Talley, N.J., Funch-Jensen, P., Janssens, J. and Whitehead, W.E. (1990) Identification of subgroups of functional gastrointestinal disorders. *Gastroenterology International* **3**, 4, 159–172.

Eypasch, E., Williams, J.I., Wood-Dauphinee, S., Ure, B.M., Schmulling, C., Neugebauer, E. and Troidl, H. (1995) Gastrointestinal Quality of Life Index: development, validation and application of a new instrument. *British Journal of Surgery* **82**, 216–222.

Fujita, S., Kusunoki, M., Shoji, Y., Owada, T. and Utsunomiya, J. (1992) Quality of life after total proctocolectomy and ileal J Pouch anal anastomosis. *Diseases of the Colon and Rectum* **35**, 1030–1039.

Fullerton, S.C. (1996) Health related quality of life *Current Opinion in Gastroenterology* **12**, 39–43.

Gill, T.M. and Feinstein, A.R. (1994) A critical appraisal of the quality of quality of life instruments. *Journal of the American Medical Association* **272**, 8, 619–624.

Glickman, S. and Kamm, M.A. (1996) Bowel dysfunction in spinal cord injury patients. *Lancet* **347**, 1651–1653.

Guyatt, G.H., Feeney, D.H. and Patrick, D.L. (1993) Measuring health-related quality of life. *Annals of Internal Medicine* **118**, 622–629.

Higginson, I.J. and Carr, A.J. (2001) Measuring quality of life: using quality of life measures in the clinical setting. *British Medical Journal* **322**, 1297–1300.

Irvine, E.J. (1996) Measuring quality of life: a review. *Scandinavian Journal of Gastroenterology Suppl.* **31**, 5–7.

Johanson, J.F. and Lafferty, J. (1996) Epidemiology of fecal incontinence: the silent affliction. *American Journal of Gastroenterology* **91**, 1, 33–36.

Khullar, V., Damiano, R., Toozs-Hobson, P. and Cardozo, L. (1998) Prevalence of faecal incontinence among women with urinary incontinence. *British Journal of Obstetrics and Gynaecology* **105**, 1211–1213.

Kleinman, A. (1988) *The illness narratives: suffering, healing and human condition.* Harper Collins.

Leigh, R.J. and Turnberg, L.A. (1982) Faecal incontinence: the unvoiced symptom. *Lancet* **1**, 1349–1351.

Lewis, F.M. (1987) The concept of control: a typology and health-related variables. Advances in Health Education and Promotion **2**, 277–309.

Ludman, L., Spitz, L. and Kiely, E.M. (1994) Social and emotional impact of faecal incontinence after surgery for anorectal abnormalities. *Archives of Disease in Childhood* **71**, 194–200.

Jorge, N.M. and Wexner, S.D. (1993) Etiology and management of fecal incontinence. *Diseases of the Colon and Rectum* **36**, 77–97.

North, C.S., Alpers, D.H., Thompson, S.J. and Spitznagel, E.L. (1996) Gastrointestinal symptoms and psychiatric disorders in the general population: Findings from NIMH epidemiologic catchment area project. *Digestive Diseases and Sciences* **41**, 4, 633–640.

Rockwood, T.H., Church, J.M., Fleshman, J.W., Kane, R.L., Mavrantonis, C., Thorson, A.G., Wexner, S.D., Bliss, D. and Lowry, A.C. (2000) Fecal Incontinence Quality of Life Scale: Quality of Life Instrument for Patients with Fecal Incontinence. *Diseases of the Colon and Rectum* **43**, 9–17.

Roper, N., Logan, W.W. and Tierney, A.J. (1985) Model of Living. In: *The elements of nursing* (2nd edn), pp. 19–27. Edinburgh: Churchill Livingstone.

Sailer, M., Bussen, D., Debus, E.S., Fuchs, K.H. and Thiede, A. (1998) Quality of life in patients with benign anorectal disorders. *British Journal of Surgery* **85**, 1716–1719.

Schuster, C.S. and Ashburn, S.S. (1980) *The process of human development.* Boston: Little Brown.

Seligman, M.E.P. (1992) *Helplessness: on depression, development and death* (2nd edn). New York: W.H. Freeman.

Sharpe, A., Read, A., Slater, B. and Varma, J. (1997) Quality of life assessment in patients with faecal incontinence. *International Journal of Colorectal Disease* **12**, 124. [Abstract]

Shipton, G. and Smith, E. (1998) *Long-term counselling.* London: Sage Publications.

Smith, P.S. and Smith, L.J. (1987) *Continence and incontinence: psychological approahes to development and treatment.* London: Helm.

Stewart, A.L., Greenfield, S., Hays, R.D.,Wells, K., Rogers, W.H., Berry, S.D., McGlynn, E.A. and Ware, J.E. (1989) Functional status and well-being of patients with chronic conditions. Results from the Medical Outcomes Study. *Journal of the American Medical Association* **262**, 907–913.

Toner, B.B., Segal, Z.V., Emmott, S., Myran, D., Ali, A., Digasbarro, I. and Stuckless, N. (1998) Cognitive-behavioral group therapy for patients with Irritable bowel syndrome. *International Journal of Group Psychotherapy* **48**, 2, 215–243.

Trezza, M., Krogh, K., Egevist, H., Bjerring, P. and Laurberg, S. (1999) Bowel problems in patients with systemic sclerosis. *Scandinavian Journal of Gastroenterology* **34**, 409–413.

Whitehead, W.E., Wald, A., Diamant, N.E., Enck, P., Pemberton, J.H. and Rao, S.S.C. (1999) Functional disorders of the anus and rectum. *Gut* **45** (Suppl. II), 55–59.

Zigmond, A.S. and Snaith, R.P. (1983) The Hospital Anxiety and Depression Scale. *Acta Psychiatrica Scandinavica* **67**, 361–370.

Chapter 6

Nursing Assessment of Adults with Faecal Incontinence

Sonya Chelvanayagam and Christine Norton

Introduction

Continence is a complex skill involving many factors, as seen in Chapter 4. The assessment outlined here is based on that used by nurse specialists in our own unit, which is within a specialist colorectal hospital (Norton and Chelvanayagam, 2000). This may need to be adapted to different circumstances and different patient groups. A bowel symptom questionnaire (Table 6.1, overleaf) and a one-week bowel diary (Figure 6.1, page 48) is always sent to patients with a first appointment. The vast majority of patients are able to fill these in and bring them to their appointment. Many comment that it was useful to think their symptoms through before they come, and feel reassured that they are not alone if there is a specific questionnaire.

The assessment interview

It is important to build a relationship of trust with the patient if the whole picture is to be openly and frankly discussed, and to establish a vocabulary of words that are mutually understood and acceptable. Even when patients have been referred specifically for faecal incontinence, there remains for many a great embarrassment and difficulty in talking. The experience seems to be similar to that described for urinary incontinence – as a taboo subject it has never been openly discussed, often not even with their partner or family, and many people have not developed constructs or frameworks to describe what is happening (Ashworth and Hagan, 1993). Some patients will not be aware of medical terms such as 'defaecation' or even 'stool' or 'anus', but are reluctant to use their usual slang terms to a professional.

A checklist (Table 6.2, page 49) has been found to be a useful tool as a basis for the assessment interview. The relevance of each item on the checklist will be discussed. The usual wording of the question to the patient is indicated in italics.

Main complaint: *What bothers you about your bowels / what is the main problem with your bowels?*

It is important to understand the patient's perspective on the problem and what is really bothering them. This may be quite different from the primary reason for referral. Circumstances surrounding the onset of the problem can give important clues as to causation. Sometimes this is clear (childbirth or a haemorrhoidectomy), or else the patient may not have made a link, so probing questions may be needed (such as coincidental traumatic life events, change in medication, menopause). Many people endure faecal incontinence for years without seeking professional help (Leigh and Turnberg, 1982) and it is necessary to explore what has triggered the present consultation – have the symptoms worsened, or has the ability to cope with symptoms been compromised by other factors, or is it a sign of positive health-seeking behaviour?

Usual bowel pattern: *How often do you open your bowels?*

There is a common misconception among the general population that 'normal' bowel habit is once per day. In fact, bowel frequency in a healthy population varies between 1–3 times a day to once in three days (Connell et al., 1965). It is probably a minority of the total population (40% of men and 33% of women) who open

Table 6.1: Bowel Symptom Questionnaire

(*Note:* in clinical practice this questionnaire is formatted over three pages)
Name: Date today:

Please tick the box that comes closest to your situation. There are no right or wrong answers. Please feel free to write any other comments on the questionnaire.

1. How often do you open your bowels on a typical day? .... times.
2. When you need to open your bowels, do you have to hurry?
   Yes No Varies
3. If yes, how long can you *usually* hang on?
   Under 2 minutes 2–4 minutes 5–10 minutes over 10 minutes
4. Would you say that usually your stools (bowel motions) are:
   Hard Normal Soft but formed Mushy Liquid Variable
5. Do you ever *not get to the toilet in time* and have a bowel accident?

Never	
Very rarely	No accidents in the past 4 weeks, but it happens sometimes
Rarely	1 accident in the past 4 weeks
Sometimes	More than 1 accident in the past 4 weeks but not 1 a week
Weekly	1 or more accidents a week but not every day
Daily	1 or more accidents a day

6. If you have accidents on the way to the toilet, does this depend on how hard your stools are?
   Yes No N/A
7. Do you get any soiling *after you have opened your bowels*?
   (same scale as question 5)
8. Do you get any bowel leakage at other times (e.g. *not* when you need to go, and *not* after you have been – leakage which just seems to happen)?:
   (same scale as question 5)
9. When is this leakage (i.e. which is *not* associated with an urge to go to the toilet or after you have opened your bowels)?
   At night in bed When walking When bending or lifting During sport or exercise
   Any time, no pattern

Table 6.1: Bowel Symptom Questionnaire (continued)

10. If you get *any* type of bowel accidents or leakage, is this: (tick all that apply):
    Loss of solid stool   Loss of liquid stool   Loss of mucus   No leakage

11. If you get *any* accidents or leakage, is this (if it varies, tick all that apply):
    No leakage   Minor stain only   Small amount (about a teaspoon full)
    Moderate amount (about a tablespoon full)   Large amount (large patch or whole bowel motion)

12. Do you need to wear a pad because of bowel leakage?
    Always   Usually   Sometimes   Never

13. If you do wear a pad, is this:
    Small pant liner   Sanitary towel size   Incontinence pad

14. Can you control wind (flatus)?
    Always   Usually   Sometimes   Never

15. Do you feel that your bowel control currently (within the past month) restricts your life?
    Not at all   A little   Quite a lot   A great deal
    If your bowel control does restrict your life, please briefly describe in what way/s:

16. Do you have any trouble emptying your bowels now?
    Yes   No
    If yes, is this: Need to strain   Unable to empty completely   Hard stools   Other (please state):

17. Please rate how good your bowel control is *now*:
    (please circle a number, where 0 = no control and 10 = perfect control):
    0 1 2 3 4 5 6 7 8 9 10

18. Any other comments about your bowels?

Thank you for your help.

St Mark's Hospital Bowel Diary

Name ____________________ Week beginning ________________

Key ☐ ✓ = bowels open in toilet ☐ ✓ = bowel accident

P = pad/pants change

Special Instructions

Please tick in the shaded column each time you open your bowels in the toilet.
Please tick the white column each time you have a bowel accident or leakage.
Write P if you need to change a pad or pants.

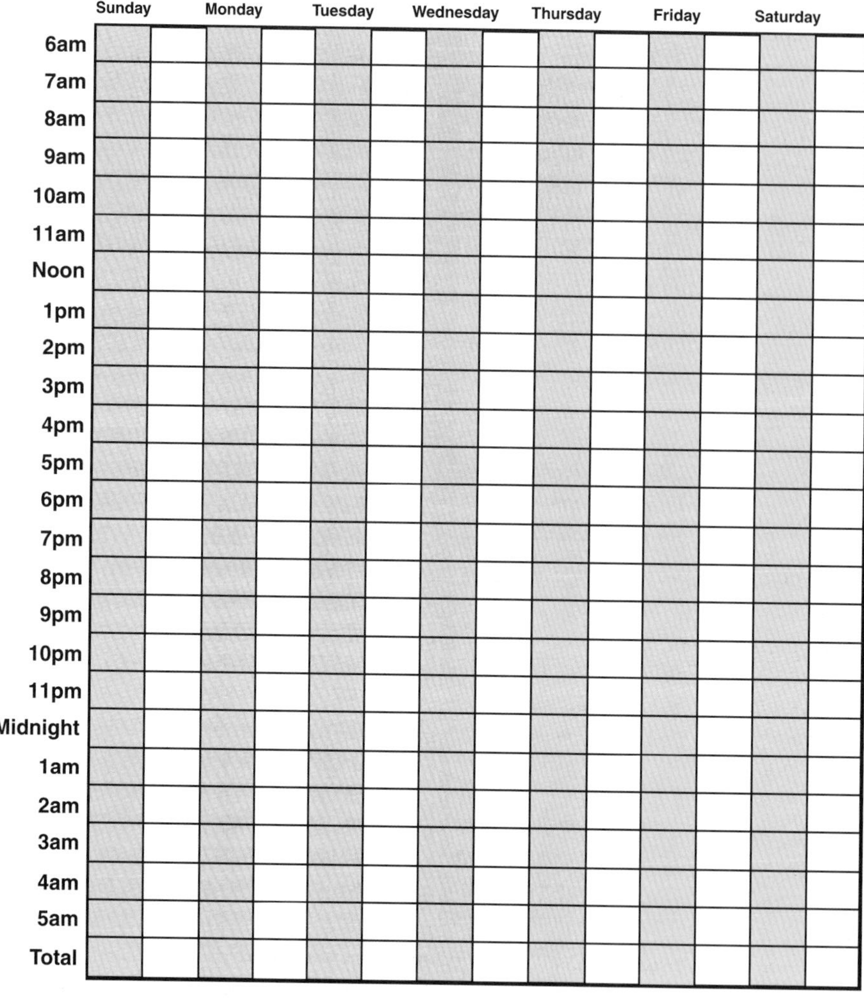

	Sunday		Monday		Tuesday		Wednesday		Thursday		Friday		Saturday	
6am														
7am														
8am														
9am														
10am														
11am														
Noon														
1pm														
2pm														
3pm														
4pm														
5pm														
6pm														
7pm														
8pm														
9pm														
10pm														
11pm														
Midnight														
1am														
2am														
3am														
4am														
5am														
Total														

Figure 6.1

Table 6.2: Assessment of Faecal Incontinence Checklist

Note: in clinical practice this assessment tool is laid out over three pages.
Main complaint
Duration of symptoms / trigger for onset
Usual bowel pattern   Any recent change?
Usual stool consistency:
1. lumps 2. Lumpy sausage 3. Cracked sausage 4. Soft smooth sausage 5. soft blobs 6. Fluffy, mushy 7. Watery, no pieces
Faecal incontinence: How often?   How much?
Urgency?   Time can defer for:
Urge incontinence:
never / seldom / sometimes / frequently
Difficulty wiping: Yes   No   Sometimes
Post-defaecation soiling: Yes   No   Sometimes
Passive soiling: Yes   No Sometimes Events causing?
Amount of flatus: Control of flatus: Good Variable / Poor
Ability to distinguish stool / flatus? Yes   No
Abdominal pain relieved by defaecation?
Other pain?
Rectal bleeding?
Mucus?
Nocturnal bowel problems?
Evacuation difficulties?
Straining?
Incomplete evacuation?
Need to digitate anally, vaginally or to support the perineum?
Painful defaecation?
Bloating?
Sensation of prolapse?
Pads / pants?
Bowel medication? Other current medication
Past medical history (include psychological).
History of depression / antidepressants?
Physical or social difficulties with toilet access?
Previous bowel treatments and results
Obstetric history: parity: Difficult deliveries or heavy babies?
Dietary influences:
Smoker?
Weight / Height / Body Mass Index
Fluids (caffeine)
Skin problems
Bladder problems
Effect on lifestyle / relationships / Emotional / psychological effect
Examination and results of anal ultrasound and ano-rectal physiology studies, transit studies and other tests

Adapted from Norton and Chelvanayagam, (2000).

their bowels once each day (Heaton et al., 1992). Most are irregular in bowel habit, with young women being the most irregular. One third of 'normal' young women open their bowels less than once per day and 1% do so less than once per week (Heaton et al., 1992). A variable bowel habit is a classic feature of the irritable bowel syndrome (IBS), particularly if combined with abdominal pain and/or bloating (Thompson et al., 1989; Drossman et al., 1994).

'Constipation' means different things to different people (Kamm and Lennard-Jones, 1994). Infrequent bowel motions, if the stool is easy to pass and not hard, are not a cause for concern or intervention. Conversely, some very constipated people can produce a stool several times per day, but only at the expense of long hours of straining on the toilet. There is, in the general population, no age-related decrease in the actual frequency of defaecation, although there seems to be an increase with age in self-report of constipation and an increase in laxative use (Harari et al., 1996). The consumption of laxatives does not necessarily prove that someone is constipated. Occasionally it is an indication of a serious mental health problem such as anorexia nervosa.

It is important to record if the patient reports a recent sustained change in the frequency of bowel motions as this may indicate underlying disease or malignancy. Any recent unexplained change in bowel habit in a patient over 40 years old should be investigated by barium enema, X-ray or by colonoscopy (see Chapter 7). Bowel cancer does not often present as incontinence as the only symptom, but up to 25% of patients may have it as one of their presenting problems (Curless et al., 1994).

Usual stool consistency: *What is your stool (bowel motion) like; is it loose, soft but formed, hard or hard pellets? Does this vary?*

It is important to record if stool consistency has altered and if the patient reports a change in stool colour. Patients with the irritable bowel syndrome are particularly prone to a very variable stool consistency. Where the patient has difficulty in describing the stool, a visual prompt may be helpful (Figure 6.2, Heaton et al., 1992). Type 3 or 4 on this 7–point scale is the most usual consistency, but in women only 56% of stool are these 'normal' types; 61% of stool are these types in men (Heaton et al., 1992). Patients have been found to be generally very accurate in assessing their own stool consistency (Bliss et al., 1999). If the stool is loose, this makes both passive and urge faecal incontinence far more likely. Pellet stool is common in slow transit constipation.

Faecal incontinence?

This will often need sensitive enquiry as many people are reluctant to admit incontinence and it is not easy to find terms that are mutually understood and acceptable. Even people attending a gastroenterologist for gut symptoms often do not volunteer the symptom of faecal incontinence to the doctor. In one study less than half of patients admitting to incontinence on a questionnaire had told the doctor about it (Johanson and Lafferty, 1996). It is also quite difficult to gauge the severity of the symptom as many people restrict their lifestyle to limit the possibility of urge incontinence, so it may actually happen very infrequently, yet still be a major problem, and many find it difficult to estimate the amount lost (minor stain, teaspoonful, tablespoonful, whole bowel motion). It is helpful to question separately about the two major symptom types of urge or passive incontinence.

Urgency and ability to defer defaecation: *When you need to open your bowels do you need to rush to get to the toilet? How long can you hold on for?*

When the rectum fills, the internal anal sphincter relaxes reflexly to enable 'sampling' of the rectal contents by the very sensitive nerve endings at the dentate line in the upper anal canal (Figure 6.3a). With normal bowel control, defaecation can be deferred for long periods of time because the urge to defaecate is opposed by voluntary contraction of the striated external anal sphincter muscle (Whitehead et al., 1981). This should generate sufficient pressure to prevent immediate stool expulsion

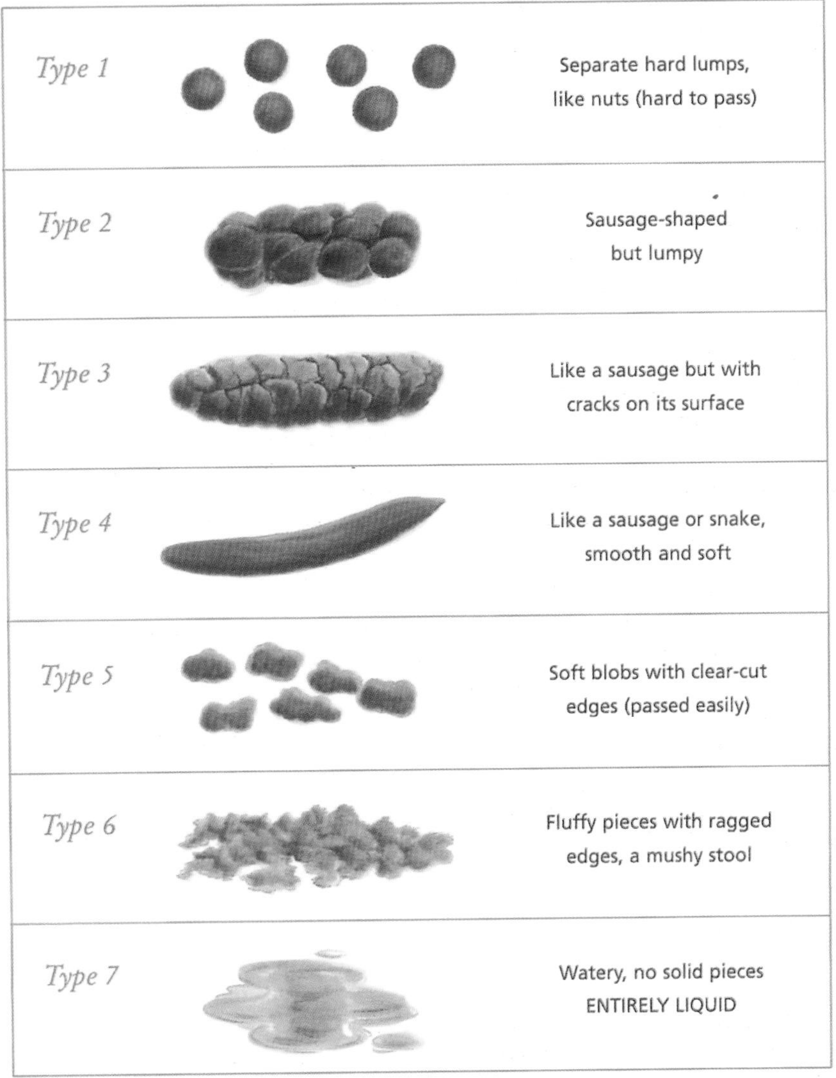

Figure 6.2 *Reproduced by permission of Norgine Ltd.*

and return the stool to the rectum (Figure 6.3(b), page 53). Retrograde peristalsis may even remove the stool away from the anal sphincter and back into the sigmoid colon in some cases. Once the urge is successfully resisted, the feeling diminishes with time, giving the individual plenty of time to find a socially convenient opportunity to defaecate. If bowel control is normal, an urge is felt with colonic peristalsis and rectal filling, but this urge will diminish, often giving up to several hours before it becomes imperative to defaecate. Indeed, it has been shown that voluntarily ignoring the call to stool can halve the frequency of defaecation and slow colonic transit (Klauser et al., 1990).

However, if the external sphincter is not functioning well, the squeeze may be insufficient to suppress the urge to defaecate, even when the stool is a normal consistency (Figure 6.4, overleaf). A reduced squeeze pressure and an inability to sustain a sub-maximal contraction has been found to correlate with the symptom of urgency (Delechenaut et al., 1992; Gee and Durdey, 1995). Patients generating high bowel pressures seen in inflammatory bowel disease or IBS may report severe urgency. Some patients with faecal incontinence generate pressure waves of very high amplitude (up to 500 cm water pressure (Herbst et al., 1997). Without adequate sphincter response to oppose this, urge incontinence is likely. Urge incontinence is very likely in instances where a patient is suffering from diarrhoea, due both to increased bowel pressures opposing sphincter function and to loose stools.

Urge incontinence: *Do you ever not get to the toilet in time and have a bowel accident?*

Urge incontinence often highlights a weakness or defect in the external anal sphincter, which is unable to oppose rectal contractions

Figure 6.3(a)
A 'sampling' of rectal contents.

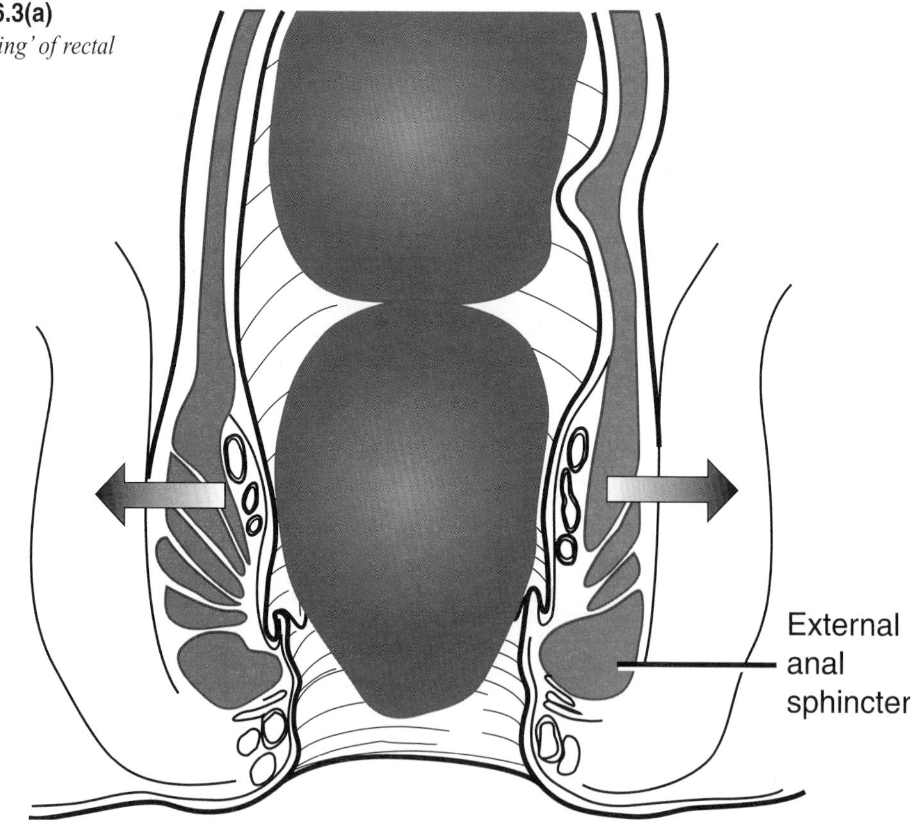

and so allow delay in defaecation (Engel et al., 1995b; Hill et al., 1994). Obstetric trauma is the most common cause of external anal sphincter damage (Sultan et al., 1994). Urgency may become a persistent problem for an individual who has suffered an episode of faecal incontinence, as the catastrophic effect leads to the fear of future accidents and so an immediate response to the urge to defaecate to try to prevent this. It is possible that a vicious circle develops – any bowel sensation is interpreted as urgent and likely to lead to incontinence – this causes great anxiety, even panic, which in turn exacerbates the sense of urgency. It is important to establish how frequently urge incontinence actually occurs and whether restrictions in activities are due to actual or feared incontinence. Some people have very infrequent episodes, but self-impose major lifestyle restrictions and never venture far from a toilet 'just in case'.

Passive soiling: *Do you have any leakage from your back passage of which you are unaware? Is this liquid or solid? Does this occur at any time or only after you have opened your bowels?*

The smooth muscle internal anal sphincter is responsible for up to 80% of resting tone in the anal canal (Kamm, 1998). A weak or disrupted sphincter will not close the anal canal completely; if the stool is loose or soft, some will remain in the anal canal and will ooze out after defaecation. Passive soiling is associated with internal anal sphincter damage on ultrasound (Engel et al., 1995b; Hill et al., 1994). It is often the result of inadvertent surgical damage (e.g. following haemorrhoidectomy or sphinctero-

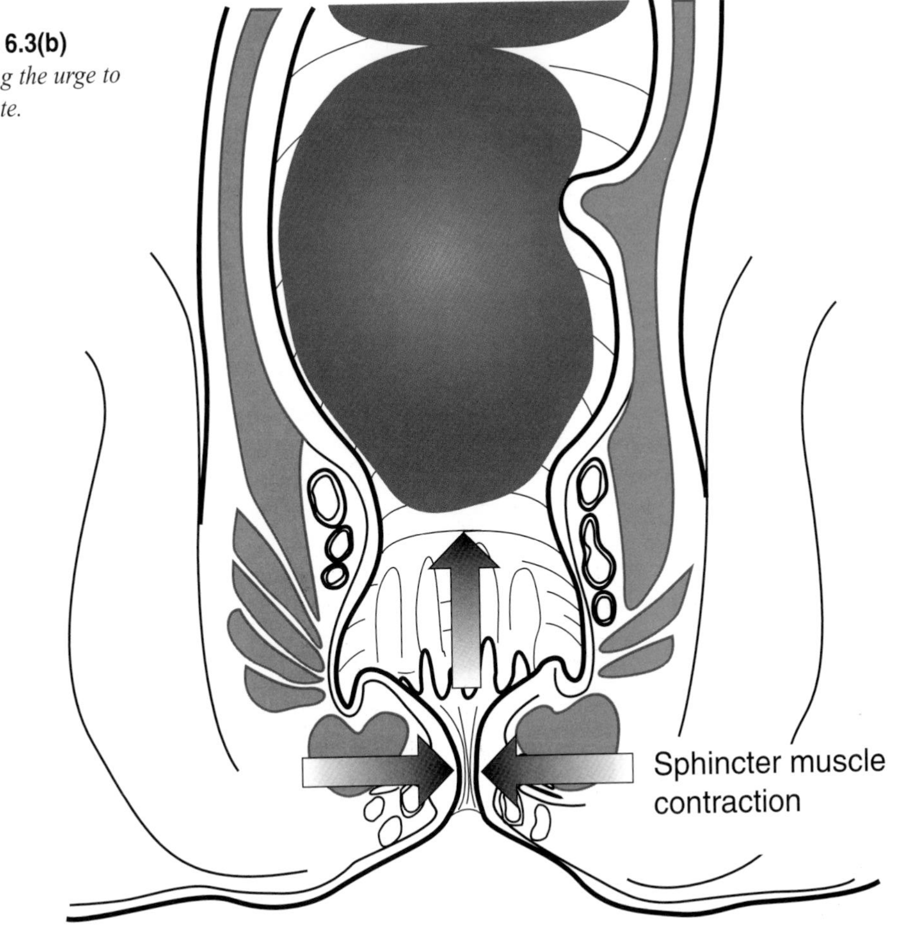

Figure 6.3(b)
Resisting the urge to defaecate.

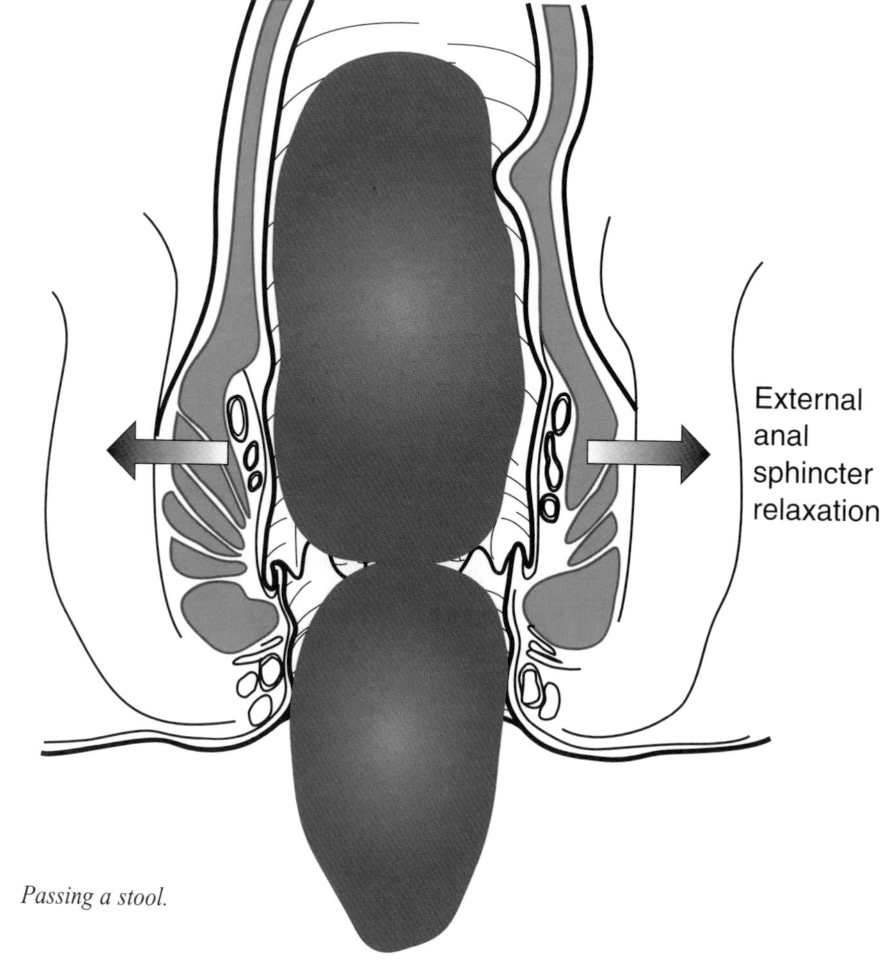

Figure 6.4 *Passing a stool.*

tomy) or may be due to idiopathic degeneration of the muscle (Vaizey et al., 1997). These patients complain of great difficulty in cleaning the anus after defaecation and subsequent soiling, possibly for several hours. Others experience passive soiling at any time without being aware of it, or loss of stool exacerbated by physical exertion such as walking or playing sport. Passive loss of solid stool or loss of copious amounts of mucus may result from a rectal prolapse.

Flatus: *Can you control wind? Are you able to tell the difference between wind and the need to empty your bowels?*

Some patients report incontinence of liquid or solid stool occurring on passing flatus because they are unable to distinguish between flatus and stool. This may because the sensory nerves involved in 'sampling' described above have been damaged (e.g. after anal surgery). Incontinence of flatus often sounds like a trivial symptom, but many people who have absolutely no control find it highly embarrassing in work, social or intimate situations.

Pain: *Do you have pain associated with opening your bowels? Is this before opening your bowels and relieved by opening your bowels, or is it a pain as you actually pass a stool?*

Abdominal pain in association with altered stool consistency, frequency or bloating, in the absence of 'organic' pathology is diagnostic of IBS (Drossman et al., 1994). Pain with an urge to defaecate may be reported by patients with inflammatory bowel disease or the irritable bowel syndrome, making it difficult to defer defaecation. They may refer to a colicky or spasmodic 'stabbing' pain. Anal pain with defaecation is often caused by haemorrhoids or an anal fissure. Chronically constipated people often report abdominal discomfort, which may be indicative of a functional rather than organic disorder, especially accompanied by bloating.

Presence of blood and mucus: *Do you pass any blood or mucus when you have your bowels open?*

Fresh blood may be passed if a patient has haemorrhoids or an anal fissure. Fresh or darker blood may indicate underlying disease or malignancy. The presence of blood and mucus in an individual with a history of straining may indicate the presence of a solitary rectal ulcer. Copious mucus with normal bowel function may indicate a villous adenoma; with disturbed bowel function, mucus is a frequent accompaniment to the irritable bowel syndrome. Passive incontinence of clear or faecal stained mucus may indicate that a rectal prolapse is present. When a patient reports passing blood and/or mucus further investigation is warranted.

Evacuation difficulties: *Do you have difficulty opening your bowels? Do you need to strain? If so, for how long? Do you ever need to insert a finger into your back passage or vagina to help stool out? Do you need to push on the area by your back passage? Does it feel as if you have not completely emptied your bowels?*

These questions examine whether the patient suffers from an evacuation difficulty. Constipation is covered in more detail in Chapters 21 and 22. It commonly co-exists with faecal incontinence in frail or disable people (Barrett, 1993). People with chronic constipation often just describe defaecation as 'unsatisfying', that it is always difficult to go and they never feel as if the bowel is properly emptied. Many repeatedly return to the toilet and some spend long periods, even hours, straining without result. Those with a very weak pelvic floor often feel unable to propel the stool out of the anal canal, as this moves down every time they strain. Some women have a rectocoele after childbirth or excessive straining. The front wall of the rectum may bulge into the vagina with attempted defaecation. Gentle backward pressure with a finger in the vagina may aid complete evacuation of any stool 'trapped' in a rectocoele. Sometimes women find it embarrassing to talk about needing to digitate and may need prompts such as 'lots of people with this problem need to help a stool out with a finger in the back passage or vagina – does this ever happen to you …?'

The symptom of incomplete defaecation may be caused by abnormally heightened sensitivity rather than a mechanical abnormality. Constipation or IBS is often associated with bloating of the abdomen: some women even report needing two sets of clothes, their normal wardrobe and clothes a size or two larger for the end of the day or for when the bowels have not been opened for several days.

Sensation of prolapse?

Some people may report a dragging feeling, or even that the rectum protrudes from the anus, particularly during or after straining. Most prolapses will reduce spontaneously after defaecation, but occasionally the patient may find it necessary to manually replace the rectum when it has prolapsed. Rectal prolapse is associated with faecal incontinence in approximately 60% of cases (Henry and Swash, 1992).

Pads or pants: *Do you need to wear a pad due to problems with leakage from your bowels? If so, what type of pad? Do you need to change your underwear during the day due to leakage? If yes, how often?*

Patients may wear pads due to urinary incontinence and so it is important to identify if pads or underwear are changed due to faecal incontinence or simply for personal preference. Also patients who describe urgency may always wear a pad due to fear of incontinence rather than actual accidents.

Medication: Many preparations can influence bowel function, either to constipate or to loosen the stool. Among the most common are analgesics and antidepressants. Non-steroidal anti-inflammatory drugs can cause loose stool or frank diarrhoea in many people.

Past medical history may give important clues as to causation of faecal incontinence. Major neurological disease, abdominal surgery, diabetes, thyroid disease, psychological disturbances and many other disorders may have an influence on bowel function. Any anal trauma may be relevant, as may unwanted anal intercourse, which has been found to be associated with internal anal sphincter damage (Engel et al., 1995a). Many women date the onset of bowel symptoms to gynaecological surgery, especially hysterectomy (Taylor et al., 1989; van Dam et al., 1997). Depression is a very common problem in clinical practice with patients with faecal incontinence and is therefore asked about specifically.

Physical or social difficulty with toilet access: Many people with physical disabilities are incontinent because of toilet access issues as much as bowel function (White, 1996). Others may need the assistance of carers. The practicalities of bowel management can be difficult for anyone with a physical impairment to manage independently. Solutions often need to be imaginative and creative, tailored to the individual's abilities, lifestyle, physical environment and the availability of help at appropriate times (Chapter 23). Many patients do not feel safe on commode chairs, and transfer from wheelchairs is often difficult. One study found that 37% of 147 patients with a spinal injury did not feel safe and 42% felt that the brakes were ineffective; 35% had falls during transfers and 23% had needed hospitalisation for the resulting injuries (Nelson et al., 1993). It may be useful to conduct a home visit or to observe the patient transferring onto a toilet or commode when toilet access in an issue.

Obstetric history: *How many babies have you had? Were forceps used for any of these deliveries? Did you tear, or did you have stitches? How heavy were the babies? Was there any problem with bowel control following the deliveries?*

Women who have had difficult deliveries, particularly assisted by forceps or involving a third-degree tear, are especially likely to report faecal incontinence (Sultan et al., 1994; Sultan et al., 1993). Prolonged labour (particularly the second stage) and heavy babies can cause trauma and damage to the anal sphincters. Postnatally, women are frequently asked about bladder function and taught the importance of pelvic floor exercises. Bowel function is much less frequently considered or mentioned. Women with pre-existing irritable bowel syndrome are known to be more likely than others without IBS to develop faecal urgency post-partum (64% vs. 10%) and poor control of flatus (35% vs. 13%), at least in the short term (Rosenberg and Whitehead, 1990).

Diet, smoking, weight and fluid intake: Many people find that what they eat influences their bowel function. A high fibre diet will soften the stool and may make it more difficult to control. Spicy food upsets some people. Others can identify a specific trigger for problems in their diet, but this can be very individual. Nicotine is thought to slow upper gut motility and increase total transit time (Scott et al., 1992), but it seems that it can speed recto-sigmoid transit (Rausch et al., 1998), and this fits with many people reporting clinically that smoking a cigarette facilitates initiation of defaecation. It is not known whether obesity has an adverse effect on bowel control. Some people with anorexia become very constipated; others abuse laxatives; a few seem to experience pelvic floor problems, possibly secondary to excessive exercise regimes or muscle wasting. Caffeine is a known gut stimulant (Brown et al., 1990) and will exacerbate urgency in many patients. Sorbitol can act as an osmotic laxative and can make stools looser if 'low calorie' or 'diet' drinks or foods are taken in quantity.

Skin problems: Some patients with faecal incontinence seem to have few problems with skin excoriation. Others suffer greatly from soreness and itching. Certainly, if there is diarrhoea, there is the possibility of small bowel digestive enzymes being in contact with the skin. If there is both urinary and faecal leakage this seems to make things worse. Some post-menopausal women may have skin problems due to hormone deficiency (and oestrogens have been suggested to have some beneficial effect on symptoms of faecal incontinence) (Donnelly et al., 1997). Where skin problems prove resistant to simple skin care and barrier creams it is worth seeking a dermatological opinion, as there may be secondary infection or a treatable skin condition.

Bladder control: *Do you have any problems with leakage from your bladder? Does urine leakage occur if you cough, sneeze or laugh? Do you need to rush to the toilet to pass water?*

Urinary incontinence may co-exist and be a sign of extensive pelvic floor failure. Referral for further investigations may be indicated. Up to a quarter of women attending a urodynamic clinic for investigation of urinary incontinence will admit to faecal incontinence on a postal questionnaire, but only 15% do so on direct questioning, emphasising the difficulty many women have in admitting this symptom (Khullar et al., 1998). Possibly surprisingly, faecal incontinence seems to be more often associated with an overactive bladder than with genuine stress incontinence, possibly reflecting the overlap of irritable bowel syndrome with an unstable bladder (Cukier et al., 1997).

Effect on lifestyle/relationships/psychological factors:

If a patient reports symptoms of faecal incontinence it is important to ascertain how this has affected their lifestyle. Some patients report feeling very restricted, planning their journeys around toilet facilities, others may become housebound. Obviously such behaviour will have a profound effect on the individual and on any partner and family. Patients often report avoiding a sexual relationship due to feeling dirty or a fear that an episode of incontinence will occur. Although intuitively and clinically it is often felt that faecal incontinence has a major negative impact on psycho-social wellbeing (Chapter 5), there have been remarkably few formal studies of this. It is known that children born with congenital ano-rectal abnormalities and with persistent faecal incontinence have a greater increased risk of behavioural and social problems than their unaffected peers (Ludman et al., 1994; Rintala, 1992). One qualitative study has documented in detail the difficulties for children and their families of growing up with faecal incontinence (Cavet, 1998), but there have been no similar studies in adults (Chapter 5).

Examination (Table 6.3, overleaf)

It has been suggested that a good history and physical examination can predict findings of ano-rectal physiology studies in many cases. A low resting tone in the anal canal on digital examination is associated with passive leakage, and there is often gaping of a 'funnel-shaped' anal introitus if gentle traction is applied away from the anal verge (Hill et al., 1994; Engel et al., 1995b). Many patients with post-defaecation soiling have trapping of soft stool in this 'funnel', which ordinary wiping with dry paper will not remove. Reduced strength and duration of voluntary contraction of the anus has been found to correlate with the symptom of urgency of defaecation (Delechenaut et al., 1992; Hill et al., 1994; Engel et al., 1995b). Urge incontinence of stool is also associated with reduced puborectalis squeeze, a reduced ano-rectal angle, and many patients also report urge and stress urinary incontinence (Hill et al., 1994).

However, estimation of resting and squeeze sphincter tone has not been found to correlate well with any objective measure of sphincter function, including continence to rectally infused saline (Read et al., 1979). Also, there is as yet no validated scale for assessing the strength or endurance of anal squeeze. Possibly, adaptation of the Oxford grading scale, used for grading of vaginal pelvic floor contraction when treating patients with Kegel exercises for urinary incontinence, would be useful (Schussler et al., 1994), but it is not known whether this would be reliable or reproducible, or have any clinical relevance. In men, digital examination has been found to be reliable except for

Table 6.3: Physical Examination Results

Inspection

Perineal soiling
Scars
Anal closure
Muscular defect
Loss of perineal body
Rectal prolapse
Muscular contraction
Perineal descent
Anal skin reflex to pin prick
Anatomic ano-rectal pathology
  Haemorrhoids
  Skin tags
  Fistula
  Mucosal ectropion
  Fissure
  Others

Palpation

Resting tone
Squeeze tone
Sphincter defects
Anal canal length
ARA
Puborectalis tone and motion
Rectal content
Soft tissue scarring
Rectocoele
Intussusception
Rectovaginal fistula

Endoscopy

Intussusception
Solitary rectal ulcer
Scarring
Mucosal defects
Neoplasm
Inflammation
  Inflammatory bowel disease
  Infectious colitis
  Others
Fistula

Source: (Jorge and Wexner, 1993)

assessment of fatigue (Wyndaele and Van Eetvelde, 1996). It is increasingly recognised that fatigue of voluntary squeeze is an important parameter of assessment, and it is possible to work out a fatigue rate index using manometry (Marcello et al., 1998). It is not known whether digital examination can accurately assess the rate of fatigue of an anal squeeze. It has been found that digital examination is especially poor at estimating resting tone (Felt-Bersma et al., 1988).

Aspects of physical examination other than the resting and squeeze tone of the anal canal should include:

- inspection of the perianal skin for skin excoriation, presence of soiling, any congenital abnormalities, and any haemorrhoids or skin tags (the latter may make perianal cleaning very difficult and lead to minor soiling problems);
- inspection of the perineum for scarring from episiotomy or tears (however, perineal inspection has been shown not to correlate well with the presence or absence of occult anal sphincter damage as seen on anal ultrasound, and an apparently intact perineum does not preclude underlying sphincter damage) (Frudinger et al., 1997);
- inspection of the posterior wall of the vagina for any rectocoele at rest and on straining;
- where there is any suspicion from the history of rectal prolapse, this will seldom be apparent if the patient is examined lying down. The best way to check for prolapse is to sit the patient on a commode or toilet, sitting forward on the toilet seat and leaning forward and ask him/her to strain as hard as she can. A prolapsing rectum will be visible or can be felt at the anal verge or below (Pemberton, 1990);
- perineal descent of greater than 2 cm on straining is considered abnormal (Pemberton, 1990);
- the contours of the lower back may suggest previously unsuspected spina bifida occulta;
- the presence of a loaded rectum may suggest constipation or faecal impaction, particularly in a frail or immobile person.

However, digital rectal examination provides an unreliable indicator of colonic loading, particularly where stools are soft and putty-like rather than hard (Ardron and Main, 1990; Barrett, 1993);
- a general assessment of physical abilities and any disabilities that might impair the individual's coping with independent toileting.

Ideally, every person presenting with unexplained faecal incontinence should have had a full medical examination to check for any rectal masses.

Rating the severity of incontinence and constipation

It is important for both clinical practice and research that a reproducible and valid estimation of the severity of the incontinence is made. Only then can the effectiveness of therapy be gauged. There have been several rating scales for faecal incontinence proposed (Jorge and Wexner, 1993; Pescatori et al., 1992; Vaizey et al., 1999). None as yet has been subject to evaluation with large patient groups to examine the ability to reflect changes in severity. The scale found to have the best clinical validity is given in Table 6.4 (Vaizey et al., 1999). It may also be useful to formally assess quality of life (Chapter 5).

It has been proposed that the criteria in Table 6.5 (overleaf) are adopted for defining constipation. Additional attempts to devise a 'score' have been devised but not as yet widely used (Agachan et al., 1996).

Conclusions

The nursing assessment outlined in this chapter gives a basis on which to plan individual care for adults with faecal incontinence. The assessment will need to be adapted for different patient groups and different settings as indicated in specific chapters of this book. If the patient brings a completed diary and bowel symptom questionnaire to the assessment interview this can greatly facilitiate the process.

Table 6.4: St Mark's Faecal Continence Score

	Never	*Rarely* <*1 mth*	*Sometimes* <*1 week*	*Usually* <*1 day*	*Always* *daily*
Solid	0	1	2	3	4
Liquid	0	1	2	3	4
Gas	0	1	2	3	4
Lifestyle	0	1	2	3	4

	No	*Yes*
Need to wear a pad/plug/change underwear for soiling	0	2
Taking constipating medicines	0	2
Lack of ability to defer defaecation for 15 minutes	0	4

Table 6.5 Standard diagnostic criteria for functional constipation

Two or more episodes for at least 3 months of:

1) Straining at defaecation at least a quarter of the time
2) Lumpy and/or hard stools at least a quarter of the time
3) A sensation of incomplete evacuation at least a quarter of the time
4) Two or fewer bowel motions in a week.

Abdominal pain is not required. Loose stools are not present, and there are insufficient criteria for irritable bowel syndrome. These criteria may not apply when the patient is taking laxatives.

Source: Thompson et al., 1992.

References

Agachan, F., Chen, T., Pfeifer, J., Reissman, P. and Wexner, S.D. (1996) A constipation scoring system to simplify evaluation and management of constipated patients. *Diseases of the Colon and Rectum* **39**, 681–685.

Ardron, M.E. and Main, A.N.H. (1990) Management of constipation. *British Medical Journal* **300**, 1400.

Ashworth, P.D. and Hagan, M.T. (1993) The meaning of incontinence: a qualitative study of non-geriatric urinary incontinence sufferers. *Journal of Advanced Nursing* **18**, 1415–1423.

Barrett, J.A. (1993) *Faecal incontinence and related problems in the older adult.* London: Edward Arnold.

Bliss, D. Z., Savik, S., Jung, H., Jensen, L. L., LeMoine, M. and Lowry, A.C. (1999) Comparison of subjective classification of stool consistency and stool water content. *Journal of Wound, Ostomy, and Continence Nursing* **26**, 137–141.

Brown, S.R., Cann, P.A. and Read, N.W. (1990) Effect of coffee on distal colon function. *Gut* **31**, 450–453.

Cavet, J. (1998) *People don't understand: children, young people and their families living with a hidden disability.* London: National Children's Bureau.

Connell, A.M., Hilton, C., Irvine, G., Lennard-Jones, J.E. and Misiewicz, J.J. (1965) Variation in bowel habit in two population samples. *British Medical Journal* **ii**, 1095–1099.

Cukier, J.M., Cortina-Borja, M. and Brading, A.F. (1997) A case control study to examine any association between idiopathic detrusor instability and gastrointestinal tract disorder, and between irritable bowel syndrome and urinary tract disorder. *British Journal of Urology* **79**, 865–878.

Curless, R., French, J., Williams, G.V. and James, O.F.W. (1994) Comparison of gastrointestinal symptoms in colorectal cancer patients and community controls with respect to age. *Gut* **35**, 1267–1270.

Delechenaut, P., Leroi, A.M., Weber, J., Touchais, J.Y., Czernichow, P. and Denis, P. (1992) Relationship between clinical symptoms of anal incontinence and the results of anorectal manometry. *Diseases of the Colon and Rectum* **35**, 847–849.

Donnelly, V., O'Connell, P.R. and O'Herlihy, C. (1997) The influence of oestrogen replacement on faecal incontinence in postmenopausal women. *British Journal of Obstetrics and Gynaecology* **104**, 311–315.

Drossman, D.A., Richer, J.E., Talley, N.J., Thompson, W.G., Corazziari, E. and Whitehead, W.E. (1994) *The functional gastrointestinal disorders.* Reston, Virginia: Degnon Associates.

Engel, A.F., Kamm, M.A. and Bartram, C.I. (1995a) Unwanted anal penetration as a physical cause of faecal incontinence. *European Journal of Gastroenterology and Hepatology* **7**, 65–67.

Engel, A.F., Kamm, M.A., Bartram, C.I. and Nicholls, R.J. (1995b) Relationship of symptoms in faecal incontinence to specific sphincter abnormalities. *International Journal of Colorectal Disease* **10**, 152–155.

Felt-Bersma, R.J.F., Klinkenberg-Knol, E.C. and Meuwissen, S.G.M. (1988) Investigation of anorectal function. *British Journal of Surgery* **75**, 53–55.

Frudinger, A., Bartram, C.I., Spencer, J. and Kamm, M.A. (1997) Perineal examination as a predictor of underlying external anal sphincter damage. *British Journal of Obstetrics and Gynaecology* **104**, 1009–1013.

Gee, A.S. and Durdey, P. (1995) Urge incontinence of faeces is a marker of severe external anal sphincter dysfunction. *British Journal of Surgery* **82**, 1179–1182.

Harari, D., Gurwitz, J.H., Avorn, J., Bohn, R. and Minaker, K.L. (1996) Bowel habit in relation to age and gender. *Archives of Internal Medicine* **156**, 315–320.

Heaton, K.W., Radvan, J., Cripps, H., Mountford, R.A., Braddon, F.E.M. and Hughes, A.O. (1992) Defaecation frequency and timing, and stool form in the general population: a prospective study. *Gut* **33**, 818–824.

Henry, M.M. and Swash, M. (1992) *Coloproctology and the pelvic floor* (2nd edn). London: Butterworth Heinemann.

Herbst, F., Kamm, M.A., Morris, G.P., Britton, K., Woloszko, J. and Nicholls, R.J. (1997) Gastrointestinal transit and prolonged ambulatory colonic motility in health and faecal incontinence. *Gut* **41**, 381–389.

Hill, J., Corson, R.J., Brandon, H., Redford, J., Faragher, E.B. and Kiff, E.S. (1994) History and examination in the assessment of patients with idiopathic faecal incontinence. *Diseases of the Colon and Rectum* **37**, 473–477.

Johanson, J.F. and Lafferty, J. (1996) Epidemiology of fecal incontinence: the silent affliction. *American Journal of Gastroenterology.* **91**, 33–36.

Jorge, J.M. and Wexner, S.D. (1993a) Etiology and management of fecal incontinence. *Diseases of the Colon & Rectum* **36**, 77–97. [Review].

Kamm, M.A. (1998) Faecal incontinence: clinical review. *British Medical Journal* **316**, 528–532.

Kamm, M.A. and Lennard-Jones, J.E. (1994) *Constipation.* Petersfield: Wrightson Biomedical Publishing Ltd.

Khullar, V., Damiano, R., Toozs-Hobson, P. and Cardozo, L. (1998) Prevalence of faecal incontinence among women with urinary incontinence. *British Journal of Obstetrics and Gynaecology* **105**, 1211–1213.

Klauser, A.G., Voderholzer, W.A., Heinrich, C.A., Schindlbeck, N.E. and Mueller-Lissner, S.A. (1990) Behavioural modification of colonic function – can constipation be learned? *Digestive Diseases and Sciences* **35**, 1271–1275.

Leigh, R.J. and Turnberg, L.A. (1982) Faecal incontinence: the unvoiced symptom. *Lancet* **1**, 1349–1351.

Ludman, L., Spitz, L. and Kiely, E.M. (1994) Social and emotional impact of faecal incontinence after surgery for anorectal abnormalities. *Archives of Disease in Childhood* **71**, 194–200.

Marcello, P.W., Barrett, R.C., Coller, J.A., Schoetz, D.J., Roberts, P.L., Murray, J.J. and Rusin, L.C. (1998) Fatigue rate index as a new measure of external sphincter function. *Diseases of the Colon and Rectum* **41**, 336–343.

Nelson, A., Malassigne, P., Amerson, T., Saltzstein, R. and Binard, J. (1993) Descriptive study of bowel care practices and equipment in spinal cord injury. *Scientific Nursing* **10**, 65–67.

Norton, C. and Chelvanayagam, S. (2000) A nursing assessment tool for adults with fecal incontinence. *Journal of Wound, Ostomy and Continence Nursing* **27**, 279–291.

Pemberton, J.H. (1990) Anorectal and pelvic floor disorders: putting physiology into practice. *Journal of Gastroenterology and Hepatology* **5** (Suppl. 1), 127–143.

Pescatori, M., Anastasio, G., Bottini, C. and Mentasti, A. (1992) New grading and scoring for anal incontinence. *Diseases of the Colon and Rectum* **35**, 482–487.

Rausch, T., Beglinger, C., Alam, N. and Meier, R. (1998) Effect of transdermal application of nicotine on colonic transit in healthy nonsmoking volunteers. *Neurogastroenterology and Motility* **10**, 263–270.

Read, N.W., Harford, W.V., Schmulen, A.C., Read, M., Santa Ana, C. and Fordtran, J.S. (1979) A clinical study of patients with faecal incontinence and diarrhoea. *Gastroenterology* **76**, 747–756.

Rintala, R. (1992) Faecal continence and quality of life in adult patients with an operated low anorectal malformation. *Journal of Pediatric Surgery* **27**, 902–905.

Rosenberg, A.J. and Whitehead, T. (1990) Achieving anal relaxation: the key to continence for encopretic children. *Gastroenterology* **99**, 1229.

Schussler, B., Laycock, J., Norton, P. and Stanton, S. (1994) *Pelvic floor re-education: principles and practice.* London: Springer-Verlag.

Scott, A.M., Kellow, J.E., Eckersley, G.M., Nolan, J.M. and Jones, M.P. (1992) Cigarette smoking and nicotine delay postprandial mouth–cecum transit time. *Digestive Diseases and Sciences* **37**, 1544–1547.

Sultan, A.H., Kamm, M.A., Hudson, C.N., Thomas, J.M. and Bartram, C.I. (1993) Anal sphincter disruption during vaginal delivery. *New England Journal of Medicine* **329**, 1905–1911.

Sultan, A.H., Kamm, M.A., Hudson, C.N. and Bartram, C.I. (1994) Third degree obstetric and sphincter tears: risk factors and outcome of primary repair. *British Medical Journal* **308**, 887–891.

Taylor, T., Smith, A.N. and Fulton, P.M. (1989) Effect of hysterectomy on bowel function. *British Medical Journal* **299**, 300–301.

Thompson, W.G., Dotevall, G., Drossman, D.A., Heaton, K.W. and Kruis, W. (1989) Irritable bowel syndrome: guidelines for diagnosis. *Gastroenterology International* **2**, 92–95.

Thompson, W.G., Creed, F., Drossman, D.A., Heaton, K.W. and Mazzacca, G. (1992) Functional bowel disorders and chronic functional abdominal pain. *Gastroenterology International* **5**, 75–91.

Vaizey, C.J., Kamm, M.A. and Bartram, C.I. (1997) Primary degeneration of the internal anal sphincter as a cause of passive faecal incontinence. *Lancet* **349**, 612–615.

Vaizey, C.J., Carapeti, E.A., Cahill, J.A. and Kamm, M.A. (1999) Prospective comparison of faecal incontinence grading systems. *Gut* **44**,77–80.

van Dam, J.H., Gosselink, M.J., Drogendijk, A.C., Hop, W.C.J. and Schouten, W.R. (1997) Changes in bowel function after hysterectomy. *Diseases of the Colon and Rectum* **40**, 1342–1347.

White, H. (1996) Aids to continence for people with physical disabilities. In: Norton, C. (ed.) *Nursing for continence* (2 edn). pp. 299–316. Beaconsfield: Beaconsfield Publishers.

Whitehead, W.E., Orr, W.C., Engel, B.T. and Schuster, M.M. (1981) External anal sphincter response to rectal distension: learned response or reflex. *Psychophysiology* **19**, 57–62.

Wyndaele, J.J. and Van Eetvelde, B. (1996) Reproducibility of digital testing of the pelvic floor muscles in men. *Archives of Physical Medicine and Rehabilitation* **77**, 1179–1181.

Chapter 7

Rectal Bleeding – When to Refer

Maggie Vance

Introduction

Patients presenting with faecal incontinence may report rectal bleeding among their symptoms. This chapter provides an overview of the differential diagnosis of rectal bleeding and discusses the signs or symptoms that should lead the nurse to seek specialist advice. A diagnostic pathway, including a rationale for diagnostic intervention and treatment choice, is presented to assist the nurse in making appropriate assessment and referrals for patients who present with rectal bleeding.

Rectal bleeding is the most common indication for referral to colorectal clinics, accounting for two-thirds of patients referred (Lamah et al., 2000). The primary cause for concern with patients who present with rectal bleeding is the possible presence of colorectal cancer. Approximately 32,000 new cases of colorectal cancer are diagnosed each year in the United Kingdom and it is the second most common cause of cancer death. Patients diagnosed with colorectal cancer may present initially with a variety of symptoms including the presence of rectal bleeding (Majumdar, 1999, Pritchard, 1998).

Although rectal bleeding is a common symptom, studies have shown that the general public are reluctant to report this symptom to their GP (Crosland and Jones, 1995). Reluctance to discuss colorectal symptoms may have serious consequences for the patient's health.

The dilemma often facing health care professionals is at what point to refer patients who present with this symptom for investigations, and how far to investigate. The answer to this problem can be complex. However, utilising the clinical skills of careful history taking and clinical examination will enable the practitioner to make the appropriate clinical decisions.

Definition of rectal bleeding

Rectal bleeding is the passage of blood from the anus. It is an abnormal event that may occur at any time during the human life cycle. Although often attributed to the presence of benign anorectal conditions, including haemorrhoids or anal fissure, the presence of neoplastic disease must be excluded (Helfand et al., 1997).

Differential diagnoses of rectal bleeding

There are many causes of rectal bleeding, the most common of which are briefly described here.

Haemorrhoids and anal fissure

These two conditions are by far the most common cause of bleeding in the general population and are covered in Chapter 11.

Inflammatory bowel disease

In ulcerative colitis the presence of rectal bleeding, caused by inflammation and ulceration of colonic mucosa, is a common presenting symptom. Bleeding is less common in Crohn's disease. Bleeding may be bright red, if distal colonic disease is present, but may be associated with symptoms of diarrhoea and the passage of mucus. Patients who are diagnosed with inflammatory bowel disease also have an increased risk of colorectal cancer.

Solitary rectal ulcer syndrome

Solitary rectal ulcers are typically, but not always, single benign ulcers found in the rectum and are thought to be caused by chronic constipation and straining. Straining causes prolapse of the rectal mucosa during defaecation, leading to mucosal trauma and ulceration. This ulceration of the rectal mucosa can cause rectal bleeding and the production of excess mucus.

Diverticulosis/Diverticular disease

Diverticular disease is the presence of diverticulae in the large intestine. A diverticulum is a single sac-like herniation of mucosa, which protrudes through the muscular layer of the colon at points of natural weakness where blood vessels penetrate the muscular layer of the colon (Young-Fadok et al., 1999). The condition is thought to be caused by raised intraluminal pressures within the colon caused by chronic constipation.

This herniation of mucosa through the muscular layer exposes the blood vessels of the colon to potential trauma and local injury from faeces. This may lead to weakness of the blood vessels, causing rupture and bleeding into the diverticulum and resulting in rectal bleeding. Diverticular bleeding can cause massive acute colonic blood loss or chronic intermittent rectal bleeding.

Neoplastic disease – adenomatous polyps and colorectal cancer

Most colorectal cancers are thought to develop from adenomatous polyps present in the colon. A polyp is a pedunculated lesion of tissue protruding above the mucosal surface into the lumen of the bowel (Schofield et al., 1993).

Polyps vary in size and shape and also in their histology and consist of two types, benign hyperplastic polyps and neoplastic polyps (adenomas). Adenomas, diagnosed by their histological appearance, may be pre-malignant and have the potential to progress to carcinoma. Theories about polyp formation and their progression from adenoma to carcinoma have been clearly documented (see Macrae et al., 1999 and Figure 7.1). Prevention and early detection of colorectal cancer concentrates on the removal of adenomas and the detection of early colorectal cancer. During the progression from adenoma to carcinoma, the polyp goes through several

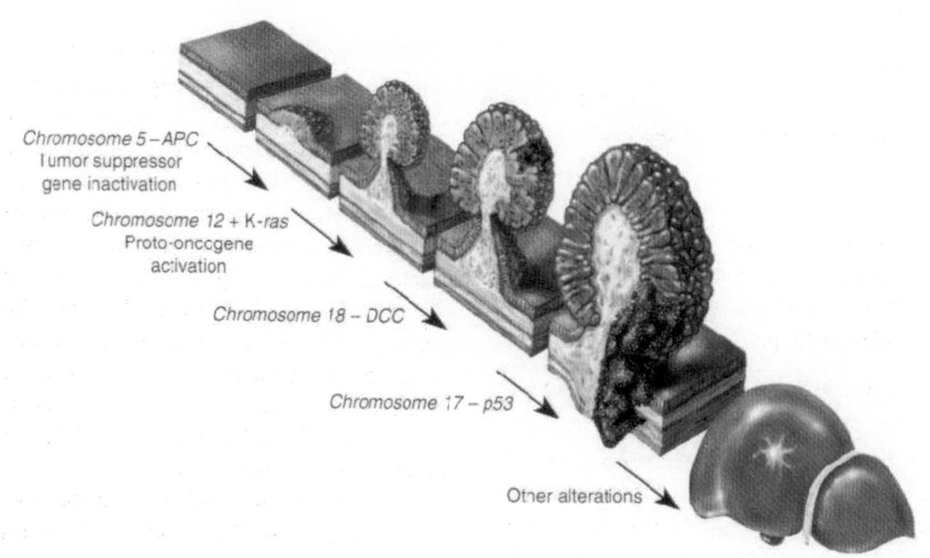

Figure 7.1 *The adenoma-carcinoma sequence.*

changes in its structure. The only indication that an adenoma is present in the colon may be the presence of occult rectal bleeding or mucus in the stool. Colorectal cancer may also cause rectal bleeding, and with rectal cancer this may be the first symptom a patient experiences. Seventy per cent of neoplastic disease of the large bowel is found in the distal (lower) colon from anus to splenic flexure.

When to refer

When a patient gives a history of rectal bleeding, regardless of the duration or type of rectal bleeding, they must initially be referred for assessment. Onward referral to hospital for diagnostic investigations will usually be indicated.

The assessment process

When a patient complains of experiencing rectal bleeding it is important to assess the following:

- nature, frequency and duration of rectal bleeding
- associated symptoms (alteration in bowel habit, pain, history of rectal prolapse, constitutional symptoms such as weight loss or anorexia)
- past medical history
- family history of colon cancer
- drug history
- abdominal physical examination for assessment for presence of palpable mass and organomegaly.

Patients may present with two different types of rectal bleeding, commonly termed as outlet bleeding and altered rectal bleeding. An assessment of the type of rectal bleeding will determine the diagnostic pathway for the patient.

Outlet rectal bleeding includes the following symptoms:

- bright red rectal bleeding only which may or may not be associated with defaecation
- blood is commonly seen on the tissue paper after defaecation or dripping in the pan of the toilet
- anal pain may be experienced with defaecation
- no abdominal pain or altered bowel habit is experienced.

Altered rectal bleeding is the presence of bleeding which may be associated with other symptoms. These can include:

- blood mixed in with stool
- blood and mucus present on defaecation
- the presence of rectal bleeding associated with an alteration in bowel habit of diarrhoea or constipation, or both
- the presence of rectal bleeding in association with abdominal pain
- associated weight loss.

Diagnostic pathway for patients with rectal bleeding

Ano-rectal examination

The ano-rectal examination is the first step of the diagnostic process and involves inspection, palpation and digital examination of the perineal area and distal rectum (see Mayer et al., 1997 for techniques). The examination enables assessment for haemorrhoids, anal fissure, rectal prolapse, and anal and distal rectal neoplastic disease.

Proctoscopy and rigid sigmoidoscopy

The passage of a proctoscope through the anal canal enables direct visualisation and enables accurate diagnosis of anal fissure and internal haemorrhoids. The proctoscope is lubricated and passed gently through the anus and rotated to enable a complete circumferential view.

Rigid sigmoidoscopy enables examination of the mid rectum with a sigmoidoscope 25 cm in length. The scope is passed through the anus and inserted into the rectum. Biopsies of abnormal areas can be taken. Although very useful for assessment of rectal mucosa, complete examination of the rectum is very difficult due to the instrument's rigidity and there is the potential for missing lesions. The presence of faeces often makes the procedure difficult and the use of rigid sigmoidoscopy for diagnostic purposes is questionable.

Flexible sigmoidoscopy and colonoscopy – rationale for choice

After an ano-rectal examination has been performed, direct visualisation of the colonic mucosa by a specialist endoscopist is necessary to complete the diagnosis of conditions which may cause rectal bleeding. Video endoscopy enables the practitioner to examine the lumen of the colon for causes of bleeding symptoms (Cotton and Williams, 1996).

Flexible sigmoidoscopy is an examination which enables the practitioner to examine the colonic mucosa extending from the anus to the splenic flexure of the colon. A fibreoptic flexible sigmoidoscope is passed through the anus and steered round the left distal colon. A picture of the lining of the bowel is relayed to a video screen enabling the practitioner to inspect the mucosa thoroughly. Patients require a phosphate enema prior to the procedure to clear the distal colon of faeces.

Patients who present with outlet bleeding with no abdominal symptoms require at least rectal examination, flexible sigmoidoscopy and proctoscopy. Rationale for the choice of this diagnostic test is based on the knowledge that approximately 70% of neoplastic colonic disease is found in the distal colon, within reach of the flexible sigmoidoscope. Although studies have shown that in 85% of rectal bleeding cases the cause for bleeding is found within the anus and rectum (Vernava et al., 1997), 15% of cases were found within the proximal colon, beyond the reach of a 15 cm rigid sigmoidoscope. Examination of the anus and rectum for patients with any type of rectal bleeding is not sufficient and is unsafe. In as yet unpublished data from St Mark's Hospital, 12% of patients who presented with only bright red rectal bleeding had neoplastic disease of which 90% was found proximal to the rectum. Of those patients with neoplastic disease, 45% also had co-existing haemorrhoids. If rigid sigmoidoscopy only had been the performed a diagnosis of haemorrhoids would have been made. However the neoplastic disease would have remained undiagnosed with potentially fatal consequences for patients who presented with the symptoms of outlet rectal bleeding only. Patients with neoplastic disease found at flexible sigmoidoscopy must have a colonoscopy at a future date to exclude the presence of further disease in the proximal colon.

Colonoscopy

Colonoscopy enables complete endoscopic examination of the large intestine with a flexible endoscope. Patients who present with altered rectal bleeding and associated symptoms must have a test that enables complete examination to exclude proximal neoplastic lesions. Barium enema also allows complete examination of the colon but is a diagnostic tool only. Colonoscopy enables therapeutic interventions, such as polypectomy (the removal of polyps) and biopsy of abnormalities to obtain a histological diagnosis. This is not possible with a barium enema.

Preparations for colonoscopy and barium enema are the same and include the intake of oral bowel preparation. The risks associated with colonoscopy are greater than those with barium enema and careful assessment of the individual patient's general condition is necessary prior to ordering either test.

The rectal bleeding clinic – a model for practice

Rapid assessment of patients with rectal bleeding is crucial in assisting with early detection of colorectal cancer. An effective way of providing this service is the development of an open access rectal bleeding clinic.

At St Mark's Hospital the rectal bleeding clinic is led by the nurse endoscopist and has been developed with the assistance of the colorectal surgeons. This partnership is crucial in providing an effective service for patients. A description of the clinic and its preliminary findings are given here. The data (as yet unpublished) show how the clinic may be effective in the early diagnosis and treatment of benign and neoplastic disorders found in patients with rectal bleeding.

Rationale for service

A nurse-led rectal bleeding clinic was set up to provide a fast-track service to examine, treat and discharge patients with benign ano-rectal conditions and screen for neoplastic disease in a single session. Patients over the age of 45 with bright red rectal bleeding were referred on first presentation to their GP.

Clinic practice

Patients are referred directly from their GP to the endoscopy unit, and referral letters are screened by a consultant surgeon and appointments arranged within a maximum 4-week period from the initial GP referral. Patients are prepared with a single phosphate enema given in the clinic. A standardised clinical protocol is utilised for all patients, which includes the following:

Symptom-related history proforma, to assess:

- nature, frequency and duration of rectal bleeding
- associated symptoms (alteration in bowel habit, pain, history of rectal prolapse, constitutional symptoms)
- past medical history
- family history of colon cancer
- drug history.

Abdominal physical examination (performed by the nurse practitioner)

Diagnostic flexible sigmoidoscopy/polypectomy (performed by the nurse practitioner)

Video proctoscopy sclerotherapy (performed by the nurse practitioner/surgeon).

Colonoscopy is performed (at a later date) in all patients with adenomas detected at flexible sigmoidoscopy. Barium enema is performed, at a later date, in patients with an incomplete sigmoidoscopic examination, failure to reach sigmoid-descending colon junction due to fixed angulated sigmoid colon (pelvic adhesions, fixed sigmoid diverticulosis).

Patients with benign ano-rectal bleeding are treated if appropriate (e.g. banding or injecting of haemorrhoids if needed), offered education and discharged on the same day, and their GP informed of findings.

All patients discharged from the clinic are followed up at one- and five-yearly intervals to assess for reoccurrence of symptoms.

Preliminary results

Complete data has been obtained on the first 220 patients referred to the clinic (118 male, 102 female; mean age 55.9 years). Indications for referral were: rectal bleeding (n = 198, 90%), bleeding with associated anal pain (n = 20, 9%), bleeding with change in bowel habit (n = 2, 1%). Complete sigmoidoscopy to the sigmoid-descending colon junction was achieved in 209 (95%) patients. Incomplete examinations in 11 (5%) patients were due to a fixed sigmoid colon. These patients were referred for barium enema. No complications were experienced at flexible sigmoidoscopy.

Of these 220 patients, 27 patients (12%) were found to have neoplastic disease including 5 (2%) with cancer and 22 (10%) with adenomas. Of those patients with neoplastic disease only 4% of lesions were within the reach of a rigid sigmoidoscope. In 96% of patients neoplastic disease was found proximal to (above) the recto-sigmoid junction. Ten patients (45%) of patients with neoplastic disease also had co-existent haemorrhoids. Twenty-two (10%) of patients had one or more adenomas found at flexible sigmoidoscopy. All of these patients went on to have a colonoscopy.

Nine patients (40%) had right-sided adenomas found at colonoscopy (transverse colon, ascending colon and caecum). These patients were entered into polyp follow-up programmes. No cancers were found at follow-up colonoscopy or barium enema.

The development of this clinic has led to a reduction in routine outpatient appointment waiting times for surgical clinics. Waiting times have been reduced from sixteen to eight weeks as a result of patients being reviewed in the one-stop rectal bleeding clinic.

Conclusions

This chapter provides an overall view of rectal bleeding; the common causes and appropriate assessment and diagnostic tests which may be utilised. Further reading will enable the practitioner to develop more in-depth knowledge of the subject. The most important points to remember are always to refer the patient on first presentation of rectal bleeding and to assess all patients seen in clinics for the presence of rectal bleeding or altered bowel habit. Patients with benign ano-rectal conditions must still be provided with health promotion about the signs and symptoms of bowel cancer to assist in the prevention and early detection of colorectal cancer, which remains the goal of every health care professional working within the field of gastroenterology and coloproctology.

References

Cotton, P. and Williams, C. (1996) *Practical gastro-intestinal endoscopy.* Oxford: Blackwell Science.

Crosland, A. and Jones, R. (1995) Rectal bleeding: prevalence and consultation behaviour. *British Medical Journal* **311**, 7003, 486–488.

Helfand, M., Marton, K.J., Zimmer-Gembeck, M.J. and Sox, H.C. (1997) History of visible rectal bleeding in a primary care population. Initial assessment and 10–year follow-up. *Journal of the American Medical Association* **227**, 10, 44–48.

Lamah, M., Ahmad, S.M., Charalampopoulos, A. and Leicester, R.J. (2000) Three-year evaluation of a rapid-access coloproctology clinic. *Digestive Surgery* **17**, 2,150–153.

Macrae, F.A. and Young, G.P. (1999) Neoplastic and nonneoplastic polyps of the colon and rectum. In: Yamada, T., Alpers, D.H., Laine, L., Owyang, C. and Powell, D.W. (eds). *Textbook of gastroenterology*, pp. 1965–1994. Philadelphia. Lippincott Williams & Wilkins.

Majumdar, S.R., Fletcher, R.H. and Evans, A.T. (1999) How does colorectal cancer present? Symptoms, duration, and clues to location. *American Journal of Gastroenterology* **94**, 10, 3039–3045.

Mayer, R., Madoff, R.D. and Goldberg, S.M. (1997) Clinical assessment. In: Nicholls, R.J. and Dozois, R.R. (eds). *Surgery of the colon and rectum*, pp. 67–84. London: Churchill Livingstone.

Pritchard, P.J. and Tjandra, J.J. (1998) Colorectal cancer. *Medical Journal of Australia* **169**, 9, 493–8.

Schofield, P.F. and Jones, D.J. (1993) Colorectal neoplasia – I: Benign colonic tumours. In: Jones, D.J. and Irving, M. (eds). *ABC of colorectal diseases,* pp. 55–57. London: BMJ Publishing Group.

Vernava, A.M., Moore, B.A., Longo, W.E. and Johnson, F.E. (1997) Lower gastrointestinal bleeding. *Diseases of the Colon and Rectum* **40**, 7, 846–858.

Young-Fadok, T.M. and Sarr, M.G. (1999) Diverticular disease of the colon. In: Yamada, T., Alpers, D.H., Laine, L., Owyang, C. and Powell, D.W. (eds). *Textbook of gastroenterology,* pp. 1926– 1944. Philadelphia: Lippincott Williams & Wilkins.

Chapter 8

Ano-rectal Physiology Investigation Techniques

Tanya Nicholls

Introduction

Ano-rectal physiology testing techniques are used for the routine clinical and diagnostic assessment of ano-rectal nerve and muscle function in patients with a variety of bowel associated disorders. The most frequent indications for these tests are faecal incontinence, difficult defaecation (including suspected cases of Hirschsprung's disease), and pre- or post-surgical assessment.

The patient consultation begins by obtaining a detailed medical, surgical and symptomatic bowel history. This gives the examiner an insight into the patient's symptoms and – more importantly – the symptom which is of most significance to the patient, and provides a basis on which to select the most appropriate tests. The patient has the opportunity to ask questions and the tests can be explained appropriately.

Unless otherwise indicated, all of the following described tests are performed with the patient in the left lateral position with the knees flexed. No bowel preparation is required; tests involving digital examination are performed last, as this may cause prolonged relaxation of the internal sphincter. Several techniques are available for each test. This chapter describes the tests used in routine clinical practice at St Mark's Hospital.

Ano-rectal manometry

Manometry is the measurement of pressure in liquids or gases. In this context it can be used for the objective measurement of high-pressure zones and is therefore an ideal technique for the assessment of anal canal sphincter function.

There are three types of manometry catheter in use:

1) Micro-balloon catheters – easy to use and to calibrate, and relatively inexpensive. These record the pressure exerted at the circumference of the balloon.
2) Water-perfused catheters – probably the most frequently used systems. They allow simultaneous recording from multiple sites, both on the longitudinal and radial axes.
3) Solid-state catheters – allow recording at multiple sites, although the orientation of the pressure transducers in relation to each other is limited due to their size.

The software used for the interpretation of results is easy to use and adaptable for a variety of operator-generated protocols (e.g. Medical Measurements Systems BV, Holland).

The resting pressure of the internal anal sphincter is responsible for approximately 80-85% of the anal canal resting tone (Fleshman, 1993). It is comprised of smooth muscle fibres, under autonomic control, maintained at near maximal contraction at all times, and its main reflex response is relaxation. Measurement of resting pressure gives some objective indication of the internal sphincter function in respect of closure of the anal canal. The external anal sphincter is comprised of striated muscle fibres under voluntary control, and contributes the remaining 15–20% of anal canal resting tone. It is maintained in a state of relaxation and its main response to an induced squeeze or coughing is contraction. The external anal sphincter is an important muscle in the voluntary deferment of defaecation and therefore the rate at which it becomes fatigued may be important. The fatigue rate index is the calculated measure of time necessary for the external anal sphincter to become completely fatigued and reach a pressure equivalent to the resting pressure.

Manometry technique

The pressure profile of the anal sphincter complex can be evaluated by performing a station pull-through technique using any of the described catheters. At St Mark's Hospital an eight-channel water-perfused catheter (Mui Scientific, Ontario, Canada) is used (Figure 8.1). This is attached to a vacuum pump and perfused with irrigated water at a rate of 0.4 ml per minute. The signal from the eight external pressure transducers passes into the UPS-2020 box (Medical Measurements Systems BV, Holland), where it is stored during the investigation and can be retrieved for analysis later. The data passes to the computer from the UPS-2020 via a power box (Medical Measurements Systems BV, Holland). A mechanical pulling device (Medical Measurements Systems BV, Holland) can be attached to the power box to allow automated extraction of the catheter at a predefined speed.

The water-perfused catheter is held horizontally at the level of the anal verge and all channels are set to zero using the protocol software. This enables the observed pressure increment to be evaluated relative to atmospheric pressure at the level of the anal canal. The catheter is passed through the anus into the rectum to a level of approximately 10 cm and then withdrawn slowly until a rise in pressure is seen on the manometry trace (Figure 8.2). The graduated markers on the surface of the catheter allow a quantitative measure of the functional anal canal length. A station pull-through technique is used to withdraw the catheter through the anus, at 0.5 cm increments along the anal canal allowing a period of at least 30 seconds rest at each position until the catheter is completely withdrawn. The area of maximum resting pressure is marked on the trace and represents the pressure exerted by the internal anal sphincter, which is maintained at near maximum contraction at all times. It is important not to rush these measurements as catheter movement caused by coughing or momentary anal canal contraction as the catheter is moved may produce artefactual readings.

The external anal sphincter is assessed using the same technique except that at each 0.5 cm increment the patient is asked to squeeze the external sphincter as if trying to stop defaecation. The squeeze pressures can be marked on the trace and represent the voluntary contraction of the external anal sphincter.

The relative squeeze pressure (which equals squeeze pressure minus resting pressure) is obtained from the software analysis, thereby supplying an objective measurement of external anal sphincter function. During ano-rectal sampling (see page 11) it is important that the external anal sphincter can maintain a contraction for long enough so that continence is maintained. Inability to maintain a suitable contraction during sampling due to a weak external anal sphincter muscle is thought to be a contributing factor in faecal incontinence.

At the level of maximum resting pressure the patient is asked to give a large cough. This elicits an involuntary contraction of the external anal sphincter and supplies additional information about external anal sphincter function. This may be significant in patients who have a poor voluntary external anal sphincter contraction on stationary manometry but an intact external anal sphincter on anal ultrasound. A normal involuntary contraction would suggest that the external anal sphincter can function within a normal predefined reference range, but that the patient is unable to consciously contract the external anal sphincter to its maximum pressure due to inco-ordination or misinterpretation of the given instructions. A normal range should be defined by each individual laboratory. It should account for differences in the type of equipment used and for age and sex variations.

There is an extremely good correlation between a poor internal anal sphincter resting pressure, passive faecal incontinence and a damaged internal anal sphincter on anal ultrasound (Marcello et al., 1998). A poor anal squeeze pressure is associated with the symptom of urge faecal incontinence and evidence of a damaged external anal sphincter on anal ultrasound.

Poor anal sphincter function associated with faecal incontinence can be caused by a number of factors, including physical damage due to obstetric trauma, sexual abuse, some surgical

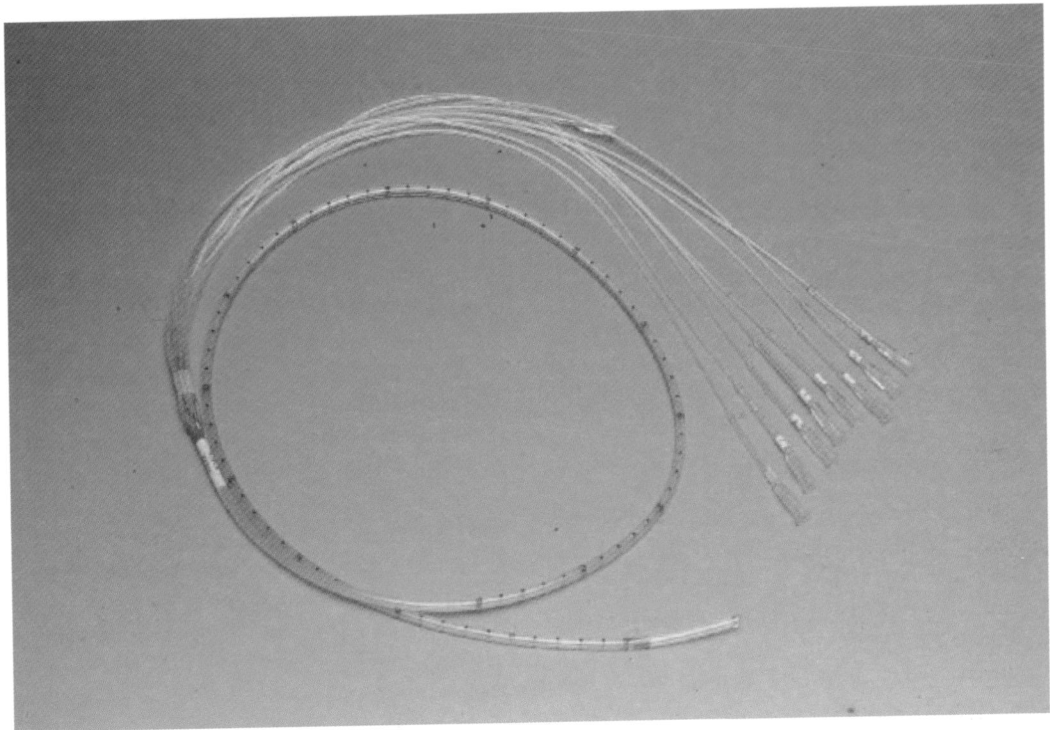

Figure 8.1 *An 8 channel water perfusion catheter (Mui Scientific, Ontario, Canada).*

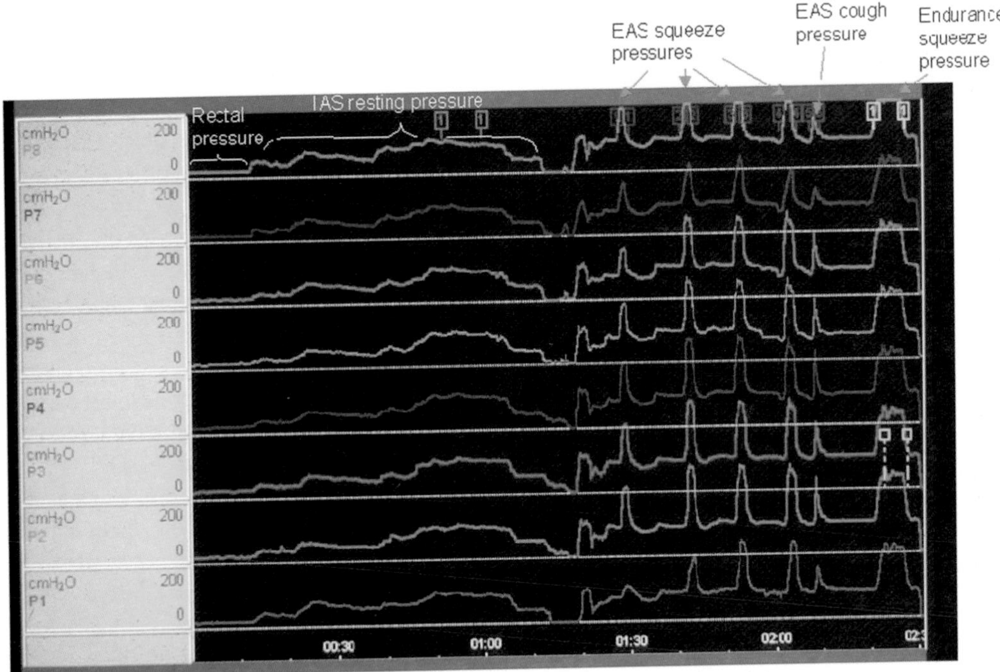

Figure 8.2 *Manometry trace produced using a station pull-through technique (Medical Measurements Systems BV, Holland).*

procedures, sphincter atrophy or sphincter degeneration.

It is possible to retrain damaged sphincter muscles so that faecal incontinence is diminished, with continence restored in some cases. However, the outcome is largely dependent on the extent and severity of muscle damage (Norton and Kamm, 1999).

A high pressure anal sphincter can lead to anal canal fissures, evacuation disorders and perianal discomfort and pain. Some evacuatory disorders (see page 252) may also be resolved by bowel retraining therapy.

Fatigue rate measurement

The fatigability of the external anal sphincter is assessed by placing the perfusion ports of the catheter in the high pressure zone which is typically 0.5 to 2.0 cm from the distal anal verge. The patient is asked to maintain a maximal anal contraction for a set period of time, usually not more than 40 seconds, because it is important to maintain squeeze pressure and not produce cycles of brief squeeze followed by rest. The fatigue rate index (FRI) can be calculated as follows:

$$FRI_{(minutes)} = \frac{(SP - RP)}{- FR}$$

where SP = squeeze pressure and RP = resting pressure in mmHG, and FR = fatigue rate in mmHg per minute.

The fatigue rate of the external sphincter muscle is an important physiological indicator. Marcello et al. (1998) estimated that it would take three minutes for the external sphincter to become completely fatigued and that patients with progressively worsening faecal incontinence have a predictably lower fatigue rate index. Bowel retraining therapy has been shown to improve the ability to maintain prolonged contraction of the external anal sphincter through specific muscle exercises (Norton and Chelvanayagam, 2001), and may therefore be of benefit in patients with symptoms of urge faecal incontinence.

Vector manometry (Vectometry)

The radial pressure profile along the anal canal can be evaluated using vectometry, which identifies segmental anal symmetry and provides information regarding anal sphincter function (Perry et al., 1990; Sentovich et al., 1997). It provides information on the geometry of the sphincter, highlighting possible deficiencies and asymmetry in the form of a three-dimensional picture (Figure 8.3 and 8.4). The derived image is relatively easy to interpret, even for an inexperienced operator. However, this is the only real significant advantage over anal ultrasound which provides more detailed structural information about the anal canal sphincter muscles. The accuracy of sphincter geometry is affected by the degree of catheter flexibility and therefore vector manometry is not a robust measurement for sphincter structure in isolation, but it may be useful when endo-anal ultrasound is not available. There is no data to support the reproducibility of vectometry to date, despite several studies reporting agreement with needle EMG and anal ultrasound (Fynes et al, 2000).

It is important to standardise this procedure so that the catheter is extracted at a predetermined speed. This is achieved with the use of an automated puller (Medical Measurements Systems BV, Holland), because manual withdrawal of the catheter can result in erratic and unreliable data. The orientation of the catheter is standardised by means of a predefined marker on its surface. The manometry catheter is passed via the anus into the rectum to a level of approximately 5 cm above the upper verge of the anal canal and is attached to the pulling device. The catheter is withdrawn initially when the anal sphincters are relaxed, and withdrawal is then repeated when the sphincter muscles are maintained at maximal contraction. A pressure profile is then obtained from the image analysis software.

The profile generated using this technique is divided into several segments of fixed length, and the maximum pressure in each segment for each channel is used to draw a three-dimensional sphincter image by means of the computer software. Vectometry identifies asymmetry and decreased sphincter pressures in the anal canal. It has been shown to be of clinical value in some studies for the identification of patients with traumatic sphincter injuries (Perry et al., 1990). However, anal ultrasound is a superior diagnostic

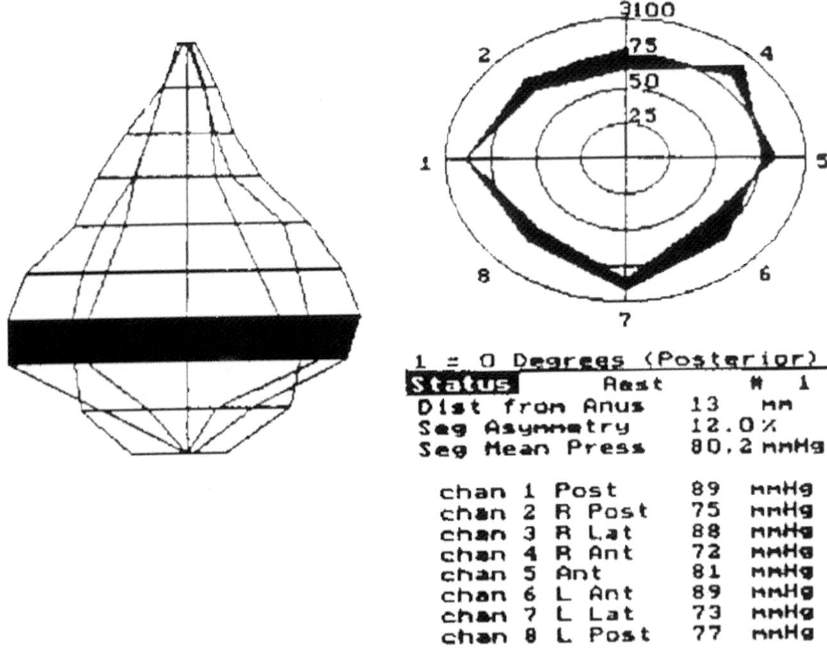

Figure 8.3 *Data from a vectometry procedure of the anal canal.*

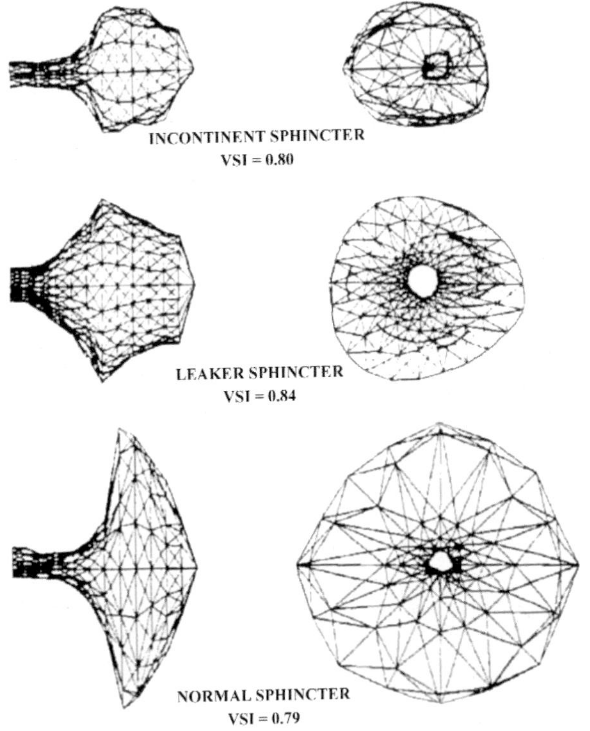

Figure 8.4 *Comparison of 3–D vector volume analysis on three different anal sphincters.*

technique, negating the use of vectometry if the choice is available.

Sensory testing

Rectal sensation

Rectal threshold, urge and maximal tolerated volume sensations can be determined by the controlled filling of the rectum with air using a latex balloon, thereby simulating the presence of stool in the rectum.

These sensations are assessed using a compliant latex balloon attached to polyvinyl tubing and a hand held 50 ml syringe (Figure 8.5). The balloon is passed through the anus into the rectum, 5 cm above the upper verge of the anal canal. To seat the balloon, 50 ml of air is perfused at a rate of approximately 50 ml per minute and the air is then withdrawn. The balloon is then continually perfused at the same rate (with periods of 30 seconds rest between each sensation) and the patient is asked to report the following sensations:

- Threshold – the first detectable change in rectal sensation
- Urge – urge to defaecate
- Pain – maximum tolerated volume.

Following this procedure the balloon is deflated but remains in the rectum, and the patient is allowed to rest before the next test.

A predetermined normal reference range should be set by individual laboratories and should allow for differences in patient age and gender. A threshold sensation below the lower limit of the normal range is often detected in patients with symptoms of irritable bowel syndrome and faecal urgency, whereas a maximum tolerated volume in excess of the upper limit of the normal range is consistent with a diagnosis of megarectum. Diamant et al., (1999) established that if the maximum tolerated volume was less than 100 ml there may be visceral hypersensitivity, poor rectal compliance, rectal irritability or patient anxiety. The clinical significance of the urge and pain threshold sensations is less well established than that of the first threshold sensation.

Recto-anal inhibitory reflex

The recto-anal inhibitory reflex is the term used to describe the reflex relaxation of the internal anal sphincter in response to rectal distension. It is often preceded by a reflex contraction of the external anal sphincter which rapidly subsides whilst the internal anal sphincter relaxes (Figure 8.6). It was first described by Gowers in 1877. The anal canal pressure gradient is increased from the proximal to the distal portion of the anal canal and allows the rectal contents to be 'sampled' by receptors in the upper part of the canal whilst continence is maintained by contraction of the external anal sphincter. The frequent spontaneous relaxations of the internal anal sphincter are called the sampling reflex.

The test for a recto-anal inhibitory reflex is performed in patients who present with chronic constipation; although absence of this reflex strongly suggests Hirschsprung's disease it is not diagnostic, and a confirmatory biopsy to demonstrate the absence of ganglia should be obtained.

The balloon remains deflated in the rectum and the manometry catheter previously used is reintroduced into the anus (water-perfused catheters must be zeroed horizontally at the level of the anal verge) so that the perfusion ports lie in the anal canal at the area of maximum resting pressure. The catheter is held in place while the balloon is inflated with 50 ml air followed by immediate deflation in one continuous smooth action. This technique can be repeated at suitable time intervals until the operator is satisfied with the result. The recto-anal inhibitory reflex can be difficult to elicit in cases where there is a low resting pressure. The manometry catheter is removed with the empty balloon still in place inside the rectum.

It may be necessary to inflate the rectum with volumes in excess of 50 ml air in patients who present with an enlarged rectum (megarectum) in order to elicit a reflex (Diamant et al., 1999).

The recto-anal inhibitory reflex remains intact in patients with extrinsic denervation but disappears with neuropathy and loss of ganglion cells of the myenteric plexus and/or atrophy and fibrosis of the internal anal sphincter (Engel et al., 1991; Chiou et al., 1989). There is no doubt that this test

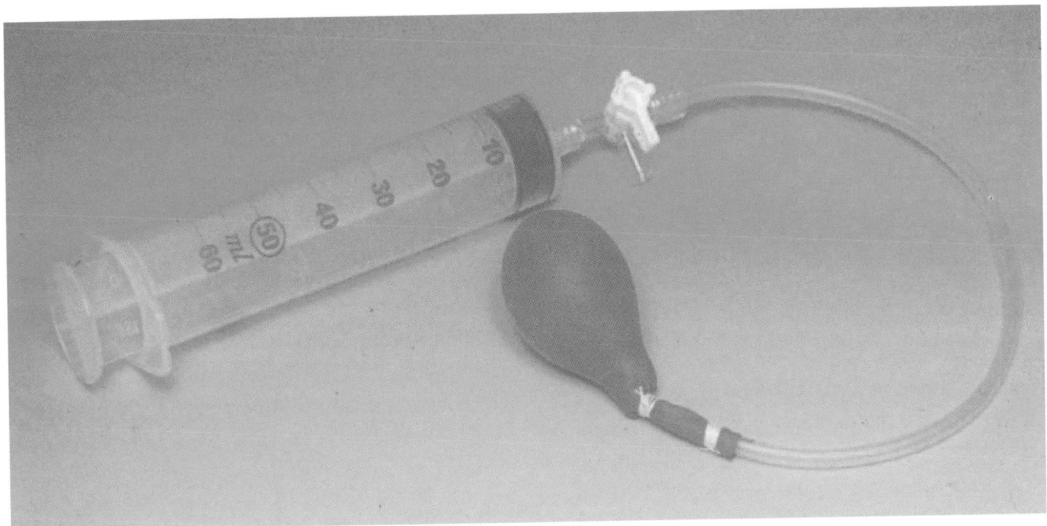

Figure 8.5 *Hand-held syringe with rectal distension balloon attached via polyvinyl tubing.*

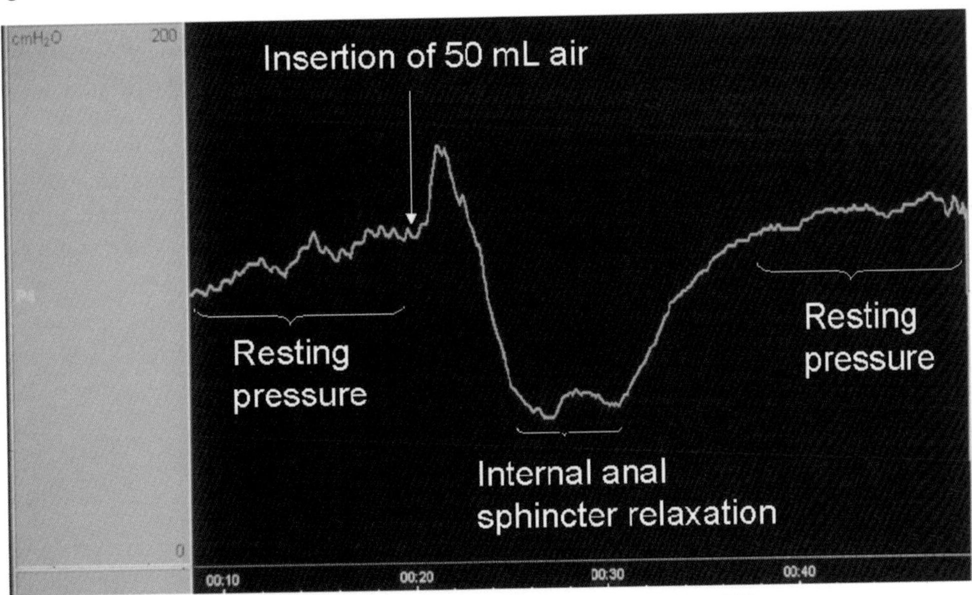

Figure 8.6 *Recto-anal inhibitory reflex (Medical Measurements Systems BV, Holland).*

remains an important screening tool for the diagnosis of Hirschsprung's disease and this was highlighted in a study by Osatakul et al. (1999). This research showed that out of 46 children investigated on the basis of clinical grounds for Hirschsprung's disease, 33 did not demonstrate a reflex and 31 of these children went on to have a positive diagnosis for Hirschsprung's disease as diagnosed by full-thickness rectal biopsy. They concluded that the overall diagnostic accuracy of using ano-rectal manometry to determine Hirschsprung's disease was 95%, with a diagnostic sensitivity of 100%.

Balloon expulsion

This is a simple test which enables the observer to assess patient co-ordination when trying to expel simulated stool in the form of a 50 ml water-filled balloon.

The balloon (which is still in the rectum) can be filled with 50 ml tepid water to simulate stool and give the patient something to push against. Traction (gentle pulling) is applied to the polyvinyl tubing attached to the balloon and the patient is asked to try and expel the balloon.

Some patients experience difficulty in trying to expel the balloon whilst in a position unusual for defaecation, i.e lying down! However, even if the balloon is not expelled, the sphincter activity during attempted expulsion can be observed. Inability to expel the balloon can be due to anismus (paradoxical contraction of the external sphincter), inadequate propulsive force or patient embarrassment. Some patients will cease respiration and strain with their head and neck to expel the balloon with great difficulty, while others will not be able to expel the balloon despite their best effort. Bowel retraining therapy (biofeedback) can be given if appropriate so that a co-ordinated defaecatory mechanism is established (see Chapter 23).

Anal canal and rectal mucosal sensation

The mucosal sensitivity of the anal canal and rectum to electrical stimulation can be assessed by using a bipolar ring electrode (Medtronic Functional Diagnostics, Skovlunde, Denmark), mounted on a suction catheter (Figure 8.7), The current is increased until the patient experiences a change in sensation. The anal canal has a greater variety of afferent nerve endings than the rectum and therefore the stimulation parameters must be adjusted to accommodate this. The mucosa of the anal canal is more sensitive to touch, temperature and pain, whereas that of the rectal mucosa (which contains more specialised sensory receptors) is more aware of sensations of fullness, urgency to defaecate and pain (Miller et al., 1988; Rogers, 1992).

Anal canal

The bipolar ring electrode is placed 1 cm above the lower verge of the anal canal. The stimulation parameters are set at a frequency of 5.0 Hz with pulse durations of 0.1 ms, which produce monophasic square waves. The current is increased until a change in anal sensation is perceived by the patient, often described as a 'prickling' or 'tapping' sensation. This procedure is repeated blind, three times to obtain the lowest most reproducible result and is reported in mA. If the patient under study has a history of anal canal

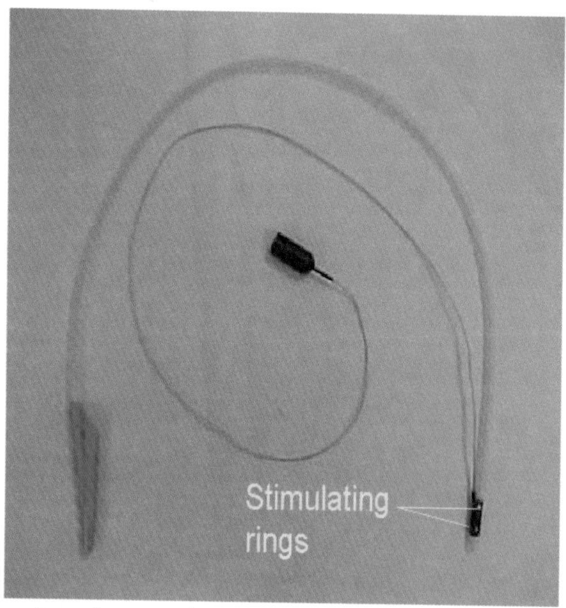

Figure 8.7 *Bipolar ring electrode mounted on a suction catheter.*

surgery, the recorded sensitivity may be persistently high as the probe may be resting against scar tissue. In this case the position of the probe should be adjusted and the procedure repeated until a convincing satisfactory result is obtained.

Rectum

The bipolar ring electrode is positioned via the anus 8 cm above the upper verge of the anal canal. The stimulation parameters are set at a frequency of 10 Hz with pulse durations of 0.5 ms which produce monophasic square waves. The current is increased until a change in sensation is perceived by the patient, often described as a 'pain' or an 'ache' in either the abdomen, back or buttocks. This procedure is repeated blind, three times to obtain the lowest most reproducible result and is reported in mA. If the recorded current is repeatedly in excess of the normal established reference range it may be due to poor contact of the electrode to the rectal mucosa. In this situation it will be necessary to remove the electrode to insert a glycerine suppository into the patient's rectum so that he or she can attempt to empty the bowel. The test can then be repeated to ensure that the documented result is a true reflection of the perceived sensation.

Anal and rectal sensation within the normal range is strongly suggestive of intact hindgut innervation. In patients with known neurological disease this can help define the role of their neuropathy in the genesis of symptoms. Reduced or absent anal sensation makes control of liquid stool or gas very difficult.

Pudendal nerve terminal motor latency (PNTML)

The pudendal nerves supply innervation for the external anal sphincter. They arise from the anterior primary rami of S2, S3 and S4 and angulate around the left and right of the ischial spine. The function of the terminal part of the pudendal nerve can be assessed by transrectally stimulating the motor nerve electrically and measuring the time taken from stimulation to the first measurable contraction of the external anal sphincter. The only commercially available device to perform this test is a St Mark's pudendal electrode (Figure 8.8), which is used to stimulate the right and left pudendal nerves. The time taken for the pulse to travel down the nerve to cause contraction of the external anal sphincter is measured in milliseconds and represents the function of the fastest conducting nerve fibres.

The St Mark's pudendal electrode is wrapped around the index finger of the operator and passed through the anus into the rectum. The finger is then bent around to the point where the pudendal nerve crosses the ischial spine. The stimulation parameters are set at a frequency of 1 Hz with pulse durations of 0.1 ms to produce monophasic

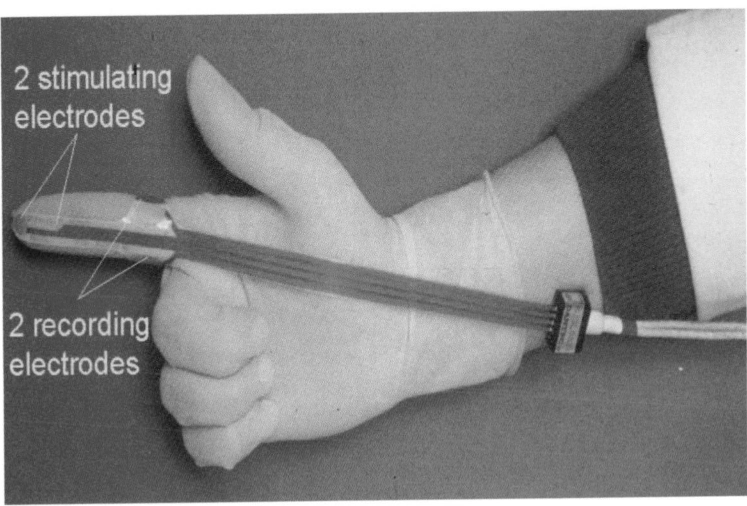

Figure 8.8 *St Mark's pudendal electrode.*

square waves. The intensity is gradually increased until a contraction of the sphincter is observed on the screen. The intensity of stimulation is then increased by 30% to produce a supramaximal stimulus (to ensure that all fibres within the nerve have been activated). This procedure is operator dependent and can be more difficult in complicated patients with a high body mass index or long anal canal. The latency is quantified using a Keypoint EMG/EP machine (Medtronic Functional Diagnostics, Skovlunde, Denmark). The equipment is set so that at the point of external anal sphincter contraction a downward deflection is recorded for the left pudendal nerve terminal motor latency and an upward deflection for the right pudendal nerve terminal motor latency (Figure 8.9). The pudendal nerve terminal motor latency can differ between the right and left side, and therefore it is important to make recordings from both sides of the pelvis.

A prolonged latency is often associated with idiopathic faecal incontinence (Swash, 1989) or descending perineum syndrome (Parks et al., 1966), caused by stretching or compression of the branches of the pudendal nerve. However, caution must be exercised in the interpretation of these results, firstly because of the difficulty in obtaining the latency and secondly because of inter-operator variability. Other factors must also be taken into consideration, e.g. pudendal nerve terminal motor latency has been shown to increase with age regardless of the continence status of the patient and a damaged nerve will still contain some fast conducting fibres which, if stimulated, will give an inaccurate representation of the overall nerve status (Cheong et al., 1995).

The clinical value of the assessment of pudendal nerve terminal motor latency is controversial. A study by Laurberg, et al. (1988) suggests that patients with prolonged latencies fare less well with anterior external anal sphincter repair, while a study by Engel et al., 1994 (which also used anal ultrasound) concluded that pudendal nerve function was not predictive of surgical results. Data generated by Rasmussen et al. (2000) support the view that idiopathic faecal incontinence in the majority of females is likely to be a result of the ageing process and that only a limited number may suffer from anal incontinence of neurogenic origin. This study also states that unilateral prolongation of pudendal nerve terminal motor latency is probably without clinical significance. Other studies highlight its lack of specificity and sensitivity. Wexner et al., 1991 demonstrated the

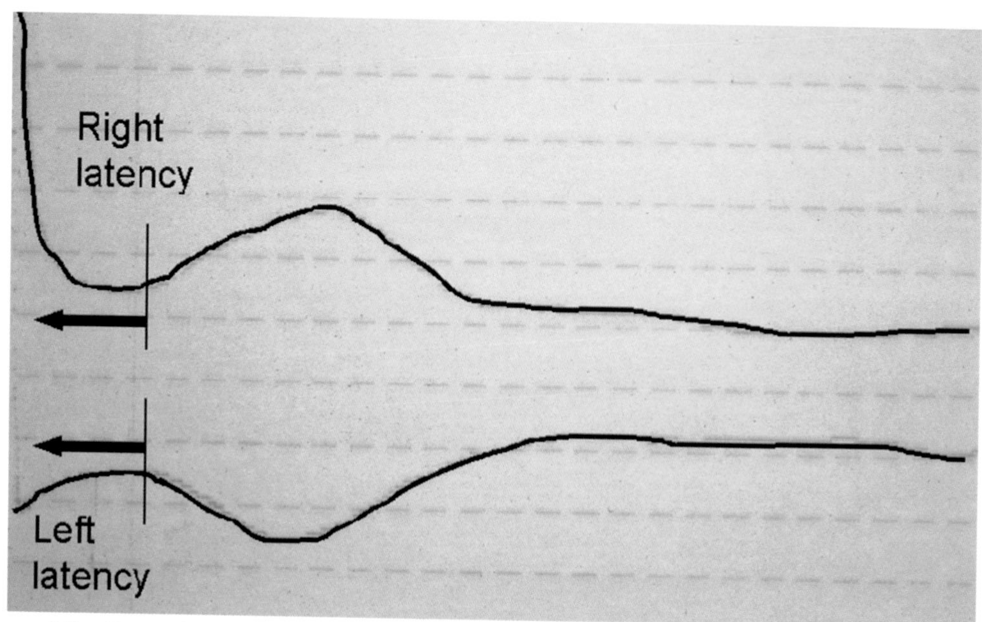

Figure 8.9 *Traces from left and right pudendal nerve terminal motor latency tests.*

lack of association in prolonged pudendal nerve terminal motor latency and external anal sphincter damage.

Perineal descent

Perineal descent can be subjectively assessed when a patient is asked to strain, with movement of the pelvic floor towards the observer. It is associated with a more obtuse ano-rectal angle and therefore with faecal incontinence (Swash et al., 1989).

Perineal descent can be quantified using the St Mark's perineometer (Figure 8.10). The metal legs are placed on the patient's ischial tuberosities with the graduated perspex rod resting on the perineum. The patient is asked to strain, and the extent of perineal descent can be quantified by recording movement of the perspex rod. It is difficult to standardise the amount a patient strains, although individuals tend to strain to a reproducible degree on most occasions. Therefore, direct comparisons of perineal descent between age and sex matched individuals are unreliable.

Perineal descent is associated with a weak pelvic floor and chronic straining to empty the bowels. It is associated with incomplete bowel emptying and can therefore be responsible for passive soiling in this patient group.

Rectal compliance testing

Compliance can be defined as the capacity of an organ to stretch to an imposed force (Whitehead and Delveaux, 1997). To preserve continence it is important that the rectum can maintain a low intraluminal pressure while being filled, i.e. that it is compliant. The compliance of a hollow viscus can be established with the use of a barostat – a pneumatic device which allows for the indirect measurement of variations in tone or any device capable of infusion and pressure measurement. The barostat (Distender Series II, G and J Electronics Inc., Ontario, Canada, Figure 8.11, overleaf) achieves this by maintaining a constant pressure in an intraluminal compliant bag, so that the volume changes of the reservoir represent the volume changes of the organ or gut wall tone. These conditions are termed isobaric. An organ that can accept an increasing volume with only a slow rise in pressure is compliant. There are a number of different protocols available for use with the barostat depending on the application and organ to be examined. They all provide

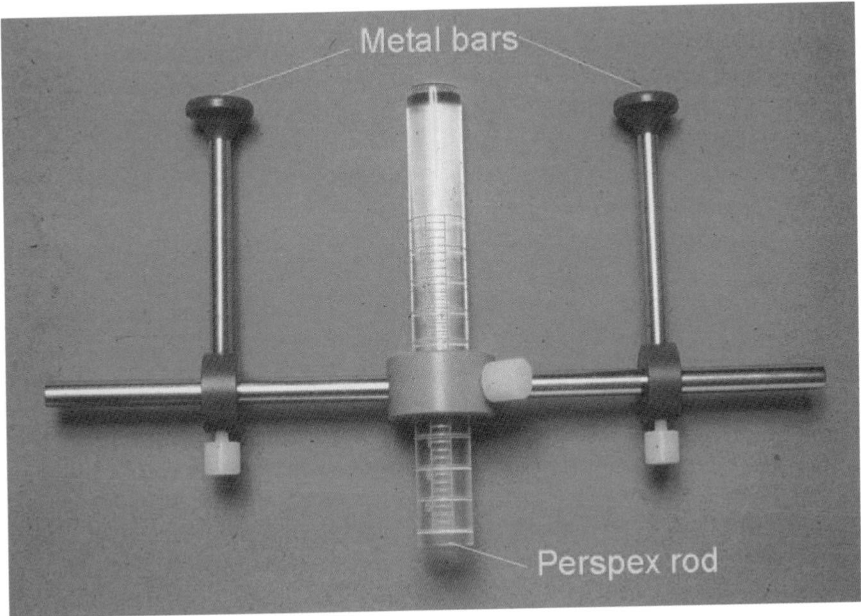

Figure 8.10 *The St Mark's perineometer.*

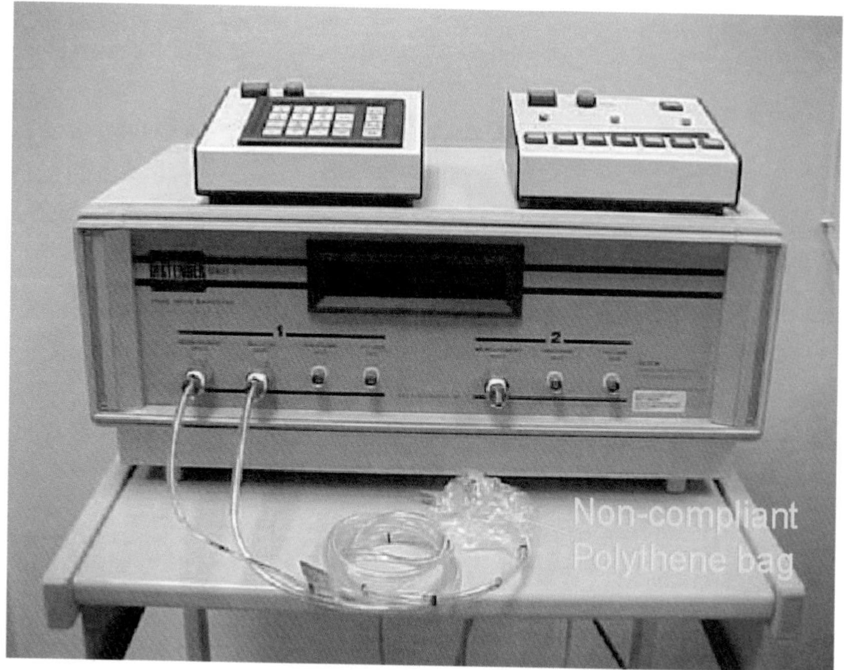

Figure 8.11 *The Barostat (Distender Series II, G and J Electronics Inc., Ontario, Canada).*

information on the pressure-volume relationships of the organ under study.

A non-compliant ultra-thin polyethylene bag with a maximum distension volume of 600 ml is placed through the anal canal into the rectum 3 cm above the proximal verge of the anal canal (as determined by stationary manometry). The bag, attached to a catheter (Mui Scientific, Ontario, Canada), is empty and connected to the barostat, and the patient is conditioned to this sensation for 60 seconds before a distension sequence is initiated. Using an ascending method of limits protocol the barostat begins to inflate the balloon. The patient is asked to tell the operator when they feel the sensations of threshold, urge and pain. These sensations can be annotated on the trace during the investigation. At the end of the test the balloon is deflated and removed from the rectum and the data is analysed.

Compliance is calculated by the change in volume divided by the change in pressure (compliance = change in volume/change in pressure). The normal reference range will depend on the type of barostat and protocol used – at present there is no multicentre normal reference range available, which makes direct comparison of data between sites impossible. Therefore it is the responsibility of individual centres to establish their own normal reference range prior to undertaking these tests.

The distension protocols available can be used to study the physiology and pathophysiology of the motor and sensory functions of the gastrointestinal tract. The barostat allows simultaneous assessment of motility and visceral sensations.

Normal rectal compliance appears to depend on an intact intrinsic nervous system and viable muscles (Marcio et al., 1993). If an abnormal rectal compliance is recorded, this indicates that the capacity of the rectum is affected and the ability to perceive distension in the rectum will be impaired, so that tests such as the recto-anal inhibitory reflex will require an increased volume of air to elicit a response. A decrease in rectal compliance is associated with irritable bowel syndrome, fibrosis and some drugs. An increase in rectal compliance can be associated with megarectum.

Saline retention test

This test is designed to stress the anal sphincter muscles in patients who have possible weakness in either the internal anal sphincter or external anal sphincter. Other substances apart from saline have been used, e.g. porridge to assess the competency of the sphincters before the closure of a stoma (Pemberton, 1990).

The patient is seated on a commode while saline is infused into the rectum via a tube. A total volume of 1500 ml is infused at a constant rate of 60 ml per minute by a pump (Diamant et al., 1999). The time and volume of the initial and final leaks can be quantified.

Patients with a weak internal anal sphincter and/or external anal sphincter have difficulty retaining the fluid. However the clinical value of this test has not been established and the results lack specificity and sensitivity, and as such cannot be used in isolation to select patients for specific therapies (Diamant et al., 1999).

Conclusions

Ano-rectal physiology testing consists of a range of tests to assess the sensation and function of the ano-rectum. No test is diagnostic on its own, and results should be interpreted with regard to the patient history, clinical examination, bowel symptoms and other investigations performed, in particular endo-anal ultrasound.

References

Cheong, D.M.O., Vaccaro, C.A., Salanga, V.D., Wexner, S.D., Phillips, R.C. and Hanson, M.R. (1995). Electrodiagnostic evaluation of faecal incontinence. *Muscle Nerve* **18**, 612–619.

Chiou, A.W-H., Lin, J. and Wang, F. (1989) Anorectal abnormalities in prospective systemic sclerosis. *Diseases of the Colon and Rectum* **32**, 417–421.

Diamant, N.E., Kamm, M.A., Wald, A. and Whitehead, W.E. (1999) American Gastroenterological Association Medical Position Statement on Anorectal Testing Techniques. *Gastroenterology* **116**, 732–760.

Engel, A.F., Kamm, M.A. and Talbot, I.C. (1991) Progressive systemic sclerosis of the internal anal sphincter leading to passive faecal incontinence. *Gut* **35**, 857–859.

Engel, A.F., Kamm, M.A., Sultan, A.H., Bartram, C.I., and Nicholls, R.J. (1994) Anterior anal sphincter repair in patients with obstetric trauma. *British Journal of Surgery* **81**, 1231–1234.

Fleshman, J.W. (1993) Anorectal motor physiology and pathophysiology. *Surgical Clinics of North America* **73**, 6, 1245–1265.

Fynes, M.M., Behan, M., O'Herlihy, C. and O'Connell, P.R. (2000) Anal vector volume analysis complements endoanal ultrasonographic assessment of postpartum anal sphincter injury. *British Journal of Surgery* **87**, 9,1209–1214.

Gowers, W.R. (1877) The automatic action of the sphincter ani. *Proceedings of the Royal Society of London* **26**, 77.

Laurberg, S., Swash, M. and Henry, M.M. (1988) Delayed external sphincter repair for obstetric tear. *British Journal of Surgery* **75**, 786–788.

Marcello, P.W., Barrett, B.S., Coller, J.A., Schoetz, D.J., Roberts, P.L., Murray, J.J. and Rusin, L.C. (1998) Fatigue rate index as a new measurement of external sphincter function. *Diseases of the Colon and Rectum* **41**, 3, 336–343.

Marcio, J., Jorge, N. and Wexner, S.D. (1993) Anorectal manometry: techniques and clinical applications. *Southern Medical Journal* **86**, 8, 924–931.

Miller, R., Bartolo, D.C.C., Roe, A., Cervero, F. and Mortenson, N.J. (1988) Anal sensation and the continence mechanism. *Diseases of the Colon and Rectum* **31**, 433–438.

Norton, C. and Chelvanayagam, S. (2001) Methodology of biofeedback for adults with fecal incontinence – a program of care. *Journal of Wound, Ostomy, and Continence Nursing* **28**, 156–168.

Norton, C. and Kamm, M.A. (1999) Outcome of biofeedback for faecal incontinence. *British Journal of Surgery* **86**, 9, 1159–1163.

Osatakul, S., Patrapinyokul, S. and Osatakul, N. (1999) The diagnostic value of anorectal manometry as a screening test for Hirschsprung's disease. *Journal of the Medical Association of Thailand* **82**, 11, 1100–1105.

Parks, A.G., Porter, N.H. and Hardcastle, J. (1966) The syndrome of the descending perineum. *Proceedings of the Royal Society of Medicine* **59**, 477–482.

Perry, R.E., Blatchford, G.J., Christensen, M.A., Thorson, A.G. and Attwood, S.E.A. (1990) Manometric diagnosis of anal sphincter injuries. *American Journal of Surgery* **159**, 112–117.

Rasmussen, O.O., Christiansen, J., Tetzschner, T. and Sorensen, M. (2000) Pudendal nerve function in idiopathic faecal incontinence. *Diseases of the Colon and Rectum* **43**, 5, 633–636.

Rogers, J. (1992) Testing for and the role of anal rectal sensation. *Baillière's Clinical Gastroenterology* **6**, 179–191.

Sentovich, S.M., Blatchford, G.J., Rivela, L.J., Lin, K., Thorson, A.G. and Christensen, M.A. (1997) Diagnosing anal sphincter injury with transanal ultrasonography and manometry. *Diseases of the Colon and Rectum* **40**, 1430–1434.

Swash, M. (1989) Electrophysiological tests. In: Read, N.W. *Pelvic floor disorders gastrointestinal motility: which test?*, pp. 257–268. Bristol: Wrightson Biomedical Publishing.

Thompson, W.G., Creed, F., Drossman, D.A., Heaton, K.W. and Mazzacca, G. (1992) Functional bowel disease and functional abdominal pain. *Gastroenterology International* **5**, 75–91.

Wexner, S.D., Marchetti, F., Salanga, V.D., Corredor, C. and Jagelman, D.G. (1991) Neurophysiologic assessment of the anal sphincters. *Diseases of the Colon and Rectum* **34**, 606–612.

Whitehead, W.E. and Delvaux, M. (1997) The working team of Glaxo Wellcome Research, UK: standardisation of barostat procedures for testing smooth muscle tone and sensory thresholds in the gastrointestinal tract. *Digestive Diseases and Sciences* **42**, 223–41.

Chapter 9

Radiographic Investigations

Andrew Williams

Anal ultrasound

The technique of anal ultrasound (endosonography) was developed as a modification of that used for staging rectal tumours using ultrasound (Hildebrandt and Feifel, 1985). A rotating transducer crystal is contained within a water-filled cone (Figure 9.1). When inserted into the anal canal it provides 360° axial images of the anal canal and its constituent structures. The investigation is usually performed with the patient lying face down in the prone position.

Images obtained using anal ultrasound are limited to a depth of 3–4 cm, beyond which the image becomes blurred. Clinically this is not a problem in anal canal imaging, as the areas of interest are well within the focal range of the transducer. Another limitation of anal endosonography is that in order to obtain a clear image, contact must be maintained with the tissue being scanned. For this reason imaging above the puborectalis, where the anal canal opens out in a funnel shape at the ano-rectal junction, is not possible.

Anal endosonography is quick to perform (usually under five minutes), relatively cheap and increasingly available. Three-dimensional reconstruction of anal endosonography has recently been developed, although not widely available (Gold et al., 1999). The clinical role that this new adjunct to anal imaging will play is at present uncertain.

The anal canal and sphincters are seen as four layers on endosonography (Figure 9.2, overleaf). The subepithelium is universally a highly reflective structure, which contrasts well against the poorly reflective internal anal sphincter. The internal anal sphincter becomes

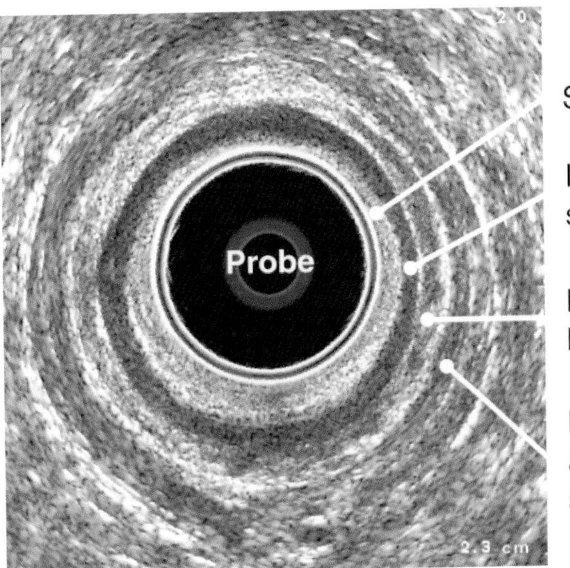

Figure 9.1 *Normal anal endosonograph showing the four layers of the anal canal.*

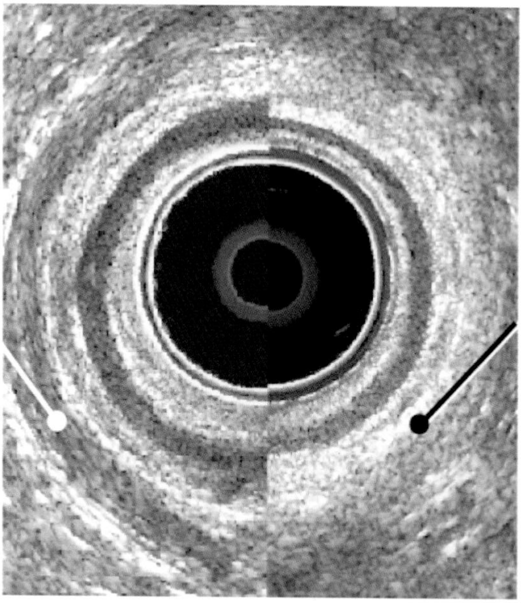

Male
External anal
sphincter-
Low reflectivity

Female
External anal
sphincter-
High reflectivity

Figure 9.2 *Differences in the normal appearance of the external anal sphincter between men and women.*

thicker and less clearly defined with increasing age, and so it is important to consider the age of the subject being scanned before any judgement on internal sphincter thickness is made. The longitudinal layer of muscle is highly reflective, giving a bright echo appearance on endosonography, which varies little between men and women. The external anal sphincter, however, varies in echogenicity depending upon the gender and age of the subject being scanned. A young male patient has a well-defined poorly reflective external anal sphincter with a striated appearance. By contrast the sphincter of a woman of the same age is much more echogenic, giving a much brighter image which is often indistinguishable from the longitudinal muscle layer (Figure 9.3). The puborectalis muscle is a sling that passes posteriorly around the cranial (upper) part of the anal canal, and has a marked striated appearance.

Anal endosonography is useful in the assessment of faecal incontinence. A pathologically thin internal anal sphincter on endosonography may be associated with reduced anal canal resting pressure and passive faecal incontinence (Vaizey et al., 1997). Abnormal increase in thickness of the internal anal sphincter is often noted in patients with solitary rectal ulcer syndrome and rectal prolapse. Faecal incontinence may follow anal surgery for a variety of conditions. The use of an anal stretch procedure for the treatment of anal fissure is now seldom performed, because a significant number of patients will develop incontinent symptoms following maximal anal dilatation. In some of these patients, endosonography will reveal internal anal sphincter disruption. The use of lateral internal anal sphincterotomy may also cause incontinent complications due to division of too great a length of internal anal sphincter. In this situation, endosonography is able to demonstrate a divided internal anal sphincter at the level of puborectalis (for the entire length of the anal canal). Finally, a small number of patients have symptoms of incontinence following haemorrhoidectomy. In this group, endosonography can demonstrate damage to either the internal or both anal sphincters, due to inadvertent sphincter muscle excision together with the vascular pedicle of the haemorrhoid during surgery.

The commonest indication for anal endosono-

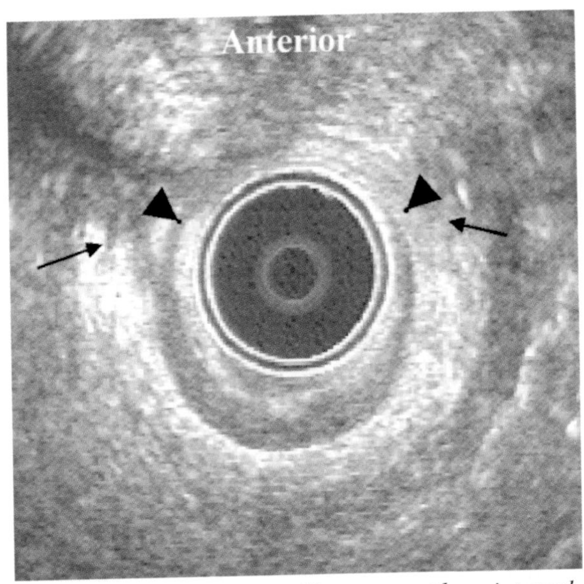

Figure 9.3 *Anal endosonography in a 28-year-old woman with an internal and external anal sphincter tear following a traumatic vaginal delivery.*

graphy is for the investigation of faecal incontinence following vaginal delivery (Bartram and Sultan, 1995). Between 11% and 35% of women will have endosonographic evidence of external anal sphincter trauma following their first vaginal delivery (Williams et al., 2000). The incidence of sphincter trauma is much higher after an instrumental delivery (Sultan et al., 1993). Anal endosonography has now largely replaced electromyographic (EMG) sphincter assessment for the diagnosis of these external anal sphincter tears. EMG sphincter measurement consisted of assessing sphincter function by inserting a needle into the external sphincter and recording muscle activity whilst asking the patient to squeeze the external sphincter. This was both a painful and inaccurate method of assessment.

Thankfully, not all women with endosonographic evidence of a sphincter tear will be symptomatic, although some previously asymptomatic women may develop incontinence as they approach the menopause. External anal sphincter tears are generally seen on endosonography as areas of discontinuity of the sphincter ring filled with hypoechoic scar tissue (Figure 9.4, overleaf). Sphincter damage may be surgically corrected with an anterior external anal sphincter repair, the results of which correlate well with the change in the post-operative endosonographic image (Engel et al., 1994). The presence of a persistent sphincter defect after surgery is strongly associated with a poor clinical outcome following surgery. Three-dimensional reconstruction of anal endosonography has enabled assessment of not only the radial extent of sphincter trauma but also the length of trauma, and is a promising adjunct to standard endosonography in sphincter assessment.

Magnetic resonance imaging (MRI)

Magnetic resonance imaging provides multi-planar images with excellent tissue differentiation. However, it requires an endo-anal receiver coil to improve imaging around the coil (within about 4 cm) to enable acquisition of images of the anal sphincters with both high resolution and tissue differentiation. Endo-coils measure between 6–10 cm in length and 7–12 mm in diameter, which increases to

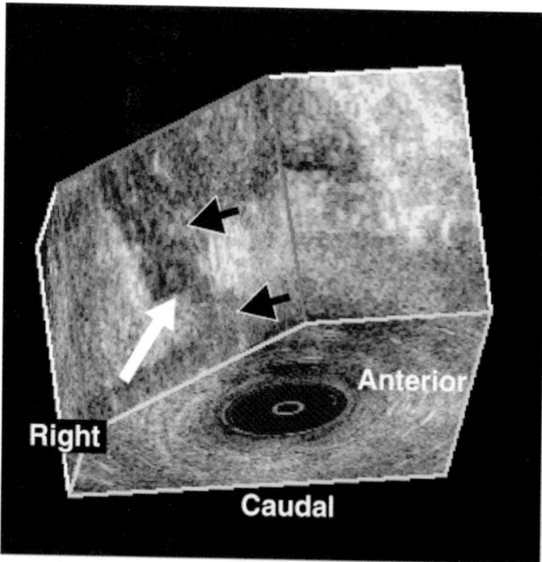

An oblique slice through the ultrasound shows the longitudinal extent of an external anal sphincter tear following a traumatic vaginal delivery, (white arrow).

The upper and lower extent of the tear are shown by the black arrows.

Figure 9.4 *Three-dimensional reconstruction of anal endosonography in a woman with an external anal sphincter tear following childbirth.*

between 17–19 mm diameter after encasement in an acetyl homopolymer (Delrin) former. The coil is inserted into the anus with the patient lying in the left lateral position, and then secured either with sandbags or with a purpose-built holder to avoid movement artefact.

Endo-anal MRI is now an established technique for examination of the anal sphincters, and much has been learnt about the anatomy of this region using endo-anal MR imaging with anatomical correlation from dissected specimens (Hussain et al., 1996). The lateral border of the external anal sphincter is well defined on endocoil MRI, especially when compared with the rather indistinct images of anal ultrasound (Figures 9.5 and 9.6).

MRI has been used to assess patients with faecal incontinence (deSouza et al., 1995). The diagnosis of sphincter defects using endocoil MRI has been validated with surgical confirmation of defect presence and extent. Endocoil MRI may be superior to anal ultrasound in the detection and assessment of external sphincter defects, due to better sphincter definition using MRI than ultrasound (Stoker et al., 2000). Magnetic resonance imaging also has the advantage of multi-planar capability – i.e. axial, sagittal and coronal images can be acquired, whilst standard anal ultrasound provides only axially orientated (cross-sectional) images. The acquisition of a volume of ultrasound data has overcome this problem. Using three-dimensional anal ultrasound, understanding of sphincter injury has increased. A direct correlation exists between the length of a defect and the arc of displacement of the two ends of the sphincter. The wider the gap between the two ends of the sphincter the greater the length of the anal canal involved in the tear.

The use of endocoil MRI has shown that faecal incontinence in the absence of a sphincter defect may be due to muscle atrophy, where the sphincter has been replaced by fat and fibrous tissue. Magnetic resonance imaging has also shown that urinary stress incontinence post-partum is associated with an increase in the signal intensity of the levator plate, suggesting fatty degeneration of the pelvic floor due to denervation. The presence of external anal sphincter atrophy on endocoil MR imaging has been associated with poor results from anterior sphincteroplasty (Briel et al., 1999).

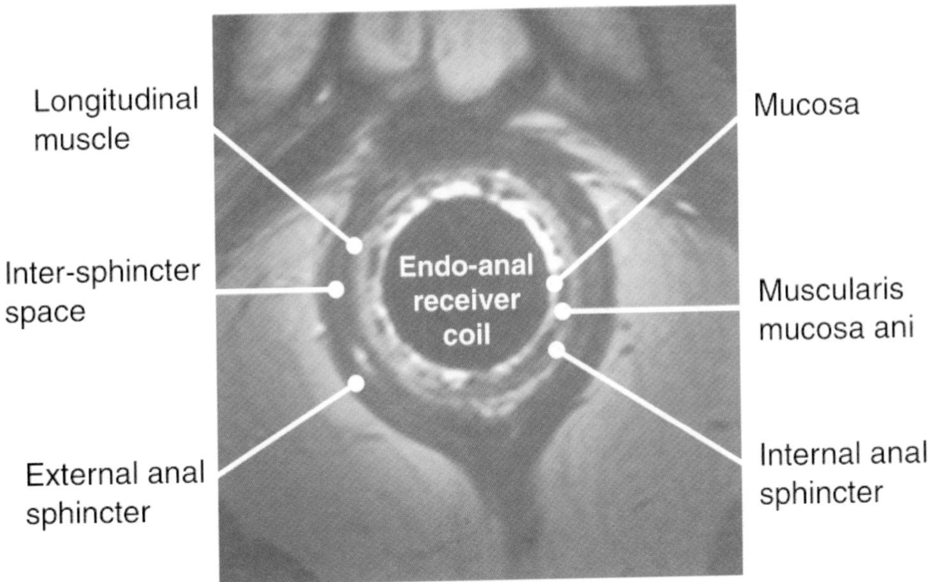

Figure 9.5 *Normal axial endo-anal receiver coil magnetic resonance image of the anal canal.*

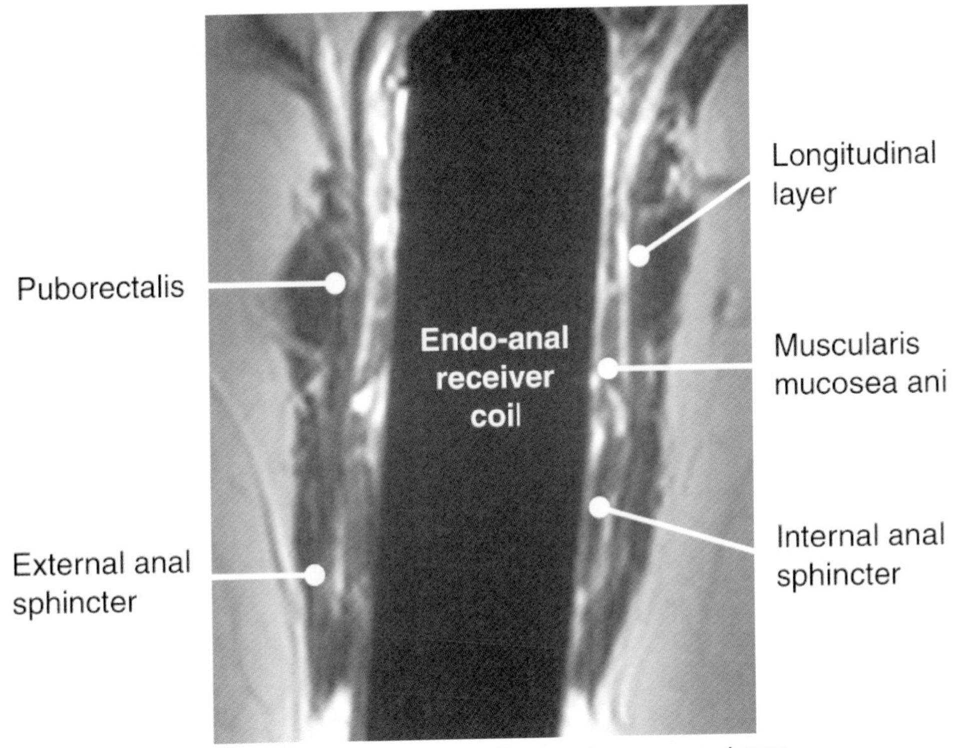

Figure 9.6 *Normal coronal endo-anal receiver coil magnetic resonance image of the anal canal.*

Defaecography / Evacuation proctography

Defaecography or evacuation proctography is a dynamic examination which provides information on ano-rectal structural changes during defaecation and assesses evacuation function. The procedure involves a video fluoroscopy recording of the patient evacuating barium paste into a specially designed commode. Barium paste is mixed with potato starch until a consistency approximating that of faeces is obtained, and the mixture is then introduced into the rectum via a rectal catheter. Barium-soaked gauze may also be inserted into the vagina in women, and barium paste applied to the perineum to aid in assessing the ano-rectal angle and perineal descent. Opacification of the small bowel with an orally ingested contrast medium, or the injection of contrast into the peritoneum (peritoneography), will reveal enterocoeles in 18% of patients with pelvic floor weakness (Halligan and Bartram, 1995).

Various anatomical changes may be noted during evacuation, namely rectocoele, enterocoele, recto-anal intussusception, rectal prolapse and changes in the ano-rectal angle (Figure 9.7). Many of these structural changes on defaecation are also found when studying asymptomatic individuals. For example, rectal intussusception is found in 80% of men and rectocoeles in 81% of women (Shorvon et al., 1989). Furthermore, defaecation patterns do not appear to be consistently related to symptomatology, manometric assessment or duration of the complaint. The only measurements that can discriminate between normal subjects and those with severe constipation are the time taken to evacuate and the completeness of evacuation. Evacuation should normally be 90% complete after the patient has the sensation of complete evacuation.

A rectocoele is thought to be significant if greater than 3 cm, or if it requires digitation (the insertion of a finger in to the vaginal or anal canal, or perineal pressure) to empty the bowel. Despite the lack of the strict discriminatory ability of defaecography, it is still a useful clinical investigation on occasions. Results can increase the confidence of the clinical diagnosis and may change the clinical diagnosis in up to

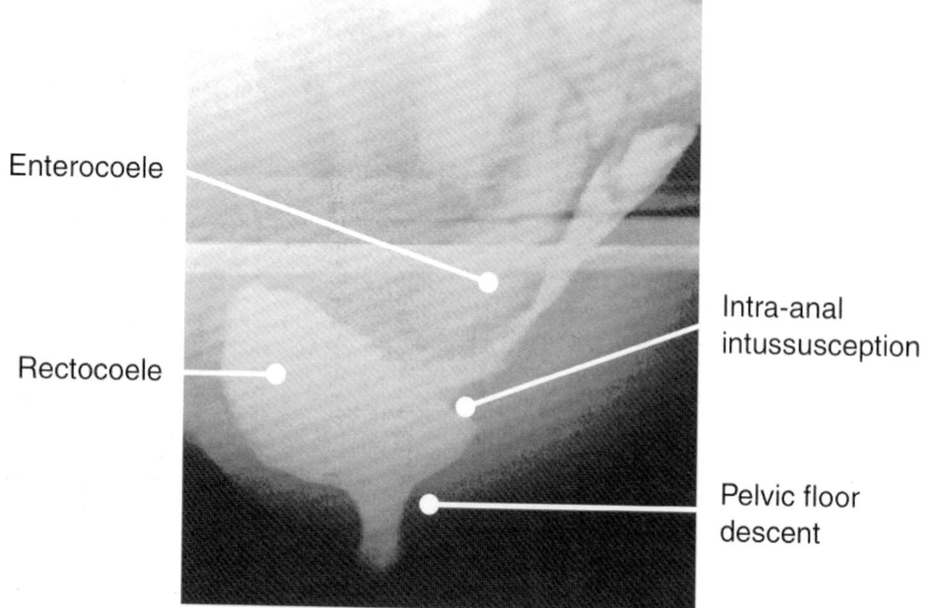

Figure 9.7 *Evacuating proctogram in a 39-year-old woman with difficult prolonged evacuation.*

18% of patients, leading to either a change in conservative treatment, surgery or the type of surgery performed (Harvey et al., 1999). It is also possible to perform proctography using MRI, with no radiation exposure and global dynamic views of the pelvic compartments.

Scintigraphy and transit measurement

Scintigraphy using technetium-labelled sulphur colloid mixed with dilute veegum powder may also be used for defaecography. The advantages of this technique are that a quantitative result is obtained and a lower dose of radiation is used than for proctography. The study, however, has the drawbacks in that it is not a dynamic study and does not correlate with patient symptoms or manometric assessment. Radioisotope testing may also be used to assess colonic transit time to diagnose idiopathic slow transit constipation. Colonic transit time is measured more easily by tracking the progress of ingested sets of radio-opaque markers with plain abdominal radiography. The standard protocol transit study requires the patient to ingest two capsules containing radio-opaque markers on three consecutive days and then taking a single plain abdominal radiograph on day five (see Chapter 21).

Conclusions

Imaging in functional anal disorders can highlight whether the disorder is due to structural damage that may be amenable to surgical intervention. Conversely it may also identify normal anatomical structure that will require further investigation. Imaging alone cannot provide all the answers but has an important role to play in the diagnostic process. Findings must always be interpreted in the light of the patient's symptoms and other clinical findings, as many of the abnormalities described in this chapter may be found in asymptomatic people.

References

Bartram, C.I. and Sultan, A.H. (1995) Anal endosonography in faecal incontinence. *Gut* **37**, 1, 4–6.

Briel, J.W., Stoker, J., Rociu, E., Lameris, J.S., Hop, W.C. and Schouten, W.R. (1999) External anal sphincter atrophy on endoanal magnetic resonance imaging adversely affects continence after sphincteroplasty. *British Journal of Surgery* **86**, 1322–1327.

deSouza, N.M., Puni, R., Gilderdale, D.J. and Bydder, G.M. (1995) Magnetic resonance imaging of the anal sphincter using an internal coil. *Magnetic Resonance Quarterly* **11**, 1, 45–56.

Engel, A.F., Kamm, M.A., Sultan, A.H., Bartram, C.I. and Nicholls, R.J. (1994) Anterior anal sphincter repair in patients with obstetric trauma. *British Journal of Surgery* **81**, 8, 1231–1234.

Gold, D.M., Bartram, C.I., Halligan, S., Humphries, K.N., Kamm, M.A. and Kmiot, W.A. (1999). Three-dimensional endoanal sonography in assessing anal canal injury. *British Journal of Surgery* **86**, 365–370.

Halligan, S. and Bartram, C.I. (1995) Evacuation proctography combined with positive contrast peritoneography to demonstrate pelvic floor hernias. *Abdominal Imaging* **20**, 5, 442–445.

Harvey, C.J., Halligan, S., Bartram, C.I., Hollings, N., Sahdev, A. and Kingston, K. (1999) Evacuation proctography: a prospective study of diagnostic and therapeutic effects. *Radiology* **211**, 223–227.

Hildebrandt, U. and Feifel, G. (1985) Preoperative staging of rectal cancer by intrarectal ultrasound. *Diseases of the Colon and Rectum* **28**, 42–46.

Hussain, S.M., Stoker, J., Zwamborn, A.W., Den Hollander, J.C., Kuiper, J.W., Entius, C.A. and Lameris, J.S. (1996) Endoanal MRI of the anal sphincter complex: correlation with cross-sectional anatomy and histology. *Journal of Anatomy* **189**, 3, 677–682.

Shorvon, P.J., McHugh, S., Diamant, N.E., Somers, S. and Stevenson, G.W. (1989) Defecography in normal volunteers: results and implications. *Gut.* **30**, 1737–1749.

Stoker, J., Rociu, E., Wiersma, T.G. and Lameris, J.S. (2000) Imaging of anorectal disease. *British Journal of Surgery* **87**, 1, 10–27.

Sultan, A.H., Kamm, M.A., Bartram, C.I. and Hudson, C.N. (1993) Anal sphincter trauma during instrumental delivery. *International Journal of Gynaecology and Obstetrics* **43**, 3, 263–270.

Vaizey, C.J., Kamm, M.A. and Bartram, C.I. (1997) Primary degeneration of the internal anal sphincter as a cause of passive faecal incontinence. *Lancet* **349**, 9052, 612–615.

Williams, A.B., Bartram, C.I., Halligan, S., Spencer, J.A., Nicholls, R.J. and Kmiot, W.A. (2000) Sphincter damage after vaginal delivery – a prospective study. *Obstetrics and Gynecology* **97**, 770–775.

Chapter 10

Investigation and Management of Chronic Diarrhoea in Adults

Sally Bell

Introduction

The term diarrhoea derives from the Greek and translates as 'to flow through'. Acute diarrhoea is usually infective in aetiology and is not dealt with in this chapter. There is a wide range of disorders that can cause chronic diarrhoea, making it a difficult diagnostic and management problem. In addition, the large number of potential tests available means that selective investigation is necessary to prevent unnecessary patient discomfort and anxiety and to conserve resources. The aim of this chapter is to outline a problem-solving approach to the investigation and management of chronic diarrhoea in adults, based on a thorough history, examination and the tailored the use of investigations.

Definition and mechanisms of chronic diarrhoea

Chronic diarrhoea in adults is defined as the frequent (more than three times per day) passage of unformed stool for one month or more (Talley and Martin, 1996). This is usually associated with an increase in faecal weight. Normal faecal weight depends on dietary fibre intake, and is less than 200g / 24 hours in the United Kingdom. Faecal weight can be measured by giving the patient a pre-weighed plastic container with a sealed lid and collecting all stools over three days. In practice, stool weight is used if there is doubt over the presence of true diarrhoea.

It is helpful to be able to identify the major mechanism of diarrhoea as this has direct relevance to the most effective treatment. The four major mechanisms of diarrhoea are:

1) Reduced intestinal absorption due to
   a) Maldigestion; pancreatic insufficiency, bile salt deficiency (bacterial overgrowth, cholestasis, drugs);
   b) Malabsorption; inflammation, infection, bowel resection, drugs, inherited defects of absorption;
2) Increased intestinal secretion, or inhibition of normal ion and water absorption (secretory diarrhoea);
3) The presence of large amounts of non absorbable, osmotically active solute (carbohydrate, a divalent ion such as magnesium, bile salts) in the gut lumen (osmotic diarrhoea);
4) Abnormal intestinal motility.

In some diseases, multiple mechanisms may coexist. For example, in Crohn's disease, diarrhoea can result from inflammation of the small and/or large intestine, bacterial overgrowth due to strictures, or bile salt malabsorption following terminal ileal resection.

History

Stool form

It is important to determine whether the patient has true diarrhoea by asking them to describe the consistency, frequency and appearance of the stools. The pattern of the diarrhoea and its associated symptoms may offer clues as to the likely cause. Large bowel disease commonly results in small volume, frequent stools, whereas urgency and tenesmus (sensation of stool present and constant urge to defaecate) are seen in rectal disease. In contrast, small bowel disease produces a large-volume watery stool. Malabsorption of fat resulting in steatorrhoea classically produces pale, bulky oily stools that are difficult to flush.

Onset

It is helpful to establish the duration of the problem and whether the onset was sudden or gradual. A long history in a well patient does not rule out organic disease, but makes the diagnosis of functional disease more likely. Many patients attribute the diarrhoea to a specific trigger event, such as recent travel or an acute episode of gastroenteritis. Not only may this provide useful clues as to the cause, e.g. infective causes or post-infective irritable bowel syndrome (IBS), but it may also reveal underlying fears that the patient may not articulate directly e.g. diarrhoea that develops after the diagnosis of cancer or inflammatory bowel disease (IBD) in a family member.

Associated symptoms

Associated symptoms such as weight loss and rectal bleeding can also provide useful clues to the likely diagnosis. Weight loss is a marker for organic disease, and is common in inflammatory bowel disease, colon cancer and malabsorption. Rectal bleeding is associated with colonic or anal pathology. Bright blood, separate from the stool, may result from local anal conditions (e.g. haemorrhoids or fissure), but is also seen in colonic disease such as rectal or colonic tumours and inflammatory bowel disease (see Chapter 11). Blood mixed with the stool is more typical of colonic disease. Bleeding is an important symptom in its own right that requires investigation to exclude colonic malignancy (see Chapter 7).

Abdominal pain is commonly associated with diarrhoea but is often not helpful in suggesting a cause. However, reproducible pain after food, particularly with abdominal distention and/or vomiting, suggests bowel obstruction, which is seen in stricturing Crohn's disease and bowel cancer. Constant severe pain radiating to the back suggests chronic pancreatitis (due to alcohol or gallstones), resulting in fat malabsorption. Pain that is out of proportion to other clinical symptoms and signs is more common in functional bowel disease, where it may be the dominant feature. As pain is a difficult symptom to quantify, it is helpful to identify whether it affects daily functioning (e.g. work or school attendance), what type and dose of medication, if any, is required (particularly narcotics such as codeine), and whether pain occurs at night (pain which wakes people from sleep is usually organic) (Talley and Martin, 1996).

Abdominal bloating is a non-specific symptom that is common in undiagnosed coeliac disease, and in irritable bowel disease in association with constipation and/or diarrhoea. Excessive dietary fibre may also result in diarrhoea and bloating.

Faecal incontinence may co-exist with or be confused with diarrhoea. Most patients will not mention it unless specifically asked. Urgency due to severe inflammation of the rectum such as in inflammatory bowel disease or radiation proctitis can produce diarrhoea, resulting in urge incontinence. Passive incontinence (loss of stool without an urge) is a separate problem often caused by poor function of the internal anal sphincter, although it can be precipitated or worsened by diarrhoea (Cheetham et al., 2001).

More unusual associated problems include lower back and buttock pain due to sacro-ileitis, large joint arthritis and skin rashes such as erythema nodosum or erythema multiforme, all of which are associated with inflammatory bowel disease. Dermatitis herpetiformis, a papulovesicular, itchy rash seen on the extensor surfaces and buttocks, is associated with coeliac disease.

Investigations

The most clinically effective and cost efficient manner of investigation is controversial, and will vary depending on the clinical likelihood of malignancy. Flexible sigmoidoscopy, colonoscopy and barium enema are all in routine use. Flexible sigmoidscopy has the advantage of only requiring an enema on the day, and should detect lesions up to the sigmoid/descending colon junction. Colonoscopy is the gold standard because the entire colon is examined and removal of polyps is possible, but it requires diet and oral preparation, and in most cases, sedation and analgesia. Barium enema is performed without sedation, and requires a similar diet and oral preparation to colonoscopy, but the removal of polyps or biopsy of lesions is not possible.

Diet

A number of dietary elements can cause or exacerbate diarrhoea (Table 10.1). Improvement in the diarrhoea following elimination of these dietary elements, with a return of symptoms after reintroducing them back into the diet, suggests that they are causal. Lactose intolerance is associated with diarrhoea, bloating, abdominal pain and excessive flatus. It is common in non-Caucasians and following small bowel mucosal damage (gastroenteritis, coeliac disease), and may coexist with the irritable bowel syndrome. Many patients are asymptomatic unless more than 10 gm of lactose (200 ml of milk) is ingested (Talley and Martin, 1996). Relief of symptoms with a two-week lactose-free diet suggests lactase deficiency.

Table 10.1: Dietary causes of diarrhoea

Excess ingestion of non- or poorly-absorbable carbohydrate

Sorbitol in elixirs, sugar-free gum and mints, pears, prunes, peaches and orange juice
Fructose from soft drinks, apples, honey, pears, cherries, dried dates, dried figs, grapes, pears and prunes
Mannitol in sugar-free products and mints
Bran and other fibre supplements

Magnesium-induced diarrhoea

Antacids
Laxatives
Food supplements

Stimulation of GI motility

Caffeine – coffee, tea and cola.

Lactose intolerance

Milk

Family history

A family history of colon cancer, inflammatory bowel disease and coeliac disease should be sought. Patients with coeliac disease may have minimal or no symptoms even if other affected family members have severe symptoms (Jennings and Howdle, 2001). The severity of the symptoms does not correlate well with gluten ingestion or histology. Thus all relatives of a confirmed case should be offered screening using anti-gliaden and anti-endomysial antibodies. As avoidance of common food elements such as gluten requires a permanent major alteration to the diet, a suspected diagnosis of coeliac disease should be confirmed before the diet is commenced.

Medication

Both prescription and over-the-counter medication are common causes of diarrhoea. A careful drug history is mandatory, with specific questions regarding over-the-counter medications such as antacids (which patients may not regard as drugs) and short-course drugs such as antibiotics or non-steroidal anti-inflammatory drugs (NSAIDs). The classes of drug most commonly implicated include antacids, antibiotics, laxatives, NSAIDs (including the newer cox-2 selective agents), anti-hypertensives and potassium supplements. Less commonly prescribed drugs such as anti-arrhythmics, bile acids, antineoplastics, and cholinergic agents are also associated with diarrhoea. Although medication-induced diarrhoea usually follows commencement of the drug, or increase in dose, occasionally it can occur after chronic usage with a stable dose.

Alcohol is an under-recognised cause of chronic diarrhoea. One third of binge drinkers have steatorrhoea, illustrating that regular ingestion is not necessary to produce symptoms. Ingestion of ethanol has been shown to reduce intestinal transit times, electrolyte and water absorption, impair digestive enzyme function, decrease pancreatic exocrine function (potentially reversible), and can lead to reduction in bile secretion in patients with liver disease (Bujanda, 2000). The type of alcoholic drink is not important. Alcohol abuse may result in chronic pancreatitis, characterised by steatorrhoea and severe unrelenting abdominal pain radiating to the back, often leading to narcotic dependence.

Infections

As chronic diarrhoea is common in patients with HIV/AIDS, a sexual history is essential. A CD4 count of less than 50 cell/mm^3, a history of homosexuality and use of antiretroviral therapy are risk factors for diarrhoea in those infected with HIV. Infections with unusual organisms are the most likely causes of diarrhoea in HIV-positive patients. However, bacterial overgrowth, lactose intolerance and drug-induced diarrhoea are also common. Cramps, bloating and diarrhoea suggest small bowel disease (e.g. *Mycobacterium avium intracellulare, Cryptosporidia, Isospora belli, Giardia)* whilst bloody stools suggest infective colitis (e.g. *Cytomegalovirus, Shigella, Campylobacter)* (Fantry, 2000).

Medical history

The past medical history may be helpful in identifying other diseases that are associated with or may contribute to diarrhoea, including iatrogenic diarrhoea following surgery, and systemic diseases. Intestinal surgery, including cholecystectomy, partial and total colonic resection, vagotomy and terminal ileal resection may be followed by diarrhoea. Terminal ileal resection of less than 100 cm may result in bile salt diarrhoea, whereas extensive resections of more than 100 cm produce causes depletion of the bile salt pool, resulting in steatorrhoea. Truncal vagotomy and gastric drainage is now an uncommon operation – nevertheless, it produces diarrhoea in up to 25% of patients. This is usually episodic, and may be explosive with associated urgency and faecal incontinence, and treatment is difficult.

Diarrhoea is a recognised complication of a number of systemic diseases including diabetes, thyrotoxicosis and scleroderma. Diarrhoea affecting type 1 (insulin-dependent) diabetics is often associated with autonomic neuropathy (nerve degeneration), seen most commonly in patients with a long history and / or poor glycaemic control. Other symptoms suggestive of autonomic neuropathy are postural dizziness due to orthostatic hypotension, impotence, urinary incontinence, and sweating associated with eating. The diarrhoea is classically episodic, frequent (10–30 times per 24 hours), with watery stool, and may be nocturnal or worse when the patient is supine. It is often associated with faecal incontinence. Other types of autonomic neuropathy can also produce diarrhoea. Small intestinal bacterial overgrowth due to impaired motility contributes to diarrhoea in diabetics and patients with scleroderma. Small intestinal bacterial overgrowth is related to stasis, and is therefore also seen after gastric surgery, in patients with small bowel diverticulosis, strictures (due to Crohn's disease or radiation), and chronic intestinal pseudo-obstruction.

Other autoimmune diseases, such as coeliac disease, arthritis and connective tissue diseases are associated with microscopic and collagenous colitis, respectively. As with all autoimmune diseases, they are more common in middle-aged women. Macroscopically the colon is normal; on biopsy, however, microscopic inflammation and a thick band of sub-epithelial collagen (in collagenous colitis) is seen. The diarrhoea is watery, large volume and associated mucus and mild colicky abdominal pain are common. Despite the volume, most patients are not dehydrated and do not lose weight. This diagnosis should be considered particularly if a patient with coeliac disease fails to respond to a gluten-free diet despite histological small bowel improvement.

The commonest cause of diarrhoea in the 'well' patient from the community is functional bowel disease, often referred to as irritable bowel syndrome. The history is often prolonged, the patient young, and non-specific associated symptoms such as bloating and abdominal pain and upper gastrointestinal symptoms (nausea, belching, dyspepsia) are common. The course is relapsing and remitting.

Relapses may be associated with periods of psychological stress. Enquiries about the effect of work, family and financial stresses on the course of the diarrhoea may suggest the diagnosis, although inflammatory bowel disease may also worsen with stress. In practice, functional bowel disease is a diagnosis of exclusion that should not be made if there are any clinical features that suggest organic rather than functional disease. These include new onset of symptoms in elderly patients, nocturnal symptoms, progressive increase in the severity of symptoms, weight loss, rectal bleeding, dehydration, and steatorrhoea. Abnormal simple investigations (raised erythrocyte sedimentation rate, anaemia, leucocytosis, or low potassium) and blood, pus or excess fat in the stool also suggest organic disease. Functional bowel disease may co-exist with other pathologies such as inflammatory bowel disease.

A psychiatric history, with specific questioning about symptoms of eating disorders (altered body image, preoccupation with weight, binge eating, induced vomiting, excessive exercise) and laxative use, is important. Laxative use is seen particularly in women who have a long history of normal investigations performed at multiple hospitals, and accounts for 10–15% of all chronic diarrhoea. Cramping abdominal pain, rectal pain, nausea and vomiting, muscle weakness, lassitude and bone pain are associated with surreptitious laxative use. Hypokalaemia, melanosis coli and rarely, digital clubbing are other features which suggest laxative use. Melanosis coli, a pigmentation of the colonic mucosa due to anthracene laxatives (senna, aloe, dantron), may be seen at endoscopy or occasionally only on histology. It develops within four months of laxative use and disappears 4–12 months after ceasing the laxatives. A high index of suspicion is required to make the diagnosis. Psychiatric assessment as part of an inpatient assessment can be helpful.

Exercise

Exercise-induced diarrhoea is not commonly seen in hospital practice, but affects about a quarter of competitive runners and may present in primary care. It is more common in younger (under 35), inexperienced runners, and tends to occur at the commencement of training or when the intensity is increased. Urgency during or immediately after running is typical, and the stools may contain blood. Gradual increase in training intensity, reduction in dietary fibre, and waiting 1–2 hours after eating before running may prevent the diarrhoea.

Demographics

Lastly, basic demographics such as age and ethnic background influence the likely diagnosis. This is shown by the increased incidence of coeliac disease in those of Irish descent, and the high incidence of lactose intolerance in non-Caucasians. Older patients (over 50) have an increased risk of colon cancer and are more prone to other disorders such as small intestinal bacterial overgrowth. In comparison, Crohn's and coeliac disease are more commonly diagnosed in younger patients. However, this is not absolute, as cancer can occur in the young, and Crohn's and coeliac disease have been diagnosed in elderly patients.

Examination

General inspection is useful to give an overall impression of the patient's nutritional status and wellbeing. Weight and height allow quick estimation of the patient's body mass index (BMI = weight in kilograms divided by the height in metres squared). For women, a BMI of greater than 18.5 is acceptable, while the corresponding figure for men is 20. Examination of the periphery should include estimation of basic nutritional status (muscle wasting, peripheral oedema and fat reserves), skin rashes (commonly found on the shin and extensor surfaces), and evidence of nutritional deficiency (see Table 10.2).

Although abdominal findings are uncommon, the presence of a mass or enlarged liver is suggestive of a tumour or metastasis, which should be excluded by appropriate imaging (usually CT scan). The sigmoid colon is often palpable in thin people and may be tender in both inflam-

Table 10.2: Clinical signs of nutrient deficiencies

Deficiency	*Clinical signs*
Iron	Pallor Glossitis Cheilosis Koilonychia
B_{12}	Peripheral neuropathy
Protein	Peripheral oedema White nails
Vitamins K and C	Petechiae / bruising

matory and functional bowel disease. The perineum should be inspected for evidence of perianal Crohn's disease (such as a fistula, or fissure), which is often associated with active rectal disease. Rectal examination is essential to exclude faecal impaction (resulting in 'overflow' diarrhoea in elderly people), and low rectal tumours. Examination and biopsy of the rectal mucosa with a rigid sigmoidoscope will identify pigmentation (laxative abuse), inflammation (ulcerative colitis, rectal Crohn's disease, radiation proctitis), ulceration (carcinoma, solitary rectal ulcer) or neoplastic disease (rectal carcinoma, villous adenoma).

Differential diagnosis and investigation

After taking a history and examining the patient it should be possible to establish a differential diagnosis that will determine the order and choice of subsequent tests. The investigation of chronic diarrhoea should be performed in a stepwise fashion, excluding common and easily treatable disorders first before rare conditions are considered. Severely ill patients should be referred and investigated urgently and may require a planned admission to coordinate tests and/or opinions.

Basic screening

As a first step, there are a number of basic screening tests that may suggest the presence of organic disease and help direct subsequent investigations. Not all of these are required if the history or examination has identified a likely cause. A full blood count and film will identify anaemia (coeliac disease, colon cancer, IBD), low mean red cell volume (iron deficiency), low red cell folate (coeliac disease, Whipple's disease), thrombocytosis (inflammation, e.g. IBD) and leucocytosis (infection, inflammation). C-reactive protein or erythrocyte sedimentation rate are helpful if elevated (inflammation, cancer, infection), but can be negative in patients with definite inflammation. Folate is absorbed in the upper small bowel and is therefore low in coeliac and Whipple's disease, whereas a low B_{12} suggests prolonged terminal ileal disease.

Stool sample

A fresh stool sample should be inspected for blood, pus and oil, and tested for red cells (inflammation, cancer, infection), white cells (inflammation, infection), fat droplets by Sudan stain (fat malabsorption), and ova (infection with giardia). The sample should then be cultured to exclude infective causes of diarrhoea. A rigid sigmoidoscopy and biopsy is particularly helpful if there is bloody diarrhoea, and may reveal features of inflammatory or infective colitis, radiation proctitis, pseudomembraneous colitis (secondary to *Clostridium difficile* overgrowth following broad-spectrum antibiotics) or microscopic colitis (on histology). Stool should be tested for *Clostridium difficile* toxin if this is clinically indicated.

Diagnosis

In well, young patients with no organic features on history or examination, normal screening tests and a normal faecal weight, further examination is not necessary unless new signs or symptoms develop. These patients are likely to have functional bowel disease.

There may be features of the history or examination that point to a specific cause of the diarrhoea, considerably narrowing or eliminating the need for further investigations. These include:

1) risk factors for infective diarrhoea, such as overseas travel, immunodeficiency (HIV/AIDS), and recent antibiotic therapy;
2) family history of coeliac disease;
3) a dietary history suggestive of lactase deficiency;
4) iatrogenic diarrhoea, for example, following intestinal surgery or radiation enteritis;
5) drug induced diarrhoea; and
6) features of a systemic disease such as diabetes, thyrotoxicosis, inflammatory bowel disease.

Further tests

Patients at special risk for infectious diarrhoea should have three separate stool specimens sent. It is important to provide the laboratory with all relevant history – special stains or PCR (polymerase chain reaction) tests may be required to detect unusual pathogens such as *Cryptosporidium, Microsporidium* and *Mycobacterium*, which are common in HIV/AIDS diarrhoea. Enterotoxigenic *E.coli* is the commonest cause of prolonged traveller's diarrhoea, although other bacteria (salmonella, shigella, campylobacter), protozoa (giardia) and helminths (strongyloides) are also found. A history of recent antibiotics should prompt a request for clostridium toxin. If stool specimens are negative, colonoscopy and ileoscopy with biopsies is the most productive test (Fantry, 2000).

In patients with a history of diarrhoea related to milk ingestion, relief of symptoms with a two-week lactose-free diet suggests lactase deficiency. Formal testing for lactose intolerance can be performed directly by measuring lactase in small bowel biopsies, or indirectly using a lactose breath hydrogen test or lactose tolerance test.

Anaemia, combined iron and folate deficiency, or a family history suggests coeliac disease. This should be investigated with anti-gliaden and anti-endomysial antibodies, followed by an upper gastrointestinal endoscopy with small bowel biopsy in those with positive antibodies. Atrophy of the small intestinal villi is characteristic of coeliac disease.

If there is no specific cause suggested by the history, it should be possible to localise the probable site of disease by the presence of key clinical features. Diarrhoea with bleeding suggests large bowel pathology, usually inflammatory or infectious colitis. Colonic carcinoma and villous adenoma can also cause bleeding with diarrhoea, and occasionally haemorrhoids can bleed during an episode of acute watery diarrhoea due to the trauma of recurrent wiping. A rigid sigmoidoscopy and rectal biopsy may demonstrate proctitis and will show the extent of the disease if it is limited to the distal sigmoid or rectum. If the rectum is normal, colonoscopy, ileoscopy and biopsies should be performed, as Crohn's disease may spare the rectum. Continuous inflammation from the rectum extending proximally a variable distance is characteristic of ulcerative colitis. Crohn's disease is typically patchy, with areas of normal mucosa between inflamed areas ('skip lesions'). The histology and endoscopic appearances enable ulcerative colitis to be distinguished from Crohn's disease in 85% of cases. In the 15% of patients with 'indeterminate' colitis, and in those with definite Crohn's disease, a small bowel barium follow-through is useful to identify whether the small bowel is affected by Crohn's disease.

Steatorrhoea on history or fat in the faeces (detected on Sudan stain) should be confirmed by a three-day faecal fat estimation. The patient should have a diet containing at least 100 grams of fat for three days prior to and during the collection. More than seven grams of fat in stool per day suggests small bowel disease (e.g. bacterial overgrowth, coeliac disease, Crohn's disease, Whipple's disease) or pancreatic insufficiency (chronic pancreatitis).

In suspected small bowel disease the likely cause will direct the order of investigations. Common and easily treatable diseases should be sought first (see Table 10.3). Pain and diarrhoea

Table 10.3: Differential diagnosis by probable site of disease

Site	*Relatively common*	*Uncommon*
Large bowel	Irritable bowel syndrome IBD Colon cancer Villous adenoma	Microscopic colitis
Small bowel	Coeliac disease Bacterial overgrowth Crohn's disease Lactase deficiency Parasitic infections Terminal ileal resection	AIDS Whipple's disease Tropical sprue Lymphoma Small Bowel ischaemia Amyloidosis Ulcerative jejunitis Radiation enteritis Zollinger-Ellison syndrome
Hepatobiliary/pancreatic	Chronic pancreatitis Post cholecystectomy	Pancreatic cancer Cystic fibrosis Extrahepatic biliary obstruction Chronic cholestatic liver disease

suggesting Crohn's disease should prompt a small bowel barium follow-through, which may demonstrate structural abnormalities such as fistula, strictures and mucosal inflammation or ulceration. Diverticula that predispose patients to bacterial overgrowth may also be seen. Diagnosis of bacterial overgrowth can be made directly from duodenal aspirates, although this is invasive and cumbersome. Indirect testing using breath tests is more common but has a low sensitivity. Empirical treatment with a course of antibiotics is an acceptable alternative in those with a risk factor for bacterial overgrowth, or high folate.

Pancreatic insufficiency is difficult to investigate. Functional tests are seldom used as they are uncomfortable, costly and have high false positive rates if not performed correctly. They have largely been replaced by therapeutic trials of enzyme replacement and structural imaging, using plain abdominal films and CT scanning of the abdomen to look for calcification and scarring associated with chronic pancreatitis, or a pancreatic mass. Dilated or irregular ducts suggestive of chronic pancreatitis may also be seen on magnetic resonance cholangiography (MRCP), or endoscopic retrograde cholangiography (ERCP). A therapeutic trial of full dose pancreatic enzyme replacement is worthwhile if pancreatic insufficiency is suspected, and should result in a reduction in stool fat content and an improvement in symptoms.

If the major feature is watery diarrhoea without any localizing symptoms, upper gastrointestinal endoscopy and colonoscopy with biopsies are the investigations of choice, looking for unusual causes of diarrhoea such as Whipple's disease and microscopic and collagenous colitis. Adequate size mucosal biopsies from rectum and colon are necessary to make the diagnosis of microscopic and collagenous colitis, as rectal biopsies alone may be normal. Mucosal biopsies may also reveal tissue deposits (amyloidosis, collagenous colitis) and rarely, organisms (Whipple's disease, schistosomiasis, spirochaetes).

The possibility of laxative abuse or factitious diarrhoea should be considered in patients with watery diarrhoea with no obvious cause. In the past, laxatives containing phenolphthalein could be detected by alkalinisation of a stool sample with a solution of sodium hydroxide. Phenolphthalein-containing laxatives are no longer available either over the counter or by prescription. Urine can be examined for a wide range of laxatives using thin-layer chromatography or high-pressure liquid chromatography. This is not always locally available, but can be used if the clinical suspicion is high. Factitious diarrhoea is usually a result of the patient adding either water or urine to the stool sample. Water is suggested by a low stool osmolality (performed on a stool specimen sent to biochemistry), while the presence of urea in the stool specimen indicates urine has been added.

In patients in whom the cause of the diarrhoea remains unclear, the presence of osmotically active substrates (which attract water into the stool) should be tested for by calculating the faecal osmotic gap. This is done by measuring the stool sodium and potassium concentration (performed by biochemistry on a stool sample), and using the formula:

$$\text{osmotic gap} = 290 - 2 \times (Na_{conc} + K_{conc})$$

An osmotic gap of 50 milliOsmols/kg or more indicates osmotically active substrates such as magnesium (antacids) or sorbitol (diet drinks and foods) (Farthing, 1996).

The next diagnostic steps are to test the response to fasting and exclude rare neuroendocrine secretory causes of diarrhoea such as Zollinger-Ellison, carcinoid and Verner Morrison syndromes. These syndromes result from oversecretion of intestinally active hormones resulting in secretory diarrhoea. The patient will need to be admitted for intravenous fluid replacement and fasted for 24–72 hours. Osmotic diarrhoea, steatorrhoea and bile acid diarrhoea improve with fasting, whereas secretory diarrhoea persists. Partial response occurs in cases of diarrhoea due to inflammatory bowel disease and bacterial overgrowth.

Neuroendocrine causes can be excluded by a combination of clinical features, measurement of the relevant hormone and/or imaging to look for the primary tumour. Patients with Zollinger-Ellison have a history of recurrent severe peptic ulceration, weight loss and diarrhoea or steatorrhoea, and have an elevated fasting plasma gastrin. Diarrhoea due to carcinoid is usually seen in those with hepatic metastases, which may result in hepatomegaly. Metastases and the primary tumour may be seen on fine cut helical CT and twenty-four hour urine collection demonstrates an elevated 5-HIAA concentration. Verner Morrison syndrome produces severe watery diarrhoea, hypokalaemia, and hypochlorydia, and is confirmed by an elevated serum vasoactive intestinal peptide (VIP) level (Farthing, 1996).

Management

Treatment of chronic diarrhoea should be specific to the underlying cause, if possible. If drug-induced diarrhoea is suspected, the drug should be stopped if possible, and an alternative sought if required. For those diseases where no specific therapy is available or effective, empirical treatment with anti-diarrhoeal drugs can be useful. Adequate doses of a single drug should be used before it is considered to have failed. The use of a single agent is preferable to low doses of multiple agents to reduce drug interactions and side effects.

The following section outlines the basics of management in some of the more common or easily treated diseases, followed by a brief overview of clinically available anti-diarrhoeal drugs.

Irritable bowel syndrome

A good relationship with the patient is essential to successful management. It is helpful to acknowledge that the symptoms are genuine, and that they are caused by a common and legitimate clinical syndrome. Explaining that any investigations done are to exclude other diseases and are likely to be negative is important to prevent 'disappointment' in patients expecting a positive diagnostic test. Often reassurance is required that the diagnosis is correct. The natural history of relapses and remissions should be outlined, with emphasis on the benign nature of IBS. An unhurried discussion covering the possible mechanisms for symptoms (abnormalities of gut sensation and motor function, influenced by diet, psychological and behavioral factors) can also be helpful. A dietary and pyschosocial history covering the relationship of symptoms to food, work, exercise and sleep may identify triggers that can be modified or avoided. Patients with diarrhoea-predominant IBS may benefit from fibre reduction, avoidance of diet foods containing sorbitol, stopping smoking, and a reduction of caffeine (tea, coffee and soft drinks) and alcohol intake. Foods that repeatedly and consistently result in symptoms should be avoided, but extreme elimination diets are unhelpful and result in vitamin and mineral deficiencies. It is common for patients with IBS to report improvement in symptoms on wheat-free or low gluten diets. This may be due to a reduction in dietary fibre contained in wheat products, and placebo effects. There is no need for a gluten-free diet in IBS, nor is it caused by colonisation of the gut by *Candida albicans*. If drug therapy is required for diarrhoea, loperamide is often effective. It is important patients understand that treatment is symptomatic and is not aimed at a cure. If there is no improvement, relaxation therapy, individual psychotherapy or hypnotherapy may have a role in selected patients (Boyce, 2001; Forbes et al., 2000; Keefer and Blanchard, 2001). The diagnosis should be reviewed if new symptoms develop or the pattern changes significantly.

Coeliac disease

Treatment involves a strict gluten-free diet for life. Gluten is present in wheat, rye and barley, and is commonly used in commercially prepared foods, so advice from an experienced dietitian and the Coeliac Society (see Appendix II) is invaluable. Improvement in symptoms usually occurs within a month. Patient should have a repeat small bowel biopsy to document healing after 6–12 months. If there is no response clinically the commonest cause is persistent ingestion of gluten (inadvertently or deliberately), incorrect diagnosis (check the small bowel histology), the development of complications (lymphoma, collagenous sprue), or another diarrhoeal disease (e.g. lactase deficiency) (Jennings and Howdle, 2001).

Inflammatory bowel disease

It is important to determine which type of inflammatory bowel disease is present, as the course of disease and type of treatment often differ. Diarrhoea is an indicator that active inflammation is present. The aim of treatment is to control inflammation and therefore to reduce symptoms. Non-specific anti-diarrhoeal drugs such as loperamide should be used only after adequate medical therapy and specialist consultation, as they can precipitate megacolon in active ulcerative colitis. A low-fibre, high-energy diet may reduce bowel frequency and pain. Treatment of IBD is reviewed by Kamm (1999).

Ulcerative colitis

Ulcerative colitis only involves the mucosa of the large bowel. The type and form of treatment of an acute attack depend on the extent of the inflammation and its severity. Rectal involvement is managed using suppositories (either salicylates (5ASA) or steroid), which have a direct effect on the mucosa and little systemic absorption. Disease that extends up to the descending colon can be managed using foam or liquid enema preparations of salicylates or steroid. Retention of topical therapy can be difficult, but improves with continuing use.

Total colitis may benefit from local treatment to ease rectal symptoms, but will require systemic therapy as well. This is used in a 'pyramid' fashion, with the next step in treatment added to the previous drug, rather than replacing it. Mild disease (less than 4 motions/day) is managed with oral salicylates (sulphasalazine or olsalazine) at full dose. Moderate to severe disease (4–6 motions/day, blood, low-grade fever, malaise) often requires a course of corticosteroids (prednisolone or budesonide), commencing at a high dose (e.g., 40 mg/day). The dose should be tapered by 5–10 mg weekly once a response is seen, to 20 mg/day, and then by 2.5–5 mg/day until the drug is withdrawn. Immunosuppression with azathioprine is used for patients who are unable to reduce their steroid dose, or require two or more courses of steroid over a short period of time. Azathioprine should be used at full dose (2 mg/kg) and may take 3–6 months to become effective. Fifteen per cent of patients do not tolerate the drug due to the development of pancreatitis, or severe flu-like symptoms. All patients require blood monitoring for the duration of use to monitor for bone marrow suppression.

Intravenous steroids are used for severe disease (more than six motions a day, severe bleeding, fever, tachycardia) that fails to improve rapidly on oral steroid, and for fulminant disease. Failure to respond to intravenous steroids after 7–10 days, or the development of toxic megacolon, is an indication for urgent colectomy. Intravenous cyclosporin is an alternative in this clinical setting; however, relapse is common and colectomy may still ultimately be required. Overall, 20% of patients with ulcerative colitis require surgery, either for fulminant colitis or disease that remains active despite maximal medical therapy.

Once remission is attained, maintenance with 5 ASA compounds (e.g. sulphasalazine 2–4 gm) reduces the risk of relapse. Steroids do not prevent relapse. In patients with more aggressive disease, relapse rates are lower on azathioprine, but the benefits need to be balanced with the possible risks of long-term immunosuppression (e.g., bone marrow suppression).

Crohn's disease

Management of Crohn's disease depends on the severity of disease and the site of involvement. Crohn's colitis is managed in a similar fashion to ulcerative colitis. The combination of terminal ileal and colonic disease is better treated with mesalazine (a coated 5ASA which is released in the distal ileum) than sulphasalazine or olsalazine, which are active in the colon only. Elemental and polymeric diet alone is as effective as steroids in active disease, but is difficult to tolerate for long periods and relapse is common on return to a normal diet. In patients who require immunosuppression but fail, or are intolerant of azathioprine, methotrexate is an alternative but it also requires blood monitoring. Infliximab, an anti-tumour necrosis factor antibody, results in remission in a third of patients, but repeated infusions are often necessary to maintain response, treatment is expensive, and the long-term safety profile is unknown. Cyclosporine is not effective orally, but an intravenous course may have a role in fulminant colitis and fistulating disease. As the disease may occur anywhere from mouth to anus, a surgical cure is not possible. However, eighty per cent of patients will require surgery at some stage to deal with limited ileo-caecal disease, obstruction due to strictures, fistula, inflammatory masses, and fulminant colitis. Surgery should aim to preserve bowel if possible, as multiple resections can result in short gut syndrome. Recurrence occurs endoscopically in almost all patients, and although this may be asymptomatic, 70% of patients with small bowel disease and 40% of those with colonic disease will require further surgery.

Maintenance therapy in Crohn's disease is more difficult than in ulcerative colitis. Mesalazine reduces relapse by a third, but high doses may be required. Oral metronidazole reduces relapse after terminal ileal resection; however long-term use is hampered by side effects such as peripheral neuropathy, which may be irreversible.

Iatrogenic diarrhoea

Management of iatrogenically induced diarrhoea is often commenced with little further investigation. For example, following terminal ileal resection, absorption of bile salts may be impaired, resulting in delivery of bile salts to the colon, causing diarrhoea. Cholestyramine, which binds bile acids, prevents them from causing diarrhoea. If there has been extensive terminal ileal resection, the pool of bile salts becomes depleted, resulting in fat malabsorption and steatorrhoea. In this setting, cholestyramine is unhelpful, but a low fat diet may reduce symptoms.

Laxative abuse

Patients who abuse laxatives typically deny laxative use even when confronted with evidence and discharge themselves from care, only to have the process of investigation repeated at another hospital, making confrontation an unhelpful manoeuvre. It should be explained that full investigation has failed to identify a cause, and that in this situation symptomatic treatment and psychological support can be helpful. This may allow patients to transfer from a somatic to a psychological expression of symptoms. It is important to stress that further investigation is not required.

Bacterial overgrowth

Treatment with oral antibiotics (e.g. metronidazole, tetracycline, or ampicillin) should produce clinical improvement. However, relapse after cessation is common if there is a cause of stasis. In this situation, long-term rotating courses of antibiotics may be required.

Lactose intolerance

Milk and high lactose dairy products (ice-cream, cream cheese, yoghurt) should be reduced until the symptoms resolve. Complete exclusion of all dairy products is usually not necessary, as many types of cheese have relatively little lactose (cottage cheese, feta, ricotta) and are tolerated in small amounts. Hard and semi-hard cheese such as cheddar are lactose-free (Moulds et al., 1998).

Collagenous and microscopic colitis

Symptomatic therapy with loperamide may be all that is required. If anti-inflammatory treatment is required, sulphasalazine is the treatment of choice due to its long-term safety profile. Oral corticosteroids are an alternative, but should be used in short courses in the same way as in inflammatory bowel disease.

Diabetes

Diabetic diarrhoea is typically refractory to commonly used anti-diarrhoeal drugs such as loperamide. Therapeutic trials of cholestyramine, antibiotics (for possible bacterial overgrowth) and opiates may be useful. Optimal glycaemic control and avoidance of excess sorbitol (used as a sweetener in some diabetic foods) may also be helpful.

Drug therapy

Anti-diarrhoeal drug therapy can be divided into two groups by the major mechanism of action of the drugs: inhibition of intestinal transit (opiates and opoids, alpha 2 adrenergic agonist) or inhibition of intestinal secretion (somatostatin analogues) (see Chapter 16).

Synthetic opioids such as loperamide (Imodium) are the most commonly used anti-diarrhoeal drugs (Moulds et al., 1998). They require dose titration to a maximum of 16 mg/day to achieve optimal effects and are generally well tolerated, although cramping abdominal pain may occur at higher doses. Loperamide should be used with care in acute colitis as toxic megacolon may be precipitated. Opiates, such as codeine and morphine, are effective but have sedative side effects. For this reason long-term use is reserved for patients with severe diarrhoea not controlled by synthetic opoids. Significant hypotension is the major side effect of clonidine, an alpha 2 adrenergic agonist that has been shown to be effective in diabetic diarrhoea, limiting its clinical use.

Octreotide is a long-acting somatostatin analogue which inhibits gut secretion and motility, and promotes water and electrolyte absorption. It is particularly useful in more unusual causes of diarrhoea such as antineoplastic drug mediated diarrhoea, VIP-mediated diarrhoea, carcinoid syndrome, high-output states in patients with short bowel syndrome, cryptosporidial or microsporidial infection in AIDS, diabetic diarrhoea, and systemic sclerosis. Side effects include a temporary increase in diarrhoea due to steatorrhoea in some patients, and gallstone formation with long-term use.

Conclusions

Assessment of chronic diarrhoea by taking a comprehensive history, thorough examination and careful selection of appropriate investigations is essential to establish cause and effective treatment. Chronic diarrhoea is a debilitating symptom that requires an empathic approach and definitive diagnosis in order to ensure effective management.

References

Boyce, P. (2001) Psychologic therapies for irritable bowel syndrome. *Current Treatment Options in Gastroenterology* **4**, 323–331.

Bujanda, L. (2000) The effects of alcohol consumption upon the gastrointestinal tract. *American Journal of Gastroenterology* **95**, 3374–3382.

Cheetham, M.J., Malouf, A.J. and Kamm, M.A. (2001) Fecal incontinence. *Gastroenterology Clinics of North America* **30**, 115–130.

Fantry, L. (2000) Gastrointestinal infections in the immunocompromised host. *Current Opinion in Gastroenterology* **16**, 45–50.

Farthing, M.J. (1996) Chronic diarrhoea: current concepts on mechanisms and management. *European Journal of Gastroenterology and Hepatology* **8**, 157–167.

Forbes, A., MacAuley, S. and Chiotakakou-Faliakou, E. (2000) Hypnotherapy and therapeutic audiotape: effective in previously unsuccessfully treated irritable bowel syndrome? *International Journal of Colorectal Disease* **15**, 328–334.

Jennings, J.S. and Howdle, P.D. (2001) Celiac disease. *Current Opinion in Gastroenterology* **17**, 118–126.

Kamm, M.A. (1999) *Inflammatory bowel disease* (2nd edn). London: Martin Dunitz.

Keefer, L. and Blanchard, E.B. (2001) The effects of relaxation response meditation on the symptoms of irritable bowel syndrome: results of a controlled treatment study. *Behaviour Research and Therapy* **39**, 801–811.

Moulds, R.F., Catto-Smith, A., Dammery, D., Desmond, P.V., Khariwala, B., King, S., Leggett, B., Martin, C.J., Pavli, P., Roberts-Thomson, I., Stewart, K., Wilson, A. and Yeomans, N. (1998) *Gastrointestinal Drug Guidelines* (2nd edn). Australia: Therapeutic Guidelines (www.tg.com.au).

Talley, N. and Martin, C.J. (eds) (1996) *Clinical gastroenterology; a practical problem-based approach*. Sydney: MacLennan & Petty.

Chapter 11

Common Ano-rectal Conditions

Gordon Buchanan and Richard Cohen

Introduction

Anorectal disorders are common and can affect anyone. Most of these conditions are not life-threatening, though they can cause considerable morbidity. They are usually diagnosed on symptoms and clinical examination, although radiological and endoscopic evaluation is sometimes necessary. This chapter discusses their presenting features, lists necessary investigations, and also outlines current treatment regimens available to practitioners.

Pruritus ani

Pruritius ani is a common and frustrating symptom complex composed of itching, burning and pain. A full history and examination are usually diagnostic for causes of pruritus. The commonest cause of pruritus ani is perianal soiling irritating the perianal skin, though pruritus (Burton et al., 1985) can be caused by other anal disorders or dermatological conditions (Table 11.1). Once present, a vicious circle of itching and increased irritation ensues which must be broken to improve symptoms.

Soiling is best demonstrated to the patient by wiping the anal margin with a moistened swab, which may reveals leakage not otherwise evident. The patient must be reassured that this does not imply that they are 'unclean', but that faecal matter is easily trapped in the perianal skin, especially if there are skin tags or cracked skin. Treatment is directed at the underlying cause, as well as general advice on avoiding soaps, creams and scratching. Patients are advised to clean themselves with a moistened tissue prior to drying the skin and to avoid excessive patting dry. A small anal plug of cotton wool often prevents faecal leakage and dietary manipulation such as the avoidance of coffee, chocolate and sorbitol-containing foodstuffs can help some people and is worth a trial.

Table 11.1: Causes of secondary pruritus ani

Anorectal conditions	Haemorrhoids
	Fissure
	Fistula
	Prolapse
	Proctitis
Dermatological conditions	Psoriasis
	Contact dermatitis
Infections	Condylomata acuminata
	Candida albicans
Neoplasia	Rectal cancer
	Villous adenoma
	Bowen's Disease

Haemorrhoids

Haemorrhoids, or 'piles', are dilated anal cushions situated within the mucosa and sub-epithelial tissues of the anal canal. The anal canal is composed of blood-filled spaces supported by a tissue matrix, surrounded by the anal sphincter complex. This arrangement forms a seal which helps to prevent the unwanted leakage of liquid and gas (Loder et al., 1994). The blood-filled spaces exist above and below the dentate line, and are characteristically arranged at the 3, 7 and 11 o'clock positions when the patient is examined in the lithotomy position. Haemorrhoids develop within this tissue and can prolapse into the anal lumen as they enlarge. External haemorrhoids can also develop on the

Table 11.2: Haemorrhoid classification and treatment by degree of prolapse

Degree	*Appearance*	*Treatments*
1st	Prolapse into lumen Evident on proctoscopy	Reassurance High fibre diet Injection sclerotherapy
2nd	Prolapse out of anus on straining Typically prolapse during defaecation Reduce spontaneously May require manual reduction	Reassurance High fibre diet Injection sclerotherapy Rubber band ligation Haemorrhoidectomy
3rd	Prolapsed haemorrhoids, and tags continually protrude from anus	Haemorrhoidectomy and / or Tag excision
4th	Thrombosed, external strangulated haemorrhoids	Ice packs, analgesia or haemorrhoidectomy

perineum, which may be associated with skin tags.

Haemorrhoids are very common in Western society, though their exact prevalence is difficult to assess as only a small proportion of patients are referred to surgeons. All age groups can be affected, but the condition is rare in children, occurring most commonly in adult males. Haemorrhoids are thought to be associated with straining caused by lack of dietary fibre, though they can be associated with conditions like portal hypertension, as the ano-rectal junction is an important portal-systemic venous anastomosis.

Common symptoms include bright red rectal bleeding, often on the toilet paper or dripping into the pan. There is usually no alteration in bowel habit, though pruritus, post-defaecation soiling and a prolapsing sensation are often present. Pain is usually a feature of strangulated haemorrhoids. Table 11.2 gives a classification of haemorrhoids, with suggested management.

Digital rectal examination and sigmoidoscopy is usually normal and haemorrhoids are best visualised on proctoscopy. After insertion, the central introducer of the proctoscope is withdrawn, allowing visualisation of the haemorrhoids bulging into the anal lumen in the 3, 7 and 11 o'clock positions (Figure 11.1), and as this instrument is withdrawn their extent is noted. Haemorrhoids often have an internal and external component. Prolapsing haemorrhoids may only be evident on straining (Figure 11.2). Third-degree haemorrhoids are evident on inspection of the anus (Figure 11.3).

Investigations, including colonoscopy (Loder et al., 1994), are performed to ensure there is no coexistent colorectal pathology. Treatments vary according to degree of symptoms and prolapse (Table 11.2). Dietary measures, injection sclerotherapy and application of Barrons bands are all instituted via outpatients, and day case haemorrhoidectomy (Carapeti et al., 1998) is feasible using several surgical strategies. Patients should be warned of the small risk of impaired continence before consenting to haemorrhoidectomy.

Thrombosed haemorrhoids can be extremely painful. The emergency treatment of thrombosed external haemorrhoids (Figure 11.4) is usually symptomatic, including analgesia, glyceryl trinitrate, stool softeners and ice packs. Surgery in this state may result in anal stenosis and is avoided in some centres for that reason.

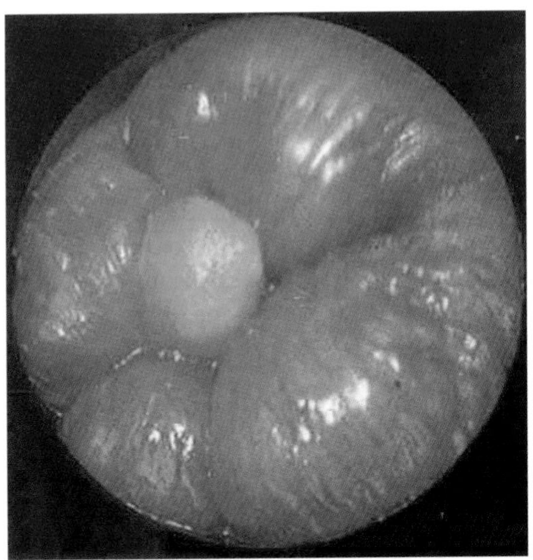

Figure 11.1 *First-degree haemorrhoids pouting into the anal lumen on proctoscopy.*

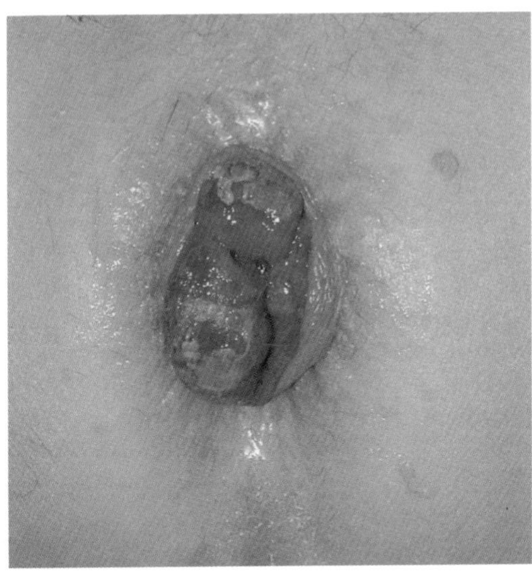

Figure 11.2 *These second-degree haemorrhoids only protrude on straining.*

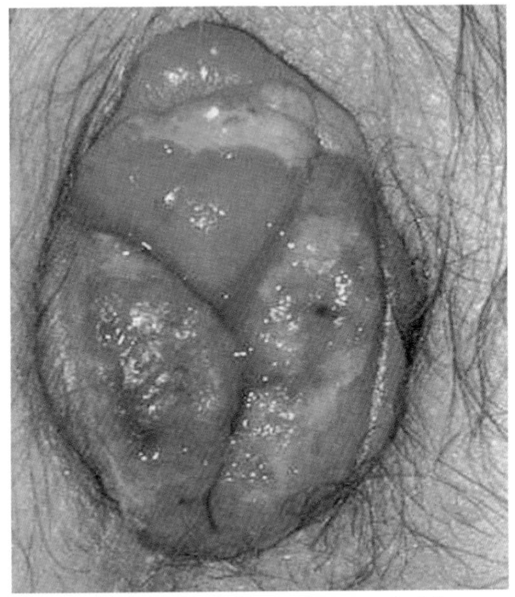

Figure 11.3 *Third-degree haemorrhoids continually prolapsed.*

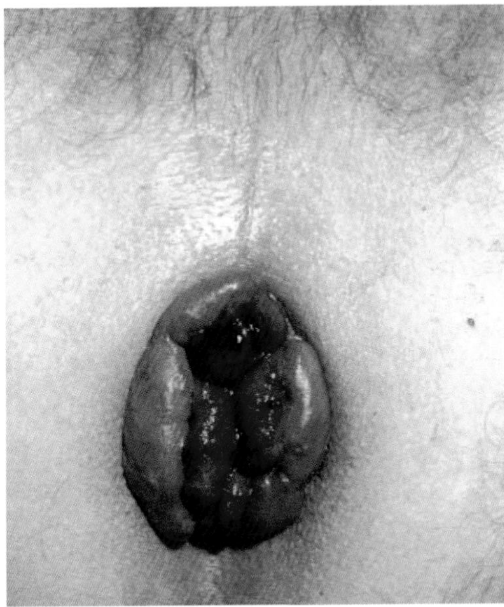

Figure 11.4 *Fourth-degree or strangulated haemorrhoids.*

Most patients achieve a satisfactory result from one or a combination of these treatments. Anal stenosis, recurrent haemorrhoids, haemorrhage, pain, and altered continence are recognised, though uncommon, operative complications.

Anal fissure

Fissure-in-ano describes a longitudinal tear of the anoderm situated below the dentate line. This may be secondary to other conditions (e.g. Crohn's disease, trauma), though usually occurs in young adults where its aetiology is unknown. There is a well-recognised association between fissure and high anal canal resting pressure (Arabi et al., 1977), although the reason for this remains unclear.

Patients commonly present with painful defaecation associated with rectal bleeding. A lump, or 'sentinel pile', is often present at the lower end of the fissure. Fissures are usually situated in the posterior midline, but can occur in the anterior midline. Gentle parting of the anal margin allows visualisation of the fissure (Figure 11.5), which is often a simple tear.

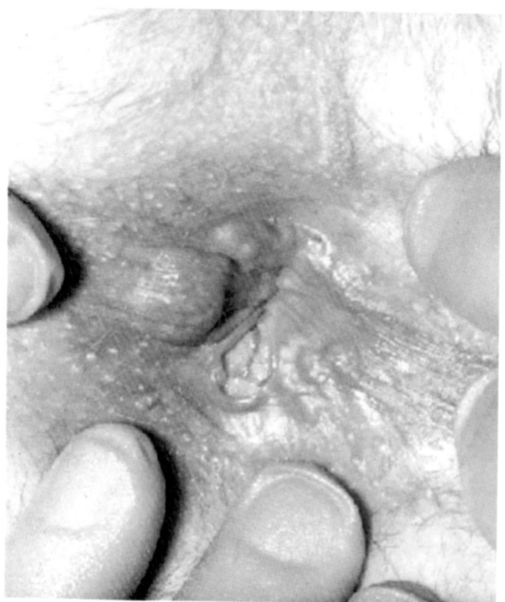

Figure 11.5 *Anal fissure situated in the posterior midline.*

When a fissure is chronic its edges may be raised and anal sphincter fibres seen within its base.

Where assessment is limited by pain, examination under anaesthetic is necessary. Surgical treatments are aimed at lowering anal canal pressure to promote healing. This can be achieved by anal stretch, or internal anal sphincterotomy. Anal stretch has largely been abandoned as it often precipitates faecal incontinence (Speakman et al., 1991). Sphincterotomy also has an associated risk of subsequent soiling. Where these options fail, advancement flaps provide an alternative surgical approach.

The recent success of reversible chemical sphincterotomy using glyceryl trinitrate (GTN) ointment, which lowers anal canal resting pressure, healing fissures in 50–80% of cases (Lund and Scholefield, 1997), has led to the wide acceptance of medical treatment as the first-line therapy for this condition, thus avoiding the attendant risks of surgery. Headaches are a recognised side effect of GTN, and diltiazem ointment seems as efficacious in healing fissures without causing headaches (Knight et al., 2001).

Anal fistula

An anal fistula is a track or cavity communicating with the ano-rectum by an identifiable internal opening. There is usually, but not always, an external opening (Marks and Ritchie, 1977). Fistulae predominate in males in the 4th decade (Marks and Ritchie, 1977), affecting one in ten thousand Europeans (Ewerth et al., 1978). 90% of fistula are idiopathic (Parks, 1961) though some are associated with Crohn's disease (Marks et al., 1981) and tuberculosis (Shukla et al., 1988).

The most popular hypothesis of the cause of anal fistula is the cryptoglandular hypothesis (Eisenhammer, 1956). This states that an infected anal gland located in the intersphincteric space leads to abscess formation. These glands cross the internal sphincter and communicate with the anal canal (Hermann and Desfosses,

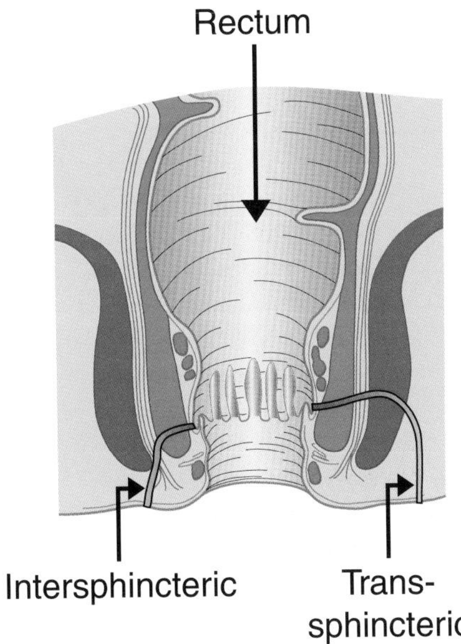

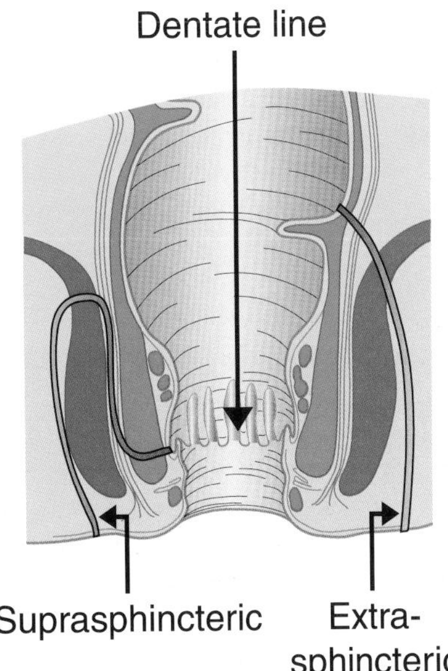

Figure 11.6 *Types of anal fistula.*

1880) at dentate line level. Pus in the intersphincteric space can track in several directions, passing through, above or between the sphincter components, usually emerging on the perianal skin to result in one of the various types of fistula (Figure 11.6) classified by Parks (Parks et al., 1976).

Perianal pain, chronic discharge and bleeding are the main presenting symptoms (Nicholls, 1996). Careful assessment, both in the awake and anaesthetised patient helps to locate the course of the fistula and any extensions. By inspecting the anus it is usually possible to see the relative position of any external openings (Figure 11.7). Palpating the anal margin with a gloved, lubricated, finger helps detect induration and elucidate the likely course of the primary track, or any horseshoeing (extension in a semi-circle around the anus). By then inserting this finger into the anal canal one attempts to feel induration, indicating the position of the internal opening, the majority of which lie in the midline posterior (Marks and Ritchie, 1977). By palpating into the rectum one can attempt to feel hard supralevator induration caused by high extensions or primary tracks. The internal opening can sometimes be directly visualised at proctoscopy.

Fistula assessment may be improved by preoperative imaging. Anal ultrasound (Figure 11.8, overleaf) is a valuable screening tool (Law and Bartram 1989), often providing helpful information (Deen et al., 1994) to the surgeon.

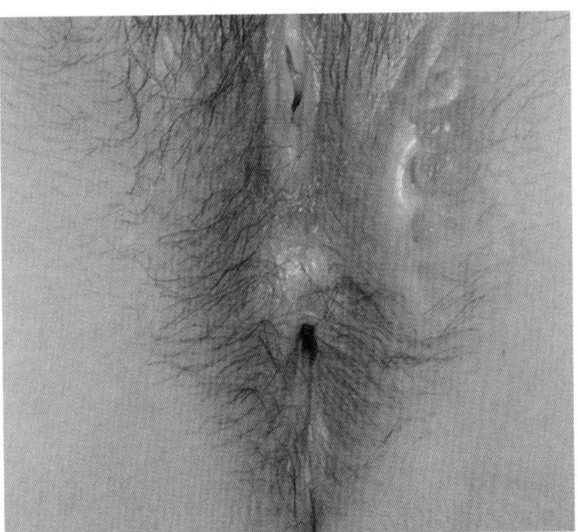

Figure 11.7 *Female with external opening of anal fistula adjacent to vagina.*

Injecting hydrogen peroxide into the external fistulous opening (Cheong et al., 1993; Poen et al., 1998) helps differentiate an active track from scarring during ultrasound. MRI is highly accurate (Beckingham et al., 1996), especially for the presence of extensions (Figure 11.9), adding important additional information to surgical findings (Lunniss et al., 1992), often better predicting clinical outcome than surgery itself (Chapple et al., 2000).

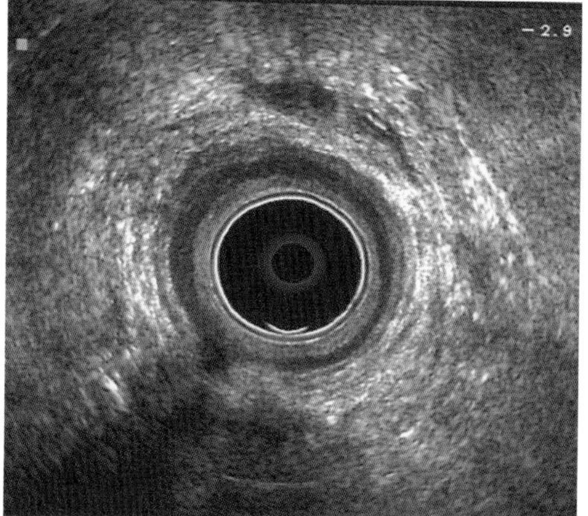

Figure 11.8 *Anal ultrasound with internal opening of fistula.*

Fistulae are usually simple (Marks and Ritchie, 1977), passing through relatively little anal sphincter, though some encompass the whole sphincter mechanism or may have secondary or horseshoe extensions. These complex fistulae are more likely to recur as sepsis is harder to eradicate, and laying open the fistula (Parks and Stitz, 1976), including sphincter mechanism, may precipitate faecal incontinence (Lunniss et al., 1994). In this circumstance, setons are often employed as part of the surgical strategy (Hamalainen and Sainio, 1997). A seton is a semi-permanent stitch introduced along the fistula track which stays *in situ* and allows drainage of the fistula when tied loosely, or slowly cuts through the sphincter muscle when tightly applied. Sphincter-preserving techniques including core out fistulectomy, advancement flaps (Hidaka et al., 1997) and the recent use of fibrin glue (Patrlj et al., 2000), have all met with varying success. Occasionally a fistula is secondary to pelvic disease, necessitating a bowel resection.

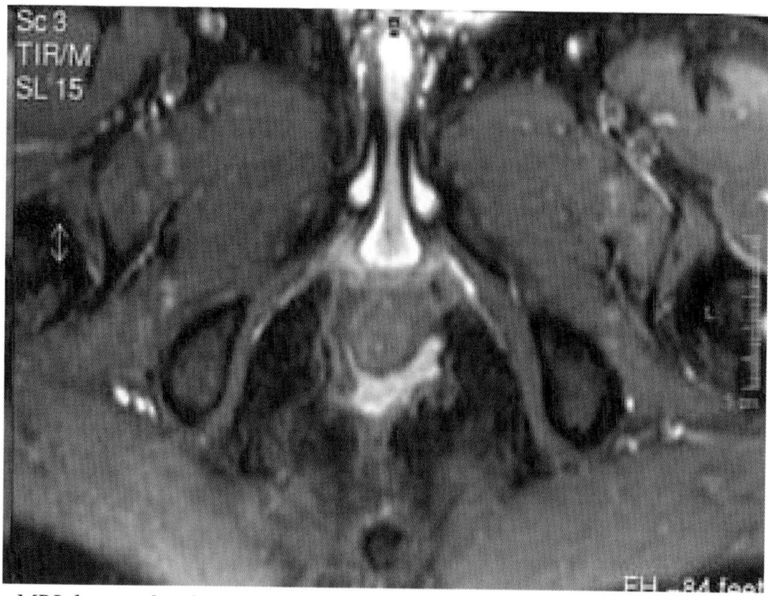

Figure 11.9 *MRI depicts fistula with horseshoe extension (fistula shows up bright).*

Rectovaginal fistula

These are usually related to obstetric trauma but are sometimes idiopathic or associated with Crohn's disease, malignant disease or pelvic irradiation. Typically, patients present with vaginal irritation and passage of flatus or faeces per vaginam. There may be a purulent discharge, and depending on aetiology incontinence often coexists. Clinical examination is usually diagnostic, though occasionally rigid sigmoidoscopy or Sims vaginal speculum into the vagina aids visualisation of the internal opening.

Management involves treatment of the underlying condition and eradication of sepsis. As most of these fistulae pass through or above the whole sphincter complex, laying the track open is likely to precipitate incontinence, so placement of setons, and advancement flaps (Kodner et al., 1993) are advocated by many.

Pilonidal sinus

Pilonidal sinus describes natal cleft suppuration due to hair follicle infection. Folliculitis leads to abscess formation, which extends into the subcutaneous fat. It is thought that surrounding hairs (Figures 11.10 and 11.11) are then sucked into the dilated follicle, inciting a foreign body reaction. This results in a subcutaneous sinus lined with granulation tissue, squamous epithelium and epithelial debris, with ensuing suppuration and discharge via the midline.

Pilonidal disease occurs mainly in young males (Jones, 1992). Initially thought to be congenital in origin, its prevalence amongst soldiers led workers to conclude that it was secondary to hair follicle infection, though why this happens remains unclear (Allen-Mersh, 1990).

It commonly presents as an acute abscess requiring surgical drainage, though chronic infection and asymptomatic forms are recognised (Bissett and Isbister, 1987). There is usually a single midline opening within the natal cleft posterior to the anus, although multiple sinuses with lateral openings are frequent (da Silva, 2000). Conservative treatment by shaving and meticulous hygiene may be adequate for mild disease, though definitive treatment is usually surgical.

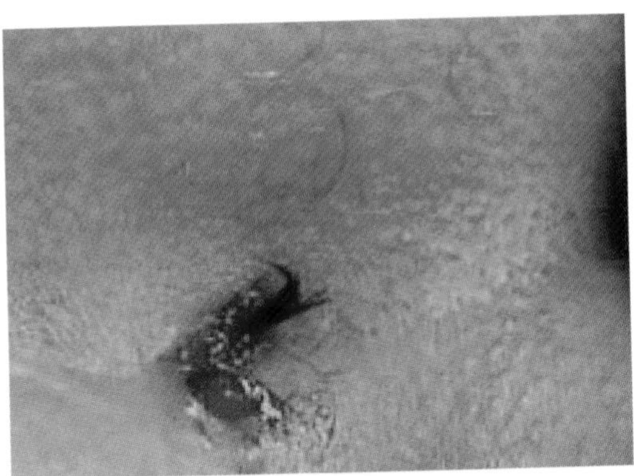

Figure 11.10 *Hairs embedded in recurrent pilonidal sinus.*

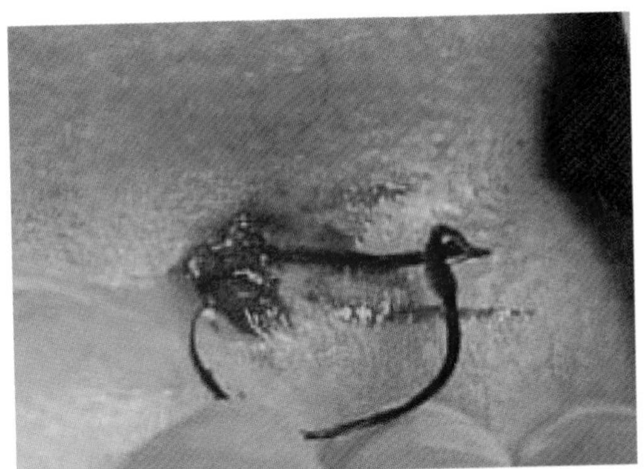

Figure 11.11 *At surgery hairs were embedded deep in sinus.*

Perianal haematoma

Patients typically present with a tender lump sited at the anal verge, approximately 2–4 cm in size, with a dark blue tinge (Figure 11.12). The term haematoma is rather imprecise (Thomson, 1982) as histological examination reveals a 'clotted venous saccule'. These lesions are frequently confused with haemorrhoids. They often subside spontaneously, and supportive measures include a cold compress and analgesia. Relief is also obtained by incision and evacuation under local anaesthesia, usually on an outpatient basis (Iseli, 1991).

Anal warts (condylomata acuminata)

Human papilloma virus types 6 and 11 usually cause benign warts; rarely, oncogenic viruses can infect patients. Condylomata acuminata is a sexually transmitted disease (STD), often affecting homosexuals, or others who practice anal intercourse. As such it may be associated with HIV and other STDs.

Warts may be single or multiple, sometimes giving a carpet appearance around the anus (Figure 11.13). Topical podophyllin (Maw and von Krogh, 2000) is useful for simple lesions, though excision by laser, cryotherapy and electrocautery are alternatives. Sharp dissection by scissors after infiltration of local anaesthetic is effective, though surgical excision of extensive lesions is often performed in stages to prevent excessive scarring.

Rectal prolapse

Full-thickness rectal prolapse is the complete eversion of the rectum through the anal canal. It is a disabling condition, where patients notice a lump which prolapses on defaecation. This sometimes reduces spontaneously, or may require manual reduction. It is often associated with bleeding, mucus discharge and symptoms of incontinence. This may be due to the weakness in pelvic musculature, or due to the physical presence of the prolapse. Some patients give a history of constipation and straining predating the prolapse.

Clinical examination may reveal weak sphincter musculature, although the prolapse may not be evident when patients are examined in the left lateral position. In order to confirm the diagnosis, patients should either be asked to squat (Figure 11.14) or be examined seated on the toilet; these manoeuvres are usually successful in demonstrating a prolapse. Occasionally the prolapse may also involve the uterus

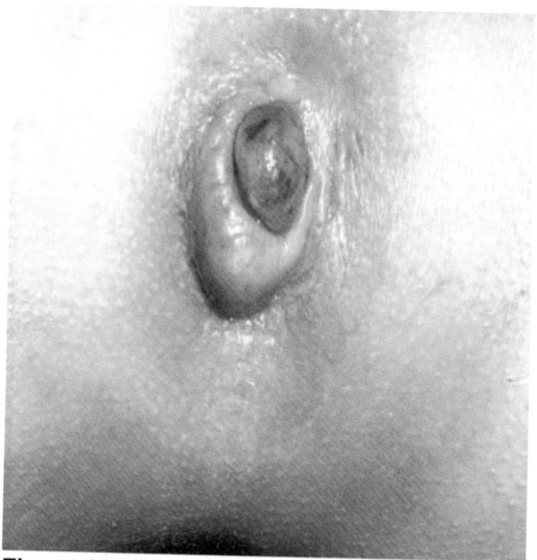

Figure 11.12 *Perianal haematoma. Blue tinge over stretched anoderm.*

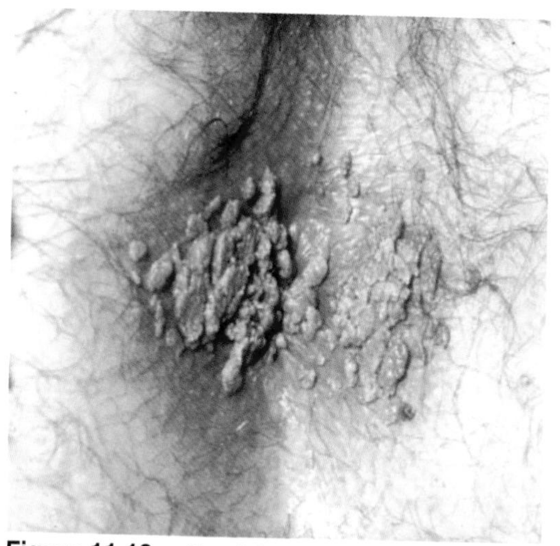

Figure 11.13 *Condylomata acuminata.*

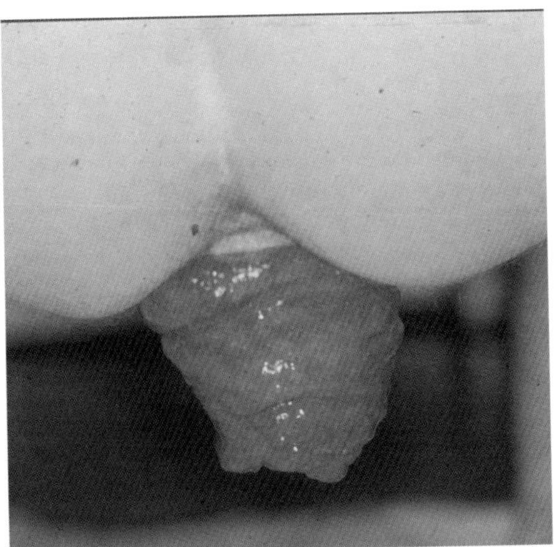

Figure 11.14 *Patient squats to demonstrate full-thickness rectal prolapse on 'bearing down'.*

(procidentia) (Bartolo, 1996). Longstanding prolapse may become irreducible, and bed elevation together with application of cold compress usually achieves reduction. If this recurs, further reduction is necessary prior to definitive surgery. Strangulation of the prolapse requires surgery (Ramanujam and Venkatesh, 1992).

The condition predominates in elderly females, though can occur in the young. Its exact aetiology is unclear, though weak pelvic musculature is often present. Some families with genetic tissue abnormalities seem predisposed.

There are numerous surgical techniques described (Wassef et al., 1986), however none is completely satisfactory. In essence, they can be divided into abdominal and perineal approaches:

1) Abdominal
   a) Open
      i) Rectopexy (often with prosthetic mesh)
      ii) Resection rectopexy
   b) Laporoscopic
2) Perineal
   a) Delormes
   b) Perineal rectosigmoidectomy

In general, perineal approaches are most commonly applied as they do not carry the attendant morbidity of abdominal surgery.

Solitary rectal ulcer syndrome

This is associated with internal intussusception and prolapse of the rectum (Sielezneff et al., 1995). Patients provide a history of multiple visits to the lavatory, associated with sitting, straining and often digitating. There may be bleeding, and proctosigmoidoscopy often shows a red ulcer, typically on the anterior rectal wall, which has characteristic histological features. Defaecating proctography is often diagnostic. As surgical treatments are often unsuccessful at treating this disorder, behavioural treatments including biofeedback (Binnie et al., 1992; Vaizey et al., 1997) represent an attractive option to aid patients.

Polyps and neoplasia

Benign and malignant neoplastic lesions can affect the ano-rectum. The squamous epithelium of the anal margin is the usual site of anal cancer, though this is rare in comparison with adenocarcinoma of the rectum. Patients usually present with a non-healing ulcer, pain and bleeding. Human Papilloma Virus is thought to predispose to this lesion (Palmer et al., 1989) which is invariably treated by chemoradiotherapy as a first line.

Rectal cancer is common, and most patients present with alteration in bowel habit and rectal bleeding. The diagnosis is usually confirmed by palpating a hard mass on digital examination, and subsequent biopsies taken on rigid sigmoidoscopy. Curative treatment for rectal cancer is surgical, though radiotherapy and chemotherapy are used for adjuvant and palliative treatment. Many patients with similar symptoms have polyps (Figure 11.15, overleaf), and these are usually evident on sigmoidoscopy. If biopsies confirm these to be adenomatous polyps, then investigation of the whole colon by ileocolonoscopy is warranted. Most polyps in the rectum can be treated by local excision.

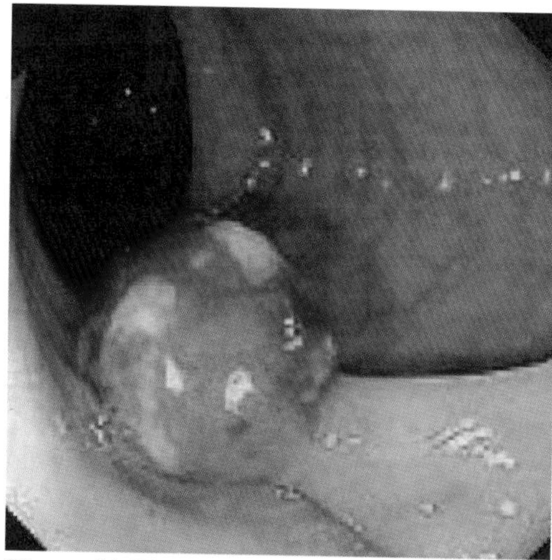

Figure 11.15 *Pedunculated polyp viewed through sigmoidoscope.*

Conclusion

This chapter has outlined the importance of careful clinical assessment in order to institute appropriate treatment for the many ano-rectal conditions which present to the practitioner.

References

Allen-Mersh, T.G. (1990) Pilonidal sinus: finding the right track for treatment. *British Journal of Surgery* **77**, 2, 123–132.

Arabi, Y., Alexander-Williams, J. and Keighley, M.R. (1977) Anal pressures in hemorrhoids and anal fissure. *American Journal of Surgery* **134**, 5, 608–610.

Bartolo, D.C. (1996) Rectal prolapse. *British Journal of Surgery* **83**, 1, 3–5.

Beckingham, I.J., Spencer, J.A., Ward, J., Dyke, G.W., Adams, C. and Ambrose, N.S. (1996) Prospective evaluation of dynamic contrast enhanced magnetic resonance imaging in the evaluation of fistula *in ano*. *British Journal of Surgery* **83**, 10, 1396–1398.

Binnie, N.R., Papachrysostomou, M., Clare, N. and Smith, A.N. (1992) Solitary rectal ulcer: the place of biofeedback and surgery in the treatment of the syndrome. *World Journal of Surgery* **16**, 5, 836–840.

Bissett, I.P. and Isbister, W.H. (1987) The management of patients with pilonidal disease – a comparative study. *Australian and New Zealand Journal of Surgery* **57**, 12, 939–942.

Burton, C.S., Eyre, R.W. and Callaway, J.L. (1985) 'Pruritus ani'. *North Carolina Medical Journal* **46**, 1, 35.

Carapeti, E.A., Kamm, M.A., McDonald, P.J. and Phillips, R.K. (1998) Double-blind randomised controlled trial of effect of metronidazole on pain after day-case haemorrhoidectomy. *Lancet* **351**, 9097, 169–172.

Chapple, K.S., Spencer, J.A., Windsor, A.C., Wilson, D., Ward, J. and Ambrose, N.S. (2000) Prognostic value of magnetic resonance imaging in the management of fistula-in-ano. *Diseases of the Colon and Rectum* **43**, 4, 511–516.

Cheong, D.M., Nogueras, J.J., Wexner, S.D. and Jagelman, D.G. (1993) Anal endosonography for recurrent anal fistulas: image enhancement with hydrogen peroxide. *Diseases of the Colon and Rectum* **36**, 12, 1158–1160.

da Silva, J.H. (2000) Pilonidal cyst: cause and treatment. *Diseases of the Colon and Rectum* **43**, 8, 1146–1156.

Deen, K.I., Williams, J.G., Hutchinson, R., Keighley, M.R. and Kumar, D. (1994) Fistulas *in ano*: endoanal ultrasonographic assessment assists decision making for surgery. *Gut* **35**, 3, 391–394.

Eisenhammer, S. (1956) The internal anal sphincter and the anorectal abscess. *Surgery, Gynecology and Obstetrics* **103**, 501–506.

Ewerth, S., Ahlberg, J., Collste, G. and Holmstrom, B. (1978) Fistula-in-ano. A six year follow up study of 143 operated patients. *Acta Chirurgica Scandinavica* **482**, 53–55.

Hamalainen, K.P. and Sainio, A.P. (1997) Cutting seton for anal fistulas: high risk of minor control defects. *Diseases of the Colon and Rectum* **40**, 12, 1443–1446.

Hermann, G. and Desfosses, L. (1880) Sur la muqueuse de la region cloacale du rectum. *Comptes Rendus de l'Academie des Sciences; Series III, Sciences de la Vie* (III) **90**, 1301–1302.

Hidaka, H., Kuroki, M., Hirokuni, T., Toyama, Y., Nagata, Y., Takano, M. and Tsuji, Y. (1997) Follow-up studies of sphincter-preserving operations for anal fistulas. *Diseases of the Colon and Rectum* **40**, 10 (Suppl.), S107–S111.

Iseli, A. (1991) Office treatment of haemorrhoids and perianal haematoma, *Australian Family Physician* **20**, 3, 284–290.

Jones, D.J. (1992) ABC of colorectal diseases. Pilonidal sinus, *British Medical Journal* **305**, 6850, 410–412.

Knight, J.S., Birks, M. and Farouk, R. (2001) Topical diltiazem ointment in the treatment of chronic anal fissure. *British Journal of Surgery*, **88**, 4, 553–556.

Kodner, I.J., Mazor, A., Shemesh, E.I., Fry, R.D., Fleshman, J.W. and Birnbaum, E.H. (1993) Endo-rectal advancement flap repair of rectovaginal and other complicated anorectal fistulas. *Surgery*, **114**, 4, 682–689.

Law, P.J. and Bartram, C.I. (1989) Anal endosonography: technique and normal anatomy. *Gastro-intestinal Radiology* **14**, 4, 349–353.

Loder, P.B., Kamm, M.A., Nicholls, R.J. and Phillips, R.K. (1994) Haemorrhoids: pathology, pathophysiology and aetiology. *British Journal of Surgery* **81**, 946–954.

Lund, J.N. and Scholefield, J.H. (1997) A randomised, prospective, double-blind, placebo-controlled trial of glyceryl trinitrate ointment in treatment of anal fissure. *Lancet* **349**, 9044, 11–14.

Lunniss, P.J., Armstrong, P., Barker, P.G., Reznek, R.H. and Phillips, R.K. (1992) Magnetic resonance imaging of anal fistulae. *Lancet* **340**, 8816, 394–396.

Lunniss, P.J., Kamm, M.A. and Phillips, R.K. (1994) Factors affecting continence after surgery for anal fistula. *British Journal of Surgery* **81**, 9, 1382–1385.

Marks, C.G. and Ritchie, J.K. (1977) Anal fistulas at St Mark's Hospital. *British Journal of Surgery* **64**, 84–91.

Marks, C.G., Ritchie, J.K. and Lockhart-Mummery, H.E. (1981) Anal fistulas in Crohn's disease. *British Journal of Surgery* **68**, 525–527.

Maw, R. and von Krogh, G. (2000) The management of anogenital [correction of anal] warts. *British Medical Journal* **321**, 7266, 910–911.

Nicholls, R.J. (1996) Clinical assessment. In: Phillips, R.K.S. and Lunniss, P.J. (eds), *Anal fistula: surgical evaluation and management.* London: Chapman and Hall Medical.

Palmer, J.G., Schofield, J.H. and Shepherd, N. (1989) Anal cancer and human papillomaviruses. *Diseases of the Colon and Rectum* **32**, 1016–1022.

Parks, A.G. (1961) Pathogenesis and treatment of fistula-in-ano. *British Medical Journal* **1**, 463–469.

Parks, A.G. and Stitz, R.W. (1976) The treatment of high fistula-in-ano. *Diseases of the Colon and Rectum* **19**, 6, 487–499.

Parks, A.G., Gordon, P.H. and Hardcastle, J.D. (1976) A classification of fistula-in-ano. *British Journal of Surgery* **63**, 1, 1–12.

Patrlj, L., Kocman, B., Martinac, M., Jadrijevic, S., Sosa, T., Sebecic, B. and Brkljacic, B. (2000) Fibrin glue–antibiotic mixture in the treatment of anal fistulae: experience with 69 cases. *Digestive Surgery* **17**, 1, 77–80.

Poen, A.C., Felt-Bersma, R.J., Eijsbouts, Q.A., Cuesta, M.A. and Meuwissen, S.G. (1998) Hydrogen peroxide-enhanced transanal ultrasound in the assessment of fistula-in-ano. *Diseases of the Colon and Rectum* **41**, 9, 1147–1152.

Ramanujam, P.S. and Venkatesh, K.S. (1992) Management of acute incarcerated rectal prolapse. *Diseases of the Colon and Rectum* **35**, 12, 1154–1156.

Shukla, H.S., Gupta, S.C., Singh, G. and Singh, P.A. (1988) Tubercular fistula *in ano. British Journal of Surgery* **75**, 1, 38–39.

Sielezneff, I., Bulgare, J.C., Sastre, B. and Sarles, J.C. (1995) Result of surgical treatment of exteriorised rectal prolapse in adults. Experience of 21 years. *Annales de Chirurgie* **49**, 5, 396–402. [In French]

Speakman, C.T., Burnett, S.J., Kamm, M.A. and Bartram, C.I. (1991) Sphincter injury after anal dilatation demonstrated by anal endosonography. *British Journal of Surgery* **78**, 12, 1429–1430.

Thomson, H. (1982) The real nature of 'perianal haematoma'. *Lancet* **2**, 8296, 467–468.

Vaizey, C.J., Roy, A.J. and Kamm, M.A. (1997) Prospective evaluation of the treatment of solitary rectal ulcer syndrome with biofeedback. *Gut* **41**, 817–820.

Wassef, R., Rothenberger, D.A. and Goldberg, S.M. (1986) Rectal prolapse. *Current Problems in Surgery* **23**, 6, 397–451.

Further reading: Phillips, R.K.S. (ed.) (2001). *A companion to specialist surgical practice: Colorectal Surgery* (2nd edn). London: W.B. Saunders.

Chapter 12

Conservative Management of Faecal Incontinence in Adults

Christine Norton and Sonya Chelvanayagam

BIOFEEDBACK

Introduction

'Biofeedback' has been widely reported as a treatment for faecal incontinence. However, many authors have failed to describe their methods in any detail. Many papers give vague reference to 'supportive measures and advice' without specifying what advice is given. This chapter describes biofeedback as it has been developed in our unit at St Mark's Hospital. It is a package of care incorporating many different elements of nursing management, as appropriate for each individual (Norton and Chelvanayagam, 2001). The biofeedback service is nurse-led: the patients are referred to the nurse as primary therapist and the nurse manages each patient's care. There is open access to other colleagues to either discuss or refer for further management. Biofeedback is the therapy of first choice for patients who do not have major anal sphincter disruption (these patients are offered the option of surgery), and whose symptoms fail to respond to simple dietary measures and medication. About three hundred new patients are seen by the service each year.

Background

Biofeedback, based originally on the principles of operant conditioning, has been the subject of over a hundred papers on faecal incontinence in the English-speaking literature. Many of these describe or evaluate the treatment in children and are not be covered in this chapter. The aim of biofeedback is to give the person immediate and accurate visual or auditory feedback on bodily functions not normally consciously appreciated or controlled, with the aim of teaching or enhancing performance of those functions.

However, closer inspection of this literature reveals many methodological problems. A systematic review of controlled trials of biofeedback for faecal incontinence in adults found only five studies in adults that have employed any type of randomisation or controls. The reviewers strongly criticised the methodological quality of most of these and failed to draw any definite conclusions or recommendations for clinical practice (Norton et al., 2003). Despite this lack of controlled studies, some reviewers have concluded that biofeedback should be the treatment of first choice for faecal incontinence (Whitehead et al., 2001), with an overall cure and improvement rate of 79% on a summation of studies (Enck, 1993).

A systematic review of all forty-six studies which included four or more patients and were published in English up until the end of 2000 (Norton and Kamm, 2001) found that in those studies with data which could be analysed, 48.6% of patients were said to be cured of symptoms of faecal incontinence following biofeedback therapy and 71.7% were reported to be improved. All but one study found that some patients were improved, and only three had an overall response rate (cure and improved combined) of under 50% of patients treated. Studies varied in the method of biofeedback used, their methodological quality, criteria for success and the outcome measures used. Eight of the forty-six studies employed some form of control, but complexity of study design or brevity of reporting made it difficult to interpret the results in most instances.

Many different techniques have been used in the name of 'biofeedback' to treat faecal incontinence. Three main modalities, with many variations and many adjunctive measures, have been described. There is a wide variety of methods used within each modality, and some studies gave very little detail on the equipment or training programme used. No two studies have described exactly the same treatment as 'biofeedback'. Studies have used between one and twenty-eight sessions over two days to one year duration of therapy (Norton and Kamm, 2001).

The first method is the use of an intra-anal electro-myographic (EMG) sensor, anal manometric probe (measuring intra-anal pressure), or perianal surface EMG electrodes to teach the patient how to exercise the anal sphincter, usually as a variation of the pelvic floor muscle (or 'Kegel') exercises more commonly used for treatment of urinary incontinence (Schussler et al., 1994). Some have used this simply to demonstrate correct isolation and use of an anal squeeze in response to rectal filling or an urge to defaecate. Others have devised a programme of home exercises, and use the clinic biofeedback sessions to demonstrate correct technique and monitor progress in achievement. Early studies tended to focus on the peak muscle strength (squeeze increment) (MacLeod, 1987), while later workers have suggested that it is the overall muscle capacity (strength and endurance of the squeeze) that is important (Chiarioni et al., 1993; Patankar et al., 1997).

The second modality is the use of a 3-balloon system to 'train' the patient to correctly identify the stimulus of rectal distension and to respond without delay by immediate and forceful EAS contraction to counteract reflex inhibition of the internal anal sphincter. Some have felt that sensory delay is an important factor in faecal incontinence, and that abolishing any delay in response to the sensation of distension is the crucial element in successful therapy (Buser and Miner, 1986; Miner et al., 1990).

The third method is the use of a rectal balloon to 'retrain' the rectal sensory threshold, usually with the aim of enabling the patient to discriminate (and thus respond to) smaller rectal volumes (Miner et al., 1990). However, tolerance of larger volumes by the use of progressive distension and urge resistance is also reported (Oresland et al., 1988; Norton and Kamm, 1999b).

One study has used anal ultrasound to show patients the contraction of the anal sphincter on a screen (Solomon et al., 2000).

Two studies have attempted to evaluate the different components of biofeedback in randomised controlled trials (Latimer et al., 1984; Miner et al., 1990). Unfortunately, both had very complex designs which makes analysis of the different components impossible from the data presented, except that improving (lowering) the threshold for sensing rectal distension did seem to be beneficial in reducing symptoms (Miner et al., 1990).

There is consensus amongst many studies that lowering the threshold for discrimination of rectal sensation of distension, and synchronising voluntary external anal sphincter contraction with reflex internal anal sphincter relaxation, are both important factors in the success of biofeedback (Enck, 1993). The role of biofeedback in abolishing any delay between experiencing an urge to defaecate and contracting the anal sphincter in response to that urge is less clear, as is the role of sphincter strengthening exercises (Miner et al., 1990).

Some studies have used sphincter exercises to improve the strength (Enck et al., 1994), duration (Chiarioni et al., 1993) and speed of recruitment of the external anal sphincter, as well as the ability to contract this muscle in isolation. Others have studied asymmetry of voluntary anal sphincter contraction using vector manometry (usually measuring squeeze pressures at 8 points circumferentially within the anus) and linked symptom improvement to the development of greater symmetry of contraction (Sangwan et al., 1995). There is disagreement as to whether any of these parameters can be improved by exercises. There is also disagreement as to whether improvement of these parameters leads to symptom improvement. Uncontrolled studies have suggested marked improvement in sphincter function and symptoms (MacLeod, 1987), whereas other more rigorous studies have found that symptom improvement is unrelated to increases in anal sphincter resting or squeeze pressures (Miner et al., 1990).

All studies agree on the crucial role of patient motivation and the patient-therapist interaction. Enck concluded that 'the mode of action is obscure' (Enck, 1993). Loening-Bauke (1990) cast doubt on the efficacy of the biofeedback itself, concluding that the major effect was the 'placebo' effect of time, attention and general advice, as a time series of patients receiving biofeedback fared no better than another series receiving conventional medical therapy. It can be debated whether these elements are 'placebo' or an essential element of patient care. A recent review of studies of biofeedback for faecal incontinence found similar results were reported, whatever method of biofeedback was used, and has suggested that 'it is possible that it does not matter which treatment intervention is used' (Heymen et al., 2001). This was confirmed in a small controlled study by the same authors (Heymen et al., 2000).

There have been several studies of the efficacy of biofeedback in patients with neurological disease. Early uncontrolled studies suggested benefit in spina bifida (Whitehead et al., 1981; Wald, 1981). However, later controlled studies have shown no benefit over well-monitored conventional therapy, including use of behaviour modification techniques and medication (Loening-Baucke et al., 1988; Whitehead et al., 1986).

The biofeedback clinic

All patients attending for biofeedback at St. Mark's Hospital are sent a one-week bowel diary and a bowel symptom questionnaire (Chapter 6, pages 46–47) to fill in and bring to their first appointment. Virtually all patients comply with this, and it is helpful in several ways. Many people are not accustomed to discuss their bowel function with other people, and some with faecal incontinence have never really talked to anyone about their symptoms. It is difficult to find an acceptable vocabulary to discuss the subject, with both baby words and slang or swear words being considered unacceptable for use with a health professional. The questionnaire helps to introduce terms that will be used in the assessment interview and gives the patient the opportunity to think through the situation and describe what is actually happening. Many people comment on feeling reassured by the questionnaire that there are other people with the same (or even worse) symptoms, and that someone finally understands what the symptoms are like. The diary and questionnaire give a baseline from which to monitor progress of treatment, and can be repeated as an outcome measure.

The first assessment interview is crucial. One hour is always allowed for this, and it may take even longer if the patient is particularly distressed or has complex problems. A detailed assessment form is used to record information and to check that no important factors are missed (Chapter 6).

Subsequent follow-up appointments usually take 40–60 minutes – a one-hour slot is allowed as often the patient will have new or unresolved issues that she/he wants to discuss. Most patients have a total of 4–6 sessions at approximately four-weekly intervals.

Elements of the package

There are many different possible elements to biofeedback treatment, and it has been developed as a package of care in our unit. The elements include: therapist-patient interaction; patient teaching; support and information; exercises to attempt to strengthen the anal sphincter and supporting pelvic floor muscles; biofeedback to enhance the ability to perform the exercises, but also to give sensitivity and co-ordination training; bowel habit training and behaviour modification to teach the patient to resist urgency; advice on diet, fluids and medication; and advice on practical management of incontinence (products, skin care, odour control, toilet adaptations and personal hygiene) (Table 12.1). Not all elements are relevant to all patients. This chapter describes the retraining aspects of this package of care; Chapter 20 describes the practical coping strategies that are also suggested to patients.

Table 12.1: Elements of the biofeedback programme

Diary and symptom questionnaire
Structured assessment
1) Patient teaching
2) Emotional support
3) Lifestyle modifications
4) Management of faecal incontinence
5) Urge resistance programme
6) Anal sphincter exercises
7) Clinic computer biofeedback
8) Home biofeedback unit

Patient teaching

Following the assessment, the nurse explains normal colonic function and bowel continence and the likely physiological and emotional generation of the patient's symptoms in the light of both the results of previous tests and the assessment. A patient-orientated explanation of normal bowel function and the causes of faecal incontinence has been published elsewhere (Norton and Kamm, 1999a). It is important to phrase this explanation in terminology adapted to each individual's needs. This is often accompanied by hand drawings and the use of anatomical models (e.g. from Adam, Rouilly Ltd – address in Appendix II). The approach is one of partnership between the patient and nurse. It has long been accepted that patient teaching is more than simple information-giving that it is an ongoing process during the patient-nurse relationship (Wilson-Barnett, 1988).

If there is any difficulty with evacuating the bowels, the advice outlined in Chapter 22 will also be given. Correct defaecation posture is particularly important for any patients who are felt to be leaking stool because of inefficient bowel emptying, and nearly all of these are advised to sit with their feet supported on a footstool (see page 261).

Resisting urgency – bowel habit training

'Bladder training' has been found helpful for people with urgency and frequency of micturition (with or without proven detrusor overactivity) (Fantl et al., 1991). This is essentially a behavioural progressive urge resistance training programme and is recommended as the treatment of first choice for an unstable bladder (Agency for Health Care Policy and Research, 1996). No similar programme has been described for faecal incontinence, although logically similar mechanisms are operant. Just as the bladder and urethral sphincter are co-ordinated to work synergistically (bladder contraction causes sphincter relaxation unless this is voluntarily opposed, and sphincter contraction can inhibit bladder contraction), so the anus and rectum are connected by feedback loops to enable synergistic function.

It is logical therefore to develop a behaviour modification programme to help people with urgency of defaecation. A progressive programme of urge resistance is recommended, starting with the non-threatening situation of sitting on the toilet. The individual has to 're-learn' that urgency which is resisted will diminish with time. This can be coupled with progressive rectal balloon distension during biofeedback sessions to aid this learning process (see below). Table 12.2 (overleaf) gives the patient instructions for this programme. It may also be helpful to keep a chart during the training period.

A suggested mechanism – can urgency be learned?

It is not difficult to imagine how a person who has had the extremely unpleasant experience of faecal incontinence may 'learn' hypervigilance

Table 12.2: Holding-on programme

Currently when you need to have your bowels open you find that you have to rush to the toilet. Your rectum (where you store the stool), your sphincter muscles and your confidence need retraining to help you overcome this problem.

Next time when you need to open your bowels:

1) Sit on the toilet and hold on for 1 minute before opening your bowels. Don't forget to take a watch/clock in with you!
   Gradually increase this to 5 minutes.
   Don't worry if you're not able to do this for the first few times but keep practising.
2) When you have mastered this, repeat the above but hold on for 10 minutes before opening your bowels. It may be helpful to take something to read with you. This stage is harder but remember you're on the toilet and therefore 'safe'.
3) Once you are able to delay opening your bowels for 10 minutes whilst sitting on the toilet, now is the time to begin to move away from the toilet. Therefore the next stage is when you want to open your bowels to sit near the toilet, either on the edge of the bath or on a chair inside or just outside the toilet area. Now hold on for 5 minutes. Once you are able to do this, repeat the exercise increasing to 10 minutes.
4) When you are able to delay opening your bowels for 10 minutes whilst off the toilet, you should now gradually move further away. Maybe sitting on the bed in your bedroom. As your muscles are now becoming stronger you should be able to hold on for 10 minutes, and as you feel more confident, increase the distance between you and the toilet.

Gradually you will find that you can increase the distance and the time away from the toilet. This may take some time to master, but obviously the more practice you have at both your sphincter exercises and this programme it will happen sooner rather than later.

and hypersensitivity to bowel contents, and experience or interpret any bowel sensation as 'urgency'. The feeling of urgency may induce an emotional reaction of anxiety, even panic if there is no readily available toilet, because of the fear of a socially apparent bowel accident. Our interioceptive perception and vocabulary is not well developed – unlike the exquisite sensitivity and discriminatory abilities of the external senses, there are limited internal sensory receptors available to the conscious mind, with fairly crude and imprecise messages received (Leder, 1990). We often find it difficult, if not impossible, to verbalise internal sensations. Women seem more aware of specific body functions than men, more attentive to their inner body state, with a higher awareness of body signals (Sherr and St Lawrence, 2000). This leaves scope for misinterpretation. However, internal sensations are difficult to ignore and an aversive call almost compels action.

We are not generally in control of autonomic functions, but the viscera are influenced by our current emotional state. Mostly we learn to ignore repetitive stimuli, except where the stimulus implies danger: unpleasant stimuli grab our attention (Leder, 1990). It has been known that anxiety is a bowel stimulant for over fifty years (Almy, 1951), increasing bowel motility and propulsive contractions (Herbst et al., 1997). Thus anxiety makes incontinence even more likely. Anxiety leads the individual to pay more attention to somatic sensations, and possibly to misinterpret or over-interpret them (Whitehead, 1989). The logical and natural reaction to this urgency is to find a toilet as quickly as possible and to empty the bowel, as stool in the toilet cannot cause social embarrassment. So, rather than ignoring the call to stool as most people would if the moment is not convenient, the person with previous experience of faecal incontinence responds as rapidly as possible, not even attempting to defer for fear of provoking an accident. Eventually the individual never has the experience of an urge to defaecate that diminishes, extreme urgency is felt all the time until the bowel is emptied, and all urges to defaecate are experienced as very urgent. A vicious circle of hypersensitivity and anxiety becomes established. There is a large psychological literature showing that attention to inner feelings tends to increase the intensity and magnitude of reported symptoms and the intensity of emotions associated with them (Mechanic, 1983). Self-consciousness arises from malfunction.

This conscious or unconscious 'learned misbehaviour' has been suggested in people with the irritable bowel syndrome (Heaton et al., 1991), who have a dissociation between rectal contents and rectal symptoms and cannot discriminate a full rectum or loose stool reliably.

In addition, some people respond to this urge with a very unfocused attempt to 'hold on' – all muscles in the body are tensed – as well as holding their breath. If the anal sphincter alone is used in such circumstances, it both helps to prevent stool expulsion and, via feedback loops, will help to inhibit rectal contractions and promote retrograde propulsion of the stool (Crowell et al., 1991; Halls, 1965). However, if intra-abdominal pressure is increased by holding the breath and contracting the abdominal muscles this could be counterproductive, adding to the propulsive pressures on the stool and increasing the likelihood of incontinence. It is also observed clinically that it is much harder to contact the anal sphincter while running than when staying still, and physical activity may also stimulate gut motility.

It is known that constipation can be behaviourally induced, with deliberately ignoring the urge to defaecate resulting in slowed colonic transit and greatly reduced stool frequency (Klauser et al., 1990). Might habitual over-responding conversely result in the increased frequency, urgency and looser stool consistency so often observed in people with faecal incontinence?

When 'holding on' is learned in childhood, this is not an explicit process – we do not actually know 'how' to do it. Parents reward their children for the socially desirable behaviour of holding stool until the potty or toilet is reached, and children modify their behaviour accordingly once they have the neuromuscular and social maturity to comply. But few could describe the explicit processes involved. This makes it very hard to regain that control once it is lost – the complex neuromuscular co-ordination was never a conscious process in the first place.

This mechanism is explained to patients with urgency, many of whom identify with the panic/urgency/increased panic vicious circle and admit that they never try to defer defaecation.

Anal sphincter exercises

A review of the literature shows no evidence-based protocols for anal sphincter exercises. An exercise programme based on more general knowledge about pelvic floor exercises and clinical experience has therefore been developed. A schedule of home exercises for the anal sphincter is individualised to each patient's initial performance. This exercise programme is being evaluated in a prospective study. A balance must be struck between asking too much, with a detrimental affect on compliance and motivation, and not doing enough to effect an improvement in muscle function. The programme that has been found to be accepted by the majority of patients is given in Table 12.3 (overleaf). Instruction on the number of repetitions of each exercise is written in by hand at the first session, and then revised verbally at subsequent sessions. A combination of maximal, submaximal and fast-twitch contractions are used (omitting the submaximal where the patient has very poor initial strength).

It seems likely that any initial improvement in performance is due to activation of existing, but under-utilised, function by teaching the patient the effective use of the sphincter and by facilitating nerve pathways as well as patient understanding as a result of teaching. Increasing muscle strength, bulk, speed of reaction and endurance will usually take many weeks of consistent exercise to become apparent.

Many of the studies of biofeedback for faecal incontinence have mentioned incidentally that patients were asked to practice contractions of the anal sphincter at home, but with very little

Table 12.3: Patient instructions for anal sphincter exercises

Note: These instructions are printed in an illustrated 8-side booklet which also includes information on the continence mechanism and tips on doing the exercises. Length of squeeze and number of repetitions is individualised, depending on what is achieved at the initial assessment (The figure in brackets below is a sample.) This booklet can be downloaded from the St Mark's Hospital website (www.bowelcontrol.org.uk).

Sit comfortably with your knees slightly apart. Now imagine that you are trying to stop yourself passing wind from the bowel. To do this you must squeeze the muscle around the back passage. Try squeezing and lifting that muscle as tightly as you can, as if you are really worried that you are about to leak. You should be able to feel the muscle move. Your buttocks, tummy and legs should not move much at all. You should be aware of the skin around the back passage tightening and being pulled up and away from your chair. Some people find it helpful to imagine that they are trying to pick up a penny from the chair with their anal sphincter muscles. You are now exercising your anal sphincter. You should not need to hold your breath when you tighten the muscles!

Now imagine that the sphincter muscle is a lift. When you squeeze as tightly as you can your lift goes up to the 4th floor. But you cannot hold it there for very long, and it will not get you safely to the toilet, as it will get tired very quickly. So now squeeze more gently, take your lift only up to the 2nd floor. Feel how much longer you can hold it than at the maximum squeeze.

Practising your exercises

1) Sit, stand or lie with your knees slightly apart. Tighten and pull up the sphincter muscles as tightly as you can. Hold tightened for at least (5) seconds, and then relax for at least 10 seconds to allow the muscle to recover.

   Repeat at least (5) times. This will work on the **strength** of your muscles.

2) Next, pull the muscles up to about half of their maximum squeeze. See how long you can hold this for. Then relax for at least 10 seconds.

   Repeat at least (5) times. This will work on the **endurance**, or staying power, of your muscles.

3) Pull up the muscles as quickly and tightly as you can and then relax and then pull up again, and see how many times you can do this before you get tired. Try for at least (5) quick pull-ups.

4) Do these exercises – (5) as hard as you can, (5) as long as you can and as many quick pull-ups as you can – at least (10) times every day.

5) As the muscles get stronger, you will find that you can hold for longer than 5 seconds, and that you can do more pull-ups each time without the muscle getting tired.

6) It takes time for exercise to make muscle stronger. You may need to exercise regularly for several months before the muscles gain their full strength.

detail as to what they were actually asked to do in most reports. Those who report their instructions vary greatly as to what was suggested. There is no evidence at all on an optimal programme, and no comparisons of different programmes. There has been one small-scale report of the use of anal sphincter exercises without biofeedback, and no comparison of the outcome from the two therapies. Many studies that have used exercises as an adjunctive therapy have allowed insufficient time for muscle hypertrophy.

In contrast, there has been a relatively large literature on the use of pelvic floor exercises (PFE) in treating urinary incontinence, and the exercise programme in Table 12.3 has been devised from this work. PFE have been shown to improve both stress and urge urinary incontinence, to increase pelvic floor muscle strength and to maintain the benefit in the long term (Schussler et al., 1994). They are seen as the treatment of first choice for women with mild to moderate stress urinary incontinence (Agency for Health Care Policy and Research, 1996). However, there has been little consensus on the optimum exercise programme, and wide variations in clinical practice have been reported, with even specialist physiotherapists recommending holding a contraction between 1–30 seconds, repeated 1–50 times per session, usually hourly throughout the day (Mantle and Versi, 1991). Wells, reviewing twenty-two studies of PFE found protocols using between 15 to 160 contractions per day, from 2 to 30 seconds (10 seconds mode), with between 5 to 100 contractions at each session (Wells, 1990). A panel of four senior experts agreed on a recommended 'standard' starting programme of 5 fast twitch and 5 slow maximal contractions, 10 times per day (Continence Foundation, 2000).

PFE are based on the presumption that it is possible to both increase the capacity of existing muscle and to hypertrophy the muscle (aerobic and anaerobic capacity) (Palmer, 1997). Strong repeated exercise increases muscle bulk, and prolonged contraction at moderate intensity increases endurance. Griffin has suggested that any performance improvement within the first 3–4 weeks of exercise is the result of improved activation of existing muscle capacity, teaching the patient how to recruit and use existing muscle most effectively (i.e. improved neuromuscular co-ordination); hypertrophy might take up to twelve weeks to become apparent, and can continue for several months after this (Griffin et al., 1994). Exercise can improve both resting and squeeze pressures in the pelvic floor (Griffin et al., 1994).

It has also been shown that teaching patients 'the knack' of using the pelvic floor muscles appropriately to counteract anticipated rises in abdominal pressure (e.g. coughing or sneezing) can significantly reduce urinary stress incontinence within one week (Miller et al., 1996). It is possible that the same principle applies in teaching patients to use the anal sphincter appropriately to resist the urge to defaecate. Simple explanation of the continence mechanism and how to contract the anal sphincter in isolation from abdominal effort seems to make a big difference for some patients. Only 60% of women are able to generate an effective pelvic floor contraction after written or verbal instruction; up to one quarter will practise counter-productively (i.e. strain) until taught the correct action digitally (Bump et al., 1991).

Wilson has found a possible preventive role for exercises. Women taught exercises postnatally had significantly lower rates of faecal incontinence than controls (4.4% vs. 10.6%) at twelve months after childbirth (Wilson et al., 1997).

Computer-assisted biofeedback

Biofeedback gives the person immediate feedback about normally subconscious body processes. Equipment is used to detect and amplify a physiologic response (Burgio and Engel, 1990). Biofeedback training is usually given with the patient lying in a lateral position, having a clear view of a computer screen which gives an immediate and clear view of pressure readings from a small air-filled manometric probe inserted into the anus in a standard position (PRS 9600, Hollister Inc.). This equipment was chosen because it is widely available to Nurse Continence Advisers and specialist continence physiotherapists in the UK. It is not as expensive as that needed for some of the 3-balloon systems popular in the USA (Schuster, 1977).

Firstly, the anal probe and feedback is used to help the patient to identify an anal sphincter contraction. Once this is achieved successfully, a range of exercises (maximal, submaximal and fast-twitch – see Figures 12.1–12.4) are practised, with plenty of verbal encouragement to improve performance. Typically, patients will initially produce a transient anal sphincter contraction which cannot be sustained beyond a few seconds. It is explained that, as the smooth muscle internal anal sphincter is inhibited reflexly for 10–20 seconds when the rectum fills, this current contraction of the external sphincter is not long enough to maintain continence until the internal sphincter has closed off again. The aim is to squeeze harder and for longer (Figure 12.5). Most people hold their breath to start with, and are encouraged to 'breathe while they squeeze'. Patients are also encouraged to experiment to find how to produce an optimum contraction. The primary effort should not be abdominal wall contraction, although it is likely that some abdominal effort is synergistic with maximal contraction (Sapsford et al., 1997; Laycock et al., 2001). Many comment that it is helpful to 'see what you are doing'. It is especially difficult for people with very weak muscle tone to tell if the correct action is produced without this biofeedback, as a weak muscle contraction gives limited direct feedback. It is essential to create awareness before exercises can be practised effectively (Burgio et al., 1986). Performance can be re-checked at each session to monitor correct practice and progress.

It is thought that biofeedback augments the effectiveness of pelvic floor exercises for urinary incontinence (Agency for Health Care Policy and Research, 1996). There are no comparative trials of exercises and biofeedback for faecal incontinence.

Balloon distension training is performed with a clinic-made rectal balloon attached to a 50 ml syringe (see Chapter 8). The balloon is introduced into the rectum via the anal canal. Progressive balloon distension is used for people with an oversensitive rectum. The balloon is inflated slowly to the point of an urge to defaecate, when filling is stopped. The patient is then encouraged to relax and is distracted by conversation. One to two minutes later the nurse enquires if the urge is still as strong. Very often it is not, and filling of the balloon is recommenced until the patient again experiences urgency. This process is repeated until the patient reaches a volume at which the urge does not diminish with time, or the urge becomes uncomfortable. The air is then let out of the balloon. This can be repeated several times during a session. The aim is for the patient to 're-learn' that the urge will diminish if it is resisted. There is only one case report in the literature of this balloon distension, used successfully for a single patient with severe diarrhoea (Schiller et al., 1979). However, in our clinical practice we have found this progressive distension useful.

Conversely, where there is a problem with an insensitive rectum, progressive balloon deflation can be used. The balloon is inflated to the sensory threshold and then repeated inflation at progressively lower volumes are made, while asking the patient to indicate when the air is felt. Some people are able to learn to discriminate lower and lower volumes. If rectal sensation is felt sooner, then the appropriate response of external anal sphincter contraction can be made. This has often been reported as the most important element in the success of biofeedback (Buser and Miner, 1986; Miner et al., 1990; Whitehead et al., 1980).

It is also possible to use surface EMG electrodes on the external anal sphincter and to ask the patient to squeeze as soon as the inflating balloon is felt. This helps to train co-ordination between rectal filling and appropriate sphincter response (contraction), and to attempt to abolish any apparent delay between sensation and response (especially important for those at-

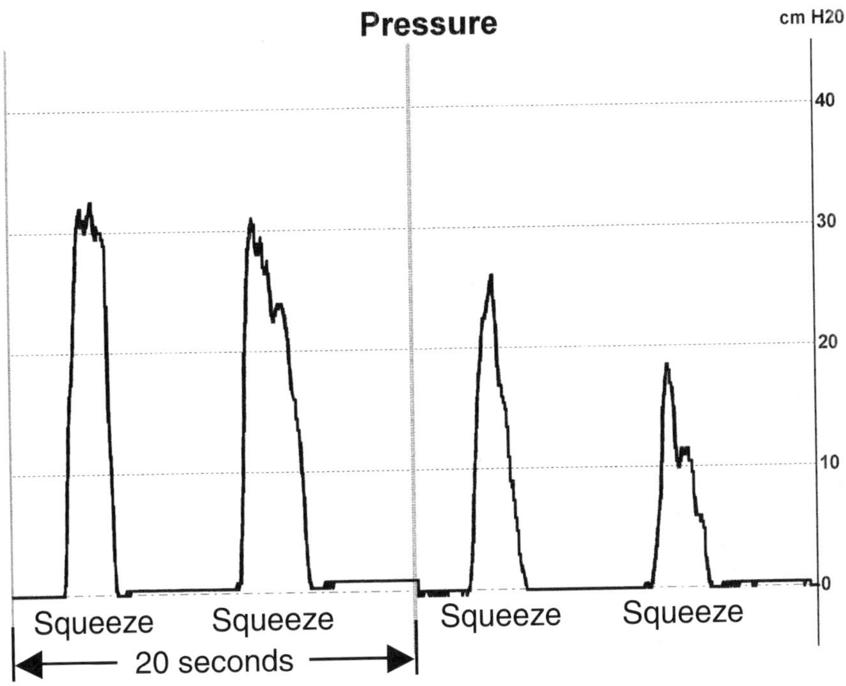

Figure 12.1 *Maximal contraction. Note: Patient is asked to squeeze as hard as they can and hold. Note successive fatigue with each squeeze.*

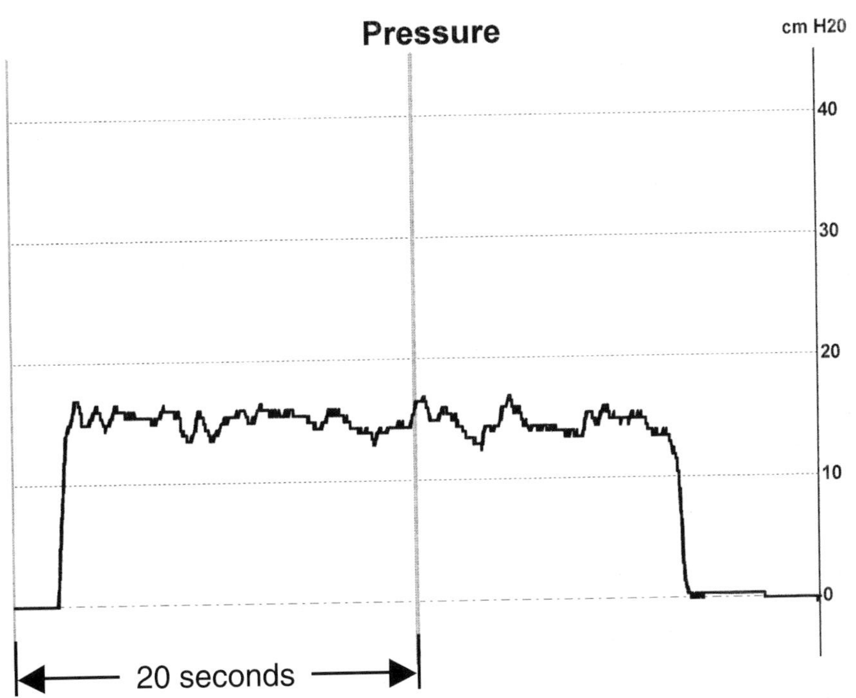

Figure 12.2 *Sub-maximal contraction. Note: Patient is asked to 'squeeze half way and hold as long as possible'.*

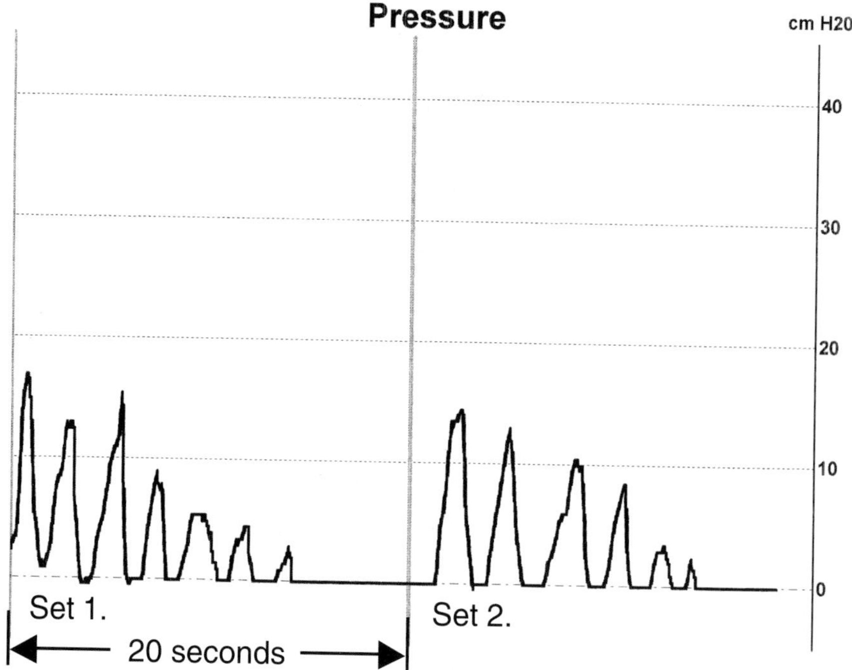

Figure 12.3 *Fast-twitch contractions. Note: Patient is asked to squeeze and relax as hard and as quickly as possible.*

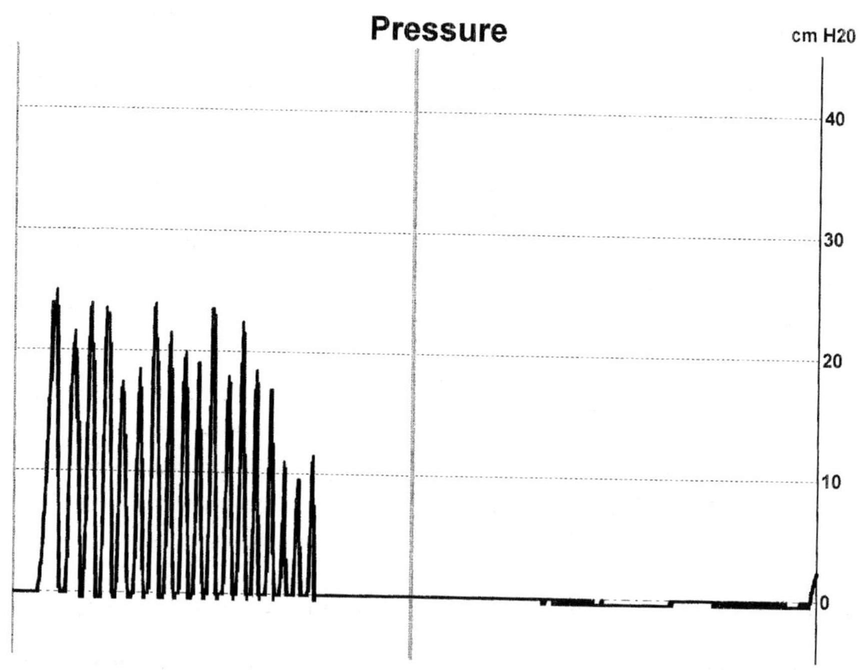

Figure 12.4 *Fast-twitch contractions after training. Note: Contractions are much faster and with less fatigue than in Fig. 12.3.*

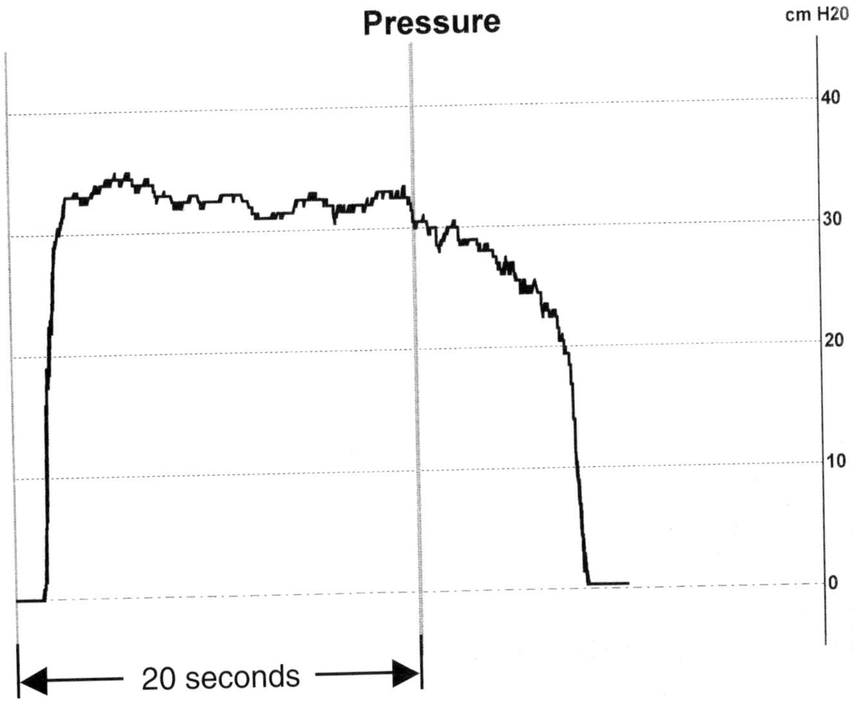

Figure 12.5 *Sustained maximal contraction after exercise programme.*

tempting to control loose stool or flatus) (Buser and Miner, 1986). A 2- or 3-balloon system is also available to allow rectal distension and monitor anal reaction. This system allows the therapist to show the patient the transient anal relaxation upon rectal distension (recto-anal inhibitory reflex) and instruct the patient on how to increase anal squeeze pressure to counteract this.

For people with ineffective evacuation, the trace from the electrodes can be used to teach appropriate relaxation on attempted balloon expulsion (simulated defaecation) and abolish any paradoxical anal contraction or 'anismus' (Preston and Lennard-Jones, 1985) (see Chapter 22). Surface EMG electrodes on the abdominal muscles can help the patient to distinguish sphincter contraction from abdominal effort and to isolate the anal sphincter.

Biofeedback sessions are usually for up to one hour at 2–4 weekly intervals, depending upon the patient's understanding and progress, and practical issues such as travelling time and work or family commitments. Many authors have used weekly sessions, but this has been found impractical for many patients. Also, as progress often takes 2–4 months to become apparent, it leads to a high number of sessions before any improvement is noted, and hence to patient and therapist discouragement and demotivation. Patients are advised not to expect instant results.

There is an increasing number of home biofeedback units available on the market. It is not known whether these enhance the effectiveness of an exercise programme. As these units are relatively expensive they are not used routinely, but they are helpful for selected patients who have difficulty in locating the correct action for the exercises and who benefit from continued feedback between clinic sessions.

Conclusions on biofeedback

An evaluation of the package of care described above found that two-thirds of patients were cured or improved in the short term (Norton and

Kamm, 1999b). Long-term results are not yet available. Patients with urge incontinence of faeces were more likely to respond that those with passive soiling, and those with intact anal sphincters derived most benefit. However, even some patients with disruption of both internal and external anal sphincters considered their symptoms 'cured' at the end of therapy. However, a subsequent controlled study, comparing patients who received advice, teaching and information (Chapter 20) with those who also did exercises, had biofeedback plus exercises or biofeedback exercises and a home exercise machine, found no significant differences in outcome between the different groups (Norton, 2001; Norton et al., 2002). It is not known which are the effective elements of the care – further work is needed to evaluate aspects of care and to characterise those patients most likely to respond. This package of care can be adopted by nurses in a variety of settings, including colorectal units and continence clinics.

ELECTRICAL STIMULATION FOR FAECAL INCONTINENCE

The first published report of electrical stimulation having an effect for faecal incontinence comes from (Caldwell, 1963), who reported the case of a 60-year-old woman who had been faecally incontinent for twenty-three years and had undergone multiple surgical operations without success. Caldwell surgically implanted electrodes in the anal sphincter, activated by an external battery stimulator, which was intended to keep her continent by continuous stimulation. However, the batteries ran down frequently, so this soon became 2–3 hours per day and within four months the stimulator was no longer needed as she had regained complete control. He later reported (Caldwell, 1965) that the same method successfully controlled rectal prolapse and faecal incontinence, although it was not clear if stimulation could be discontinued (i.e. did the stimulation control symptoms, or was there a therapeutic effect?).

Subsequently needle EMG and an anal plug electrode were tried (Hopkinson and Lightwood, 1966; Hopkinson, 1975; Keighley and Fielding, 1983), with encouraging initial results.

Sylvester and Keilty (1987) reported a pilot study of interferential stimulation in 7 women. Treatment was given 3 times per week for a total of 12 sessions using four suction electrodes (two on the thighs, two on the posterior superior iliac spine, aiming for cross-over of interferential current at the anal sphincter). The regime was 10 minutes of 10–100 Hz swing, followed by 10 minutes of 45–90 Hz at maximum tolerated mA. One month later both resting and squeeze pressures had increased, but only 2 of the 7 had any symptomatic benefit, and this was short-lived. Interferential stimulation is seldom used for this indication today.

Mills et al. (1990) used skin electrode stimulation for patients mostly with proven pudendal neuropathy and faecal incontinence, some of whom had had previous unsuccessful surgery and/or physiotherapy. Of 20 patients who completed therapy 6 were continent, 3 much improved, 4 improved, 4 slightly improved, 3 were the same. Some of the improved patients regressed once treatment stopped. The best results were with patients who had external sphincter weakness; poorer results were obtained with internal sphincter or both sphincter weakness. Overall, 65% who completed were improved.

Fox et al. (1991), have reported that surface perianal stimulation in the laboratory can increase the strength of voluntary anal sphincter contraction (measured by simultaneous manometry) by 30–40%. They emphasised the importance of selecting the correct frequency (10–20 Hz for resting tone and endurance, 30–60 Hz for squeeze tone). They used a home battery stimulator with a fixed pulse width of 300 microseconds and other variable parameters. The stimulation was given via an internal or skin electrode, with an indifferent lumbosacral electrode. Of 49 attendees 38 (77.5%) gained complete clinical continence and 3 improved and were continuing treatment, i.e. a failure rate of 16.3%. It is not clear from the report how many of these received the electrical stimulation, which was part of a package of conservative treatments including biofeedback, cones, dietary advice, exercise and medication.

Pescatori et al. (1991) report 15 consecutive patients referred for faecal incontinence (10 women, 5 men, mean age 42 years) who received transanal electrical stimulation. All had previously tried dietary measures, antidiarrhoeal agents and pelvic floor exercises (30 daily contractions of 30 seconds each). A stimulator with an anal plug at 20 Hz, and with a stimulus duration of 10 seconds, with an indifferent electrode on the flank was used for 30 minutes per day for 10 consecutive days. With electrical stimulation symptoms improved in 10, with marked improvement in 4 of these, but none became totally continent. The poorest results were in the most severe cases. There was no change in resting tone or rectal sensation, but a significant improvement in voluntary contraction in responders, with no change in non-responders. One responder relapsed at six months, but improved again with a further course, and one non-responder improved by using the stimulator at home for one month. Ten days would not be considered by many as sufficient time for this therapy.

Scheuer et al. (1994) report disappointing results in ten female patients aged a mean of 53 years with neurogenic (pelvic floor denervation on EMG) faecal incontinence. All had total incontinence without any sensation of urge and had little or no voluntary squeeze. Two patients reported some improvement, with a return of the feeling of urge and ability to defer defaecation for 10–15 minutes. The other eight were unchanged. There was no significant change in resting or squeeze pressures. However, in an editorial comment following this article, Rowedder suggests that there would be very little hope of improvement in this denervated group and that the stimulation parameters were not correct for denervated muscle.

Electrical stimulation parameters

There have been significant advances in both understanding of the effect of electrical stimulation on muscle and nerve, and in the technology to deliver stimulation. Frequency of the current measures the number of pulses per second (pps) or cycles per second (cps), expressed in Hertz (Hz). Pulse width is measured in microseconds (expressed as microseconds that the pulse remains positive for). Longer pulses are generally more uncomfortable (hence the well-recognised discomfort associated with faradism). 250 microseconds is a commonly-accepted pulse width. Denervated muscle needs very long pulse widths to activate it (over 300 microseconds) and this is painful. Electrical stimulation is generally felt by sensory nerves before the muscle starts to contract; discomfort often decreases once the contraction starts.

Slow twitch muscle (‘red muscle’, Type 1 fibres) form approximately 70–80% of the levator ani; Type 2 fast-twitch fibres (‘white’) approximately 20–30%, with some intermediate fibres. The external anal sphincter is similarly composed. Slow twitch muscle is naturally stimulated by the anterior horn cells at 5–20 pps. The natural firing frequency for fast twitch fibres, used only in circumstances requiring extra force or speed, is 20–60 pps. Stimulation between 10–20 Hz will therefore cause a smooth tetanic contraction of Type 1 fibres, but will have limited, if any, effect, on Type 2 fibres. Stimulation at higher frequencies should affect both types of fibres, and above about 35 Hz there will be almost no perceptible relaxation between pulses. At 50 Hz there should be a smooth tetanic contraction. It is possible to convert fast to slow muscle by continuous stimulation at low frequency, but it soon reverts once stimulation is discontinued. Choice of frequency is really a balance of comfort vs. effectiveness. Higher frequencies are more comfortable at a given intensity, but will cause fatigue more quickly. This can be partly ameliorated by selecting a duty cycle with sufficient rest periods; the weaker the muscle is, the longer the rest periods should be.

It is known that if there has been partial denervation (e.g. during childbirth) there will be some neronal sprouting and reinnervation by adjacent nerves. Electrical stimulation could interfere with this process, as it is known to enhance neuronal axonal sprouting. For this reason it is usual to wait at least six weeks after any injury before starting electrical stimulation, and then to commence on low frequencies.

There are many possible pulse shapes, for example square or ramped, and there is no evidence as to which shape is most effective or comfortable. To prevent fatigue, it is now accepted that a duty cycle which alternates several seconds of stimulation on with several seconds off, and off time greater than or equal to on time, is desirable. The weaker the muscle, the greater off time needed to prevent fatigue. It is also possible to ramp onset and the end of the current to increase comfort. A 20% ramp is built into some machines. Patients tend to tolerate a more intense current with ramping.

Resistance is encountered at the electrode/tissue interface (measured in ohms). Resistance is lower at moist, as opposed to dry, surfaces and will therefore be less with an intra-anal probe than with surface skin electrodes.

Contraindications to the use of electrical stimulation include a pacemaker or other electrical implant, pregnancy, within six weeks of obstetric anal sphincter injury, inflammatory bowel disease, painful perianal conditions and radiation proctitis. It is customary not to use stimulation with patients with malignancies in the UK (although this is not true elsewhere), and, as blood pressure can rise, this should be monitored in patients with a heart condition.

Conclusions on electrical stimulation

There are many methodological problems with the published literature, such that it is reasonable to conclude that electrical stimulation for faecal incontinence has never been properly evaluated in a controlled manner. A recent review of controlled trials of electrical stimulation (Hosker et al., 2000) found only one controlled trial in the world literature. There are no controlled studies comparing different stimulation parameters, or active with sham stimulation. Most studies have been very small. Many of the studies have used inappropriate stimulation parameters – particularly too low a frequency – for optimum effect. Some have not even stated their parameters. Many have used very few treatments, or over a period of time too short to reasonably expect change. Some have used home exercise as well (often instructions not stated), so it is not possible to tell which has an effect. Only one study has compared biofeedback and exercise with adjunctive electrical stimulation, but in this study different therapists were used to compare vaginal biofeedback with anal biofeedback plus electrical stimulation, and so electrical stimulation was not the only variable; the difference in outcome found could have been the effect of a different therapist or biofeedback method (Fynes et al., 1999).

In conclusion, given the reasonable success rates of electrical stimulation for urinary incontinence (Schussler et al, 1994), this is a treatment modality which warrants proper investigation.

Conclusions

Biofeedback and electrical stimulation are suitable treatment modalities for most patients with faecal incontinence. Conservative measures will be the first line of treatment for the majority of patients. They can also be used as a adjunct to surgery or where previous surgery has failed to resolve symptoms.

References

Agency for Health Care Policy and Research (1996) *Urinary incontinence in adults: acute and chronic management*. 96–0682. Rockville, Maryland, USA: US Department of Health and Human Services.

Almy, T.P. (1951) Experimental studies on the irritable colon. *American Journal of Medicine* **10**, 60–67.

Bump, R.C., Hurt, W.G., Fantl, J.A. and Wyman, J.F. (1991) Assessment of Kegel pelvic muscle exercise performance after brief verbal instruction. *American Journal of Obstetrics and Gynecology* **165**, 322–329.

Burgio, K.L. and Engel, B.T. (1990) Biofeedback-assisted behavioral training for elderly men and women. *Journal of the American Geriatrics Society* **38**, 338–340.

Burgio, K.L., Robinson, J.C. and Engel, B.T. (1986) The role of biofeedback in Kegel exercise training for stress urinary incontinence. *American Journal of Obstetrics and Gynecology* **154**, 58–64.

Buser, W.D. and Miner, P.B. (1986) Delayed rectal sensation with faecal incontinence. Successful treatment using anorectal manometry. *Gastroenterology* **91**, 1186–1191.

Caldwell, K.P.S. (1963) The electrical control of sphincter incompetence. *Lancet* **ii**, 174–175.

Caldwell, K.P.S. (1965) A new treatment for rectal prolapse. *Proceedings of the Royal Society of Medicine* **58**, 792.

Chiarioni, G., Scattolini, C., Bonfante, F. and Vantini, I. (1993) Liquid stool incontinence with severe urgency: anorectal function and effective biofeedback treatment. *Gut* **34**, 1576–1580.

Continence Foundation (2000) *Pelvic floor exercises*. London: Continence Foundation.

Crowell, M.D., Bassotti, G., Cheskin, L.J., Schuster, M.M. and Whitehead, W.E. (1991) Method for prolonged ambulatory monitoring of high amplitude propagated contractions from the colon. *American Journal of Physiology* **261**, G263–G268.

Enck, P. (1993) Biofeedback training in disordered defaecation. A critical review. *Digestive Diseases and Sciences* **38**, 1953–1960.

Enck, P., Daublin, G., Lubke, H.J. and Strohmeyer, G. (1994) Long-term efficacy of biofeedback training for faecal incontinence. *Diseases of the Colon and Rectum* **37**, 997–1001.

Fantl, J.A., Wyman, J.F., McClish, D.K., Harkins, S.W., Elswick, R.K., Taylor, J.R. and Hadley, E.C. (1991) Efficacy of bladder training in older women with urinary incontinence. *Journal of the American Medical Association* **265**, 609–613.

Fox, J., Sylvestre, L. and Freeman, J.B. (1991) Rectal incontinence: a team approach. *Physiotherapy* **77**, 665–672.

Fynes, M.M., Marshall, K., Cassidy, M., Behan, M., Walsh, D., O'Connell, P.R. and O'Herlihy, C. (1999) A prospective, randomised study comparing the effect of augmented biofeedback with sensory biofeedback alone on fecal incontinence after obstetric trauma. *Diseases of the Colon and Rectum* **42**, 753–758.

Griffin, C., Dougherty, M.C. and Yarandi, H. (1994) Pelvic muscles during rest: responses to pelvic muscle exercise. *Nursing Research* **43**, 164–167.

Halls, J. (1965) Bowel content shift during normal defaecation. *Proceedings of the Royal Society of Medicine* **58**, 859–860.

Heaton, K.W., Ghosh, S. and Braddon, F.E.M. (1991) How bad are the symptoms and bowel dysfunction of patients with the irritable bowel syndrome? A prospective, controlled study with emphasis on stool form. *Gut* **32**, 73–79.

Herbst, F., Kamm, M.A., Morris, G.P., Britton, K., Woloszko, J. and Nicholls, R.J. (1997) Gastrointestinal transit and prolonged ambulatory colonic motility in health and faecal incontinence. *Gut* **41**, 381–389.

Heymen, S., Pikarsky, A.J., Weiss, E.G., Vickers, D., Nogueras, J.J. and Wexner, S. (2000) A prospective randomised trial comparing four biofeedback techniques for patients with faecal incontinence. *Colorectal Disease* **2**, 88–92.

Heymen, S., Jones, K.R., Ringel, Y., Scarlett, Y. and Whitehead, W.E. (2001) Biofeedback treatment of fecal incontinence: a critical review. *Diseases of the Colon and Rectum* **44**, 728–736.

Hopkinson, B.R. (1975) Electronic activation of the sphincters in the treatment of rectal prolapse. *Proceedings of the Royal Society of Medicine* **68**, 21–22.

Hopkinson, B.R. and Lightwood, R. (1966) Electrical treatment of anal incontinence. *Lancet* **1**, 297–298.

Hosker, G., Norton, C. and Brazzelli, M. (2000) Electrical stimulation for faecal incontinence in adults. *Cochrane Database of Systematic Reviews* [computer file] **2**, CD001310 (www.cochrane.org).

Keighley, M.R.B. and Fielding, J.W.L. (1983) Management of faecal incontinence and results of surgical treatment. *British Journal of Surgery* **70**, 463–468.

Klauser, A.G., Voderholzer, W.A., Heinrich, C.A., Schindlbeck, N.E. and Mueller-Lissner, S.A. (1990) Behavioural modification of colonic function – can constipation be learned? *Digestive Diseases and Sciences* **35**, 1271–1275.

Latimer, P.R., Campbell, D. and Kasperski, J. (1984) A components analysis of biofeedback in the treatment of faecal incontinence. *Biofeedback and Self-Regulation* **9**, 311–324.

Laycock, J., Chiarelli, P., Haslam, J., Lavender, R., Mann, K. and Naylor, D. (2001) Pelvic floor exercises: are we teaching them correctly? *Neurourology and Urodynamics* **20**, 427–428. [Abstract]

Leder, D. (1990) *The absent body*. Chicago: University of Chicago Press.

Loening-Baucke, V. (1990) Efficacy of biofeedback training in improving faecal incontinence and anorectal physiologic function. *Gut* **31**, 1395–1402.

Loening-Baucke, V., Desch, L. and Wolraich, M. (1988) Biofeedback training for patients with myelomeningocele and faecal incontinence. *Developmental Medicine and Child Neurology* **30**, 781–790.

MacLeod, J.H. (1987) Management of anal incontinence by biofeedback. *Gastroenterology* **93**, 291–294.

Mantle, J. and Versi, E. (1991) Physiotherapy for stress incontinence: a national survey. *British Medical Journal* **302**, 753–755.

Mechanic, D. (1983) Adolescent health and illness behavior: review of the literature and a new hypothesis for the study of stress. *Journal of Human Stress* **9**, 4–13.

Miller, J.M., Ashton-Miller, J.A. and DeLancy, J.O.L. (1996) The knack: a precisely timed pelvic muscle contraction can be used within a week to reduce leakage in urinary stress incontinence. *Gerontologist* **36**, 328.

Mills, P.M., Deakin, M. and Kiff, E.S. (1990) Percutaneous electrical stimulation for ano-rectal incontinence. *Physiotherapy* **76**, 433–438.

Miner, P.B., Donnelly, T.C. and Read, N.W. (1990) Investigation of the mode of action of biofeedback in the treatment of faecal incontinence. *Digestive Diseases and Sciences* **35**, 1291–1298.

Norton, C.S. (2001) Biofeedback and nursing management for adults with faecal incontinence. Unpublished PhD thesis: Kings College, London.

Norton, C. and Kamm, M.A. (1999a) *Bowel control – information and practical advice*. Beaconsfield: Beaconsfield Publishers.

Norton, C. and Kamm, M.A. (1999b) Outcome of biofeedback for faecal incontinence. *British Journal of Surgery* **86**, 1159–1163.

Norton, C. and Kamm, M.A. (2001) Anal sphincter biofeedback and pelvic floor exercise for faecal incontinence in adults – a systematic review. *Alimentary Pharmacology and Therapeutics* **15**, 1147–1154.

Norton, C., Hosker, G. and Brazzelli, M. (2003) Effectiveness of biofeedback and/or sphincter exercises for the treatment of faecal incontinence in adults. *Cochrane electronic library* (www.cochrane.org).

Norton, C. and Chelvanayagam, S. (2001) Methodology of biofeedback for adults with fecal incontinence – a program of care. *Journal of Wound, Ostomy and Continence Nursing* **28**, 156–168.

Norton, C., Chelvanayagam, S. and Kamm, M.A. (2002) A randomised controlled trial of biofeedback for faecal incontinence. *Gut* **50**, supplement 11, A61, Abstract 221.

Oresland, T., Fasth, S., Nordgren, S., Swenson, L. and Akervall, S. (1988) Does balloon dilatation and anal sphincter training improve ileo-anal pouch function? *International Journal of Colorectal Disease* **3**, 153–157.

Palmer, M.H. (1997) Pelvic muscle rehabilitation: where do we go from here? *Journal of Wound, Ostomy and Continence Nursing* **24**, 98–105.

Patankar, S.K., Ferrara, A., Larach, S.W., Williamson, P.R., Perozo, S.E., Levy, J.R. and Mills, J. (1997) Electromyographic assessment of biofeedback training for faecal incontinence and chronic constipation. *Diseases of the Colon and Rectum* **40**, 907–911.

Pescatori, M., Pavesio, R., Anastasio, G. and Daini, S. (1991) Transanal electrostimulation for faecal incontinence: clinical, psychologic and manometric prospective study. *Diseases of the Colon and Rectum* **34**, 540–545.

Preston, D.M. and Lennard-Jones, J.E. (1985) Anismus in chronic constipation. *Digestive Diseases and Sciences* **30**, 413–418.

Sangwan, Y.P., Coller, J.A., Barrett, R.C., Roberts, P.L., Murray, J.J. and Schoetz, D.J., Jr. (1995) Can manometric parameters predict response to biofeedback therapy in fecal incontinence? *Diseases of the Colon and Rectum* **38**, 1021–1025.

Sapsford, R.R., Hodges, P.W. and Richardson, C.A. (1997) Activation of the abdominal muscles is a normal response to contraction of the pelvic floor muscles. *Proceedings of the International Continence Society* Yokohama, Japan, Abstract **117**, pp. 31–32.

Scheuer, M., Kuijpers, H.C. and Bleijenberg, G. (1994) Effect of electrostimulation on sphincter function in neurogenic fecal continence. *Diseases of the Colon and Rectum* **37**, 590–593.

Schiller, L.R., Santa Ana, C., Davis, G.R. and Fordtran, J.S. (1979) Faecal incontinence in chronic diarrhoea: report of a case with improvement after training with rectally infused saline. *Gastroenterology* **77**, 751–753.

Schussler, B., Laycock, J., Norton, P. and Stanton, S. (1994) *Pelvic floor re-education: principles and practice*. London: Springer-Verlag.

Schuster, M.M. (1977) Biofeedback treatment of gastrointestinal disorders. *Medical Clinics of North America* **61**, 907–912.

Sherr, L. and St Lawrence, J. (2000) *Women, health and the mind*. Chichester: John Wiley & Sons.

Solomon, M.J., Rex, J., Eyers, A.A., Stewart, P. and Roberts, R. (2000) Biofeedback for fecal incontinence using transanal ultrasonography: novel approach. *Diseases of the Colon and Rectum* **43**, 788–792.

Sylvester, K.L. and Keilty, S.E.J. (1987) A pilot study to investigate the use of interferential in the treatment of ano-rectal incontinence. *Physiotherapy* **73**, 207–208.

Wald, A. (1981) Biofeedback therapy for faecal incontinence. *Annals of Internal Medicine* **95**, 146–149.

Wells, T.J. (1990) Pelvic (floor) muscle exercise. *Journal of the American Geriatrics Society* **38**, 333–337.

Whitehead, W.E. (1989) Effects of psychological factors on gastrointestinal function. In: Snape, W.J. (ed.) *Pathogenesis of functional bowel disease*, pp. 37–53. New York: Plenum Medical Book Company.

Whitehead, W.E., Engel, B.T. and Schuster, M.M. (1980) Perception of rectal distension is necessary to prevent faecal incontinence. *Advances in Physiological Science* **17**, 203–209.

Whitehead, W.E., Parker, L.H., Masek, B.J., Cataldo, M.F. and Freeman, J.M. (1981) Biofeedback treatment of faecal incontinence in patients with myelomeningocele. *Developmental Medicine and Child Neurology* **23**, 313–322.

Whitehead, W.E., Parker, L., Bosmajian, L., Morrill-Corbin, E.D., Middaugh, S., Garwood, M., Cataldo, M.F. and Freeman, J. (1986) Treatment of fecal incontinence in children with spina bifida: comparison of biofeedback and behavior modification. *Archives of Physical Medicine and Rehabilitation* **67**, 218–224.

Whitehead, W.E., Wald, A. and Norton, N.J. (2001) Treatment options for fecal incontinence: consensus conference report. *Diseases of the Colon and Rectum* **44**, 131–144.

Wilson, P.D., Herbison, G.P., Glazener, C.M.A., Lang, G., Gee, H. and MacArthur, C. (1997) Postnatal incontinence: a multicentre randomised controlled trial of conservative treatment. *Neurourology and Urodynamics* **16**, 349–350.

Wilson-Barnett, J. (1988) Patient teaching or patient counselling? *Journal of Advanced Nursing* **13**, 215–222.

Chapter 13

Bowel Care in Old Age

Danielle Harari

Introduction

Both constipation and faecal incontinence are frequent health concerns for elderly people. The number of general practitioner visits for constipation increase markedly among people over 65 years, and one-third of community-dwelling elderly people use laxatives regularly. Self-reported constipation in older people has been associated with anxiety, depression and poor health perception, while clinical constipation in frail individuals may lead to serious complications such as faecal impaction, sigmoid volvulus (twisting of the sigmoid colon, which is an acute abdominal emergency), and urinary retention. Few medical symptoms cause as much distress and social isolation as faecal incontinence, a condition which places older people at greater risk of morbidity, dependency, hospital admissions and nursing home placement.

Epidemiology of constipation in older people

The commonly held belief that constipation is an inevitable consequence of getting older stems partly from questionnaire studies showing a marked increase in self-reported constipation with age. Thirty-four per cent of women and 26% of men aged over 65 and living at home report constipation (Donald et al., 1985; Talley et al., 1992; Whitehead et al., 1989). This preponderance of women over men is seen up until the eighth decade, when the sexes become more equal in prevalence (Donald et al., 1985; Talley et al., 1992; Whitehead et al., 1989; Harari et al., 1996). Yet, despite this high rate of subjective constipation in older people, there is no reduction in actual frequency of bowel movements with ageing; 1–7% of both young and older community-dwellers report two or fewer bowel movements a week (Harari et al., 1996; Harari et al., 1997). This consistent bowel pattern in relation to age persists even after statistically adjusting for the greater amount of laxatives used by elderly people (Harari et al., 1997). This suggests that bowel-related symptoms other than infrequent bowel movements drive self-reporting of constipation in older people.

The symptoms reported are in fact straining and passage of hard stools. Of older individuals who report constipation, 65% report persistent straining, and 39% report hard bowel movements, implying that they are suffering primarily from difficulties with rectal evacuation (Talley et al., 1992; Harari et al., 1997). The current standardised definitions of constipation appropriately incorporate specific bowel symptoms, instead of using subjective self-reporting (Table 13.1). By these definitions, functional constipation affects 17% and rectal outlet delay 21% of people who live in their own home aged 65 years and over (Talley et al., 1992).

Constipation in the nursing home is an even greater problem, with 47% of residents reporting constipation, 17% having two or fewer bowel movements per week, and 30% reporting persistent straining (Harari et al., 1994). Nursing home residents with constipation are at high risk of developing faecal impaction and overflow incontinence. Indeed, faecal impaction is the main reason for hospitalisation in 27% of frail older people admitted to hospital (Read et al., 1985). Over half of nursing home residents nevertheless take laxatives at least once daily, prompting speculation that non-pharmacological approaches to manage constipation may

Table 13.1: Current standardised definitions of constipation

Functional or slow-transit constipation

2 or more of the following symptoms present for at least 3 months:

2 or fewer bowel movements per week

Straining on more than 1 in 4 occasions

Hard stools on more 1 in 4 occasions

Feeling of incomplete evacuation on more than 1 in 4 occasions

Rectal outlet delay

Feeling of anal blockage on more than 1 in 4 occasions *and*

Prolonged defaecation (>10 minutes to complete bowel movement)

OR

Need for self-digitation (pressing in or around the anus to aid evacuation) on any occasion

be under-utilised in this setting (Harari et al., 1995; Brocklehurst et al, 1999).

Epidemiology of faecal incontinence in older people

Faecal incontinence affects 3–18% of people aged 65 and over living at home, and up to 30% of those in the acute hospital setting (Prosser et al., 1997; Tobin et al., 1986; Chassagne et al., 1999). The prevalence of faecal incontinence increases markedly beyond the age of 80. However, only one in eight of older individuals with daily faecal incontinence will volunteer the problem to their general practitioner (Prosser et al., 1997) and, regrettably, doctors and nurses do not routinely enquire about the symptom. This hidden problem therefore leads to social isolation and a downward spiral of psychological distress, dependency and poor health. The condition takes its toll on carers also; faecal incontinence surpasses even dementia as a leading reason for requesting nursing home placement. Within nursing homes, up to 52% of residents suffer from faecal incontinence, yet only 4% of chronically incontinent long-term care patients are referred to their general practitioners for assessment of this problem (Tobin et al., 1986). A recent study observed that over a 10-month period, 20% of nursing home patients with no prior history of faecal incontinence developed the condition in long-term care (Chassagne et al., 1999).

The ageing bowel / pathogenesis of constipation and incontinence

Gut transit time and colonic motility are actually no different in healthy elderly and young subjects, supporting the epidemiological findings of a consistent bowel pattern with ageing (Loening-Baucke and Anuras, 1984). In contrast, elderly people with chronic illness reporting constipation have prolonged total gut transit time of 4–9 days (normal < 3 days), with evacuation being most strikingly delayed through the lowest part of the large bowel and the rectum. Nursing home residents have even more prolonged transit times of up to three weeks in those least mobile, making them highly susceptible to slow-transit constipation and overflow faecal incontinence (Brocklehurst et al., 1983). Colonic function appears to be more influenced by factors associated with ageing (such as chronic disease, immobility and medications), than by ageing itself.

Ano-rectal function in healthy older people is characterised by a tendency towards an age-related reduction in internal anal sphincter tone (resting pressure), and a more definite decline in external anal sphincter and pelvic muscle strength, especially in older women who have had children (McHugh and Diamant, 1987). There are several types of ano-rectal abnormalities in older people with constipation or faecal incontinence:

Ano-rectal problems

Dyschezia

Most commonly seen in frail elderly people is rectal dyschezia, characterised by reduced tone, increased compliance and impaired sensation, such that a greater degree of rectal distension is required to induce the defaecatory mechanism (Read et al., 1985). These patients have recurrent rectal impactions, a frequent consequence of which is faecal soiling. Faecal soiling affects 28% of older people, and is a symptom rarely elicited by doctors or nurses (O'Keefe and Talley, 1991).

Pelvic dyssynergia

Patients with rectal outlet delay may have pelvic dyssynergia, also termed 'anismus', which is failure to relax the pelvic and external sphincter muscles during attempted defaecation. The decline in strength in these muscles seen with ageing, particularly in women, further contributes to evacuation difficulties.

Irritable bowel syndrome

Some patients with a longstanding history of constipation will have increased rectal tone and reduced compliance indicative of irritable bowel syndrome; these patients often complain of difficult passage of small faecal pellets, and abdominal pain and distension relieved by defaecation (O'Keefe and Talley, 1991).

Other abnormalities

Ano-rectal abnormalities leading to faecal incontinence are external anal sphincter and pelvic floor weakness (most commonly due to pudendal neuropathy caused by a combination of childbirth trauma and age-related attrition), and weakness of the internal anal sphincter due to conditions such as diabetes mellitus (Camilleri, 1996) or spinal cord disease, or to specific ano-rectal disease (e.g. rectal prolapse).

Causes of constipation in older people (Table 13.2)

Immobility is a primary risk factor, and greater physical activity in elderly people reduces the symptoms of constipation. Constipation is a common side effect of drug therapy in older people. The drugs most implicated are iron supplements, calcium supplements, calcium channel blockers, opiates, and non-steroidal anti-inflammatory drugs. Another important group of drugs affecting the bowel are those with anticholinergic properties (e.g. antipsychotics, tricyclic antidepressants, oxybutynin) which may induce irreversible colonic laxity with long-term use (Harari et al., 1995).

Patients with neurological diseases often rank constipation as being the foremost symptom affecting their quality of life. Patients with Parkinson's disease in particular suffer severe evacuation difficulties from both slow-transit constipation and pelvic dyssynergia (Edwards et al., 1992). Patients who have had diabetes for many years commonly develop autonomic neuropathy, where intrinsic nerve pathways throughout the body, including the gut wall, become damaged (Camilleri, 1996). These individuals are markedly constipated, with bacterial overgrowth in the sluggish gut causing further problems of nocturnal diarrhoea.

Low dietary fibre intake is common in older people and is a potentially modifiable factor. Older people are especially prone to dehydration through impairment of the thirst sensation – a low fluid intake slows gut transit and reduces stool output. Metabolic imbalances of hypothyroidism, kidney failure, low potassium level and high calcium level are identified through simple blood tests and should not be overlooked, particularly in severe cases of con-

Table 13.2: Causes of constipation in older people

Slow-transit constipation

Immobility

Drugs: anticholinergic agents (antidepressants, antipsychotics, oxybutynin), opiates, iron supplements, calcium supplements, calcium-channel blockers, aluminium-containing antacids, diuretics

Neurological diseases: Parkinson's disease, diabetes mellitus, stroke

Dietary deficiencies: low intake of fibre/ carbohydrate, dehydration

Metabolic problems: hypothyroidism, kidney failure, hypercalcaemia, hypokalaemia

Colon tumour

Rectal outlet delay

Sacral cord disease

Dementia

Depression

Lack of privacy

Ano-rectal disease

Weak abdominal muscles

Self-reported constipation

Misperceptions regarding bowel habit

Anxiety / depression

stipation. Patients with depression and dementia may ignore the urge to move their bowels, predisposing them to recurrent rectal impactions which stretch and desensitise the rectum, ultimately leading to rectal dyschezia. Older patients frequently have weak abdominal muscles, limiting their ability to push down effectively during defaecation. Diminishing height with age may mean that it is no longer possible to sit on the toilet with the feet well-supported, making effective abdominal effort more difficult (see Chapter 22). Sometimes the simple provision of a footstool can make a great difference to the ability to evacuate the rectum effectively.

Causes of faecal incontinence in older people

A primary cause of faecal incontinence in elderly patients is overflow incontinence secondary to constipation and stool impaction. This is a treatable, preventable and frequently overlooked condition. Overflow has been shown to be the underlying problem in 52% of nursing home residents with longstanding faecal incontinence (Tobin and Brocklehurst, 1986); all too often untreated overflow incontinence leads to acute hospitalisation for these frail older patients.

Dementia-related incontinence is caused by lack of voluntary control by the brain over the external sphincter in combination with a loss of awareness of the need for continence, often misunderstanding the environment and with difficulty in communicating needs. Dementia affects 46% of nursing home residents with chronic faecal incontinence (Tobin and Brocklehurst, 1986). These individuals are very commonly incontinent of urine also (Johanson et al., 1997).

Functional incontinence occurs in individuals who are unable to access the toilet in time, due to impairments in mobility, dexterity, communication or vision. These patients may even have normal lower gut function. The functional aspect is also a significant factor in nursing homes where immobility – and in particular the need for assistance in transferring from bed to chair – greatly increases the risk of incontinence (Brocklehurst et al, 1983; Johanson et al., 1997). Those who are dependent on carers to assist with toileting may feel too embarrassed to ask for help when it is needed and so defer defaecation. Confusion may affect memory of the location of the toilet or how/why to ask for assistance. Toileting regimens may not match an individual's natural bowel habit. Repeated delay will eventually lead to harder stools which are difficult to evacuate.

Older patients with external anal sphincter weakness (possibly related to previous obstetric trauma or age-related changes) will have varying degrees of incontinence depending on the laxity of the muscle, but even a slightly weakened sphincter will be easily overwhelmed by a very loose stool (Johanson et al., 1997). The more common (and reversible) causes of loose stools in this population are excessive use of laxatives (in particular Codanthramer (Brocklehurst et al., 1999) and agents administered to prepare the bowel for diagnostic procedures such as Picolax), lactose intolerance (associated with symptoms of bloating and cramping after taking milk products), dietary factors (bran, caffeine, fruit sugars), and antibiotic-related diarrhoea.

Assessment and diagnosis of constipation and faecal incontinence

Assessment of bowel problems in an older person should also include a comprehensive evaluation of the patient's physical and psychosocial functioning, in order to identify all contributing factors. For an objective measurement of bowel pattern, have the patient or carer keep a simple stool chart for one week to document frequency, consistency and continence.

Table 13.3 lists the important aspects of assessment for constipation. A careful bowel symptom history will point to whether constipation is largely slow-transit (i.e. the stool does not get to the rectum) or due to rectal outlet delay (i.e. the stool is not evacuated from the rectum). The two often coexist. Some frailer patients with constipation may not report any bowel-related symptoms, and may even have regular bowel movements despite significant impaction. This emphasises the importance of a thorough and objective bowel assessment in all older people with risk factors, especially in acute hospital and nursing home settings.

An empty rectum on digital rectal examination does not exclude the diagnosis of constipation; a plain abdominal radiograph is needed where clinical suspicion (such as a positive bowel symptom history) is present. The presence of faeces in the caecum on an abdominal X-ray (Figure 13.1) correlates well with prolonged transit time, and is a 'spot diagnosis' for slow-transit constipation in the present author's clinical experience. The radiograph is also useful in diagnosing colonic dysmotility (Figure 13.2), as well as acute complications of constipation such as bowel obstruction from impaction (Figure 13.3), and sigmoid volvulus.

Table 13.4 summarises the clinical evaluation of faecal incontinence in older people, with emphasis on comprehensive evaluation of the individual. There is much room for improvement in this clinical area; observation of practice suggests a lack of thoroughness by doctors and nurses in assessing faecal incontinence in older people in all settings (community, acute hospital, and nursing home), with failure to obtain an accurate symptom history or to perform rectal examinations.

It is helpful to document the type of incontinence. Constant leakage of loose stool or stool-stained mucus is associated with overflow around an impaction. Patients with dementia-related incontinence often pass complete bowel movements, especially after meals in response to the gastrocolic reflex (a reflexic response to food or drink in the stomach enhancing muscular activity of the large bowel). Patients with

Table 13.3: Assessment and diagnosis of constipation in older people

Bowel history

Number of bowel movements per week

Stool consistency

Straining / symptoms of rectal outlet delay

Duration of constipation

Faecal / urinary incontinence

Abdominal pain relieved by evacuation

Rectal pain or bleeding

Laxative use, prior and current

General history

Mood and cognition
Symptoms of systemic illness (e.g. weight loss, malaise)
Diet

Specific physical examination

Digital rectal examination including sphincter tone

Perianal sensation / cutaneous anal reflex

Abdominal palpation, auscultation

Tests

Indications for plain abdominal radiograph:
Empty rectum with clinical suspicion of constipation
Possible faecal impaction
Evaluation for bowel dysmotility / redundant sigmoid loop / volvulus

Indications for colonscopy or barium enema:
Systemic illness (weight loss, anaemia etc.)
New-onset faecal impaction without prior history of constipation

Blood tests:
Full blood count, potassium, urea, creatinine, glucose and calcium levels, thyroid function

weakness of the anal sphincters tend to leak small amounts of stool – where external anal sphincter weakness predominates the patient often reports urgency prior to leaking, while those with internal sphincter laxity tend to have unconscious leakage of stool (Kamm, 1998).

Evaluation of toilet access should be multidisciplinary and include a broad functional assessment, e.g. the Barthel Index (Collins et al., 1988), vision test (count fingers), upper limb dexterity assessment (undoing buttons), and cognitive measure (e.g. Mini-Mental State Examination (Folstein et al., 1975). The health care provider should be aware of the physical layout of the patient's home, and in particular bathroom details (location, distance from main living area, width of doorway for accommodating walking aids, presence of grab rails or raised toilet seat). Low lighting levels, high degree of clutter and hard-to-manage clothing

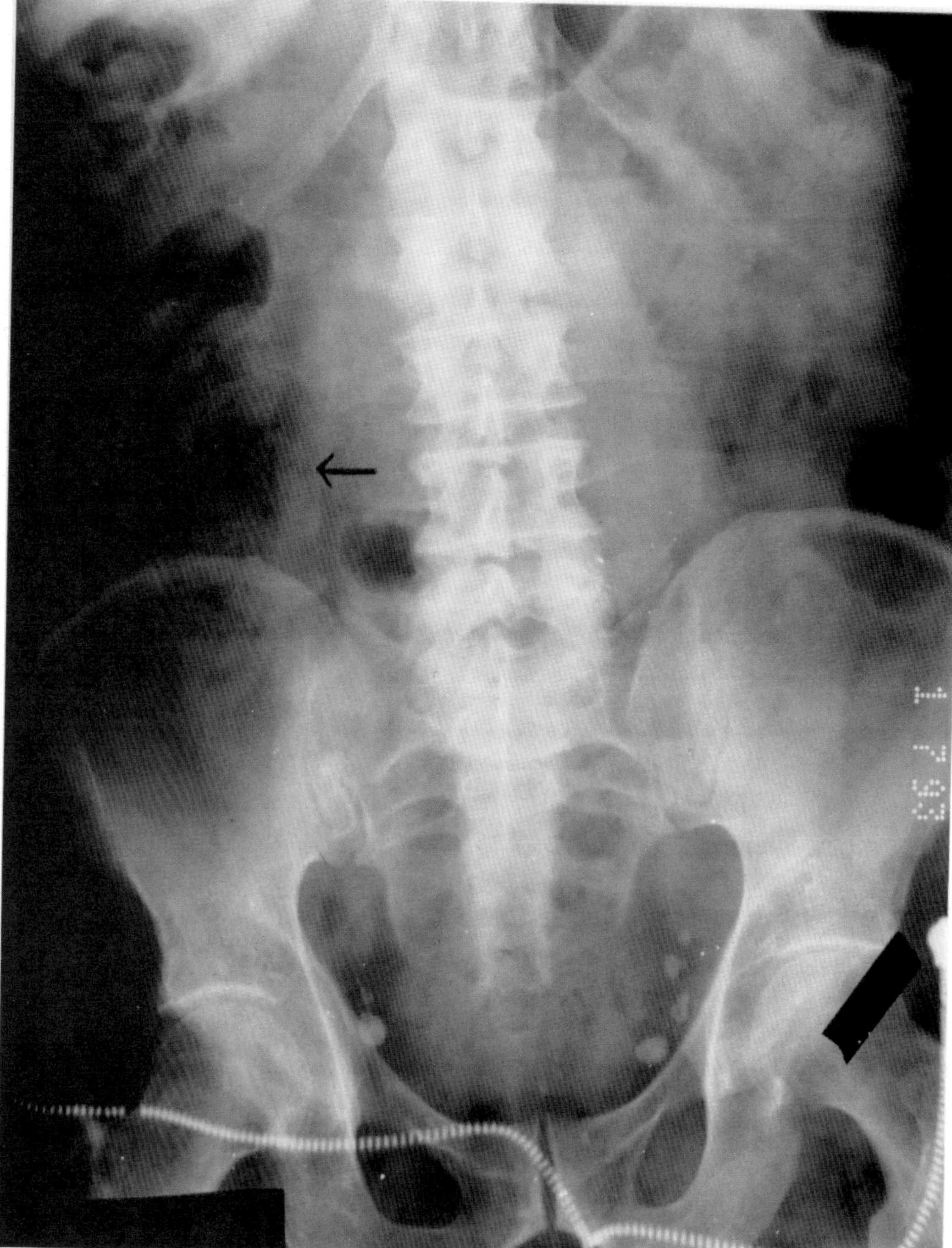

Figure 13.1 *Abdominal radiograph of a 73-year-old man with chronic schizophrenia who has taken anticholinergic psychiatric drugs for many years. This was his third hospital admission for colonic impaction. The arrow points to the caecum, which is full of stool. Faecoliths are visible in the pelvic region as roundish calcifications.*

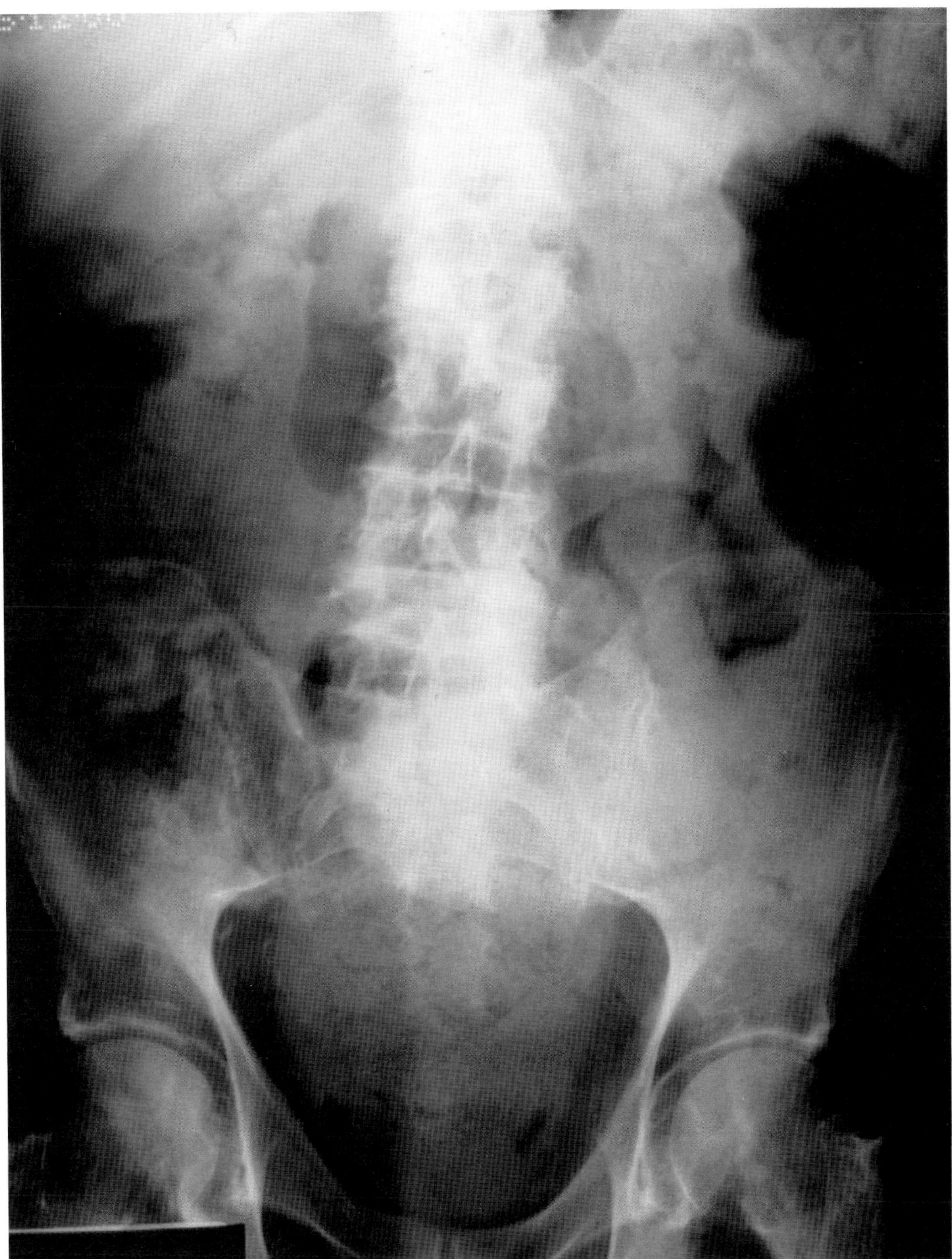

Figure 13.2 *Abdominal radiograph of a 79-year-old woman who suffered a stroke six months previously. She has symptoms of rectal outlet delay and slow-transit constipation. The rectum contains a large bolus of hard stool, and there is moderate stool retention in the caecum and right-sided colon. The colon shows excess gas shadows with dilatation of large and small bowel and a smooth gut outline on the left suggesting chronic bowel dysmotility.*

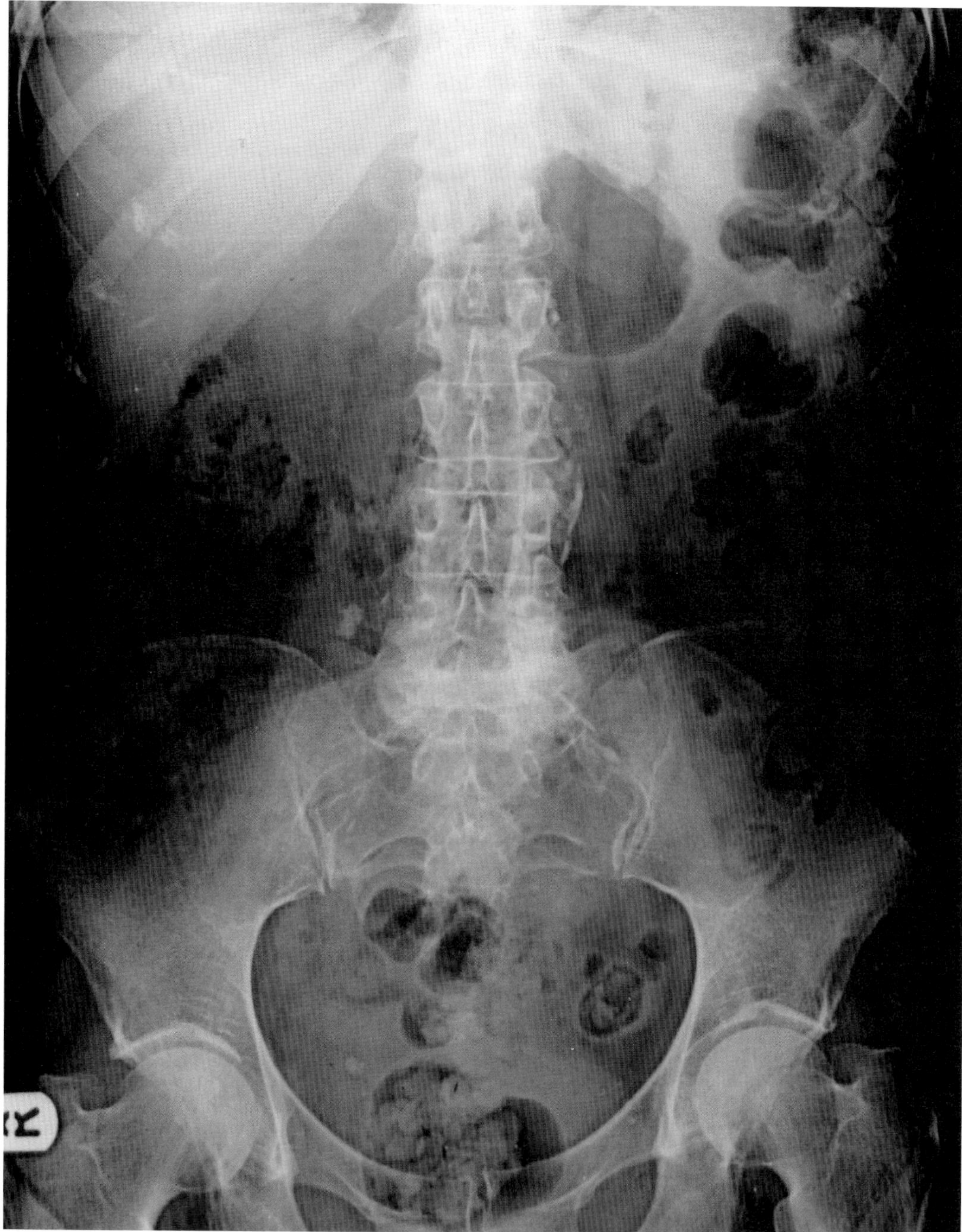

Figure 13.3 *Abdominal radiograph of an 83-year-old man with Parkinson's disease and symptoms of continuous faecal leakage. As his carer at home, his wife was changing his clothing up to six times a day. The rectum and lower colon are completely impacted with stool, and the dilated loop of bowel on the left side of the film implies obstruction. He was admitted to an intermediate care centre and treated with enemas and laxatives, resulting in complete resolution of his incontinence.*

Table 13.4: Assessment and diagnosis of faecal incontinence in older people

Emphasis in older people is on a *structured clinical approach* to identify all contributing factors for faecal incontinence

History

Duration of faecal incontinence

Frequency of episodes

Type (soiling, small amounts, complete bowel movement)

Stool consistency

Stool-stained mucus

Passive or urge faecal incontinence

Constipation symptoms / current laxative use

Systemic illness (confusion, depression, weight loss, anaemia)

Antibiotic use

General examination

Abbreviated Mental Status Examination (score of 6 or less out of 10 suggests significant cognitive impairment)

Mood assessment (for depression)

Neurological profile

Toilet access

Evaluate ability to use toilet based on muscle strength, coordination, vision, limb function, and cognition

Place in context of current living environment

Specific examination

Abdominal inspection for distension and tenderness

Perineal inspection for skin breakdown, dermatitis, surgical scars

Observe for excessive downward motion of the pelvic floor when asking patient to bear down in the lateral lying position

Digital examination for stool impaction

Digital examination for evaluation of impaired sphincter tone –
- Anal gaping, and/or easy insertion of finger (internal sphincter)
- Reduced squeeze pressure (external sphincter)

Ask patient to strain while sitting on commode and observe for rectal prolapse

Tests

An abdominal Xray should be performed to look for stool impaction in the colon

In the case of diarrhoea – send stool sample for culture, including *C. difficile*

Blood tests for full blood count, glucose, urea and electrolytes, thyroxine may also be relevant, as well as observation of the process of getting to and onto the toilet and assessment of stability and safety (support, stability and safety) (Faden, 2002).

Digital examination can assess anal sphincter tone reasonably well. Easy finger insertion with gaping of the anus on finger removal indicates poor internal sphincter tone, while reduced squeeze pressure around the finger when asking the patient to 'squeeze and pull up' suggests external sphincter weakness. A rectal examination is also essential for identifying stool impaction.

It should be noted that impaction may be with hard or soft stool. All incontinent patients without evidence of rectal stool impaction should ideally undergo a plain abdominal X-ray to establish or rule out the diagnosis of overflow (Figure 13.3). Diarrhoea persisting for more than two days requires medical evaluation for the presence of infection and other causes.

Complications of constipation and faecal incontinence

Overflow faecal incontinence is the most important complication of constipation in older people because it is both common and preventable. In addition to overflow incontinence, clinical features of stool impaction in older patients are anorexia, abdominal discomfort and distension, unexplained fever, confusion, and importantly in frailer patients, a non-specific clinical deterioration.

Faecalomas are stool pellets which have been retained in the colon for so long that they have become calcified (Figure 13.1). They are seen in constipated patients with diverticular disease. These pellets may rarely perforate the bowel (stercoral perforation of the colon), causing acute abdominal pain and a high mortality.

Sigmoid volvulus occurs when the lower part of the colon, distended with stool and gas, twists upon itself, compromising its mesenteric blood supply. Treatment with a flatus tube to remove the gas and 'straighten out' the twisted colon is often effective. Rarely, patients may need surgical intervention. Patients with neurological disease affecting the gut (such as Parkinson's disease), those with psychiatric disease and long-term users of anticholinergic drugs are at greatest risk of this complication.

Prolonged straining at stool can result in rectal prolapse, which may in turn lead to problems with incontinence. A large rectal impaction can impinge on the bladder neck and cause significant urinary retention and incontinence.

Complications of faecal incontinence include pressure sores, dermatitis, urinary tract infections, and most importantly, psychosocial distress for both patient and carer.

Treatment of constipation

Non-pharmacological treatment of constipation in older people

It seems likely that much constipation in older adults could be prevented by attention to diet, fluid intake, mobility, and ensuring toilet access with privacy and similar measures. In mild constipation, elderly people should be treated initially with non-pharmacological measures, and these should remain the mainstay of treatment even when laxatives are necessary (Table 13.5). Education as to what constitutes normal bowel habit corrects patient misperceptions, and thereby may address self-reported constipation in some cases. In those with clinical constipation, toileting habits should be assessed with emphasis placed on comfort and privacy, particularly in institutional settings. Individuals should be encouraged to attempt defaecation within half an hour of breakfast to take advantage of the gastrocolic reflex. Where straining is predominant, elevation of the legs while seated on the toilet will facilitate more effective use of the abdominal muscles.

Increasing dietary bran has been associated in a systematic review with increased stool weight and decreased transit time in healthy and constipated adults (Tramonte et al., 1997). Coarse bran, although more effective than refined fibre

Table 13.5: Non-pharmacologic treatment of constipation

Education

What constitutes normal bowel habit / correction of misperceptions

Misuse of laxatives

Toileting

Comfort and privacy

15–30 minutes after breakfast (gastrocolic reflex)

Straining

Treat haemorrhoids and other ano-rectal conditions

Elevation of legs onto footstool while seated on toilet

Fibre

Crude fibre intake of 6–10 grams with adequate fluid intake

Bloating, flatulence and irregular bowel habit may reduce compliance

Raw bran may cause malabsorption of calcium and iron

Fluids

Minimum intake of 1500 ml (approx. 8 glasses) of fluid per day

Increase intake in summer, and in acute illness

Exercise

Regular exercise program within functional limitations

Regular erect posture maintenance in bedridden patients

Medications

Eliminate, reduce the dosage, or substitute other medications for those which predispose to constipation eg. nortriptyline for amitriptyline

Metabolic disturbances

Restore normal levels

Physical disimpaction

Manual disimpaction for rectal impaction – use scissoring action of fingers, may need local anaesthetic (e.g. lidocaine jelly) to reduce discomfort in softening stool, is less palatable, and may significantly reduce calcium and iron absorption from the gut. Dietary fibre should therefore be recommended to older people in the form of wholegrain bread, fresh fruit, seeded berries, vegetables, beans, lentils, etc. Porridge, baked beans and fruit such as prunes or rhubarb may be acceptable and palatable. Caution should be exercised and fibre introduced gradually, as it can result in significant abdominal distension, discomfort and flatulence in patients with slow colonic transit. Daily fluid intake should be at least 1500 ml to avoid dehydration (in the absence of medical restrictions), and a programme of regular exercise should be encouraged, within individual functional limitations. Positioning immobile elderly patients out of bed and into a chair for up to 60-minute periods (with chair-lifts at 15-minute intervals for prevention of pressure ulcers) may have similar beneficial effects. Daily exercise in bed and the use of abdominal massage have been shown to reduce laxative and enema use in chairfast geriatric long-stay patients, although transit time was unaffected (Resende et al., 1993). Increasing the oportunities to use the toilet has been found to increase defaecation in the toilet (Ouslander et al., 1996).

Laxative and enema treatment of constipation in older people

Currently the annual cost of laxative prescriptions in the UK is approaching £50 million, costing the National Health Service more than anti-hypertensive or diabetic drugs (Petticrew et al., 1997). There have been very few comparative studies of laxatives in the elderly, and the published trials generally lack statistical power because of insufficient patient numbers (Petticrew et al., 1997). Table 13.6 summarises the pharmacological treatment of constipation in older people in the form of guideline protocols. The following summarises available information on the most commonly used laxatives in the elderly:

Senna as a stimulant laxative works through direct stimulation of the nerves within the gut wall, both enhancing transit and softening stool. Studies have shown senna to be safe in elderly people, and it is the preferred stimulant laxative for treatment of slow-transit constipation (Passmore et al., 1993).

Codanthramer should generally be avoided as it causes unpleasant perineal skin irritation in patients with faecal or urinary incontinence, and has recently been associated with increased risk of incontinence in nursing home residents (Brocklehurst et al., 1999).

Bisacodyl may cause nausea and electrolyte imbalance if taken by mouth, but is useful in suppository form for treating rectal outlet delay.

Bulk laxatives (e.g. Fybogel) work by drawing in water, whilst being resistant to bacterial breakdown. They hasten transit, soften and bulk stool, and have been shown to facilitate rectal evacuation in older people (Tramonte et al., 1997). They may cause transient bloating and flatulence, and a good fluid intake is needed to avoid colonic retention of bulky stool. Whilst currently under-prescribed, bulk laxatives should be considered the first-line laxative in treatment of chronic constipation in elderly people.

Lactulose is an osmotic laxative which helps to retain fluid in the gut lumen. It has been shown to prevent constipation in frail nursing home residents, and to effectively treat chronic constipation in ambulatory older patients. Lactulose may cause bloating and abdominal discomfort, especially if taken in combination with a high fruit intake.

Polyethylene glycol (Movicol) is a more potent osmolar laxative which appears to effectively and safely treat faecal impaction in elderly nursing home residents (Puxty et al., 1986). It is as effective and better tolerated than sodium picosulphate in older people as a bowel preparation for colonoscopy or barium enema.

Suppositories may help to initiate defaecation. One or two glycerin suppositories are often sufficient. Bisacodyl suppositories provide added chemical stimulation if needed.

Enemas are useful for acute disimpaction and for preventing recurrent impactions in people

Table 13.6: Pharmacological treatment of constipation in older people

Slow-transit constipation

Bulk laxative 1–3 times daily with fluids to achieve comfortable evacuation at least 3 times weekly

In less mobile individuals, in those with questionable fluid intake, or in people intolerant of bulk laxatives, give lactulose 15–30 ml 1–2 times daily

If constipation symptoms persist, *add* senna 1–3 tablets at bedtime

Rectal outlet delay

Manual disimpaction where necessary, followed by a tap water, phosphate or sodium citrate enema for initial clearance

Glycerine suppository once weekly to once daily after breakfast as required to achieve comfortable evacuation

If symptoms persist, change to bisacodyl suppository every other day

Bulk laxative once daily to soften stool and facilitate emptying

Colonic faecal impaction

Arachis oil retention enema daily for 3 days for initial disimpaction

Check daily for signs of bowel obstruction i.e. nausea or vomitting, abdominal discomfort, abdominal distension, reduced or absent bowel sounds. Continue giving daily enemas without laxatives until signs of obstruction resolve.

When obstruction resolves, give senna 2–3 tablets at bedtime *and* lactulose 30 ml twice daily. Continue daily tap-water enemas until there is no further result.

If stool retention persists, give polyethylene glycol (Movicol) ½–1 sachet daily with fluids and daily tap-water enemas until clear.

When impaction resolves, continue maintenance regimen of senna 2 tablets at bedtime and lactulose 10–30 ml twice daily to prevent recurrence.

with hypotonic bowel or rectum. It may be necessary to use an enema to disimpact the rectum prior to commencing oral therapy. *Phosphate* enemas should be used with caution in people with renal failure (no more than once weekly), and likewise *sodium citrate* enemas (Micolette) may worsen oedema in patients with heart failure because of their high salt content. *Tap water* enemas are the safest method when repeated enemas are required in elderly people. *Arachis oil* retention enemas can be very helpful for moving hard impacted stool, even when patients have trouble retaining the fluid due to weak sphincter muscles.

Treatment of faecal incontinence

The Royal College of Physicians working party on incontinence concluded that faecal incontinence is poorly managed in current clinical practice (RCP, 1996), and this view has been supported by several researchers observing care directed toward older patients with incontinence in acute care hospitals, nursing homes and general practice surgeries.

There are very few published trials of treatment of faecal incontinence in older people. Tobin and Brocklehurst (1986) evaluated a therapeutic intervention in 52 nursing home

Table 13.7: Management of faecal incontinence in older people

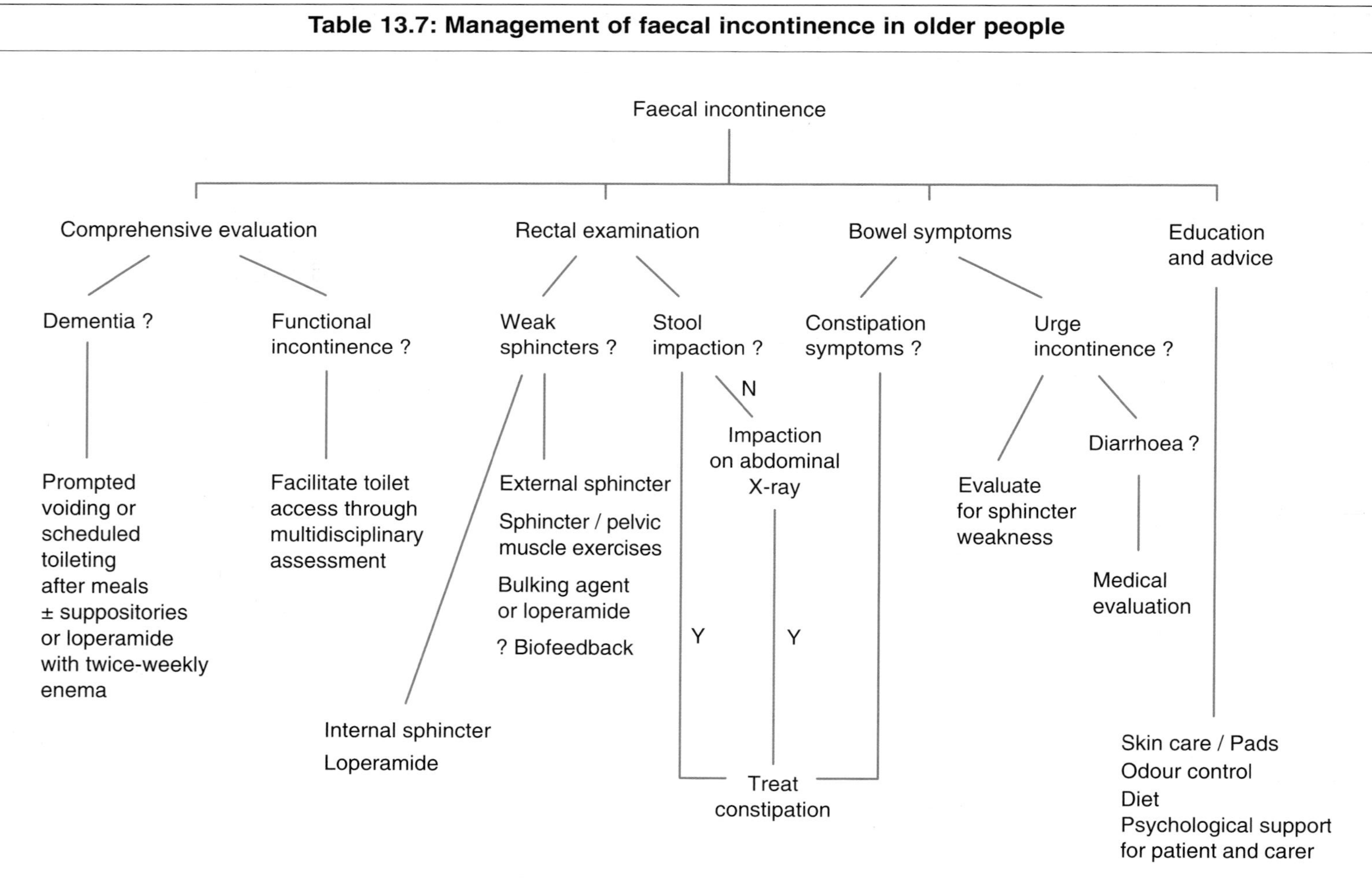

residents with faecal incontinence, based on treatment recommendations to primary care physicians. The researchers classified patients with rectal impaction and continuous faecal soiling as having overflow and recommended treatment with enemas until no further response, followed by lactulose; complete resolution of incontinence was achieved in 94% of those in whom full treatment compliance could be obtained. Another nursing home study found that treatment of constipation was only effective in improving overflow incontinence in 206 elderly residents when long-lasting and complete rectal emptying could be achieved using daily lactulose, daily suppositories and weekly tap-water enemas (Chassagne et al., 2000). These studies emphasise the therapeutic importance of a thorough and complete bowel programme for patients with overflow incontinence. It seems likely that measures to prevent or treat chronic constipation have a major role in preventing subsequent impaction with faecal incontinence.

Treatment of dementia-related incontinence depends on the severity of cognitive impairment. Prompted voiding should be attempted in those with mild to moderate dementia. Ouslander et al. (1996) showed that prompted voiding programmes significantly increased the number of continent bowel movements in an uncontrolled study of elderly nursing home residents with dementia-related incontinence over a period of a few weeks. The nursing literature suggests however that guidelines on prompted voiding for patients with faecal incontinence are frequently not adhered to in current practice, particularly in the acute hospital setting. Scheduled toileting after meals, aided by suppositories to ensure more complete emptying, is the next step-wise approach, followed by a bowel programme of controlled evacuation in those with persistent incontinence. Tobin and Brocklehurst (1986) evaluated such a bowel programme in the nursing home, consisting of daily codeine phosphate and twice-weekly enemas; continence was achieved in 75% of those fully treated. Use of loperamide as a constipating agent (e.g. 2 mg at night) is an alternative approach. However, this must be monitored carefully to ensure that impaction does not develop.

In patients with external sphincter weakness, there is some evidence that biofeedback and sphincter and pelvic floor muscle strengthening exercises have a clinically beneficial effect (Norton et al., 2000). However, this approach is unlikely to help more than a minority of highly selected older patients who have intact cognition, good motivation and preserved ano-rectal sensation. Judicious use of loperamide (in the absence of constipation) has been shown to make the problem of faecal incontinence secondary to internal anal sphincter dysfunction more manageable (Sun et al, 1997).

A crucial aspect of managing bowel incontinence in older patients is providing education and advice to patients and their carers.

Self-management through dietary change (e.g. limiting or increasing – depending on causation – caffeine, fruit etc.), pelvic muscle strengthening exercises, bowel retraining, and dose-response manipulation of bowel medications (laxatives, suppositories or loperamide) should be strongly encouraged through using written materials combined with face-to-face teaching. Health promotion research shows that self-management education of older people with chronic medical illnesses improves self-esteem and general health perception, regardless of whether disease-related clinical outcomes also improve. Advice on skin care, odour control and continence aids is very important for patients and carers. Finally, greater emphasis needs to be placed on systematic and effective management of faecal incontinence in older people, backed up by sound communication between doctors and nurses, especially in the nursing home and acute hospital setting. Table 13.7 summarises the management of faecal incontinence in algorithmic form.

References

Barrett, J.A., Brocklehurst, J.C., Kiff, E.S., Ferguson, G. and Faragher, E.B. (1990) Rectal motility studies in faecally incontinent geriatric patients. *Age and Ageing* **19**, 311–317.

Brocklehurst, J., Dickinson, E. and Windsor, J. (1999) Laxatives and faecal incontinence in long-term care. *Nursing Standard* **52**, 32–36.

Brocklehurst, J.C., Kirkland, J.L. and Martin, J. (1983) Constipation in long-stay elderly patients: its treatment and prevention by lactulose, poloxalkol-dihydroxyanthroquinolone and phosphate enemas. *Gerontology* **29**, 181–184.

Camilleri, M. (1996) Gastrointestinal problems in diabetes. *Endocrinology and Metabolism Clinics of North America* **25**, 361–378.

Chassagne, P., Landrin, I. and Neveu, C. (1999) Fecal incontinence in the institutionalised elderly: incidence, risk factors and prognosis. *American Journal of Medicine* **106**, 185–190.

Chassagne, P., Jego, A. and Gloc, P. (2000) Does treatment of constipation improve faecal incontinence in institutionalised patients. *Age and Ageing* **29**, 159–164.

Collins, C., Wade, D.T., Davies, S. and Horne, V. (1988) The Barthel ADL Index: a reliability study. *International Disability Studies* **10**, 63.

Donald, I.P., Smith, R.G., Cruikshank, J.G., Elton, R.A. and Stoddart, M.E. (1985) A study of constipation in the elderly living at home. *Gerontology* **31**, 112–118.

Edwards, L.L., Quigly, E.M.M. and Pfeiffer, R.F. (1992) Gastrointestinal dysfunction in Parkinson's disease. *Neurology* **42**, 726–732.

Folstein, M.F., Folstein, S.E. and McHugh, P.R. (1975) 'Mini-Mental State': a practical method for grading the cognitive state of patients for the clinician. *Journal of Psychiatric Research* **12**, 189–198.

Harari, D., Gurwitz, J.H., Choodnovskiy, I., Avorn, J. and Minaker, K.L. (1994) Constipation: assessment and management in an institutionalised population. *Journal of the American Geriatrics Society* **42**, 1–6.

Harari, D., Gurwitz, J.H., Choodnovskiy, I., Avorn, J. and Minaker, K.L. (1995) Correlates of regular laxative use in frail elderly persons. *American Journal of Medicine* **99**, 4, 513–518.

Harari, D., Gurwitz, J.H., Avorn, J., Bohn, R. and Minaker, K.L. (1996) Bowel habits in relation to age and gender: findings from the National Health Interview Survey and clinical implications. *Archives of Internal Medicine* **156**, 315–320.

Harari, D., Gurwitz, J.H., Avorn, J., Bohn, R. and Minaker, K.L. (1997) How do older persons define constipation? *Journal of General Internal Medicine* **12**, 63–66.

Johanson, J.F., Irizarry, F. and Doughty, A. (1997) Risk factors for fecal incontinence in a nursing home population. *Journal of Clinical Gastroenterology* **24**, 156–160.

Kamm, M.A. (1998) Faecal incontinence. *British Medical Journal* **316**, 528–532.

Loening-Baucke, V. and Anuras, S. (1984) Sigmoidal and rectal motility in healthy elderly. *Journal of the American Geriatrics Society* **32**, 887–891.

McHugh, S.M. and Diamant, N.E. (1987) Effect of age, gender, and parity on anal canal pressures. *Digestive Diseases and Sciences* **32**, 7, 726–736.

Norton, C., Hosker, G. and Brazzelli, M. (2000) Biofeedback and/or sphincter exercises for the treatment of faecal incontinence in adults. *Cochrane Database Systematic Reviews* **2**, CD002111.

O'Keefe, E. and Talley, N.J. (1991) Irritable bowel syndrome in the elderly. *Clinics in Geriatric Medicine* **7**, 265–286.

Ouslander, J.G., Simmons, S., Schnelle, J., Uman, G. and Fingold, S. (1996) Effects of prompted voiding on fecal incontinence among nursing home residents. *Journal of the American Geriatrics Society* **44**, 424–428.

Passmore, A.P., Wilson-Davies, K. and Stoker, C. (1993) Chronic constipation in long stay elderly patients: a comparison of lactulose and a senna-fibre combination. *British Medical Journal* **307**, 769–771.

Petticrew, M., Watt, I. and Sheldon, T. (1997) Systematic review of the effectiveness of laxatives in the elderly. *Health Technology Assessment* **1**, 13, 1–52.

Prosser, S. and Dobbs, F. (1997) Case-finding incontinence in the over-75s. *British Journal of General Practice* **47**, 498–500.

Puxty, J.A. and Fox, R.A. (1986) Golytely: a new approach to faecal impaction in old age. *Age and Ageing* **15**, 3, 182–184.

Read, N.W., Abouzekry, L., Read, M.G., Howell, P., Ottewell, D. and Donnelly, T.C. (1985) Anorectal function in elderly patients with faecal impaction. *Gastroenterology* **89**, 959–966.

Resende, T.L., Brocklehurst, J.C. and O'Neill, P.A. (1993) A pilot study on the effect of exercise and abdominal massage on bowel habit in continuing care patients. *Clinical Rehabilitation* **7**, 204–209.

Royal College of Physicians (1996) *Incontinence: report of a working party*. London: RCP.

Sun, W.M., Read, N.W. and Verlinden, M. (1997) Effects of loperamide oxide on gastrointestinal transit time and anorectal function in patients with chronic diarrhoea and faecal incontinence. *Scandinavian Journal of Gastroenterology* **32**, 34–38.

Talley, N.J., O'Keefe, E., Zinsmeister, A.R. and Melton, L.J. (1992) Prevalence of gastrointestinal symptoms in the elderly: a population-based study. *Gastroenterology* **102**, 895–901.

Tobin, G.W. and Brocklehurst, J.C. (1986) Faecal incontinence in residential homes for the elderly: prevalence, aetiology and management. *Age and Ageing* **15**, 41–46.

Tramonte, S.M., Brand, M.B., Mulrow, C.D., Amato, M.G., O'Keefe, M.E. and Ramirez, G. (1997) The treatment of chronic constipation in adults. A systematic review. *Journal of General Internal Medicine* **12**, 15–24.

Whitehead, W.E., Drinkwater, D., Cheskin, L.J., Heller, B.R. and Schuster, M.M. (1989) Constipation in the elderly living at home: definition, prevalence and relationship to lifestyle and health status. *Journal of the American Geriatrics Society* **37**, 423–429.

Further reading

Potter, J., Norton, C. and Cottenden, A. (2002) *Bowel care in older people*. London: Royal College of Physicians.

Chapter 14

Surgical Treatment of Faecal Incontinence

Andrew Malouf

Introduction

Surgery for faecal incontinence should be reserved for patients with ongoing troublesome symptoms who have failed to respond to other measures. Intervention should be based on symptomatology and its influence on quality of life. Several surgical approaches are available for different types of faecal incontinence, and these often markedly improve symptoms. It is important to appreciate that incontinence is a symptom, and that in the absence of specific correctable local pathologies, surgical intervention is unlikely to restore ongoing perfect continence. This should be addressed during pre-operative patient counselling, and realistic goals and patient expectations defined. It is also important to appreciate that symptom improvement, though infrequently complete, is often sufficient to achieve patient satisfaction and improve quality of life (Malouf et al., 2000a). This chapter will discuss surgical techniques and outcomes.

Surgical interventions must be closely tailored to individual patients. The traditional mainstays have been overlapping sphincter repair for anterior obstetric-related trauma or defects from external sphincter trauma at other sites, and post-anal repair for 'idiopathic' or 'neurogenic' faecal incontinence associated with pudendal nerve damage. Colostomy is traditionally used for end-stage symptoms after prior failed attempts at surgical restoration of continence, or in patients in whom other procedures are felt to be inappropriate. Recent surgical advances include dynamic graciliplasty, artificial anal sphincter implantation, and antegrade continence enema procedures. Newer still, direct sacral nerve stimulation and injection augmentation of the internal sphincter have emerged as potentially valuable treatments. With all surgical procedures continence is less likely to be achieved in the presence of chronic diarrhoeal states, as following surgery continence is frequently incomplete for liquid stool.

Local ano-rectal conditions causing incontinence

Anal and perianal lesions such as skin tags, prolapsing piles and ano-rectal polyps, can all produce passive or post-defaecation soiling by associated mucus discharge or prevention of adequate anal canal closure or perianal cleaning. In the absence of occult sphincter injury, neuropathy, or more generalised rectal pathology, eradication of these local pathologies, often by surgery, usually produces resolution of symptoms. These conditions are discussed in more detail in Chapter 11. However, anal surgery does itself carry a small risk of *de novo* faecal incontinence, and must always be performed with great care.

Incontinence associated with full-thickness rectal prolapse

Full thickness rectal prolapse is associated with some degree of faecal incontinence in about 75% of patients (Jacobs et al., 1997; Williams et al., 1991). Incontinence is usually passive and associated with a reversible recto-anal inhibition, where the presence of the prolapse in the upper anal canal provokes reflex anal relaxation (Farouk et al., 1994). Faecal urgency and urge incontinence are uncommon. Intussusception into the upper anal canal induces the recto-anal inhibitory reflex, resulting in chronic internal sphincter relaxation, a fall in resting anal canal pressure, and clinical sphincter laxity. Prolapse also generates abnormally high rectal pressure waves, creating a pressure gradient across the already inhibited internal sphincter. Pudendal neuropathy is also frequently present and may contribute to incontinence (Malouf et al., 1999). In addition, prolapsed rectal mucosa will usually itself also produce mucus discharge.

Surgical correction of prolapse improves continence in up to 75% of patients. Surgery is aimed at restoring normal physiology and, in particular, restoring a positive pressure gradient between the sphincters and rectum. Objectives include elimination of the prolapse, with the retention of a compliant rectal reservoir and a functioning anal sphincter. When the prolapse protrudes into the anus there is inhibition of anal canal closure; sphincter recovery relates to reversal of this recto-anal inhibition (Farouk et al., 1994), and continence can be restored even in patients with very poor pre-operative sphincter function. Following surgery, resting pressures rise but remain similar to those of incontinent patients with no history of prolapse; squeeze pressures are unaltered (Matheson and Keighley, 1981). High-pressure rectal waves are abolished, so that rectal pressures no longer exceed those of the weak internal sphincter (Malouf and Bartolo, 1999).

In general, abdominal procedures (such as suture, mesh or resection rectopexy) are more likely to improve incontinence than perineal procedures such as Delorme's or Altmeiere's operations (Madoff et al., 1992; Deen et al., 1994). The best continence results appear to be achieved by resection rectopexy (Duthie and Bartolo, 1992).

Overlapping external anal sphincter repair (Figure 14.1, overleaf)

Structural anal sphincter damage is the commonest cause of faecal incontinence seen in surgical practice. This most frequently relates to anterior sphincter trauma during childbirth (Sultan et al., 1993), but may occur following anal surgery such as fistulotomy or sphincterotomy, or following direct accidental trauma. External sphincter defects are usually single, but are often associated with a concurrent internal sphincter defect. Patients with obstetric injury present with faecal urgency and urge incontinence from external sphincter dysfunction, with or without accompanying passive incontinence from internal sphincter dysfunction.

Surgery aims to restore anatomical continuity between the muscle ends of the disrupted external sphincter. End-to-end repair, without muscle overlap, gives only mediocre results even in the short term (Arnaud et al., 1991). Superior results have been consistently shown using an overlapping repair technique. Through an anterior semicircular perianal incision, a skin flap is raised and the underlying external sphincter ends and intervening scar tissue exposed and mobilised. Division of the scar tissue enables a formal overlap repair, using non-absorbable sutures. Both muscle and scar are overlapped. Scar tissue enables more secure suture placement and reduces the risk of sutures cutting out. It is unknown whether the addition of simultaneous internal sphincter repair is of added clinical benefit.

Patients undergo pre-operative mechanical bowel preparation, and operation is carried out under antibiotic cover, usually in the lithotomy position. The central portion of the wound is often left open at the end of the procedure to minimise tension on the skin edges. This also enables drainage, and healing is usually uneventful over 2–3 weeks. Post-operative 'confinement of the bowels' (restricting oral intake to clear fluids only for up to 5 days), and defunctioning stomas (Hasegawa et al., 2000), have not been shown to alter results, though stomas may be useful for more complex or repeat repairs. It is important to avoid post-operative constipation which may lead to damage of the repair during straining or the passage of a hard stool. However, once healing has been attained (4–8 weeks), keeping the stool firm rather than soft may help to maximise the benefit of surgery.

Successful outcome with overlapping repair is consistently reported in about 75% of patients

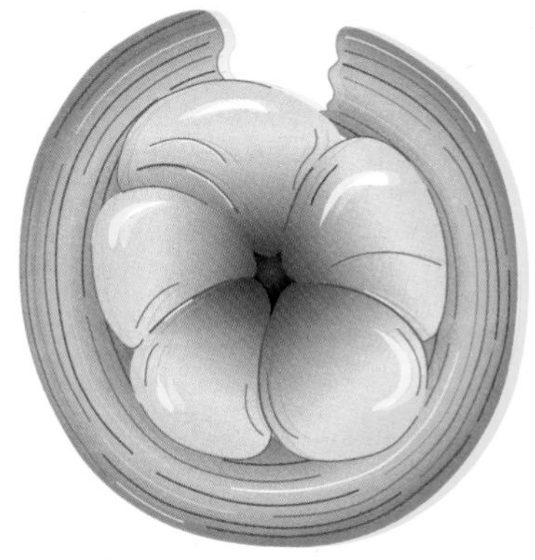

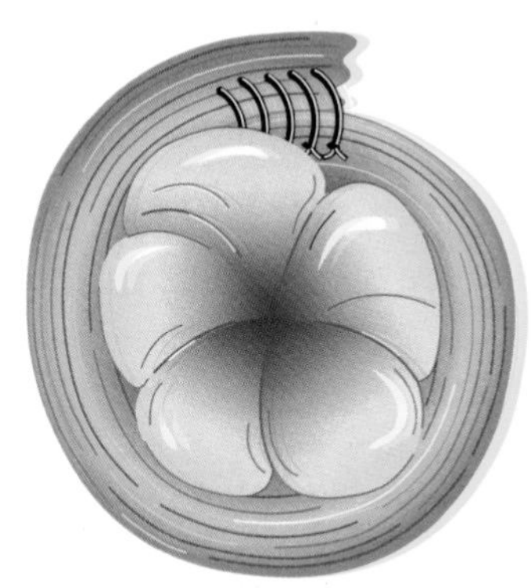

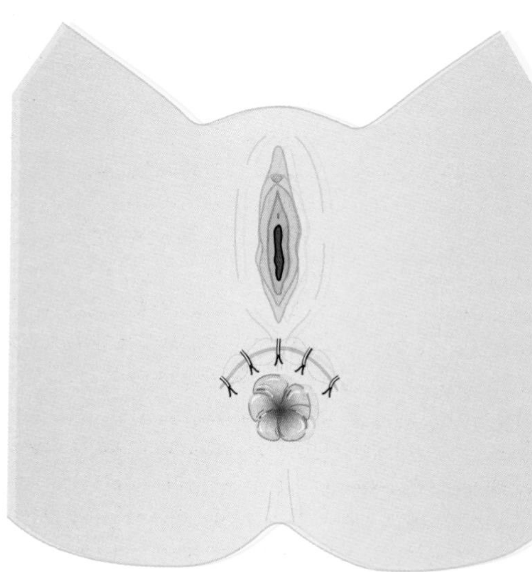

Figures 14.1 *Overlapping anal sphincter repair.*

in the short term (Briel et al., 1998; Young et al., 1998; Ctercteko et al., 1988), with continence to both solid and liquid stool, and high rates of patient satisfaction. Good outcome is associated with restoration of circumferential integrity of the external sphincter muscle, leading to an increased ability to squeeze (Engel et al., 1994a). Repair also improves maximum resting pressure and increases functional anal canal length. The addition of an anterior levatorplasty, where the medial aspects of the puborectalis muscles are plicated deep to the external sphincter, may improve results, but available data are limited.

Outcome failure appears to be more common in the presence of a coexisting pudendal neuropathy, but age itself, the timing of onset of symptoms after obstetric delivery, and the duration of symptoms prior to sphincter repair do not adversely affect outcome. Some patients with poor outcome have persisting external sphincter defects on ultrasound (Engel et al., 1994a).

Reports on the long-term results of overlapping sphincter repair are few (Malouf et al., 2000a; Londono-Schimmer et al., 1994). It is apparent, however, that at least for obstetric-related trauma, results deteriorate with time (Malouf et al., 2000a). In the only longitudinal study of overlapping repair for obstetric-related defects followed for a minimum of five years, only 50% of patients were regarded as long-term successes on the criteria of continence, despite the fact that interim analysis at a median of 15 months after repair showed continence to solid and liquid stool in 80% of the same cohort of patients. At a minimum of five years follow-up, no patient was fully continent to stool and flatus. Fifteen per cent had required further surgery for incontinence, nearly a third reported the onset of a new evacuation disorder not present prior to surgery, and the majority of patients still had at least some faecal urgency, urge faecal incontinence, and passive faecal soiling. Sixteen per cent of patients reported an overall deterioration in symptoms compared to before surgery. Despite these figures, however, over 70% of patients reported improved bowel control compared to before surgery, nearly two- thirds rated symptom improvement as 50% or more, and 50% of patients rated satisfaction with the long term results of surgery as 8 or more out of 10 (Malouf et al., 2000a). These results suggest that even minor symptom improvement may be enough to satisfy patients and improve lifestyle. They also highlight the need for adequate patient counselling prior to surgery, and the need to establish realistic goals and expectations.

Sphincter repair is a relatively straightforward procedure with little operative morbidity. Patients failing to achieve satisfactory continence with an overlapping repair may be considered for a repeat repair. The largest published series of repeat sphincter repairs reported improvement in patient symptoms by 50% or more in 15 of 23 patients at a mean follow-up of 20 months (Pinedo et al., 1999). The long-term results of repeat sphincter repair remain unknown.

Internal anal sphincter repair

Structural internal sphincter damage can arise in combination with obstetric injury, following anal dilatation, lateral sphincterotomy, and after surgery for anal fistula. Defects manifest as passive incontinence associated with a low resting anal pressure. Although it is technically feasible to perform surgical internal sphincter repair, reported outcome is poor, with persistence of defects visible on anal ultrasound, low resting pressures, and incomplete continence (Leroi et al., 1997; Morgan et al., 1997). Failure may relate to sutures not holding the thin muscle together initially, or to later breakdown of the repair. The procedure is rarely performed in isolation.

Insertion of a cutaneous (skin) flap into the area of an internal sphincter defect (rotation, island or advancement anoplasty) has shown short-term improvement in all of 13 patients in the only report of this procedure (Morgan et al., 1997). No long-term results are available, and further evaluation is required.

Injection augmentation of the internal anal sphincter

Internal sphincter dysfunction causing passive incontinence can be treated by internal sphincter augmentation using injected material to bulk tissues, either locally at sites where the muscle is deficient, or circumferentially if the whole of the muscle is degenerate or fragmented. Promising short-term results have been reported in small uncontrolled studies using autologous fat (Shafik, 1995), Teflon paste (Shafik, 1993), Gax collagen (Kumar et al., 1998), or Bioplastique (Malouf et al., 2001). More than one injection session may be required, but collectively, 75% of patients reported responded to treatment. The long-term results, however, are not yet known, and the procedure requires further evaluation. At present, injectable materials are relatively expensive and there is the potential for local infection, migration of the injected material, and discomfort.

Post-anal repair

Post-anal repair (Figure 14.2, overleaf) has been the traditional surgical approach for the treatment of idiopathic or neurogenic faecal incontinence. It was thought to improve continence by restoring the normal ano-rectal angle (which is often obtuse in these patients), by increasing functional anal canal length, and by modifying anal sensation (Orrom et al., 1991; Henry, 1987) although the mechanism for this was unclear. Patients require pre-operative mechanical bowel preparation and perioperative antibiotics. Defunctioning stomas are unnecessary. A semicircular incision is made behind the anus, and dissection is continued up to the levator ani within the intersphincteric plane. Stitches are placed in the levator, puborectalis and external sphincter using non-absorbable sutures. Levator sutures are placed as a lattice to minimise tissue tension, puborectalis sutures progress from a lattice to muscle approximation as sutures become more superficial, and external sphincter sutures secure the muscle bellies together. Whether

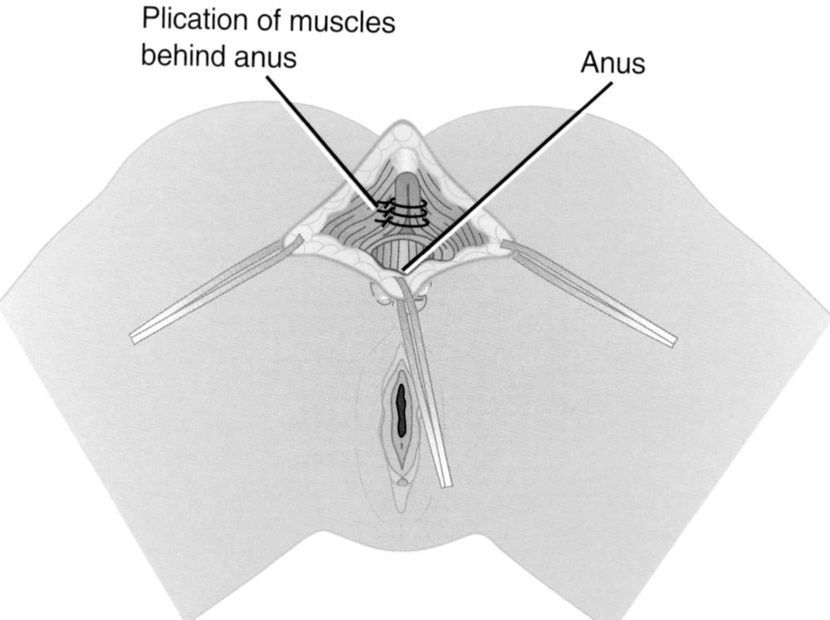

Figure 14.2 *Post-anal repair.*

additional internal sphincter plication improves results remains unclear. Wounds are closed in a 'Y' shape to minimise skin tension.

The short-term results of post-anal repair are good, with improvement in continence being widely reported in 60–85% of patients (Keighley, 1984; Rainey et al., 1990; Braun et al., 1991). There appears to be no clear clinical or physiological parameter predictive of outcome. Longer-term follow-up, however, shows that continence deteriorates with time, with as few as 21% of patients continent a median of 3.5–6 years after surgery (Engel et al., 1994b; Setti Carraro and Nicholls, 1994; Yoshioka and Keighley, 1989). One study of 116 patients followed a median of 59 months (Yoshioka and Keighley, 1989) found that 60% still had faecal urgency, 76% still leaked faeces, and 52% still wore pads for incontinence. Longer-term deterioration of results may relate to an ongoing neuropathic process. The operation is now used less widely than previously. It may have an additional role in patients without structural sphincter defects with ongoing incontinence after rectal prolapse surgery (Setti Carraro and Nicholls, 1994).

Total pelvic floor repair

The disappointing long-term results of post-anal repair for neurogenic or idiopathic incontinence led to the development of the total pelvic floor repair. This combines a post-anal repair with an anterior sphincter plication and levatorplasty to further enhance the anal high pressure zone. Though continence improves in a majority of patients in the short term, long-term continence rates may be as low as 14% (Keighley and Korsgen, 1996), and the procedure has not been widely adopted.

Anal neosphincters

Patients with troublesome symptoms in the presence of gross structural sphincter damage, or failed previous attempts at surgical restoration of continence, may be considered for a neosphincter procedure. These utilise either biological tissue, or implant a prosthesis.

Dynamic graciloplasty

Dynamic graciloplasty involves transposing the gracilis muscle from the inner thigh to the

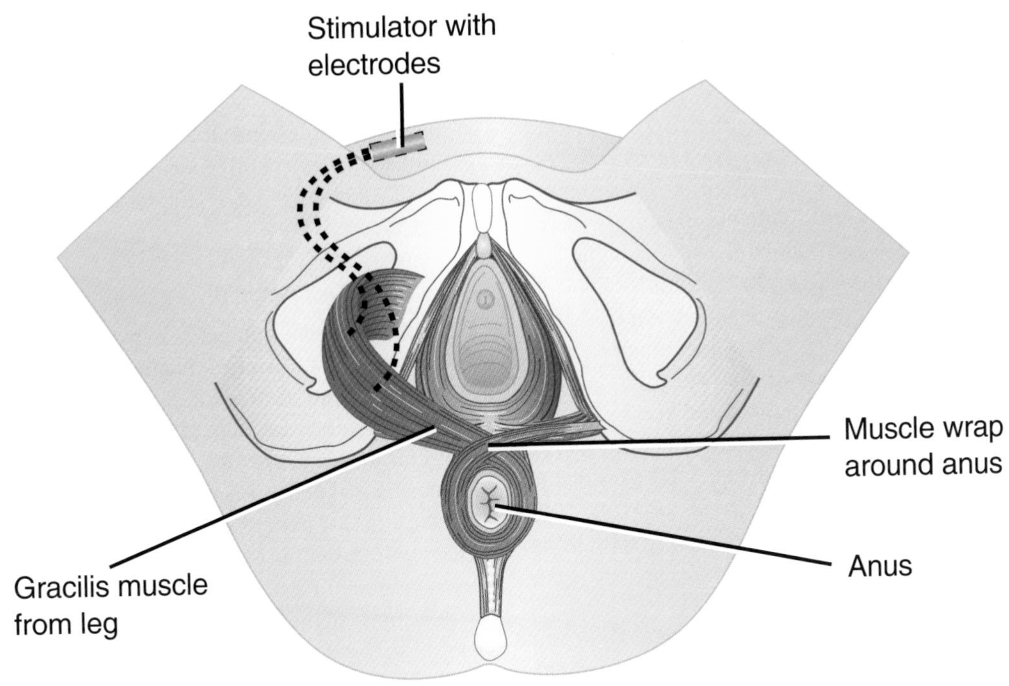

Figure 14.3 *Dynamic graciloplasty.*

perineum to create a neoanus, which is then electrically stimulated to produce a maintained tonic contraction (Figure 14.3). The muscle is completely mobilised distal to its proximal neurovascular bundle using either one long or three shorter medial thigh incisions, and its tendon is detached from the tibia. A tunnel is created around the anus via either one anterior perineal or two lateral perianal incisions, through which the transposed gracilis muscle is wrapped around the anus to create a neo-sphincter, and its tendon secured. Attention should be paid not to place tension on the blood or nerve supply.

Stimulating electrodes are operatively secured either around the nerve, or more commonly directly into the muscle, and tunnelled subcutaneously to a pulse generator (battery) implanted in the anterior abdominal wall deep to the anterior rectus sheath. Once wounds are healed, the gracilis undergoes a standardised programme of increasing stimulation over several weeks working up to continuous stimulation, which converts the type 2 fatigue-prone skeletal muscle to a type 1 fatigue-resistant muscle.

Improved or normal continence can be achieved in up to 70% of patients followed short term with associated improvement in lifestyle (Baeten et al., 2000). The procedure has been shown to be cost effective compared with the long-term use of pads or defunctioning colostomy. The operation itself, however, is relatively complex, and continence does come at a cost of morbidity rates of up to 50%. Some morbidity is minor or related to electrical device failure, and this should reduce with further technological development. However, more significant morbidity such as sepsis, pressure necrosis, perielectrode fibrosis and lead migration can lead to functional failure. Failures can sometimes be salvaged by a second contralateral graciloplasty.

Much of the ongoing morbidity from dynamic

graciloplasty relates to the development of new, or the exacerbation of pre-existing rectal evacuation difficulties, and associated faecal impaction, which can be chronic or intermittent. These frequently necessitate the use of regular evacuation aids such as suppositories or enemas, but these are not always sufficient for symptom alleviation. Patients with pre-existing evacuation disorders are probably not suitable for graciloplasty. Graciloplasty should also be avoided in the presence of inflammatory bowel disease. There is a well documented steep surgical learning curve for dynamic graciloplasty, and outcome appears to correlate closely with surgical experience (Madoff et al., 1999). This suggests the procedure should be limited to specialised centres.

An inherent aspect of dynamic gracilpolasty is that the electrical components, in particular the battery, have a limited functional lifespan, and are expected to require replacement at undefined intervals. Batteries may last up to nine years.

Dynamic graciloplasty has also been used successfully for perineal reconstruction following abdominoperineal excision of the rectum for cancer (Cavina, 1996). Long-term follow-up has shown that it is both oncologically safe, and maintains satisfactory continence in the majority of patients. To date, however, it is not widely used for this indication.

In general, it is felt that patients with acquired incontinence, such as obstetric-related injury or direct sphincter trauma, achieve better overall results than patients with idiopathic or neurogenic incontinence, or those having total anorectal reconstruction after abdominoperineal excision (Madoff et al., 1999).

Gluteus maximus transposition

This uncommonly performed procedure involves bilateral mobilisation of the inferior parts of the gluteus maximi muscles, and construction of a neoanus by muscle wrapping of the anal canal. Encouraging early results (Devesa et al., 1992) may be further improved by electrically stimulating the muscle via implanted electrodes connected to a pulse generator (dynamic gluteoplasty) (Guelinckx et al., 1996). The procedure is technically challenging, however, experience is limited, and it has not been widely adopted. In addition, transposed gluteus maximus requires higher stimulation amplitudes than transposed gracilis to achieve continence, reducing the lifespan of implanted stimulators (Vaizey et al., 1998).

Artificial anal sphincter

The artificial anal sphincter is a silastic prosthetic implant utilising a manually controlled hydrostatic pressure system (Figure 14.4). Current systems are a modification of earlier artificial urinary sphincters, and incorporate three principal components (a cuff, a hydrostatic reservoir, and a pump) linked by silastic tubing. The whole system is fluid filled, and operates by producing anal canal occlusion by shifting fluid within the system. The cuff is placed around the anal canal and occludes the canal when filled with fluid from a pressure-regulated reservoir implanted in the anterior abdominal wall deep to the anterior rectus sheath. Cuffs of varying width and length, and reservoirs of different pressure ranges, are available to suit individual patient anatomy. A pump containing valves and a resistor placed in the labia majora in a female, or scrotum in a male, enables patient-controlled transfer of fluid to and from the cuff. Pumping transfers fluid from the perianal cuff to the reservoir, to allow passage of a stool during defaecation. The cuff refills spontaneously over a few minutes by the hydrostatic pressure within the reservoir. The pump also contains a deactivation button which renders the system inactive during the healing phase after operation, or if subsequent transanal surgery is required.

Full mechanical bowel preparation and early post-operative laxatives are used to prevent impaction during the healing phase. Strict aseptic technique and prophylactic antibiotics are essential to avoid sepsis of an implanted prosthesis within a potentially contaminated operative field. The cuff is placed through either a transverse perineal body incision, or bilateral perianal incisions. To minimise the risk of the device eroding through the skin with subsequent

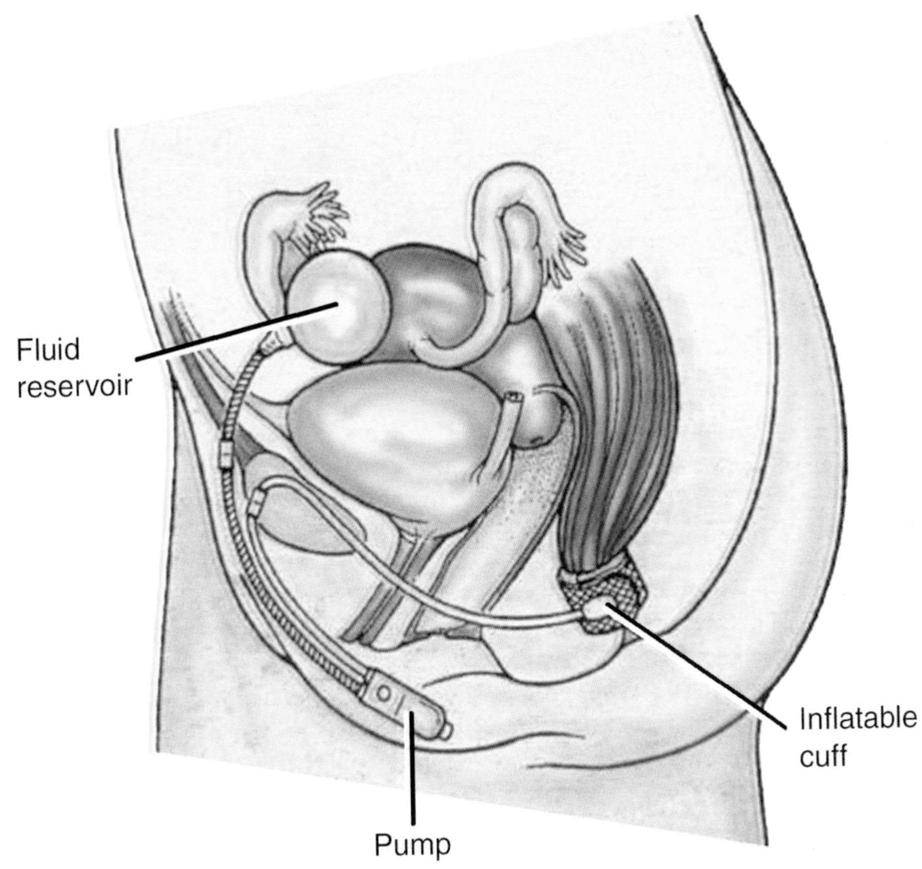

Figure 14.4 *Artificial anal sphincter.*

sepsis, the cuff is placed encircling the anal canal as high as possible, ideally against the inferior surface of the levators. The reservoir is placed deep to the anterior rectus sheath via a small transverse incision, and the pump placed through the same incision in the labia majora or scrotum. The pump, reservoir and cuff are connected by subcutaneously tunnelled tubing. A defunctioning colostomy is unnecessary. Patients with active or recurrent perianal sepsis, inflammatory bowel disease, or extensive perianal scarring are not suitable for artificial anal sphincter placement because of a markedly increased risk of implant sepsis and erosion.

Although first reported for the treatment of faecal incontinence in 1987, published experience using both earlier urinary systems and devices subsequently modified for the bowel remains limited to small numbers. Continence is achieved in up to 75% of patients in the short to medium term (Rullier et al., 2000), but associated morbidity is considerable, and the majority of this relates to implant sepsis (Malouf et al., 2000b). If sepsis becomes established, it is rarely controlled by antibiotics and drainage, and removal of the whole system is usually necessary. Failure and subsequent removal due to either sepsis or functional failure may be as high as two-thirds in the medium term. Sometimes continence can be restored after an initial functional failure by replacing defective individual components that have ruptured or malfunctioned, or replacing a whole system.

As with dynamic graciloplasty, rectal evacuation difficulty can be a major cause of ongoing morbidity after implantation, particularly in those with a pre-existing evacuation disorder or

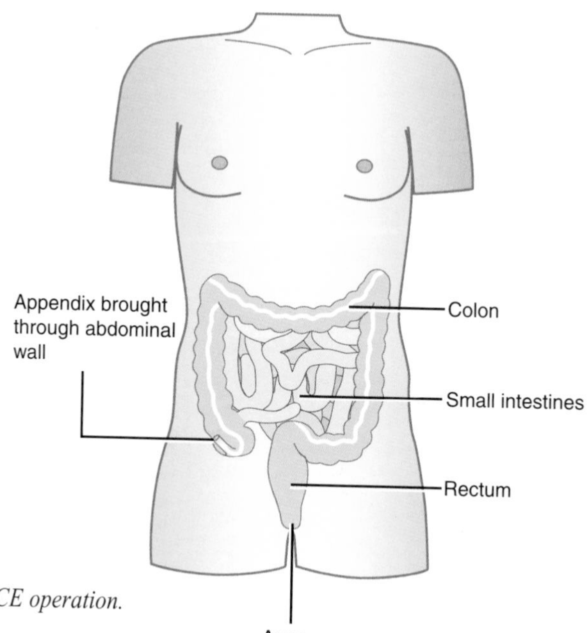

Figure 14.5a *The ACE operation.*

those with altered pre-operative ano-rectal sensation, who should probably not be considered for implantation. Suppositories, enemas or oral laxatives may help in management.

The only report of long-term follow-up of implanted artificial anal sphincters (Christiansen et al., 1999) showed 50% of patients had improved continence at a minimum follow-up of 5 years, with better outcome seen in patients after a failed sphincter repair than in patients with an underlying neurological disorder. The removal rate due to sepsis was 18%, and the revision rate of still-functioning prostheses was 63%. Revisions were less common with the newer systems modified for the bowel. It also highlighted the need for enemas in patients with rectal evacuation difficulty.

The precise roles of the artificial anal sphincter and dynamic graciloplasty remain to be defined. They may indeed prove interchangeable for similar patient groups, and failure of one procedure may well be salvaged by performance of the other. They both, however, have similar limitations in patients with pre-existing rectal evacuation disorders and those with altered ano-rectal sensation. Both should also be avoided in the presence of chronic diarrhoeal states and in inflammatory bowel disease. Graciloplasty is probably preferable to an artificial anal sphincter in the presence of a history of anal sepsis, because of the lesser risk of development of sepsis with biological as opposed to foreign material. Further work is required to clarify patient selection for both procedures.

Antegrade continence enema (ACE) procedures and colonic conduits

An alternative approach to direct sphincter surgery involves the creation of a small right-sided colonic stoma, through which irrigation is performed to produce predictable complete colonic cleansing so that leakage and unexpected evacuation is minimised (Figures 14.5a,b). Irrigation involves instillation of 3–4 litres of warm tap water over an hour or so, though transit through the colon and evacuation of instillate can take up to two hours and hence be time-consuming. The antegrade continence enema (ACE) or Malone procedure has been used mostly in children with congenital disorders (Shankar et al., 1998; Hensle et al., 1998), and uses the appendix, or in the absence of the appendix, a

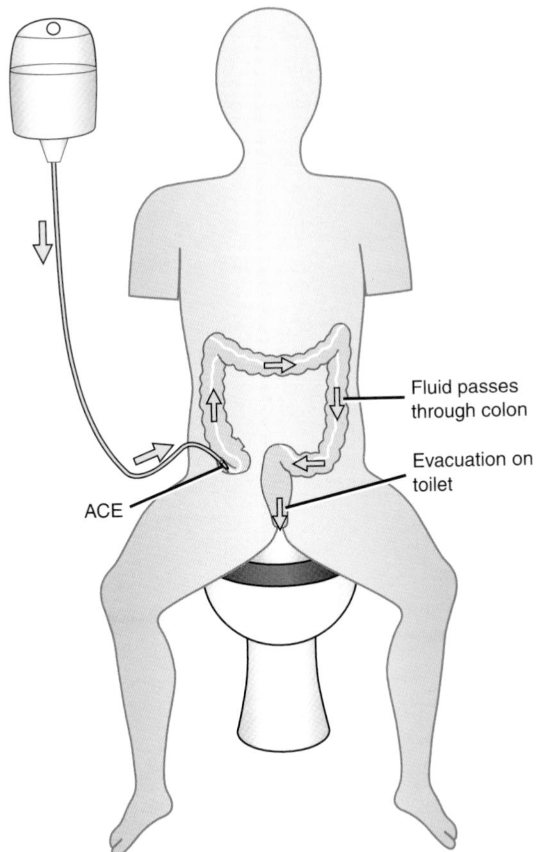

Figure 14.5b *Irrigating the ACE.*

conduit fashioned from a flap of caecum (Malone et al., 1990; Kiely et al., 1995).

Improved continence has been reported in up to 75% of patients in the short term (Shankar et al., 1998; Hensle et al., 1998), with associated improved quality of life (Shankar et al., 1998), though results appear not to be as good in wheelchair-bound children with spinal neuropathy. Similar results have been shown in small numbers of adults (Krough and Laurberg, 1998). Abdominal pain and bloating can be a problem with irrigation. Longer-term problems relate mostly to stoma narrowing or stenosis, which may require dilatation or revision. Other problems include reflux of irrigation fluid into the ileum, and loss of responsiveness to infused fluid over time. A few patients experience leakage of flatus or liquid stool from the ACE.

Limited experience using continent sigmoid and transverse colon valved conduits in adults has also been reported (Hughes and Williams, 1995; Maw et al., 1996). Though promising (Stuchfield, 1995), procedures are technically demanding, have attendant morbidity, and have not been widely adopted.

Sacral nerve stimulation

Direct electrical stimulation of the sacral nerves has been successfully used for urological disorders since the early 1980s. Its recent application to small numbers of patients with faecal incontinence has shown promising early results. The earliest report (Matzel et al., 1995), at a follow-up of six months, described restoration of continence in 3 patients with a structurally intact but weak external sphincter using S3 nerve stimulation. A study assessing the short-term effects of direct sacral nerve stimulation showed restoration of continence in 8 of 9 evaluable patients (Vaizey et al., 1999). This related to calmed rectal activity, a possible facilitation of external anal sphincter contraction, and reduced episodes of spontaneous internal anal sphincter relaxation. Malouf et al. (2000c) reported dramatic reduction in incontinent episodes, and improvement in continence scores, at medium-term follow-up in five patients with internal anal sphincter weakness. Complication rates are low, the procedure is technically straightforward, and it enables the unique ability to assess the clinical response to treatment over a short period of time prior to making a decision to going on to permanent implantation.

Sacral nerve stimulation involves three phases. The first, acute percutaneous nerve evaluation (PNE), assesses the acute clinical response to direct nerve stimulation via stimulating needles placed percutaneously through the sacral foramena adjacent to the sacral nerves (Figure 14.6). This can be done as a day case under general anaesthetic, or as an outpatient procedure using local nerve block. Stimulation produces visible anal contraction and perineal lifting, often combined with flexor hallucis brevis contraction, noted by flexion of the great toe. The level producing maximal response to stimulation is usually S3, but may be S4. If an acute reaction is demonstrated, the needle is substituted by a stimulating wire, which is left in situ over a 1–3 week period via an attachment to an external pulse generator to assess the clinical effect on continence over this test period. This is known as the subchronic nerve evaluation phase. Patients clinically responding to stimulation with improvement in symptoms of incontinence then go on to the third phase of treatment, operative placement of a permanent stimulating sacral electrode, and an implantable pulse generator. This requires a 4–5 cm midsacral incision through which the same foramen used for the test stimulation is identified and cannulated with the stimulating electrode, and connected via a subcutaneously tunnelled lead to an implantable pulse generator placed deep to the rectus fascia in the anterior abdominal wall or in the buttock. Stimulation intensity can be adjusted using a patient-controlled handheld programmer to maintain continence.

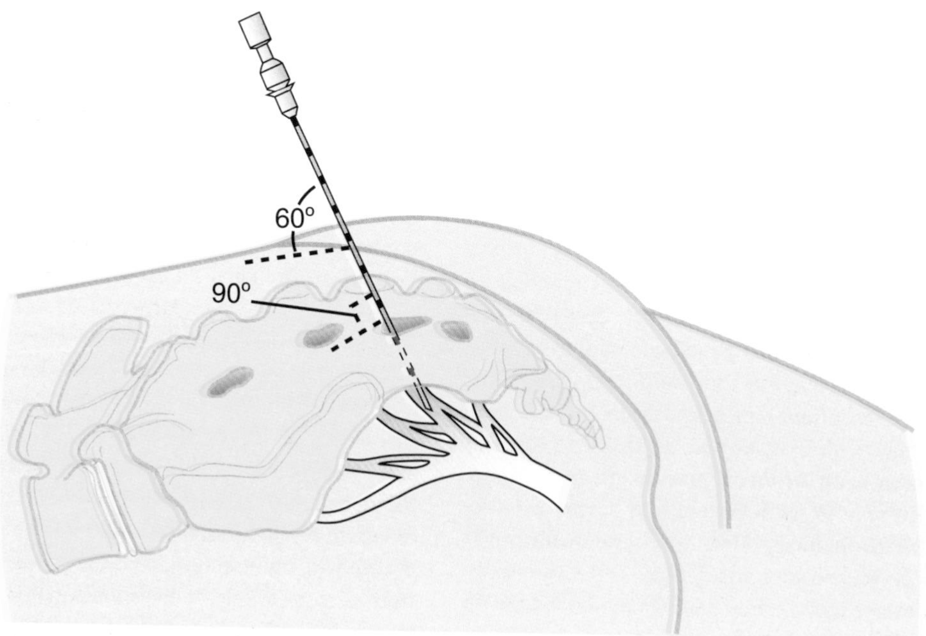

Figure 14.6 *PNE insertion for sacral nerve stimulation.*

Precise indications for sacral nerve stimulation for faecal incontinence remain to be defined. Patients with structurally intact but weak either internal or external sphincters appear most likely to benefit. Preliminary results from a prospective multicentre study also suggest benefit for some patients with an intact overlapping sphincter repair but ongoing incontinence, and some patients with constipation may also benefit, for reasons which are not yet clear (unpublished data from St Mark's Hospital). Longer-term results are awaited.

Colostomy

Formation of a colostomy is reserved for patients with intractable symptoms after failed continence surgery, or those felt unsuitable, or not desiring alternative surgical approaches. This can make a major positive contribution to quality of life (see Chapter 15) (Craven and Etchells, 1998). Adequate pre-operative information and counselling are crucial to successful adaptation and acceptance of the stoma by the patient. Colostomy is usually an end sigmoid stoma created flush with the abdominal wall skin, with the distal end being closed and left in the pelvis. Surgery is sometimes performed through a left iliac fossa incision, with or without laparoscopic assistance, avoiding the midline laparotomy that is more commonly required in more obese patients or those who have had abdominal surgery. Faecal diversion should not be considered as treatment failure. For the majority, reliable colonic emptying into a continent stomal appliance gives relief from incapacitating symptoms, and returns life to as close to normal as possible. With a stoma, dietary and pharmacological manipulation of the gut is often unnecessary, and the unpredictability of incontinence is resolved. Stomal irrigation can further improve predictable gut emptying so that bags are not required to be worn at all times. Though soiling from rectal stump secretion may occur, this is usually easily controlled with intermittent suppositories and is not commonly a major problem. Despite this, however, up to a quarter of patients are unable to come to terms with a stoma. In addition, the cumulative risk over a patient's lifetime of complications associated with stomas may amount to 50%. The commonest relate to peristomal herniation, prolapse, and small bowel obstruction.

Conclusions

Surgical treatment needs to be specifically tailored to individuals. A common cause of faecal incontinence is obstetric-related anterior sphincter trauma, and the majority of these patients achieve at least a good short-term result with direct overlapping repair. Although the longer-term results are not necessarily maintained, the majority improve continence, and though not perfect, this is enough to satisfy many patients. Repeat sphincter repair can also be performed with a reasonable chance of success. Isolated internal sphincter repair for passive incontinence is disappointing. Small short-term series report encouraging results using injection augmentation of the internal sphincter, though further work is required. Patients with neurogenic or idiopathic incontinence are sometimes managed with a post-anal repair, with good short-term results, although on long-term follow-up only a minority maintain continence.

In patients with major structural damage, advanced neurological abnormalities, or failed previous surgery for incontinence, dynamic graciloplasty or an artificial anal sphincter are appropriate options. Both have up to 75% early success rates, but associated morbidity is appreciable, and particularly relates to sepsis. Implantable components are also expensive. Limited long-term data are available for both procedures, but it appears that efficacy deteriorates with time. Further technological refinement may improve results. Even in the absence of pre-operative constipation, rectal evacuant aids are frequently required.

Other procedures such as antegrade colonic enemas and colonic conduits, though encouraging in limited reports with intermediate term follow-up, are not universally applicable and have not been widely adopted. This may change as experience with these procedures grows.

Sacral nerve stimulation offers a promising novel approach for patients with structurally intact but weak sphincters, or with a sonographically intact overlap repair with poor functional outcome. Reports to date, however, are limited and further assessment is required.

Defunctioning colostomy remains a valuable procedure for intractable incontinence unresponsive to other measures, or when more complex surgical procedures are unsuitable or undesired by an individual patient. This can often liberate patients by restoring bowel control.

It is important to remember that incontinence is a functional problem, and that as such, no single operation will improve all patients with any particular aetiology. Patients need to be adequately counselled as to the realistic expectation of success of individual procedures, and in particular, that the long-term results of most of these procedures remain far from clear at present.

References

Arnaud, A., Sarles, J.C., Sielezneff, I., Orsoni, P. and Joly, A. (1991) Sphincter repair without overlapping for fecal incontinence. *Diseases of the Colon and Rectum* **34**, 744–747.

Baeten, C.G., Bailey, H.R., Bakka, A., Belliveau, P., Berg, E., Buie, W.D. et al. (2000) Safety and efficacy of dynamic graciloplasty for fecal incontinence: report of a prospective, multicenter trial. Dynamic Graciloplasty Therapy Study Group. *Diseases of the Colon and Rectum* **43**, 743–751.

Braun, J., Tons, C., Schippers, E., Fass, J. and Schumpelick, V. (1991) Results of Parks postanal repair in idiopathic anal insufficiency. *Chirurg* **62**, 206–210. [In German]

Briel, J.W., de Boer, L.M., Hop, W.C. and Schouten, W.R. (1998) Clinical outcome of anterior overlapping external anal sphincter repair with internal anal sphincter imbrication. *Diseases of the Colon and Rectum* **41**, 209–214.

Cavina, E. (1996) Outcome of restorative perineal graciloplasty with simultaneous excision of the anus and rectum for cancer. A ten-year experience with 81 patients. *Diseases of the Colon and Rectum* **39**, 182–190.

Christiansen, J., Rasmussen, O. and Lindorff-Larson, K. (1999) Long-term results of artificial anal sphincter implantation for severe anal incontinence. *Annals of Surgery* **230**, 45–48.

Craven, M.L. and Etchells, J. (1998) A review of the outcome of stoma surgery on spinal cord injured patients. *Journal of Advanced Nursing* **27**, 922–926.

Ctercteko, G.C., Fazio, V.W., Jagelman, D.G., Lavery, I.C., Weakley, F.L. and Melia, M. (1988) Anal sphincter repair: a report of 60 cases and review of the literature. *Australian and New Zealand Journal of Surgery* **58**, 703–710.

Deen, K.I., Grant, E., Billingham, C. and Keighley, M.R. (1994) Abdominal resection rectopexy with pelvic floor repair *versus* perineal rectosigmoidectomy and pelvic floor repair for full-thickness rectal prolapse. *British Journal of Surgery* **81**, 302–304.

Devesa, J.M., Vincente, E., Enrique, J.M., Nuno, J., Bucheli, P., de Blas, G. and Villanueva, M.G. (1992) Total fecal incontinence – a new method of gluteus maximus transposition: preliminary results and report of previous experience. *Diseases of the Colon and Rectum* **35**, 339–349.

Duthie, G.S. and Bartolo, D.C.C. (1992) Abdominal rectopexy for rectal prolapse: a comparison of techniques. *British Journal of Surgery* **79**, 107–113.

Engel, A.F., Sultan, A.H., Kamm, M.A., Bartram, C.I. and Nicholls, R.J. (1994a) Anterior anal sphincter repair in patients with obstetric trauma. *British Journal of Surgery* **81**, 1231–1234.

Engel, A.F., van Baal, S.J. and Brummelkamp, W.H. (1994b) Late results of postanal repair for idiopathic faecal incontinence. *European Journal of Surgery* **160**, 637–640.

Farouk, R., Duthie, G.S., MacGregor, A.B. and Bartolo, D.C. (1994) Rectoanal inhibition and incontinence in patients with rectal prolapse. *British Journal of Surgery* **81**, 743–746.

Guelinckx, P.J., Sinsel, N.K. and Gruwez, J.A. (1996) Anal sphincter reconstruction with the gluteus maximus muscle: anatomic and physiologic considerations concerning conventional and dynamic gluteoplasty. *Plastic and Reconstructive Surgery* **98**, 303–304.

Hasegawa, H., Yoshioka, K. and Keighley, M.R. (2000) Randomised trial of fecal diversion for sphincter repair. *Diseases of the Colon and Rectum* **43**, 961–964.

Henry, M.M. (1987) Pathogenesis and management of fecal incontinence in the adult. *Gastroenterology Clinics of North America* **16**, 35–45.

Hensle, T.W., Reiley, E.A. and Chang, D.T. (1998) The Malone antegrade continence enema procedure in the management of patients with spina bifida.

Journal of the American College of Surgery **186**, 669–674.

Hughes, S.F. and Williams, N.S. (1995) Continent conduit for the treatment of faecal incontinence associated with disordered evacuation. *British Journal of Surgery* **82**, 1318–1320.

Jacobs, L.K., Lin, Y.J. and Orkin, B.A. (1997) The best operation for rectal prolapse. *Surgical Clinics of North America* **77**, 49–70.

Keighley, M.R. (1984) Postanal repair for faecal incontinence. *Journal of the Royal Society of Medicine* **77**, 285–288.

Keighley, M.R.B. and Korsgen, S. (1996) Long term results and predictive parameters of outcome following total pelvic floor repair. *Diseases of the Colon and Rectum* **39**, A15.

Kiely, M.A., Kaji, D.M., Duque, M., Wild, J. and Galansky, S.H. (1995) The Malone antegrade continence enema for neurogenic and structural fecal incontinence and constipation. *Journal of Urology* **154**, 759–761.

Krogh, K. and Laurberg, S. (1998) Malone antegrade enema for faecal incontinence and constipation in adults. *British Journal of Surgery* **85**, 974–977.

Kumar, D. and Benson, M. (1998) Gluteraldehyde cross-linked collagen in the treatment of faecal incontinence. *British Journal of Surgery* **85**, 978–979.

Leroi, A.-M., Kamm, M.A., Weber, J., Denis, P. and Hawley, P.R. (1997) Internal anal sphincter repair. *International Journal of Colorectal Disease* **12**, 243–245.

Londono-Schimmer, E.E., Garcia-Duperly, R., Nicholls, R.J., Ritchie, J.K., Hawley, P.R. and Thomson, J.P. (1994) Overlapping anal sphincter repair for faecal incontinence due to sphincter trauma: five year follow-up functional results. *International Journal of Colorectal Disease* **9**, 110–113.

Madoff, R.D., Williams, J.G., Wong, W.D., Rothenberger, D.A. and Goldberg, S.M. (1992) Long-term functional results of colon resection and rectopexy for overt rectal prolapse. *American Journal of Gastroenterology* **87**, 101–104.

Madoff, R.D., Rosen, H.R., Baeten, C.G., LaFontaine, L.J., Cavina, E., Devesa, M. et al. (1999) Safety and efficacy of dynamic muscle plasty for anal incontinence: lessons from a prospective, multicentre trial. *Gastroenterology* **116**, 549–556.

Malone, P.S., Ransley, P.G. and Kiely, E.M. (1990) Preliminary report: the antegrade continence enema. *Lancet* **336**, 1217–1218.

Malouf, A.J. and Bartolo, D.C.C. (1999) Rectal prolapse. In: Wexner, S.D. (ed.) *Protocols in general surgery: laparoscopic colorectal surgery*, Chapter 10. New York: Wiley-Liss.

Malouf, A.J., Cadogan, M.D. and Bartolo, D.C.C. (1999) Chapter 3.21: The Anal Canal. In: *Surgery*. Ed. V.W. Fazio. London: Mosby International.

Malouf, A., Norton, C., Nicholls, R.J. and Kamm, M.A. (2000a) Long-term results of anterior overlapping anal sphincter repair for obstetric trauma. *Lancet* **355**, 260–265.

Malouf, A.J., Vaizey, C.J., Kamm, M.A. and Nicholls, R.J. (2000b) Reassessing artificial bowel sphincters *Lancet* **355**, 2219–2220. [Letter]

Malouf, A.J., Vaizey, C.J., Nicholls, R.J. and Kamm, M.A. (2000c) Permanent sacral nerve stimulation for fecal incontinence. *Annals of Surgery* **232**, 143–148.

Malouf, A.J., Vaizey, C.J., Norton, C.S. and Kamm, M.A. (2001) Internal anal sphincter augmentation for faecal incontinence using injectable silicone biomaterial. *Diseases of the Colon and Rectum* **44**, 595–600.

Matheson, D.M. and Keighley, M.R.B. (1981) Manometric evaluation of rectal prolapse and faecal incontinence. *Gut* **22**, 126–129.

Matzel, K.E., Stadelmaier, U., Hohenfellner, M. and Gall, F.P. (1995) Electrical stimulation of spinal nerves for treatment of faecal incontinence. *Lancet* **346**, 1124–1127.

Maw, A., Hughes, F., Doherty, A., Stuchfield, B. and Williams, N. (1996) The continent colonic conduit for the treatment of evacuatort disorders of the colon and rectum. *International Journal of Colorectal Disease* **11**, 140.

Morgan, B., Patel, B., Beynon, J. and Carr, N.D. (1997) Surgical management of anorectal incontinence due to internal anal sphincter deficiency. *British Journal of Surgery* **84**, 226–230.

Orrom, W.J., Miller, R., Cornes, H., Duthie, G., Mortensen, N.J. and Bartolo, D.C. (1991) Comparison of anterior sphincteroplasty and postanal repair in the treatment of idiopathic fecal incontinence. *Diseases of the Colon and Rectum* **34**, 305–310.

Pinedo, G., Vaizey, C.J., Nicholls, R.J., Roach, S., Halligan, S. and Kamm, M.A. (1999) Results of repeat anal sphincter repair. *British Journal of Surgery* **86**, 66–69.

Rainey, J.B., Donaldson, D.R. and Thomson, J.P. (1990) Postanal repair: which patients derive most benefit? *Journal of the Royal College of Surgeons of Edinburgh* **35**, 101–105.

Rullier, E., Zerbib, F., Laurent, C., Caudry, M. and Saric, J. (2000) Morbidity and functional outcome after double dynamic graciloplasty for anorectal reconstruction. *British Journal of Surgery* **87**, 909–913.

Setti Carraro, P. and Nicholls, R.J. (1994) Postanal repair for faecal incontinence after rectopexy. *British Journal of Surgery* **81**, 305–307.

Setti Carraro, P., Kamm, M.A. and Nicholls, R.J. (1994) Long-term results of postanal repair for neurogenic faecal incontinence. *British Journal of Surgery* **81**, 140–144.

Shafik, A. (1993) Polytetrafluoroethylene injection for the treatment of partial faecal incontinence. *International Surgery* **78**, 159–161.

Shafik, A. (1995) Perianal injection of autologous fat for treatment of sphincteric incontinence. *Diseases of the Colon and Rectum* **38**, 583–587.

Shankar, K.R., Losty, P.D., Kenny, S.E., Booth, J.M., Turnock, R.R., Lamont, G.L., Rintala, R.J. and Lloyd, D.A. (1998) Functional results following the antegrade continence enema procedure. *British Journal of Surgery* **85**, 980–982.

Stuchfield, B. (1995) The continent colonic conduit in the management of severe constipation. *British Journal of Nursing* **4**, 1012–1016.

Sultan, A.H., Kamm, M.A., Hudson, C.N. and Bartram, C.I. (1993) Anal sphincter disruption during vaginal delivery. *New England Journal of Medicine* **329**, 1905–1911.

Vaizey, C.J., Kamm, M.A. and Nicholls, R.J. (1998) Recent advances in the surgical treatment of faecal incontinence. *British Journal of Surgery* **85**, 596–603.

Vaizey, C.J., Kamm, M.A., Turner, I., Nicholls, R.J. and Woloszko, J. (1999) Effects of short term sacral nerve stimulation on anal and rectal function in patients with anal incontinence. *Gut* **44**, 407–412.

Williams, J.G., Wong, W.D., Jensen, L., Rothenberger, D.A. and Goldberg, S.M. (1991) Incontinence and rectal prolapse: a prospective manometric study. *Diseases of the Colon and Rectum* **34**, 209–216.

Yoshioka, K. and Keighley, M.R. (1989) Critical assessment of the quality of continence after post-anal repair for faecal incontinence. *British Journal of Surgery* **76**, 1054–1057.

Young, C.J., Mathur, M.N., Eyers, A.A. and Solomon, M.J. (1998) Successful overlapping anal sphincter repair: relationship to patient age, neuropathy, and colostomy formation. *Diseases of the Colon and Rectum* **41**, 344–349.

Chapter 15

A Stoma for Incontinence?

Julia Williams

Introduction

Stoma surgery is often viewed as a last-resort treatment for a patient with faecal incontinence, and may be perceived in a negative manner. It has been referred to in the literature as a 'high price to pay for a cure' (Devlin et al., 1971). In fact a stoma has the potential to improve the patient's quality of life, especially in those patients with a spinal injury (Stone et al., 1990; Craven and Etchells, 1998).

Appearance is a very important concept in the Western world and it influences how a person is perceived and valued by others and how the person values themselves. The known psychological impact of stoma surgery may inhibit early discussion of the option by healthcare professionals, as it may be thought that in resolving the problem of faecal incontinence, another problem is caused. This chapter explores the issues relating to the suitability of a stoma as a modality of treatment for someone who is faecally incontinent.

Culturally and socially, bodily waste is viewed within Western societies as a private function best dealt with in the privacy of the individual's own home. Achieving continence is regarded as one of the major milestones in childhood, and very early on we learn that our bodily waste is seen as dirty and that it has the potential to be harmful to ourselves and others. When and where a child or adult goes to the toilet is governed by what is deemed as socially acceptable, which usually means within the confines of a lavatory where the waste can be cleanly flushed away. If bodily waste is found on the floor or on a chair it is considered 'a matter out of place' (Douglas, 1966: cited Littlewood and Holden, 1991), and is likely to offend others and hence be deemed to be socially unacceptable.

What is a stoma?

A stoma can be viewed as a false anus constructed surgically from the bowel so to protrude through the abdominal wall, thus allowing for the passage of bodily waste into a conveniently placed appliance (see Figure 15.1). The word 'stoma' derives from the Greek word meaning

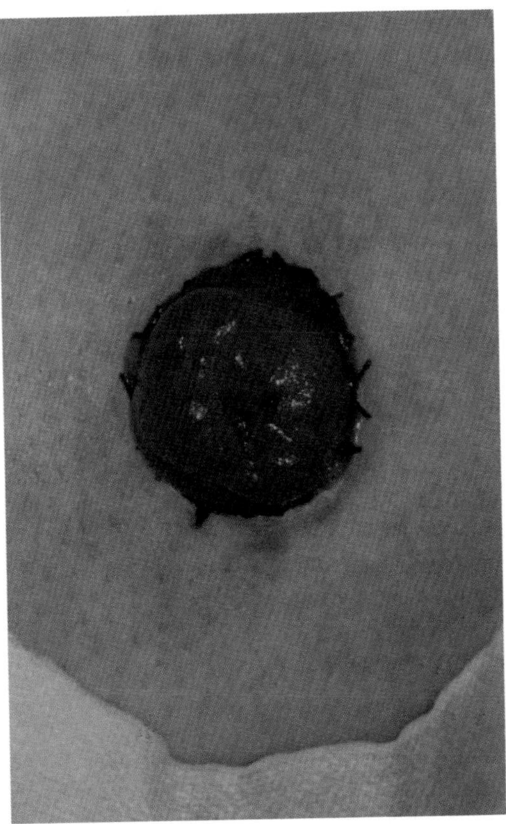

Figure 15.1 *Stoma.*

opening or mouth. It is unclear as to how many people are living with a stoma, but estimates suggest approximately 80,000 people have a stoma in the UK (Department of Health, 1998) and around 15,000 new stomas are formed by surgeons in the UK each year (Department of Health, 1998). These will either be temporary or permanent.

Delvin (1985) describes three categories of stoma:

1) Input stomas – a temporary stoma used for feeding purposes, e.g. gastrostomy
2) Diverting stomas – usually a temporary stoma that creates a diversion of effluent thus allowing a diseased gut and/or an anastomosis to heal, e.g. loop ileostomy
3) Output stomas – a permanent stoma as an outlet for elimination of body waste, e.g. colostomy, ileostomy, and urostomy

A wide range of pathological, congenital and traumatic conditions necessitate the formation of a stoma (Nicholls, 1996). The type and anatomical position of the stoma will determine the nature, the frequency, the consistency and the odour of the bodily waste passed, thus requiring different types of appliance fittings. For example, a colostomy will have an output that is soft to firm and therefore is collected in a closed appliance, whereas an ileostomy will have a soft to liquid output and be better managed with a drainable appliance (see Figure 15.2). A urostomy will eliminate urine and will require an appliance with a tap. A person with a stoma will have no muscular control over their elimination and hence the need to wear an appliance. The appliance not only collects the waste but also acts as a protection for the peristomal skin. It could be viewed that someone with a stoma is permanently 'incontinent' but within a controlled environment, i.e. the wearing of a bag.

Some people react with horror and distaste when told that they may require a stoma, for this type of surgery has a profound effect on the mind as well as the body. It reverses the healthy body image people usually have of themselves (Salter, 1997) and therefore requires a great deal of adaptation and acceptance, both physically and psychologically. Stoma formation can result in feelings of inadequacy, vulnerability and dirtiness and is therefore not associated with positive aspects of life. The visible presence of the stoma, to some, is a constant reminder of previous illness and/or trauma. This may result in the person with a stoma considering whether they are still attractive to potential sexual partners or how they will be intimate with another person ever again. There may be concerns as to whether the appliance will get in the way of lovemaking, and how close will they let some-

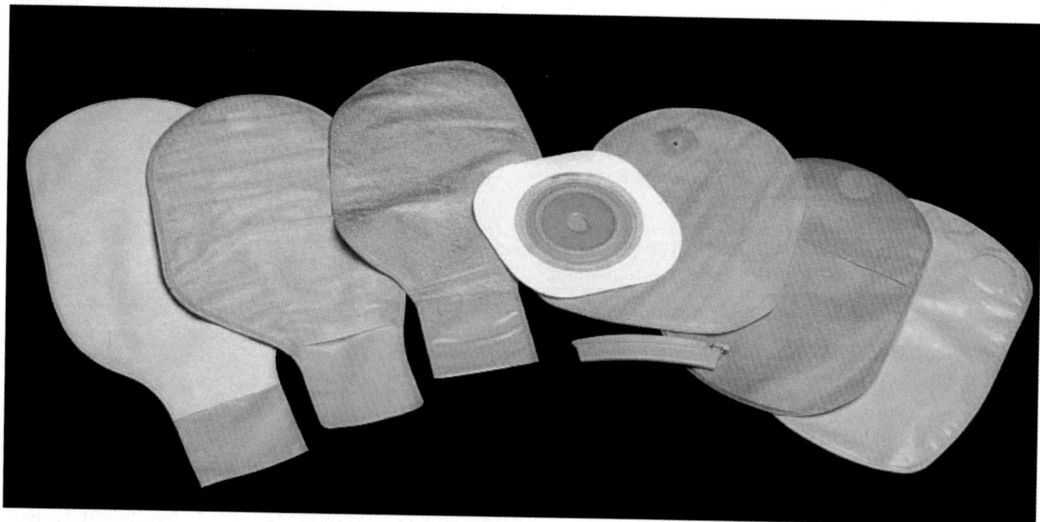

Figure 15.2 *Closed and drainable appliances.*

one get to them in the knowledge that they have faeces in a bag that happens to be attached to their abdomen. And what about the appliance? Is it likely to leak? Is it visible, does it smell or will it disguise the sound of passing wind? Many of these concerns are likely to mirror those thoughts and feelings of being faecally incontinent (Nugent et al., 1999).

A shared concern amongst people with a new stoma is whether others might detect the stoma; this results in the tendency to avoid social situations. Appearance on the outside is as important as appearance on the inside, and many people with a stoma lack the confidence to deal with a social situation. The nurse specialist in stoma care is in a prime position not only to assist the patient in coming to terms with their adaptation but also to suggest alternatives to wearing an appliance, in order that patients can adapt and regain their confidence to re-establish or tackle new social situations.

Options for ostomists

Having a stoma may not always necessitate wearing a bag at all times. Several alternatives may be considered.

Biodegradable appliance

This type of appliance has been available to ostomists since the late 1980s. Its usage is variable and many people will only use this appliance if staying away from home for any period of time. It offers patients an element of normality when they visit the toilet. The appliance is designed to flush reliably in any toilet that is capable of flushing normal toilet paper. The disposal of the soiled appliance and cleaning materials is thus kept to a minimum (see Figure 15.3). Once flushed, the biodegradable appliance immediately enters the main sewage system and begins to break down, allowing the waste to biodegrade normally.

Advantages of this appliance include having to carry less items such as cleaning equipment and a disposal bag, reduction in time to change the appliance and less mess to dispose of (if any), and gives greater confidence to change appliance whenever needed. As with all other stoma appliances, the biodegradable appliance is available on prescription via the patient's general practitioner.

The colostomy plug

The colostomy plug will not leave the person completely appliance-free but its main aim is to regain 'control' over bodily functions. It has been pioneered since the mid 1980s and involves the use of a soft foam plug, which is gently inserted into the stoma. This then expands, blocking the expulsion of faeces whilst filtering flatus (Soliani et al. 1992).

The colostomy plug system consists of a plug and a base plate (see Figure 15.4, overleaf). It is available as a one- or two-piece system. A closed pouch is worn in between plug applications. Considerable motivation is needed to use this system, as it can take four to six weeks

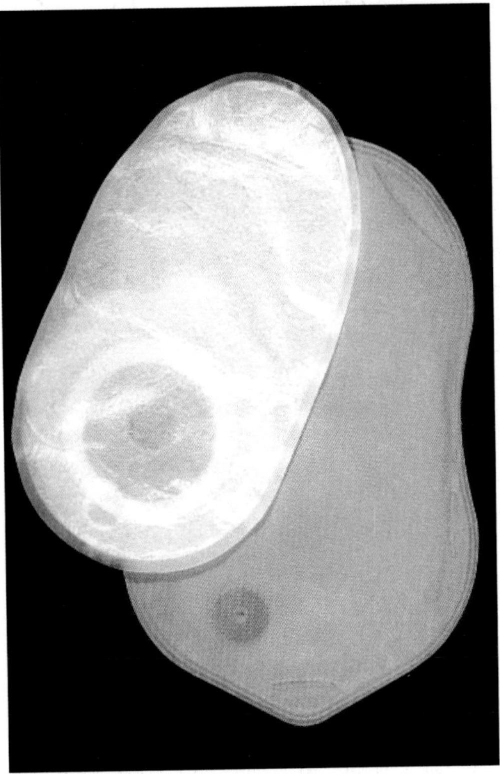

Figure 15.3 *Biodegradable appliances.*

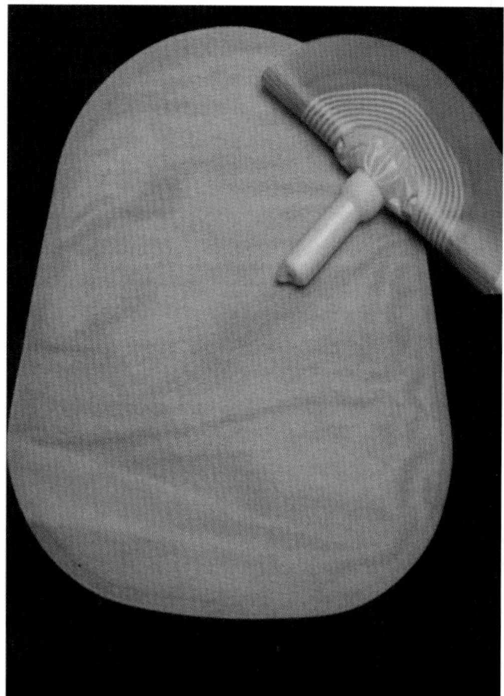

Figure 15.4 *Colostomy plug.*

before a regime is established (Table 15.1). A colostomy plug can be used in association with colostomy irrigation, as discussed below.

Colostomy irrigation

Colostomy irrigation is a technique, usually taught by the nurse specialist in stoma care, which allows cleansing of the large bowel by introducing water through the stoma via a cone and irrigating equipment (see Figures 15.5 and 15.6). Once the procedure is completed, the ostomist will not require the use of a stoma appliance but will be able to use a small stoma cap over the stoma. When a stoma has been formed for incontinence, irrigation is used to gain some control over bowel habit.

The precise origin of colostomy irrigation is unknown. Early records indicate that a French surgeon introduced the notion in the late 1700s. It is unclear as to how many people with a colostomy use this technique. There are suggestions that no more than 5% of all people with a colostomy irrigate in the UK (Wade, 1989; MacDonald, 1991; O'Bichere, 1999). It is not clear why so few people use irrigation, as studies have shown that colostomy irrigation has the potential to improve quality of life greatly by providing freedom to carry out everyday activities without fear of a bowel action, thus giving some ostomists the confidence not to use a stoma appliance at all. Remarkably, it remains under-utilised primarily because many people believe that the time required to perform effective colostomy irrigation can be put to better use. Some nurse specialists also feel that it is time-consuming to teach the patient the basic principles, whilst others do not have the facilities to teach the patient within their stoma care departments and thus the patient will require several home visits.

The main advantage of colostomy irrigation for the patient is the ability to regain 'control' over bowel actions, so that in some respect the patient is 'continent' again. This should ultimately lead to increased self-esteem and self-image, allowing their quality of life to improve. Irrigators report being able to eat a more varied diet, as flatus and mucus are greatly reduced. A year's supply of irrigating equipment costs a lot less than the equivalent in stoma appliances since irrigating equipment is reusable. Some ostomists are allergic to some appliances, and irrigation is an ideal way of reducing allergic reactions.

There are however disadvantages. The main difficulty is time. The procedure itself can take up to an hour as frequently as every day, but in the main this is on alternate days. The procedure should never be hurried, as a rushed poor technique increases the risk of bowel perforation or incomplete bowel emptying. For busy households with only one bathroom this may cause some difficulty and disruption to daily routines. If irrigation is practised for some time there is evidence to suggest that the bowel becomes sluggish, and therefore if irrigation is stopped for any reason long-term aperients may be required. Table 15.2 (overleaf) highlights which ostomists may be suitable for this procedure.

Table 15.1: Teaching plan for colostomy plug users

Days (approx.)		***Comments***
1–5	Learning how to use 2-piece system	It is recommended to use base plate of this system with a closed appliance. Base plate should be renewed between 3 to 5 days. Closed appliance should be renewed as used.
6	The first plug. This should be inserted after bowel action. It is recommended this is worn for six hours (as tolerated) and then removed and replaced with usual closed appliance	Some discomfort may be felt. Reassurance should be given that this will ease with time and further plug installations. Allow time for faecal waste to discharge before installing new plug.
7–11	Wear plug for up to six hours (as tolerated) each day	Faecal leakage is likely to occur or the plug may be pushed out as a result of faecal waste or flatus. Reassurance will be required. Patients can become despondent at this point because they are losing rather than gaining control.
11–13	Increase plug wearing time to 7 hours each day (as tolerated)	Adaptation can take place over the next few days as the patient learns and senses when the plug requires removal.
14–18	Increase plug wearing time to 8 hours each day (as tolerated)	Length of time that plug is tolerated to be recorded. Length of time will vary depending on diet, consistency of faecal waste and amount of flatus formed.
19–22	Increase plug wearing time to 9–10 hours each day (as tolerated)	If tolerated, patient should be encouraged to increase length of time plug is in place.
23–26	Increase plug wearing time up to 12 hours each day (as tolerated)	Always carry extra supplies in case of leakages.
27–45	Gain confidence with the system	It will take several weeks to build up wear time.

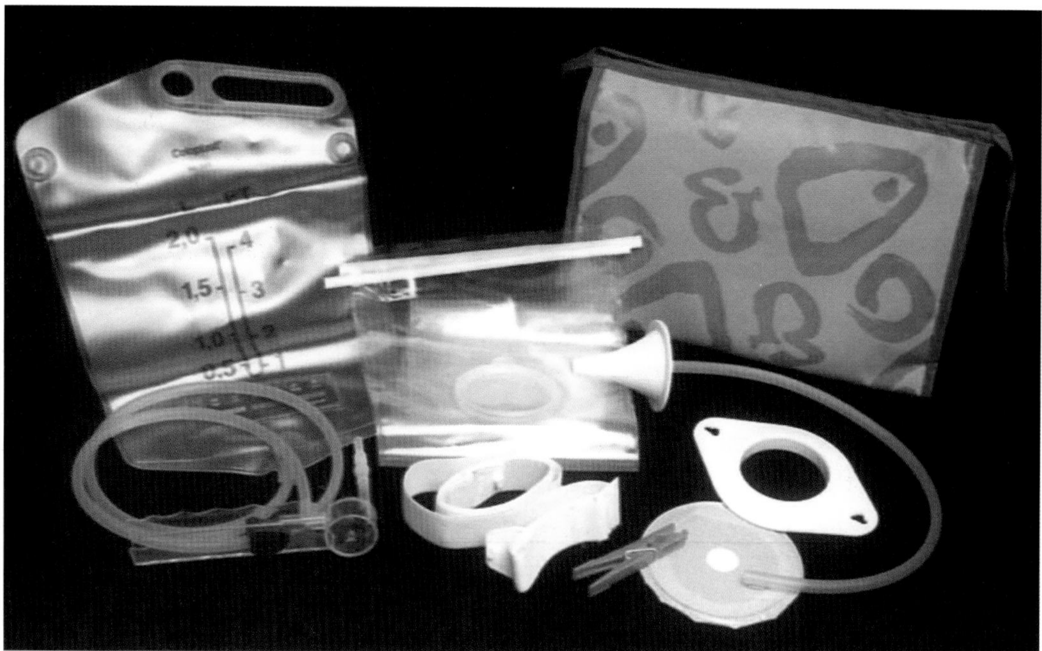

Figure 15.5 *Colostomy irrigating equipment.*

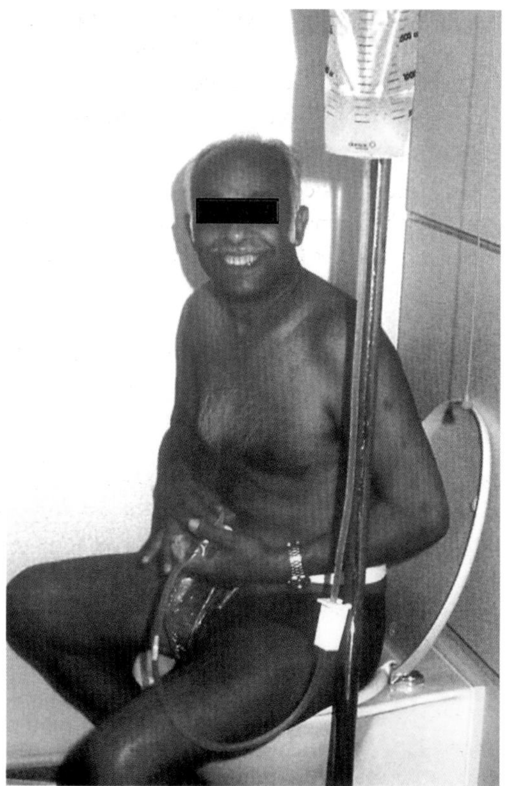

Figure 15.6 *Patient irrigating.*

Table 15.2: Patients suitable for colostomy irrigation
End colostomy with a formed stool
No evidence of stomal complications, e.g. hernia, prolapse or stenosis
No evidence of inflammatory bowel disease
Keen, motivated and committed
No physical impairments, e.g. poor eyesight, poor dexterity
Supportive social network
Adequate toilet facilities, e.g. separate toilet and bathroom
No medical history of heart disease or renal impairment
Calm, patient and relaxed outlook
Consultant's approval

Biofeedback training

Reboa et al. (1985) used biofeedback techniques with patients with a permanent colostomy to improve colostomy continence. The treatment used balloon distension to improve sensitivity to intestinal distension as near to the colostomy as possible. The aim was to learn how to control a bowel action. Fifteen out of eighteen patients reported good objective and subjective results in the ability to control flatus and bowel evacuations. Certainly this is an area which requires further investigation.

Incontinence versus a stoma

Both faecal incontinence and having a stoma can have a detrimental effect on body image and sexuality. So which is preferable? A stoma is never mandatory, and health professionals should present it as a choice, avoiding any pressure to decide one way or the other. Each individual must decide for themselves. There are several factors that need to be taken into consideration.

To some extent the various parts of our bodies form essential parts of our personality. It therefore follows that any injury to a body part is likely to result in loss of self-image and self-esteem. If a person is happy with the physical aspects of themselves, then they are likely to express positive feelings of self-esteem (Wesner, 1982). In contrast, a person who is unhappy with their physical appearance is likely to express negative feelings of self-esteem (Burnard and Morrison, 1990). Somebody with faecal incontinence is likely already to be experiencing some degree of altered body image and sexuality changes prior to discussion of the option of stoma surgery. Counselling as to the possible benefits and disadvantages of a stoma need to be discussed sensitively.

People have different coping mechanisms. Both stoma patients and those who are faecally incontinent may feel stigmatised by their families, society and employers. When an individual has a hidden stigma such as faecal incontinence or a stoma, their pathology is not apparent and they are left with the dilemma to 'decide to tell or not to, to let on or not to, to lie or not to lie' about their hidden disability (Price, 1990). Public attitudes form a serious barrier for some patients to cope with (Chelvanayagam and Norton, 2000) since incontinence is socially unacceptable, a fact that is acknowledged from early childhood. Beitz (1999) suggests that patients distance themselves from bodies that they cannot control and which render them socially unacceptable. In many instances it is a long time before individuals will seek professional help and support, as this incontinent sufferer describes:

> *'When this system breaks down it violates something intrinsic to our sense of worth. I was still clearly adult; I no longer felt human. That function of my body had become animal-like. I dealt with what was happening by denying it. The fact that it kept happening did not deter me from this denial. It would never happen again, I told myself after each occurrence. I was the only person I spoke to about it, and even I would not listen.'*
>
> (Unknown sufferer, quoted in Littlewood and Holden, 1991).

The patient's success in coping depends upon his or her personal strategies and social support. How we cope and accept support is determined by relationships and experiences throughout our lives – for example, our families, friends, work colleagues and the environment setting (Price, 1990). Friends and family play an important role in the readjustment to life with a stoma or faecal incontinence. It is felt that if they portray a positive attitude towards the person then in turn they will perceive themselves in a positive manner. If family and friends are able to provide a setting whereby the alteration in body image may be integrated into society, it will remind them of their personal worth and allow the development of ways to talk comfortably about their changed circumstances (Price, 1993). However, to date there has been no literature defining which patients will react positively to formation of a stoma to manage faecal incontinence, and it is not known what factors are important in preoperative assessment.

Adapting to stressful events may be facilitated by adequate social support (Baider et al., 1998). Support groups enable interactions with others that share common experiences, allowing the sharing of knowledge, mutual acceptance and moral support that is not available from people who have not experienced it. Most adapt psychosocially to living with a stoma (Rolstad and Nemer, 1985). However, it is estimated that 20% experience long-term difficulties (Dozois et al., 1980) such as peristomal skin excoriation, prolapsed stoma, herniation, retraction and stenosis (McCahon, 1999). There is no evidence as to whether poeple who have a stoma for incontinence adapt any differently to those who have a stoma for other reasons.

One female colostomist describes life as:

'I live a full and normal life; I eat and drink what I want, I travel, work full-time, have relationships with men and try to live life to the full.'
(Unknown cited: White 1997).

Conclusions

No comparative study has yet been undertaken to see how quality of life might be improved following stoma formation for people with faecal incontinence, although there are indications that specific groups react very positively (e.g. Stone et al., 1990). It is therefore the responsibility of the healthcare professional to address these issues with the faecally incontinent patient on an individual basis. The formation of a stoma is not necessarily a 'cure' for all problems associated with faecal incontinence, but it should be considered as a modality of surgical treatment for those individuals who are experiencing incontinence which has not been amenable to other conservative or surgical treatments.

References

Baider, L., Koch, U., Esacon, R. and Kaplan de-Noir, T. (1998) Prospective study of cancer patients and their spouses: the weakness of marital strength. *Psycho-Oncology* **7**, 49–56.

Beitz, J. (1999) The lived experience of having an ileoanal reservoir: a phenomenologic study. *Journal of Wound Ostomy and Continence Nursing* **26**, 4, 185–200.

Burnard, J. and Morrison, L. (1990) Body image and physical appearance. *Surgical Nurse* **3**, 4–8.

Chelvanayagam, S. and Norton, C. (2000) Quality of life with faecal continence problems. *Nursing Times plus* **96**, 31, 15–17.

Craven, M.L. and Etchells, J. (1988) A review of the outcome of stoma surgery on spinal cord injured patients. *Journal of Advanced Nursing* **27**, 922–926.

Department of Health Statistics (1998) London: HMSO.

Devlin, H.B. (1985) *Stoma care today.* Oxford: Medical Education Sources.

Devlin, H.B., Plant, J. and Griffin, M. (1971) Aftermath of anorectal cancer. *British Medical Journal* **14**, 413–418.

Dozois, R., Kelly, K., Beart, R. and Bahrs, O. (1980) Improved results with continent ileostomy. *Annals of Surgery* **192**, 319–324.

Goffman, E. (1963) *Notes on the management of spoiled identity*. New York: Prentice Hall.

Littlewood, J. and Holden, P. (1991) *Anthropology and nursing*. London: Routledge.

Johanson, J.F. and Lafferty, J. (1996) Epidemiology of fecal incontinence: the silent affliction. *American Journal of Gastroenterology* **91**, 33–36.

Kamm, M. (1998) Faecal incontinence – clinical review. *British Medical Journal* **316**, 528–532.

McCahon, S. (1999) Faecal stomas. In: Porrett, T. and Daniel, N. (eds) *Essential coloproctology for nurses*. London: Whurr Publishers, 165–187.

MacDonald, K. (1991) Colostomy irrigation: an option worth considering. *Professional Nurse* **7**, 15–16 and 18–19.

Nicholls, R.J. (1996) Surgical procedures. In: Myers, C. (ed.) *Stoma care nursing – a patient-centred approach,* 90–122. London: Arnold.

Norton, C. (1997) Faecal incontinence in adults 2: treatment and management. *British Journal of Nursing* **6**, 1, 23–26.

Nugent, K.P., Patankar, S.K., Stewart, B., Pantakar, R. and Johnson, C.D. (1999) Quality of life in stoma patients. *Diseases of the Colon and Rectum* **42**, 1569–1574.

Price, B. (1990) *Body image – nursing concepts and care*. London: Prentice Hall.

Price, B. (1993) How to make an assessment of altered body image in stoma patients. *Eurostoma* **4**, Autumn, 14.

Reboa, G., Frascio, M., Zanolla, R., Pitto, G. and Berti Riboli, E. (1985) Biofeedback training to obtain continence in permanent colostomy: experience of two centers. *Diseases of the Colon and Rectum* **28**, 419–421.

Rolstad, B. and Nemer, F. (1985) Management problems associated with ileoanal reservoir. *Journal of Enterostomal Therapy* **12**, 2, 41–48.

Salter, M. (1997) *Altered body image – the nurse's role* (2nd edn) London: Baillière Tindall.

Smith, L.J. and Smith, P.S. (1993) In: Barrett, J.A. (ed.) *Faecal incontinence and related problems in the older adult*, 173–206. London: Edward Arnold.

Soliani, P., Carbognani, P., Piccolo, P., Sabbagh, R. and Cudazzo, E. (1992) Colostomy plug devices: a possible new approach to the problem of incontinence. *Diseases of the Colon and Rectum* **35**, 969–974.

Stone, J., Wolfe, V.A., Nino-Murcia, M. and Perkash, I. (1990) Colostomy as treatment for complications of spinal cord injury. *Archives of Physical Medicine and Rehabilitation* **71**, 514–518.

Wade, B (1989) *A stoma for life – a study of stoma care nurses and their patients*. London: Scutari Press.

Wesner, A. (1982) The impact of mutilating surgery or trauma on body image. *International Nursing Review* **29**, 3, 86–90.

White, C. (1997) *Living with a stoma*. London: Sheldon Press.

Manufacturers producing ostomy products

Product	**Manufacturer**
Biodegradable appliance	Symphony, SIMS Portex Ltd, Boundary Road, Hythe CT21 6JL. Tel. 01303 208049 www.portex.com
	Impact, Clinimed Ltd, Cavell House, Knaves Beech Way, Loudwater, Bucks HP10 9QY. Tel. 0800 585125 www.clinimed.com
Colostomy plug	Conseal Colostomy System, Coloplast Ltd (see below)
Colostomy irrigation sets	Coloplast Ltd, Peterborough Business Park, Peterborough PE2 0FX. Tel. 01733 392000 www.coloplast.com
	Dansac Ltd, Victory House, Vision Park, Histon CB4 4ZR. Tel. 0800 581117 www.dansac.com
	Hollister Ltd, Rectory Court, 42 Broad Street, Wokingham RG11 1AB. Tel. 0800 521377 www.hollister.co.uk

Chapter 16

Drug Therapy for Faecal Incontinence

Mark Cheetham

Introduction

Current drugs used in the treatment of faecal incontinence may be classified as constipating agents, bulking agents and evacuation aids (Table 16.1). Individual drugs within these three groups are further considered below.

Table 16.1: Drugs used in the treatment of faecal incontinence

Category	*Examples of drugs*
Constipating agents	loperamide (Imodium) codeine phosphate co-phenotrope (Lomotil)
Stool bulking agents	ispaghula bran methylcellulose
Evacuation aids	polyethylene glycol (PEG) magnesium sulphate glycerin suppositories Bisacodyl
Antidepressants	amitriptyline
Novel treatments	topical phenylephrine sodium valproate
Hormone replacement therapy	topical or systemic

Constipating agents

Constipating agents act by reducing stool volume and improving stool consistency. They are useful in a variety of situations associated with faecal incontinence. Caution must be exercised in using these drugs in patients with pre-existing constipation. The principal drugs used at present are loperamide, codeine phosphate and co-phenotrope. Currently none of these drugs are licensed for use in the treatment of faecal incontinence.

Loperamide

Loperamide (trade name Imodium) is the most commonly used drug used in the treatment of faecal incontinence. This drug is a synthetic opioid with a low side-effect profile. Loperamide is currently licensed for the treatment of diarrhoea and for improving a liquid stoma effluent. The principle action of loperamide is to increase gut transit time (Sun et al., 1997) (and thus increase the amount of water absorbed from stool). Loperamide also reduces small bowel fluid secretion by modulation of the calcium-calmodulin system. Patients treated with loperamide have a reduced stool volume and a firmer stool consistency (Sun et al., 1997; Read et al., 1982; Herbst et al., 1998). Additional actions of loperamide are to reduce the amount of internal anal sphincter relaxation associated with rectal distension and to reduce rectal contractions. There appears to be minimal alteration of anal canal resting pressure in man following the administration of loperamide. All published randomised controlled trials have assessed the use of loperamide to treat faecal incontinence associated with chronic diarrhoea or in patients who have had ileoanal pouch surgery (see Table 16.2). However, clinical experience suggests that low doses of loperamide are effective in

Table 16.2: Randomised controlled trials of drug therapy for the treatment of faecal incontinence

Study	*Drugs used*	*Participants*	*Main findings*
Palmer et al., 1980	Loperamide, codeine phosphate and co-phenotrope	30 patients with chronic diarrhoea and faecal urgency	All drugs reduced stool weight and frequency. Co-phenotrope was the least effective
Harford et al., 1980	Co-phenotrope and placebo	15 patients with chronic diarrhoea and faecal incontinence	Co-phenotrope reduced stool weight and frequency
Read et al., 1982	Loperamide 4 mg and placebo	26 patients with chronic diarrhoea and faecal incontinence	Loperamide reduced stool weight and frequency together with reduced episodes of incontinence and urgency
Kusunoki et al., 1990	Sodium valproate and placebo	17 patients with ileoanal pouches	Reduction in incontinence episodes and improved stool consistency
Hallgren et al., 1994	Loperamide 4mg and placebo	30 patients with ileoanal pouches	Loperamide reduced stool frequency and weight
Sun et al., 1997	Loperamide oxide and placebo	11 patients with chronic diarrhoea and faecal incontinence	Loperamide oxide increased transit time and reduced stool weight with improvement in symptoms
Carapeti et al., 2000a	Topical 10% phenylephrine and placebo	12 patients with faecal incontinence and ileoanal pouches	50% of patients treated with phenylephrine improved continence
Carapeti et al., 2000b	Topical 10% phenylephrine and placebo	36 patients with faecal incontinence related to weak but intact anal sphincters	No overall benefit for patients treated with phenylephrine

reducing and controlling faecal incontinence even when stool consistency is normal.

The most common side effect of loperamide administration is constipation (Palmer et al., 1980). This may be minimised by commencing at a low dose and by careful titration of the dose to the patient's symptoms. Loperamide is usually started in a low dose of 1 to 2 mg once a day, and the patient is instructed to titrate the dose of the drug according to stool consistency and symptoms. Some patients find that doses less than 2 mg are optimal, in this situation loperamide syrup (1 mg of loperamide in 5 ml) allows more accurate titration. Alternatives to this regimen are to use half tablets of loperamide (i.e. 1 mg) once a day, or to use loperamide on alternate days. Patients with liquid stool (for example patients with ileoanal pouches, or those with short bowel syndrome) may require doses of up to 32 mg of loperamide a day. It is important to give the patient adequate information regarding the drug and how to adjust the dose. A patient information sheet as in Figure 16.1 is a useful adjunct to the effective use of anti-diarrhoeal agents. Loperamide is contra-indicated in acute colitis, as toxic megacolon can be precipitated, and it should be used with caution in patients with ulcerative colitis.

Codeine phosphate

Codeine phosphate is also a useful agent in the treatment of faecal incontinence. It is a naturally-occurring opiate which also acts to prolong transit time. It is prescribed in tablet or syrup form in doses of 30-120 mg daily in divided doses. The use of codeine is limited by the relatively high incidence of side effects, principally drowsiness. Additionally, long-term usage of codeine may be associated with tolerance – that is, a higher dose is required to cause the same effect. Despite these problems, codeine is a useful agent in the treatment of faecal incontinence. It may be given in addition to loperamide when maximal doses have failed to reduce symptoms.

Co-phenotrope

Co-phenotrope (trade name Lomotil) is used by some clinicians to treat faecal incontinence. This preparation consists of a synthetic opioid (diphenoxylate) and an anti-cholergic agent (atropine). The mechanism of action of diphenoxylate is similar to that of loperamide. Atropine also reduces gut motility, although it is added principally to reduce the abuse potential of diphenoxylate. There is a relatively high incidence of side effects associated with co-phenotrope (Gattuso and Kamm, 1994), principally related to the atropine content (dry mouth, confusion and urinary retention). For these reasons, co-phenotrope is not usually recommended for the treatment of faecal incontinence. However, some patients are not troubled by the side effects, and for this group the drug remains useful.

Antidepressants

Tricyclic antidepressants such as amitriptyline have been used in the treatment of faecal incontinence. Their main effect is via their anti-cholinergic actions, which prolong gut transit time and increase water absorption from stool (Santoro et al., 2000). Central side effects (such as dry mouth, blurred vision and drowsiness) are relatively common. As there are no comparative trials of the use of these agents for the treatment of faecal incontinence, their use should be restricted to those patients requiring tricyclics for another indication.

Stool bulking agents

Stool bulking agents are used by some doctors in the treatment of faecal incontinence. They are all supplements of non-digestible fibre, for example ispaguala husk, bran or methyl-cellulose. These drugs act by retaining water from within the gut, producing an increased stool volume and a looser stool consistency. However, larger volumes of soft stool may be more difficult for incontinent patients to retain, particularly in those with weak anal sphincters. They may have a limited role to play in the

Table 16.3: Information for patients taking loperamide (Imodium)

You have been prescribed loperamide (also sometimes known as Imodium) for your bowel problem. This information sheet is designed to give you some more information about this medication.

What is loperamide?

Loperamide is one of a group of drugs called anti-diarrhoeals. These drugs are designed to thicken your stools and so to reduce diarrhoea. It will also firm up slightly soft stools.

How does it work?

Loperamide works by slowing down the passage of food through the gut and encouraging more uptake by the body of water from the waste in the lower bowel. The longer food takes to pass through the gut, the more time there is for water to be absorbed from it through the gut wall. The stools that are then produced are thicker and firmer.

What dose do I take?

A suggested starting dose of loperamide will have been discussed with you. People vary a lot in their response to this medicine. It sometimes needs some experimentation to find the dose that will control your bowels without constipating you. The more you take the firmer your stools should become. If you take more than you need you may feel constipated. If you do not take enough your stools will remain loose or soft. It is usual to start on a low dose and build it up slowly over a few days so that you can judge how you body is responding.

Loperamide comes in capsules / tablets or as a syrup. As the syrup is often used for children it can only be obtained on prescription in the UK.

Amount you take	*Actual dose of loperamide*
1 capsule / tablet	2 milligrams
1 teaspoon (5 ml)	1 milligram
1 half teaspoon (2.5 ml)	Half a milligram

It is best to take loperamide half an hour before a meal. This will help to slow down the usual gut activity that is stimulated by eating. Most people find that the bowel is most active in the morning and so loperamide will help most if taken before breakfast. The medicine starts to work within half an hour of taking it and is effective for 8–12 hours. This means that doses taken after lunch are not likely to help much if all your problems are in the morning. However, a dose last thing at night may help with early morning frequency. Loperamide is a very safe drug which is not addictive. It can be taken in doses of up to 8 capsules (16 milligrams) per day over long periods of time. Do not take more than 16 milligrams per day without medical advice.

If you have any further questions please do not hesitate to ask.

treatment of faecal incontinence associated with persistent loose stools, by helping to bind the stool together. There are no published randomised controlled trials which have assessed the efficacy of fibre supplements in reducing symptoms of faecal incontinence.

Evacuation aids

In patients with constipation and faecal incontinence, the use of evacuation aids may allow predictable emptying of the rectum with full continence in the intervening period. This regimen may be useful in patients with post-defaecation soiling associated with incomplete rectal emptying. Glycerine suppositories are often used in this context. If these are ineffective, the use of bisacodyl suppositories may be indicated. In addition to lubrication, bisacodyl suppositories have a mild rectal stimulant action. Mini-enemas containing either phosphate or a lubricant achieve a similar result, and may be required in refractory cases. Rectal washouts via a Foley catheter placed in the rectum also cause effectively predictable emptying. Proprietary devices with a balloon to occlude the anal canal are available for patients who are unable to retain the instilled solution due to sphincter weakness (See Chapter 17).

Patients with overflow incontinence related to faecal impaction usually require more aggressive treatment. In such patients an osmotic laxative such as magnesium sulphate or polyethylene glycol (PEG) are the agents of choice. These drugs are taken by mouth and act by retaining water within the gut lumen; the net result is liquid stool. By titrating the dose to stool consistency and symptoms, it is possible to ensure predictable rectal emptying. This may need to be combined with enemas, at least initially. Such a strategy is particularly useful in the medical treatment of patients with megarectum (Gattuso and Kamm, 1997).

When faecal incontinence cannot be controlled in any other way, a patient may choose to stop spontaneous evacuation altogether using anti-diarrhoeal agents (see above) and then empty the rectum at a planned time using suppositories, enema or washouts. Great care is needed so that impaction does not develop. Although not ideal, this regime may allow the faecally incontinent person a degree of control that cannot be obtained otherwise, thereby improving quality of life (Tobin and Brocklehurst, 1986).

Novel treatments

Sodium valproate

A cross-over study comparing the use of sodium valproate with placebo in patients with ileoanal pouches demonstrated that valproate increased anal canal resting pressure and reduced episodes of soiling (Kusunoki et al., 1990) (see Table 16.2, page 175). However, in this study patients were only treated for 7 days. There was a high incidence of side effects in the patients treated with valproate – 6 out of the 17 patients experienced nausea with 2 experiencing severe abdominal pain. No studies have assessed longer-term administration of sodium valproate for this indication and it is not in current clinical use.

Topical phenylephrine

The internal anal sphincter receives a stimulatory innervation from the sympathetic nervous system. Laboratory studies have shown that application of the alpha-1 agent phenylephrine causes contraction of isolated human internal anal sphincter strips (Regadas et al., 1993). Recent work has demonstrated that application of a gel containing phenylephrine to the anus of volunteers increases anal canal resting pressure (Carapeti et al., 1999). In this study, 10% phenylephrine gel was found to be the optimal concentration, increases resting anal pressure by a mean of 33% for up to 7 hours. A study in patients with faecal incontinence following ileoanal pouch surgery demonstrated reduced episodes of incontinence in 50% of the patients treated (Carapeti et al., 2000a) (see Table 16.2, page 175). Topically applied phenylephrine has also been shown to increase anal canal resting pressure in patients with faecal incontinence due to a weak internal sphincter, although higher concentrations seem to be required (Cheetham et al., 2001). Clinical studies are in progress to assess the effectiveness and safety of this drug in the treatment of faecal incontinence. Early results have been disappointing (Carapeti et al., 2000b).

Hormone replacement therapy

Prevalence studies often suggest a lower prevalence of urinary incontinence in women in the immediate post-menopausal years than in younger women (Tobin and Brocklehurst, 1986). This casts some doubt on the common assertion of patients that symptoms started at menopause and on the role of hormone deficiency in causation of pelvic floor symptoms.

Hormone replacement therapy (HRT) is commonly used in clinical practice to treat urinary incontinence in post-menopausal women. However, objective evidence for efficacy is lacking, although subjective rating of symptoms by patients may improve (Fantl et al., 1994). The preventative value of hormone replacement is unknown, although oestrogen receptors throughout the female genito-urinary tract and in the pelvic floor musculature make this a possibility.

One study has suggested some benefit from HRT in post-menopausal women with faecal incontinence (Donnelly et al., 1997). Resting and squeeze pressures were increased, as was the maximum volume tolerated in the rectum. The presence of an anal sphincter defect did not preclude symptomatic benefit. 90% of women reported some improvement and 25% became symptom-free. These results must be viewed with caution as it was a small (20 patient) uncontrolled study, and it has been suggested that subjective wellbeing rather than objective improvement may be the mode of action (Fantl et al., 1994). However, it does raise the question of the role of prophylactic HRT in preventing faecal incontinence in older women. It is known that hormone replacement can increase collagen and elastic tissue in the pelvic floor, that there are oestrogen receptors in the external anal sphincter (Haadem et al., 1991) and that anal pressures have a tendency to decrease with advancing age (Laurberg and Swash, 1989). It is theoretically possible that HRT could decrease or even reverse this trend. It would need a very large longitudinal study to investigate this. Meanwhile clinically post-menopausal women in whom HRT is not contraindicated may be considered for a trial of therapy, particularly if there are also signs of atrophic changes vaginally.

Conclusions

Pharmacological therapy is useful in many patients with faecal incontinence. It may be used either as an adjunct to surgery or behavioural therapy, or alone in patients unsuitable for other therapies. Constipating agents, in particular loperamide, are the most useful drugs. Randomised controlled trials have largely concentrated on the treatment of patients with liquid stool (those with chronic diarrhoea or following ileoanal pouch surgery). However, experience suggests that low doses of anti-diarrhoeals taken regularly will reduce symptoms of faecal incontinence, even in patients with a normal stool consistency. In selected patients, evacuation aids may allow rectal emptying to be performed predictably with intervening continence. Stool-bulking agents have only a limited role to play in the treatment of faecal incontinence. Topically applied medication used to increase anal canal resting pressure may have a future role to play in the treatment of faecal incontinence.

References

Carapeti, E.A., Kamm, M.A., Evans, B.K. and Phillips, R.K. (1999) Topical phenylephrine increases anal sphincter resting pressure. *British Journal of Surgery* **86**, 267–270.

Carapeti, E.A., Kamm, M.A., Nicholls, R.J. and Phillips, R.K. (2000a) Randomised, controlled trial of topical phenylephrine for fecal incontinence in patients after ileoanal pouch construction. *Diseases of the Colon and Rectum* **43**, 1059–1063.

Carapeti, E.A., Kamm, M.A. and Phillips, R.K. (2000b) Randomised controlled trial of topical phenylephrine in the treatment of faecal incontinence. *British Journal of Surgery* **87**, 38–42.

Cheetham, M.J., Kamm, M.A. and Phillips, R.K. (2001) Topical phenylephrine increases anal canal resting pressure in patients with faecal incontinence. *Gut* **48**, 356–359.

Donnelly, V., O'Connell, P.R. and O'Herlihy, C. (1997) The influence of oestrogen replacement on faecal incontinence in postmenopausal women. *British Journal of Obstetrics and Gynaecology* **104**, 311–315.

Fantl, J.A., Cardozo, L. and McClish, D.K. (1994) Estrogen therapy in the management of urinary incontinence in postmenopausal women: a meta-analysis. First report of the Hormones and Urogenital Therapy Committee. *Obstetrics and Gynecology* **83**, 12–18.

Gattuso, J.M. and Kamm, M.A. (1994) Adverse effects of drugs used in the management of constipation and diarrhoea. *Drug Safety* **10**, 47–65.

Gattuso, J.M. and Kamm, M.A. (1997) Clinical features of idiopathic megarectum and idiopathic megacolon. *Gut* **41**, 93–99.

Haadem, K., Ling, L., Ferno, M. and Graffner, H. (1991) Estrogen receptors in the external anal sphincter. *American Journal of Obstetrics and Gynecology* **164**, 609–610.

Herbst, F., Kamm, M.A. and Nicholls, R.J. (1998) Effects of loperamide on ileoanal pouch function. *British Journal of Surgery* **85**, 1428–1432.

Kusunoki, M., Shoji, Y., Ikeuchi, H., Yamagata, K., Yamamura, T. and Utsunomiya, J. (1990) Usefulness of valproate sodium for treatment of incontinence after ileoanal anastomosis. *Surgery* **107**, 311–315.

Laurberg, S. and Swash, M. (1989) Effects of aging on the anorectal sphincters and their innervation. *Diseases of the Colon and Rectum* **32**, 737–742.

Palmer, K.R., Corbett, C.L. and Holdsworth, C.D. (1980) Double-blind cross-over study comparing loperamide, codeine and diphenoxylate in the treatment of chronic diarrhea. *Gastroenterology* **79**, 1272–1275.

Read, M., Read, N.W., Barber, D.C. and Duthie, H.L. (1982) Effects of loperamide on anal sphincter function in patients complaining of chronic diarrhea with fecal incontinence and urgency. *Digestive Diseases and Sciences* **27**, 807–814.

Regadas, F.S., Batista, L.K., Albuquerque, J.L. and Capaz, F.R. (1993) Pharmacological study of the internal anal sphincter in patients with chronic anal fissure. *British Journal of Surgery* **80**, 799–801.

Santoro, G.A., Eitan, B.Z., Pryde, A. and Bartolo, D.C. (2000) Open study of low-dose amitriptyline in the treatment of patients with idiopathic fecal incontinence. *Diseases of the Colon and Rectum* **43**, 1676–1681.

Sun, W.M., Read, N.W. and Verlinden, M. (1997) Effects of loperamide oxide on gastrointestinal transit time and anorectal function in patients with chronic diarrhoea and faecal incontinence. *Scandinavian Journal of Gastroenterology* **32**, 34–38.

Tobin, G.W. and Brocklehurst, J.C. (1986) Faecal incontinence in residential homes for the elderly: prevalence, aetiology and management. *Age and Ageing* **15**, 41–46.

Chapter 17

Bowel Dysfunction: Assessment and Management in the Neurological Patient

Paul Wiesel and Sally Bell

Introduction

Faecal incontinence and constipation are common in people with neurological disease or injury. Up to 70% of people with multiple sclerosis (MS) report monthly episodes of incontinence (Chia et al., 1995) and up to 80% of spinal cord injury (SCI) individuals complain of constipation (Glickman and Kamm 1996). Consequently many people with neurological conditions suffer emotional distress and limit their participation in social activities and/or work.

The medical literature is confusing. 'Neurogenic incontinence' can denote both incontinence secondary to damage to the pudendal nerve during childbirth or be associated with major neurological injury or disease such as autonomic diabetic neuropathy. For the purpose of this chapter, 'neurogenic bowel' refers to incontinence and constipation that occurs in patients with any chronic pathological process affecting the nervous system.

Management of the neurogenic bowel must be undertaken with the recognition that one may be treading a fine line between helping constipation and precipitating faecal incontinence. An individualised bowel programme should be designed for each patient, based on physical and psychological conditions, and consistent with life style and personal goals. Neurogenic bowel management also carries significant resource implications.

Epidemiology of the neurogenic bowel

The prevalence of faecal incontinence and constipation varies from 1% to 20% of the general adult population depending which definitions are applied (see Chapter 3). The prevalence of bowel dysfunction in people suffering from neurological disease or injury is higher.

Stroke is the commonest cause of neurological damage in Western countries, with an annual incidence rate between 300 and 500 per 100,000 population. Faecal incontinence has been reported by 23% of 135 consecutive stroke patients within one year (Brocklehurst et al., 1985). Older patients, women and those with the most severe strokes seemed to be most at risk (Nakayama et al., 1997).

Multiple sclerosis affects approximately one million young adults worldwide. Two-thirds of patients with MS complain of bowel problems (Hinds et al., 1990). The prevalence of constipation and/or faecal incontinence ranges from 39% to 73% (Chia et al., 1995; Nordenbo et al., 1996; Sullivan and Ebers, 1983). Bowel dysfunction is a source of considerable psychosocial disability for MS patients. In a study of 890 patients, the main factors limiting the ability of MS sufferers to work were spasticity, incoordination and bladder and bowel symptoms (Bauer et al., 1965), indicating that bowel dysfunction is a major hurdle to full rehabilitation.

Spinal cord injury is relatively common, with approximately 400,000 SCI individuals currently living in the UK. Glickman and Kamm reported that 95% of 115 consecutive SCI outpatients required at least one therapeutic procedure to initiate defaecation, and 50% needed help to manage their bowel (Glickman and Kamm, 1996). Faecal incontinence is reported by 15–25% of patients discharged from rehabilitation units (Krogh et al., 1997; Subbarao, 1987). Bowel function is a source of distress in over half of patients, and this is associated with the time required for bowel management and the frequency of incontinence (Glickman and Kamm, 1996). In many surveys of SCI, subjects rank bowel dysfunction as one of their major life-limiting problems (Glickman and Kamm, 1996; Hanson and Franklin, 1976; Stone et al., 1990; White et al., 1993).

Parkinson's disease affects one in a thousand people, and constipation and evacuation disorders are common in these patients, with slow transit or evacuation difficulty-type constipation in up to 50% of patients (Edwards et al., 1992).

Autonomic neuropathy (disease or degeneration of the autonomic nervous system) is associated with a wide range of gastrointestinal manifestations, such as nausea, bloating, vomiting, abdominal pain, constipation and faecal incontinence. Most knowledge is based on studies of diabetes mellitus. Constipation has been reported in 12% to 88% of diabetic patients, with a debated direct correlation with the incidence of autonomic neuropathy (Clouse and Lustman, 1989; Feldman and Schiller, 1983). Twenty per cent of diabetics complain of faecal urgency and episodes of incontinence, with evidence of decreased rectal sensation or impaired function of the anal sphincters, or both (Wald and Tunuguntla, 1984; Caruana and Wald, 1991; Sun et al., 1996).

Neurophysiology of the gastrointestinal tract

The neurological control of the bowel is the result of an intricate balance between the extrinsic nervous system, the enteric nervous system, and the intestinal smooth muscle cells.

The extrinsic nervous system

The extrinsic nervous system of the bowel is the nervous system which is external to the bowel itself. It consists of autonomic, sensory and motor nerves (Figure 17.1).

The **autonomic (smooth muscle, involuntary)** nervous system of the bowel comprises an integrated complex system of parasympathetic (predominantly stimulating motility) and sympathetic (predominantly inhibiting motility) fibres. The parasympathetic vagal nerves originate from the medulla within the brain and supply motor and sensory input to the proximal (upper) colon. The parasympathetic sacral nerves originate from the spinal level S2 to S4 and contain both motor and sensory fibres to distal (lower) colon.

The sympathetic nerve supply arises from between the tenth thoracic and third lumbar segments. It is composed of fibres that synapse with enteric ganglionic plexuses within the colon wall.

Somatic (voluntary) nerves provide both sensory and motor supply to the large bowel and pelvic floor, via the vagus, the nervi erigentes (from S2 to S4), direct sacral root branches (from S1 to S5) and the pudendal nerve.

The enteric nervous system

The enteric nervous system is the internal nervous system of the gut itself. It has an essential role in the control of motility, blood flow, water and electrolyte transport, and acid secretion in the digestive tract. This system is organised in ganglionated plexuses within the bowel wall itself and is separated from the autonomic nervous system. The enteric nervous system has several components: sensory receptors (mechano- and chemoreceptors), interneurons (processing input and controlling effector units, motor and secretory) and effector motor neurones involved in motility of the gut. Enteric nervous control of the bowel is modulated through connections from the autonomic nervous system to the brain. The enteric nervous system has the unique capacity to mediate reflex activity independently of input from the central nervous system. This is why even people with complete destruction of central neurological input to the bowel maintain some gut motility – the intrinsic nervous system keeps the bowel working to at least some extent (unlike the bladder, which can become totally atonic).

A neurogenic bowel can result from any pathological processes involving any component of the central nervous system, and/or the

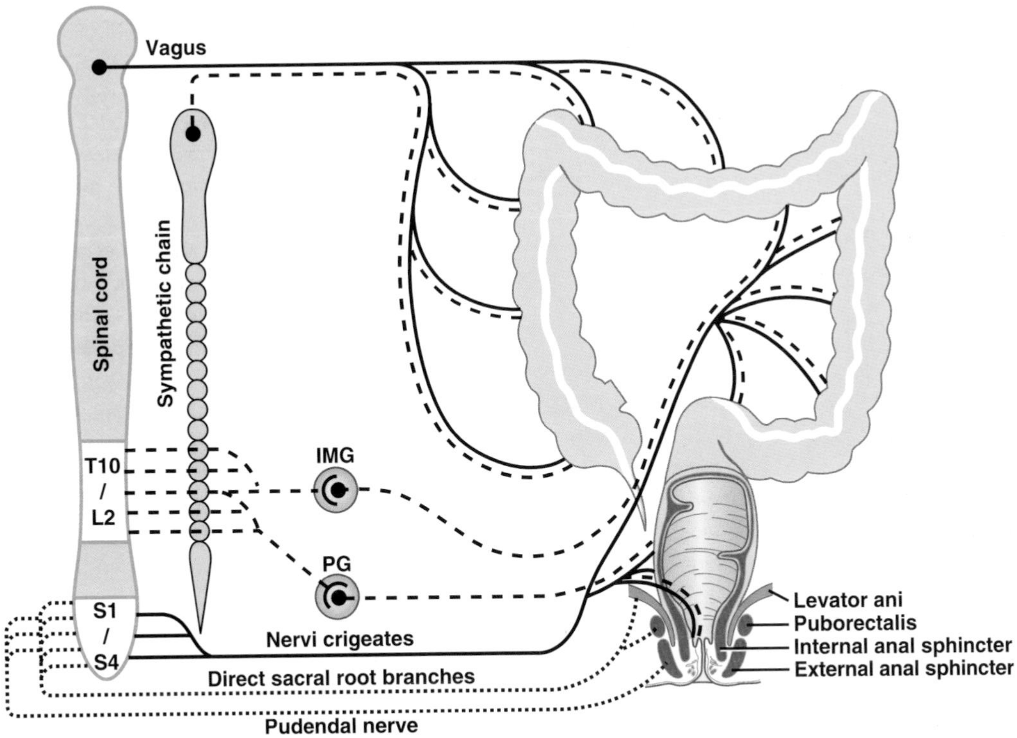

Figure 17.1 *The extrinsic nervous system of the bowel and pelvic floor.*

The extrinsic nervous system of the bowel and the pelvic floor consists of the parasympathetic vagal and sacral innervation (solid lines) and the sympathetic outflow from intermediolateral column of the spinal cord (dashed lines). The parasympathetic system is composed of pre-ganglionic fibers that synapse with pre-programmed circuits in the ganglionated enteric plexuses within the colon wall. The sympathetic nerves synapse in the prevertebral coeliac (PG), superior and inferior mesenteric (IMG) ganglia. Sensory and motor innervation of the bowel and pelvic floor occurs through the vagus, the nervi erigentes, direct sacral root branches and the pudendal nerve. Mixed nerves supply the somatic voluntary musculature of the pelvic floor and the external anal sphincter (dotted lines).

Modified from Stiens, et al., *Archives of Physical Medicine and Rehabilitation* 1997; **78**: S89.

extrinsic and the intrinsic innervation of the bowel. Bowel dysfunction can either be directly due to the neuropathological process (e.g. spinal cord injury), to common causes unrelated to the neurological disease (e.g. low dietary fibre, insufficient liquid intake, difficulty accessing the toilet), or to a combination of the neuropathological process and unrelated factors. Damage to the frontal lobe of the brain can lead to emotional disturbance, altered social relationships relating to bowel behaviour, lack of voluntary control of the pelvic floor or ignoring the call to stool because of reduced awareness. When sensory (afferent) input to the brain is impaired, a call to stool may be diminished and be responsible for constipation or faecal incontinence. Both can also coexist if incontinence is secondary to faecal impaction (misleadingly labelled 'overflow diarrhoea'). Moreover, impaired anorectal sensation may co-exist with impaired mobility and inability to cope with urgent defaecation. Thus, bowel function and continence can be altered as a result of multiple causes including: altered cognitive function, loss of mobility and independence in toileting, loss of control of the pelvic floor striated musculature, loss of ano-rectal and pelvic floor sensory function, colonic dysmotility and/or use of drugs and subsequent side effects on colonic motility and sensory function.

Assessment of the neurogenic bowel

Assessment of bowel dysfunction in neurologically impaired patients requires a holistic approach that takes into account the patient's environment, physical and psychological disabilities, and general medical conditions (Table 17.1). This will usually require a multidisciplinary team.

Assessment of the environment is essential. Bowel management is often a source of difficulty in the reintegration into the home and the community for the disabled person. This will include assessment of available health and social care resources, so that impractical and unrealistic care plans are avoided. A social worker will often become involved to assess the local healthcare network and availability of community support for which an individual may qualify. Family and social supports should be assessed in collaboration with the patient, the general practitioner and the family. Home assessment will require a home visit by an occupational therapist. Some disabled people have bowel problems that are only related to toilet accessibility (see Chapter 23).

Assessment of the individual

Assessment of the individual with a neurological disorder or injury should include assessment of impairment/disability/handicap, psychological/cognitive function and compliance with previous and current treatment.

A neurological examination will yield information about the completeness, the level, and severity of the impairment and disability. This is made easier with a validated scoring system. A physiotherapist or a rehabilitation therapist should assess the handicap: i.e. sitting tolerance, upper body strength, hand and arm function, spasticity, and transfer skills.

A drug history should be obtained, as a number of drugs commonly prescribed to neurological patients have the potential to alter bowel function: for example, oxybutynin, diuretics, antacids, antidepressants and narcotic drugs may decrease bowel motility; whereas antibiotics and dantrolene sodium may provoke soft stool, diarrhoea and faecal incontinence.

An assessment of cognitive function includes the individual's ability to learn and to direct others in assisting in the provision of bowel care. Awareness of the level of cognitive function allows the design of a realistic bowel programme. For people with severe cognitive impairment or learning disabilities, this assessment may need referral to specialised units (e.g. a neuropsychologist).

Assessment of mood can be made by the hospital anxiety and depression scale (Zigmond and Snaith, 1983). Referral to local psychiatric or psychological services may be considered for those patients where there is clinical suspicion of mood disturbance. Low mood or anxiety states may lead to inaccurate assessment of cognitive function. Coping strategies and compliance are important, as many bowel care regimes fail due to poor compliance and inadequate coping strategies (Wineman et al., 1994). This may be aggravated by altered cognitive function, mood disturbances, the level of support available or unrealistic goals.

Assessment of goals, lifestyle and commitments will enable the setting of appropriate aims for bowel care. For example, the bowel programme of a young woman who is wheelchair independent and works full-time will probably be different to that of a bedbound elderly man cared for by his wife. Self-rated quality of life can help to identify areas of specific need and monitor the outcome of bowel care programs. Patients and clinicians may disagree on perception of health and disability (Rothwell et al., 1997).

The whole individual assessment should be

Table 17.1: The assessment of the neurogenic bowel

The assessment of the neurogenic bowel is seen as a holistic approach to assessing the bowel of a neurological patient in her/his environment. In brackets is the most appropriate method (see text for details).

ENVIRONMENT ASSESSMENT

- Community and health care (community liaison team, social worker)
- Socio-familial (general practitioner, social worker)
- Home, workplace (visits)

INDIVIDUAL ASSESSMENT

- Impairment, disability and handicap
- Cognitive function, ability to learn and to direct others
- Mood, coping strategies, compliance, quality-of-life
- Concomitant diseases and drugs

BOWEL ASSESSMENT

- Past/current gastrointestinal symptoms (questionnaire, bowel diary)
- Past/current bowel programme (relatives, carers)

- **Motor assessment**
- Abdominal wall (physical examination)
- Pelvic floor (physical examination, balloon expulsion, defaecography)
- Anal sphincters (physical examination, ano-rectal manometry, endoanal ultrasonography)

- **Sensory assessment**
- Sacral reflexes (physical examination)
- Ano-rectal thresholds (balloon distension, mucosal electrostimulation)

- **Motility assessment**
- Bowel transit (radio-opaque markers colonic transit study)

repeated whenever progression or relapse of the neurological process occurs.

Assessment of bowel function

This involves a thorough history, full neurological and gastroenterological examination, and in some cases targeted investigation.

A gastrointestinal assessment should include symptoms and disease prior to the neurological disease or injury (e.g. abdominal surgery, inflammatory bowel diseases, irritable bowel syndrome, laxative dependency) and current gastrointestinal symptoms.

Symptom diaries, filled in over 1–2 weeks (Chapter 6), are useful adjuncts, particularly when memory is impaired. Constipation and faecal incontinence embrace a range of symptoms, with different meanings for different individuals. In neurological patients, constipation can be defined as small, unsatisfactory, inefficient or absent bowel movements after two or more attempts at toileting or bowel care. Faecal incontinence is the involuntary loss of faeces and/or flatus, and is generally characterised as urge incontinence or passive leakage. No published criteria have been validated in neurological patients.

Details of past bowel care programmes should be obtained. It is important to clarify the reasons for failure if this failed, as frequently inadequate techniques, or wrong dosage or timing of drugs can be found. The patient should be asked about her/his satisfaction with the programme to determine whether there are specific problem areas. Duration of care and the occurrence of complications should be recorded (faecal incontinence, constipation, difficult evacuation, nausea, abdominal distension, pain, rectal bleeding, pressure sores, dysreflexia). The current bowel programme over the last two weeks should be detailed, including: diet, fibre intake (this may require a one-week food record and assessment by a dietitian), use of assistive methods for defaecation, and the dosage and timing of pharmacological agents. Family members and carers often provide helpful additional information.

Physical examination

This includes assessment of the abdominal wall, pelvic floor musculature, anal sphincter and rectum. It will focus on the neurological system.

Assessment of the abdominal wall (looking for hernias) and muscles is done at rest, during voluntary contraction of the muscles and involuntary response to coughing and sneezing.

Assessment of the pelvic floor is performed at rest and during straining. A decreased tone and weak muscles will be seen when somatic motor neurones in the S2–S3 segments of the anterior horn of the spinal cord are impaired. Spastic muscles incapable of relaxation are present in some MS patients. Perineal descent is sometimes seen as a result of chronic straining, which can cause external rectal prolapse and eventually passive leakage of stool.

Assessment of the anal sphincters starts with examination of the sacral reflexes. These consist of motor responses in the pelvic floor and sphincter muscles, evoked by physical or electrical stimulation of sensory receptors (Uher and Swash, 1998). The *anocutaneous reflex* is a contraction of the external anal sphincter (EAS) in response to touch or pin stimulus to the perianal skin (all 4 quadrants to be assessed), which is mediated by the pudendal nerves (S2–S5). The *bulbocavernous reflex* is elicited by pinching or pricking the dorsal glans penis or by pressing the clitoris, and palpating for EAS contraction within the anal canal. Presence of both reflexes suggests the integrity of a conus-mediated (S2–S3) reflex activity. *Anal cough reflex* is a contraction of the EAS elicited by a rise in intra-abdominal pressure during vigorous coughing or sneezing. This reflex can be detected after spinal cord trans-section and might be initiated by stretch receptors in the EAS and/or surrounding muscles.

Digital examination of the anal sphincters will give a notion of the resting tone. Strength of the EAS and puborectalis can be assessed by requesting the patient to tighten the pelvic floor as if to prevent defaecation and to cough. Digital rectal examination should also exclude stool impaction (rock-hard stool), rectocoele or a tumour.

Sensory assessment of the lower limbs, pelvic floor and anus is performed with the pin-prick technique.

Further investigations of constipation and faecal incontinence

These will follow a thorough assessment, and the choice of test will depend on the clinical problem. Frequently neurological patients will benefit from objective assessment of their bowel dysfunction. Investigations assist in excluding treatable non-neurological causes of bowel dysfunction, and are used to identify those patients who may be candidates for more invasive management such as surgery. Investigation of other bowel symptoms such as rectal bleeding or weight loss may be indicated (see Chapter 7). Although haemorrhoids are frequent in neurological patients, rectal bleeding should never be attributed to them without proper investigations.

Ano-rectal physiology tests (see Chapter 8 for more detail)

Manometry is important to define weakness of one or both sphincter muscles. Manometry also allows recognition of the inability to evacuate adequately from the rectum related to a lack of sphincter relaxation, also named 'anismus' or 'pelvic floor dyssynergia'. Balloon expulsion test with a 50 ml water-filled rectal balloon will help identify those patients with pelvic floor dyssynergia (Jameson et al., 1994).

Balloon distension with an air-filled rectal balloon will provide a gross measurement of sensory function and compliance. The thresholds for the first perceived sensation (smallest volume of rectal distension), the sensation of urgency to defecate, and the maximum tolerable volume are measured. These thresholds depend on the neural balance between the ability to feel, retain and tolerate rectal content by inhibiting defaecation and by voluntary contracting the pelvic floor muscles (Caruana et al., 1991). Local diseases (e.g. proctitis) can also alter these thresholds. The recto-anal inhibitory reflex (RAIR) is induced by rapid rectal distension. A sudden fall in anal pressure is caused by internal anal sphincter relaxation. RAIR seems to be mediated by intramural myenteric neurones – it is not abolished by spinal transsection but is abolished in Hirschprung's disease.

Mucosal electrostimulation using an electrical stimulus passed across the anal and rectal mucosa can obtain a quantitative assessment of ano-rectal innervation and may help distinguish between functional and neurological disorders (Kamm and Lennard-Jones, 1990). When it is uncertain whether constipation is directly related to impaired central innervation of the gut, or is 'idiopathic', this test may be helpful. In patients with neurological disease affecting the hindgut innervation, the rectal mucosal electrical sensory threshold is usually grossly abnormal. Previous studies in patients with cord injury have demonstrated the sensitivity of electrical sensation testing in defining impaired innervation (Emmanuel and Kamm, 1999). In some patients its normality may provide a reassuring basis on which to try to behaviourally correct the constipation, in the expectation that the bowel dysfunction is reversible.

Radiological investigations

Endoanal ultrasonography and transit studies may be indicated in incontinence or constipation respectively (see Chapter 9). *Defaecography* and *proctography* are reserved for patients in whom abnormalities, such as slow or incomplete rectal emptying, failure of puborectalis and anal sphincter muscles relaxation, a rectal prolapse, a rectocoele, or a megarectum are clinically suspected.

In summary, a methodical history will assess the patient's environment, impairment, disability, handicap, coping strategies and compliance. Careful physical examination should show which element of the bowel function is essentially impaired. Targeted investigations will verify whether constipation is predominantly due to impaired colonic motility or inadequate evacuation, and faecal incontinence mostly due to a weak anal sphincter or to impaired sensory function.

Autonomic dysreflexia

Autonomic dysreflexia (also known as hyperreflexia or dysautonomia) is a potentially life-threatening complication (Banwell et al., 1993), that can occur in some people with a spinal cord injury at level T6 or above (those with injuries at T6 to T10 may also be susceptible). Patients usually present with elevated blood pressure and bradycardia. If not treated promptly and correctly, it may lead to seizures, stroke and death. The pathophysiology of dysreflexia is related to an overactivity of the sympathetic nervous system. Noxious stimuli to intact sensory nerves below the injury lead to relatively unopposed sympathetic outflow and blood pressure elevations. Parasympathetic outflow through the vagus nerve can cause reflexive bradycardia but cannot compensate for severe vasoconstriction. Anything that would have been painful, uncomfortable or physically irritating before the injury may cause dysreflexia. Symptoms are a restless feeling and shortening of breath, pounding severe headache, blurred vision and dizziness, nasal congestion, goose pimples, profuse sweating, and flushing or blotching of the skin (particularly above the level of injury). Most causes are related to the bladder, such as a blockage in a drainage device, an infection, bladder spasms, or stones. The second most common cause is a full bowel. Any stimulus to the rectum, such as digital stimulation or manual evacuation, can also trigger dysreflexia. Treatment must be initiated quickly: head elevation, pressure release, adequate urinary drainage system, or emptying the bowel, as appropriate. Other possible causes are: fractures, appendicitis, sexual intercourse, period pains, pregnancy or labour. Blood pressure should be treated until the cause is found and eliminated.

Prevention is very important, as most causes can be avoided. Medications to treat dysreflexia and prevent increases in blood pressure may be given prior to bowel care: a rectal anaesthetic ointment – ten minutes before, glycerol trinitrate 250 mcg, nitroglycerine paste 2 inches – on the skin above level of injury, nifedipine 10 mg – not sublingual, as it can cause abrupt hypotension. Blood pressure should be monitored for at least two hours after it has stabilised at under 150 mmHg systolic. If dysreflexia persists, alternatives for bowel care must be considered (e.g. surgical approaches). Table 17.2 (overleaf) gives a patient information sheet about autonomic dysreflexia (reproduced by permission of Spain Rehabilitation Center, USA).

Management of the neurogenic bowel

Bowel management in neurological patients is currently empirical, based on clinical experience rather than research-based evidence. While there is a considerable literature on the prevalence and pathophysiology of bowel dysfunction in neurological disease or injury, there has been remarkably little research done on practical management. There are about 150 non-randomised non-controlled non-comparative and anecdotal trials on different methods of managing a neurogenic bowel. Most methods emphasise the importance of a high fibre diet, drinking more fluid, triggering the gastro-colic response by a hot drink, increasing physical activity, a scheduled regular bowel routine and discouraging the long-term use of laxatives, and frequently advocate rectal stimulation with suppositories. There is no evidence to support any of these recommendations (Wiesel et al., 2001). A practical approach is whenever possible to tailor the bowel management to the specific problems revealed by the assessment described in Table 17.1. However, there are a number of general principles that apply. Many people will need active bowel management, rather than waiting for problems or complications to develop.

Managing the bowel will consider the person, within the context of more general problems and the daily environment (Table 17.3, page 192). The bowel programme will be a personalised plan designed to help the neurological patient gain control of her/his bowel, taking into account attendant care, personal obligations and goals. It should provide predictable and effective elimination of stool, and is designed to be easily applied in the individual's home setting. It should be reviewed as needed, and at least once a year to ensure ongoing relevance. A bowel diary is a key part of this review. 'Bowel care' is the term employed for assisted elimination of stool and may be part of the bowel programme. It consists mainly of conservative assistive and pharmacological methods. For a few patients, surgical methods will have to be considered.

Bowel programmes

A safe, private and pleasant environment is the first step in a successful bowel programme. This may require appropriate equipment such as hand rails, transfer board, a raised and padded commode seat, back support, safety straps, foot blocks, a suppository inserter or a digital stimulator, anal plugs, continence products, roll-in shower chair and other home adaptations (see Chapter 23). The type of equipment required is based on the individual's functional status and the living environment as assessed by physiotherapists and occupational therapists. Prevention of pressure sores should be addressed when bowel care is prolonged (for example the use of a padded seat or commode). Perineal cleaning can be problematic with limited dexterity, and will sometimes be the cause of minor soiling. A conventional U-shaped toilet seat (opening in either the front, the sides, or the rear) usually allows adequate access, and in particular cases a perineal shower or bidet can be helpful. Regional and national patient associations are a useful source of support and information on how to obtain or purchase equipment (see Appendix II). The Internet provides an opportunity for disabled people to get information and purchase products. However, material and information provided by commercial sites should be handled with caution, and in most instances suitable equipment should be available through health or social services.

Independent bowel care is ideal but not possible for some patients. The patient may be able to direct a carer. Carers who are involved in bowel management should obtain informed consent, especially when invasive procedures like digital examination and manual evacuation are required (Addison and Smith, 2000). Psychosocial difficulties are frequent in disabled patients. Emotional support for both patient and carer is important to improve compliance with and success of any bowel care regime. This may require formal counselling and regular respite for the carer. Excessive involvement in bowel management of the partner, family members, relatives or friends may not be appropriate in many cases.

Communication between the patient, carer, district nurse, general practitioner (GP) and the multidisciplinary assessment team is vital. A clear written bowel care regime with a single contact person in times of difficulty is useful. Often issues of dose titration or adjustment of routine can be dealt with over the phone, saving an immobile patient an unnecessary trip to outpatients or the GP's surgery, and preventing inappropriate attendance at accident and emergency departments.

Bowel training, with behavioural modification of self-initiating defaecation and positive reinforcement of this process, have successfully prevented constipation and soiling in children with neurological bowel (Jeffries et al., 1982; King et al., 1994; Younoszai, 1992). Preliminary data on bowel training in cerebrovascular accidents patients (CVA) and SCI adults are encouraging (Badiali et al., 1997; Munchiando and Kendall, 1993; Stiens et al., 1997; Venn et al., 1992).

Scheduling bowel evacuation after a meal should be encouraged to take advantage of the gastro-colic response. Delaying bowel movements is frequent in disabled patients but is usually unwise. Eventually the rectum will adapt to increased bulk of stool, the urge to defaecate might progressively diminish, the rectum can even dilate (megarectum) and result in impaction. Although investigators have reported some impairment of the gastro-colic response in a few SCI and MS patients, results have been inconsistent and it is worth trying to utilise this response for many people.

Fibre intake should be adequate on the premise that the bowel will respond with a decrease in transit time and an increase in stool frequency. Contradictory results have been published in neurological and disabled patients when high fibre diet was consumed (Ashraf et al., 1997; Astarloa et al., 1992; Badiali et al., 1997; Cameron et al., 1996; Levine et al., 1992; Liebl et al., 1990). However, it has been shown that the average daily fibre intake is low in SCI (between 7 and 14 grams per day) (Kirk et al., 1997). There is indeed a fundamental difference between adequate (more than 25 g/day) and 'excessive' fibre diet. Consultation with a dietician can be helpful to clarify misconceptions and provide sound advice.

An adequate fluid intake is recommended. Some individuals may try to solve common bladder problems (incontinence, urgency, frequent catheter bag emptying) by drastically reducing their fluid intake. Dehydration may occur, triggering fluid reabsorption from the faeces which can then harden and be difficult to evacuate. Similarly, prolonged colonic transit time (i.e. secondary to drugs) can result in excessive fluid absorption and hardened stool.

Table 17.2: Autonomic dysreflexia – information sheet

AUTONOMIC DYSREFLEXIA

Autonomic dysreflexia (AD) is a potentially life-threatening condition that occurs in individuals with a spinal cord injury at level T6 or above. Patients usually present with elevated blood pressure and bradycardia. Noxious stimuli to intact sensory nerves below the injury lead to relatively unopposed sympathetic outflow and dangerous blood pressure elevations. Parasympathetic outflow through cranial nerve X (vagus) can cause reflexive bradycardia but can't compensate for severe vasoconstriction.

Common signs and symptoms may include

BRADYCARDIA	CHILLS WITHOUT FEVER
HYPERTENSION	SEIZURES
POUNDING HEADACHE	SWEATING ABOVE LEVEL OF INJURY
NASAL CONGESTION	SKIN FLUSHING ABOVE LEVEL OF INJURY
BRONCHOSPASM	GOOSE BUMPS ABOVE LEVEL OF INJURY
BLURRED VISION	APPREHENSION OR ANXIETY

Follow the examination tree below to eliminate any noxious stimuli below level of injury. A drop in blood pressure will occur with the removal of the stimuli. Seizures, stroke, or death may occur if stimuli are not immediately removed.

Examination tree

Sit up and take blood pressure in both arms (repeat blood pressure every 3 minutes and between steps).
Important note – Normal systolic BP for an individual with an SCI above T6 can be in the 90-110 mm Hg range. If blood pressure is elevated, give medications as indicated. Use an antihypertensive with rapid onset and short duration while the causes of AD are being investigated.

Look for noxious stimuli below level of injury

Check Bladder for Distension: Catheterize bladder using 2% lidocaine jelly. If indwelling catheter already in place, inspect for kinks, folds, constrictions or obstructions. Irrigate or replace the catheter to ensure patency – RELIEF? – collect U/A and C/S (irritation may be due to infection). Assess for any urologic obstruction such as kidney or bladder stones.

Check Bowel: Anesthetize using lidocaine jelly 2% (wait 5 minutes) prior to checking for impaction. Remove impaction and recheck blood pressure – RELIEF? – Evaluate for high impaction.

Table 17.2: Autonomic dysreflexia – information sheet (continued)

Check Skin: Remove constricting clothing – RELIEF? – Examine for pressure ulcers – Does repositioning lower blood pressure? – Examine for insect bites – Treat – RELIEF? – Examine seat cushion and wheelchair for sharp or hard objects – Evaluate environmental temperature – Do symptoms change as environmental and patient's temperature change? – Evaluate recent surgical sites – Treat symptoms – RELIEF? – Observe for ingrown toenails – Anesthetize, debride, treat for infection – RELIEF?

Evaluate for Gastrocolic Irritation: Tube feeding given recently? – Too rapid? – Treat – RELIEF? – Too cold? – Treat – RELIEF? – Too large a volume? – Treat – RELIEF?

Gender Specific: Males: Genitalia pinched? – Correct – RELIEF? – Condom catheter too tight? – Remove catheter – RELIEF? – Reflexogenic erection? – Remove condom catheter and clothing – RELIEF?
Females: Menstrual cramping? – Treat – RELIEF? – Uterine contractions? – Treat – Evaluate follow-up – Vaginitis? – Treat symptoms and infection

Treatment reminders

1) Sit patient up.
2) Check BP often and treat elevated systolic blood pressure (> 150) until cause is found and eliminated.
3) Medications commonly used for elevated BP are:
   a) Nitroglycerine paste. Apply 1-2 inches to skin q2hrs above the level of injury. May wipe off if BP stable and reapply if needed. Avoid sublingual which can cause abrupt hypotension.
   b) Nifedipine 10 mg capsule (immediate release form). May repeat in 20-30 minutes If needed. Avoid sublingual which can cause abrupt hypotension.
   c) IV-Antihypertensives. These are secondary agents to be utilized In a monitored setting.
4) Treat symptomatic hypotension by laying down the individual and elevating the legs.
5) Anesthetize noxious stimuli prior to removal to prevent exacerbation of AD.
6) Monitor symptoms and BP for at least 2 hours after the resolution of an AD episode.
7) Admit the patient if response to treatment is poor or cause has not been identified. AD can lead to seizures, stroke, or death.

Authors: Amie B. Jackson MD and Anthony S. Burns MD
Acknowledgement: Autonomic Dysreflexia poster published by The Univerisity of Alabama at Birmingham Rehabilitation Research and Training Center on Secondary Conditions of Spinal Cord Injury and the UAB Model SCI System of Care. UAB RRTC is supported by grant #H133B980016 from the National Institute on Disability and Rehabilitation Research, Office of Special Education and Rehabilitative Services, United States Department of Education, Washington, D.C.

Although target fluid intake will essentially depend on renal function and bladder management, adequate fluid intake is advised for the prevention of hard stool. A loaded bowel may interfere with urethral or suprapubic catheter drainage.

Bladder management is closely linked with the bowel. Frequently neurological patients have both a neurogenic bladder and a neurogenic bowel (Bauer et al., 1965; Hanson and Franklin, 1976; Kang et al., 1996). Moreover, bladder catheterisation may diminish the use of a toilet and lessen opportunities to empty the bowel. Co-operative management with a urological team will sometimes be needed.

Assistive methods

A number of methods may assist effective emptying of the rectum when this does not happen adequately or spontaneously.

Abdominal massage, push-ups, Valsalva manoeuvre (holding the breath and forcibly trying to exhale against a closed glottis, thereby creating raised intra-abdominal pressure and a bearing-down effect), deep breathing and forward-leaning position are some of the techniques used to assist bowel emptying. Although very little research has been done on the use of these techniques (Ernst, 1999), they may aid bowel evacuation by increasing abdominal pressure. In a survey of 277 individuals with SCI, the seated position was rated as faster, more effective and more convenient than bowel care completed in bed (Nelson et al., 1993). To minimise the risk of vesico-ureteral reflux, Valsalva should not be performed with a full bladder and is contraindicated for individuals with cardiac problems and hypertension. Prolonged straining may eventually predispose to haemorrhoids and even rectal prolapse.

Digital ano-rectal stimulation (Figure 17.2) triggers peristalsis of the left colon. It is performed by gently inserting a gloved lubricated finger into the rectum and slowly rotating the finger in a circular movement against the rectal mucosa. Rotation is continued until relaxation of the bowel wall is felt, flatus passes, stool passes, or the internal anal sphincter contracts. It should last 20 seconds, and stimulation longer

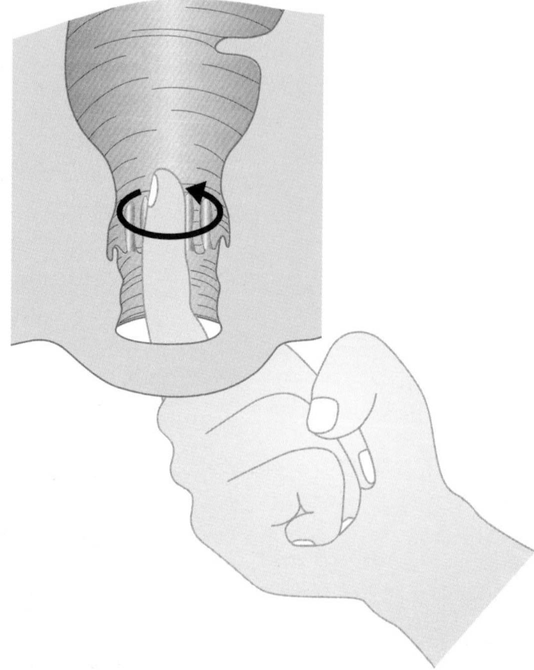

Figure 17.2 *Digital stimulation.*

than one minute is seldom necessary. Stimulation is repeated every 5 to 10 minutes until stool evacuation is complete, or no stool has been passed after at last two stimulations. Individuals who lack sufficient hand function for gloving and digital stimulation may be candidates for a digital stimulator. Applied mostly to people with high SCI injury (Glickman and Kamm, 1996), CVA patients may also benefit from a programme of daily digital stimulation (Munchiando and Kendall, 1993). It is as yet unproven if this method is effective in other neurological patients, but it should be considered.

Manual evacuation is the digital removal of faeces from the rectum. This method should only be performed when required, after informed consent, and by skilled persons. The Royal College of Nursing has recently reviewed the procedure and safety points (Addison and Smith, 2000). Manual evacuation is performed by inserting a gloved lubricated finger into the rectum to break up or hook stool and pull it out. Anaesthetic ointment should be used to decrease the noxious stimuli and avoid producing autonomic dysreflexia in those prone to this (see above). Many people with low SCI injury rely on this method once or more per day to stay continent (Glickman and Kamm, 1996), and there is often no viable alternative to the long-term use of manual evacuation in those with low SCI.

Biofeedback aims to condition patients to be more sensitive to a stimulus distending the rectum and to improve pelvic floor function. It has been shown that biofeedback is effective in constipation and faecal incontinence in some MS adults with limited disability and a non-progressive disease course (Wiesel et al., 2000).

Management of constipation and faecal incontinence in neurological disease

Prevention and management of constipation

Prevention of constipation should be the first objective. Some people will prefer constipation to faecal incontinence, either to avoid soiling or as being more socially acceptable. However, this is associated with complications such as impaction, 'overflow diarrhoea', bladder infections, increased spasticity, or the life-threatening autonomic dysreflexia in SCI patients. Patient and carers' education should be undertaken to ensure regular bowel emptying by means of general measures and assistive methods.

Attention to diet and a balanced increase in diverse sources of fibre may be sufficient to relieve mild constipation in some patients. For further information see Murray and Emmanuel (2002). Nevertheless, when patients are complaining of constipation, pharmacological methods to assist bowel emptying will often be required. Bulk-forming agents, rectal stimulants, oral laxatives and enemas should be tried according to patient's assessment and preferences. Surgical options should be discussed early in the management and considered at an appropriate time if conservative methods are not any longer realistic. In selected cases a progressive approach to the most suitable surgical method can be made by starting with retrograde enema, moving to antegrade colonic enema (ACE), and then perhaps considering a stoma. Complex surgery should be performed in specialised centres. Specific details of each of these methods are given below.

Conservative measures for constipation

Bulk-forming agents consist of natural (ispaghula or psyllium) or synthetic polysaccharides or cellulose derivatives (methylcellulose) that act in a manner similar to dietary fibre. These indigestible agents increase the intraluminal water content and overall volume of stool. In a single-blind non-randomised trial, twelve Parkinson's patients treated by eight weeks of psyllium showed a significant increase in stool frequency and in stool weight (Ashraf et al., 1997). Bulk-forming laxatives should not be considered in patients with severe slow transit constipation, because they only add more load to an inefficient bowel and cause more symptoms. The rare risk of allergic reactions to psyllium in sensitised people should perhaps discourage its use (Sussman and Dorian, 1990). These agents (ispaghula, methylcellulose) have a role in the management of constipation, and patients should be encouraged to achieve adequate dietary fibre with a supplement of natural bran, if fibre intake is less than 25–30 g/day.

Faecal softeners include different oils (mineral, paraffin, arachis) which are given orally or by enema to penetrate or lower the surface tension and therefore soften stool. Randomised controlled trials are lacking to determine the role of stool softeners in the prevention and treatment of constipation (Hurdon et al., 2000). Many oral faecal softeners may increase the uptake and toxicity of drugs, interfere with the absorption of fat-soluble vitamins and give rise to lipoid pneumonia if inhaled (Gattuso and Kamm 1993). The authors regard the evidence for the efficacy of oral faecal softeners as unproved and unsafe, discouraging further use.

Rectal stimulants (e.g. glycerine, bisacodyl*)* can be used alone or in combination with digital stimulation when this latter alone is inefficient. They have the advantage of predictability in terms of time of response and can trigger a bowel movement fifteen to thirty minutes after insertion. A glycerin suppository acts as a mild local stimulus and lubricating agent. Bisacodyl is a contact irritant that acts directly on the colonic mucosa, producing peristalsis throughout the colon. Glycerin is used in individuals who experience adverse reactions to the bisacodyl suppository, have a fast response to bisacodyl, or are making a transition from bisacodyl to mechanical stimulation. Bisacodyl may be compounded with a vegetable oil or a polyethylene glycol (PEG) base. There is strong evidence that PEG–based bisacodyl suppositories can produce significantly more rapid onset of defaecation and shorten the total bowel care time in SCI patients when compared to hydrogenated vegetable oil–based bisacodyl suppositories (Frisbie, 1997; House and Stiens, 1997; Stiens, 1995; Stiens et al., 1998). Carbon dioxide generating suppositories produce reflex – explosive and unpredictable – defaecation in response to colonic dilatation, they are not recommended. It may be necessary to remove stool prior to the insertion of a suppository against the rectal mucosa. When hand function is insufficient a suppository inserter can be used (Figure 17.3).

Oral laxatives can be prescribed to increase bowel frequency if other measures have failed, and particularly when transit is documented to be slow. Any laxatives should be titrated to produce a satisfactory response without causing liquid stools and faecal incontinence. Every agent should be tried for a minimum of 3–4 weeks before progressing to the next agent. All laxatives share, to some degree, the potential for dose-dependent side effects, including abdominal cramping, diarrhoea and electrolyte imbalance. Although the chronic ingestion of anthranoid laxatives (senna) has been blamed for the development of the cathartic colon – an

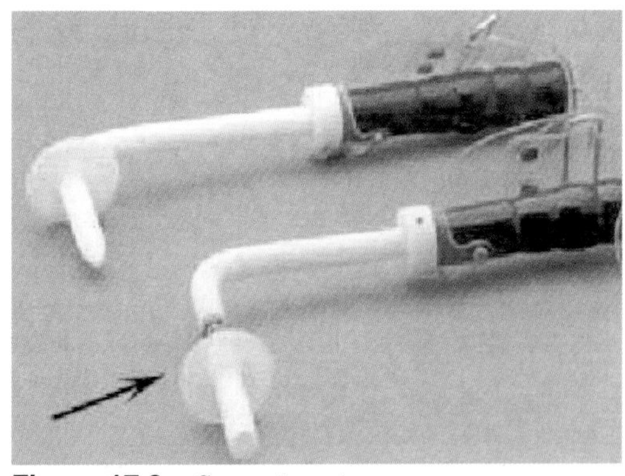

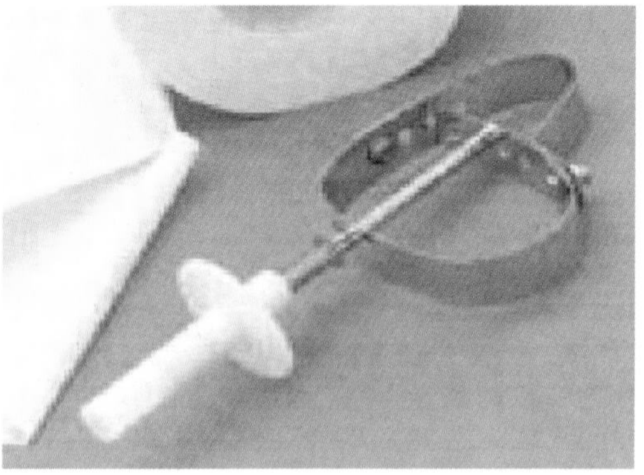

Figure 17.3 *Suppository inserters.*

atonic non-functioning colon – there are no definitive studies which have demonstrated this (Gattuso and Kamm, 1994).

Osmotic laxatives include mixed-electrolyte solutions containing polyethylene glycol (PEG, e.g. Movicol) or nonabsorbable sugars (lactulose, lactitol and sorbitol) that cause distension and stimulation of the bowel. PEG solutions act more rapidly with stronger efficacy and less side effects than nonabsorbable sugars (Attar et al., 1999; Corazziari et al., 2000; DiPalma et al., 2000). After four weeks, patients treated with PEG had a higher bowel frequency than patients treated with lactulose (Attar et al., 1999). In two double-blind, placebo controlled, parallel group studies, patients treated with small daily doses of PEG reported higher bowel frequency, less frequently straining at defaecation and reduced consumption of laxative, when compared to the placebo group (Corazziari et al., 2000; DiPalma et al., 2000). Nonabsorbable sugars are associated with the production of gases due to colonic fermentation, bloating, cramping and flatulence. By lowering the stool pH they also are aggressive to the skin and present a greater risk of pressure sores if faecal incontinence is present. Besides, PEG solutions were recently found to be safe to treat faecal impaction (Culbert et al., 1998; Ferguson et al., 1999; Ungar 2000), which could be useful when manual evacuation by a trained person fails. Although no trial has yet specifically included neurological patients, the efficacy of PEG solutions for constipation, the possibility of fine-tuning the prescription and the good tolerance, are reasons to make this agent an attractive osmotic laxative.

Saline oral laxatives (salts of sodium, magnesium or potassium) contain relatively nonabsorbable cations and anions that osmotically increase intralumenal water content and stimulate motility. They induce complete bowel evacuation in two to six hours and may give rise to electrolyte imbalance and water retention.

Stimulant oral laxatives include polyphenolic compounds (bisacodyl, phenolphthalein, sodium picosulphate) and anthraquinone-containing substances obtained from senna. Phenolphthalein is best avoided because it undergoes an enterohepatic circulation and can cause a rash. Sodium picosulfate is hydrolysed by colonic bacterial flora. Bisacodyl is hydrolysed by intestinal enzymes and can act on both the small and the large intestine to stimulate motor activity and to inhibit glucose and sodium absorption. Its effect on the small bowel is a disadvantage, in comparison with that of anthranoid glycosides, and it could be difficult to adjust the dose to produce soft, formed stools. Senna increases propulsive activity by altering electrolyte transport and increasing intraluminal fluid; it also exerts a direct stimulant effect on the myenteric plexus, which increases motility. Senna is widely used among neurological patients, and is best taken in the evening or at bedtime with the aim of producing a normal stool next morning. Senna and Bisacodyl are reliable and effective agents, which can be titrated to produce a satisfactory response without causing the stools to become liquid and / or cause excessive urgency (Gattuso and Kamm, 1994; Schiller, 1999).

Small-volume enemas have been recently used to assist impaired defaecation. A 4 ml liquid suppository mini-enema is a combination of liquid docusate and glycerine in a PEG base. In SCI patients a mini-enema (Therevac) shortened the time between insertion of the stimulant and evacuation (Dunn and Galka, 1994; House and Stiens, 1997). Although availability of these mini-enemas and cost are currently problematic, larger trials are urgently needed.

Large-volume enemas (tap water, phosphate) should be reserved for special cases when all other conservative methods have failed. Sodium, potassium or phosphate enemas act directly on colonic mucosa, causing an influx of water and electrolyte which stimulate bowel evacuation in response to distension. Their onset of action is rapid and unpredictable (two to six hours). Frequently they result in abdominal cramping and watery bowel movements. There is a risk of electrolyte disturbances, recto-anal trauma, bowel perforation, bacteraemia and colonic infections. Large-volume enemas should be if possible avoided in the routine management of the neurogenic bowel for reasons related to side effects, the need for independent self-administration, healthcare cost and the availability of other conservative or surgical methods.

Retrograde colonic irrigation (bowel washout) is sometimes used in Europe and Japan. Most methods of irrigation have been derived from colostomy irrigation techniques. Hand-warm tap water or saline solutions are instilled through a catheter incorporating an inflatable rectal balloon, or via an anal cone, and have been successfully used in spina bifida and meningomyelocele children (Blair et al., 1992; de Kort et al., 1997; Eire et al., 1998) (Figure 17.4: Shandling catheter). A closed rectal washout system which infuses liquid by gravity through a retention-cuffed speculum inserted in the rectum has been developed for people with faecal incontinence (Iwama et al., 1989). Seventy-nine per cent of 32 ambulatory patients who suffered mainly from soiling were helped by a daily rectal washout (Briel et al., 1997).

Pulsed irrigation enhanced evacuation is a mechanically-assisted method of clearing faecal impaction using intermittent pulsed irrigation of small amounts of warm tap water administered rectally (Kokoszka et al., 1994). The procedure is supposed to rehydrate faeces, to break up impacted stools and to promote peristalsis (Puet et al., 1997). However, safety, complexity, comfort and cost of this procedure have yet to be fully evaluated. No reports have yet been published on its efficacy for routine bowel care, and therefore it cannot be recommended for that purpose.

Surgical options for constipation

An antegrade continence enema (ACE) is made possible after a surgical procedure (Malone procedure) giving direct access to the caecum through the appendix or a 'neo-appendix' by means of a small stoma and use of a small catheter (Malone et al., 1990) (see Chapter 14). Enemas are usually performed daily or on alternate days, using tap water or a mixture of phosphate and saline. Bowel management and quality of life improved in some adults with severe neurogenic bowel dysfunction (Christensen et al., 2000). Response to washout is individual, and it is worth experimenting with volumes, temperatures and fluids, with or without the addition of enemas, to find the optimum. If constipation is severe in patients with intractable and disabling soiling, it might be worthwhile to treat these patients with an ACE. This procedure could also be a 'bridge' towards the acceptance of a stoma. The technique has relatively little morbidity except for abdominal pain during enema and stoma stenosis that may require dilation or surgical

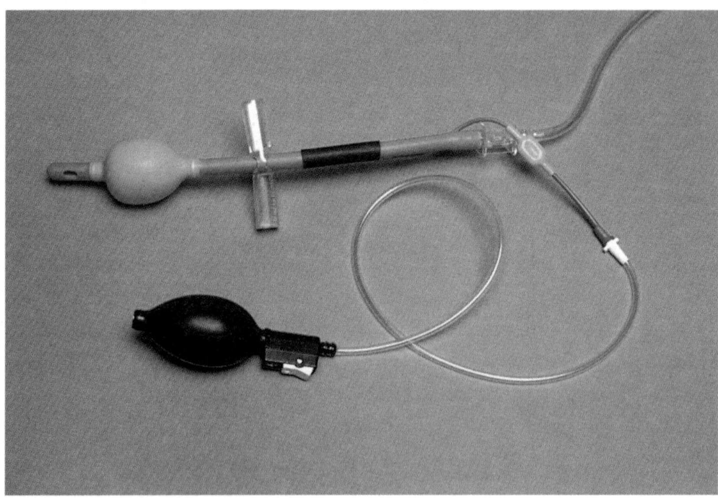

Figure 17.4 *Shandling catheter.*

revision. It has been successful in neurological children for managing combined constipation and faecal incontinence (Driver et al., 1998; Liptak and Revell, 1992). Preliminary reports in adult patients with severe faecal incontinence or impaired bowel evacuation are encouraging (Christensen et al., 2000; Krogh and Laurberg, 1998; Teichman et al., 1998a; Yang and Stiens, 2000). Overall satisfaction with the ACE was high or very high. Faecal incontinence, toileting time, bowel medications, impact on social activities and quality of life were reduced. This procedure can be discussed for selected patients with intractable constipation and faecal incontinence (Bruce et al., 1999) in whom conservative management of bowel care has failed, or in bowel related dysreflexia (Teichman et al., 1998b).

A stoma to shorten and simplify bowel care and to improve quality of life has been advocated in SCI (Craven and Etchells, 1998; Kelly et al., 1999; Saltzstein and Romano, 1990; Stone et al., 1990). When bowel emptying is ineffective using conservative methods or when bowel care requires unacceptable amount of time, inaccessible resources, or triggers complications (pressure sores, dysreflexia), a stoma is an appropriate alternative (see Chapter 15). Terminal ileostomy or terminal colostomy should be preferred rather than segmental resection of the bowel. Broad assessment of body image, lifestyle issue and independence in management of the stoma should be considered. A stoma has been used to deal with faecal incontinence in SCI patients (Frisbie et al., 1986).

Direct electrical stimulation of sacral anterior root has been attempted to promote bowel emptying in people with SCI. Stimulation is achieved by radio-frequency activation of a subcutaneous receiver (Brindley stimulator) that stimulates S2, S3, and S4 nerve roots bilaterally. Studies that have reported beneficial effects on colonic transit time, frequency of defaecation and time required for defaecation, have been based on observations and uncontrolled small series (Binnie et al., 1991; Chia et al., 1996; MacDonagh et al., 1990; Varma et al., 1986). This invasive procedure requires sacral dorsal rhizotomy in an attempt to prevent autonomic dysreflexia. This method has a high morbidity, especially when stimulation fails or devices have to be removed because of infection, leaving the patient with a flaccid bowel (from rhizothomy) which is extremely difficult to manage.

Direct electrical stimulation of posterior sacral nerves for treatment of faecal incontinence has also shown very promising preliminary results in some patients with weak, but structurally intact, anal sphincters (Malouf et al., 2000; Matzel et al., 1995). The posterior nerves are approached through the sacral foramen in a much less invasive technique than the anterior approach.

Management of faecal incontinence

Non-neurological causes of faecal incontinence should be addressed and treated: e.g. anal sphincter damage (obstetric or surgical), or infectious diarrhoea (e.g. *Clostridium difficile*). As previously mentioned, faecal incontinence might be secondary to constipation or impaction, and this should be managed first.

An anal plug has been marketed to help control faecal continence (see page 232). Impaired ano-rectal sensation is probably an important factor in enhancing tolerance of the plug and so it is particularly helpful for people with spinal lesions such as spina bifida.

Behavioural techniques, biofeedback and pelvic floor exercises may help where there is no structural sphincter damage, and may be useful as an adjunct to other treatments. Uncontrolled studies reported an efficacy of biofeedback for improving faecal continence in patients with myelomeningocele (Wald, 1983; Whitehead et al., 1981), spina bifida (Shepherd et al., 1983), and sacral agenesis (Benninga et al., 1994). In some incomplete SCI, preliminary results showed that biofeedback could be useful to recover continence (Monnerjahn C., Presentation at Annual Meeting of International Medical Society of Paraplegia, Copenhagen 1999). Biofeedback may thus play a role for those neurological patients in whom rectal sensation and the ability to contract voluntarily their pelvic floor muscles are preserved, and who can co-operate in the process of training (Wald and Tunuguntla, 1984; Wiesel et al., 2000).

Loperamide has been shown to have mainly an antisecretory effect at the mucosal level, accompanied by motor effects when it reaches the myenteric opiate receptors (Awouters et al., 1993) (see Chapter 16). Patients who experience urge incontinence of faeces associated with loose stool, or who have a passive anal seepage of soft stool, may benefit from a low dose of loperamide, although there are no data on use in patients with neurological disorders. Lower doses (syrup formulation) than those used in diarrhoea may help selected patients by inhibiting colonic motility and rectal filling, especially when given on an intermittent basis when needed, such as before leaving the house. If used in this fashion, neurological patients need to be observed closely for the development of constipation and loperamide will usually only be used in conjunction with a bowel evacuation programme.

Summary

Management of the neurogenic bowel starts with the adaptation of the patient's environment and his or her education (Table 17.2). A bowel programme will be designed to ensure satisfactory bowel care and prevent constipation and faecal incontinence. **When constipation occurs**, efforts are made to increase fluid and fibre intake and to use postprandial increases in colonic motility (gastro-colic response). Fibre is the most physiological approach in most patients. Rectal stimulants might be the first step, especially when colonic transit is normal but constipation predominantly terminal. An alternative to rectal stimulants is a small-volume enema. In case of failure, or when the rectal route is not practicable, an osmotic laxative should be tried. Stimulant laxatives should be deferred until patients do not respond to initial measures. **When faecal incontinence occurs**, behavioural techniques and pelvic floor exercises should be attempted. If constipation is not present, antidiarrheal drugs at appropriate dosage might be helpful. Surgical methods are considered when patients are unresponsive to medical therapy. Every method proposed should also consider the acceptability to the patient as well as cost aspects.

Educational strategies for the neurogenic patient

The success of any bowel management programme hinges on compliance. In a study addressing compliance with bowel medications, two-thirds of 114 participants were taking bowel medication when discharged from hospital. However, one month later 24% had reduced or stopped taking medication (Graham and Kunkle, 1996). A telephone survey questionnaire administered to 171 adults with a mean duration of SCI of 9 years and mean age of 40 years showed similar results on long-term outcomes of bowel management (Kirk et al., 1997). Bowel continence has been shown to be correlated to compliance in young adults with spina bifida (King et al., 1994). A variety of factors may contribute to nonadherence to a prescribed bowel programme, including impairment of cognitive function, misunderstanding of the prescription, inapplicability in the home setting, reluctance to cope with a disability, unwillingness to perform a complicated programme, acceptance of bowel symptoms, a lack of resources (home setting, carers, finance), and a lack of education about bowel function and management.

Education strategies should begin in the rehabilitation unit following full assessment. Education should centre on the patient, but carer(s) should also be included. The programme should describe the anatomy and the physiology of bowel function, the process of defaecation and bowel continence, the goals of a bowel programme, the safe and effective use of all methods prescribed for the bowel care, the bowel medications (type, purpose, dose, frequency, side effects and potential drug interactions), complications of the neurogenic bowel and ways to prevent and treat them, and methods to use in case of failure. Reinforcement

Table 17.3: The management of the neurogenic bowel

The management of the neurogenic bowel should offer the best method based on the assessment of the patient and his/her environment (see text for details).

Environment management

- Community and home (adapted, safe and pleasant, financial support)
- Carers (informed consent, ethical, skilled, empathetic)

Individual management

- Emotional (carers, relatives, professionals)
- Concomitant diseases, side-effects of drugs
- Bladder management (collaboration with urological team)

Bowel Management

- *Bowel programme*
  Routine (scheduling, gastrocolic response)
  Diet (healthy), fibre, fluid intake (accordance with the bladder)
- *Bowel care*
- *Assistive methods*
  Massage, push-ups, Valsalva manoeuvre, deep breathing and forward-leaning position
  Digital stimulation
  Manual evacuation
  Behavioural methods (biofeedback)
- *Pharmacological methods*
  Laxatives (bulk-forming, faecal softeners, osmotic, stimulant)
  Retrograde colonic irrigation (enema, pulsed irrigation enhanced evacuation)
  Constipating drugs (Loperamide, codeine phosphate)
- *Surgical methods*
  Antegrade continence enema procedure (Malone procedure)
  Stoma (ileostomy, colostomy)
  Sacral nerves neuromodulation (transcutaneous, direct anterior and direct posterior)

of the education should be provided when monitoring the effectiveness of the bowel programme. This approach has been successfully tested in SCI (Minton, 1983). See Appendix II for useful addresses and websites, such as www.spinal.co.uk/help/bowl.htm (sic).

Conclusions

Neurological disability is common and is often complicated by bowel problems such as constipation and faecal incontinence. Pathological involvement of the nervous system at any level may alter the motor function of the pelvic floor and abdominal muscles, bowel motility, the ascending afferent sensory function to the brain and the descending neuromodulation of visceral sensation from the brain. Although the neurophysiological pathways have been described, our understanding of enteric neurobiology is at a very early stage. This chapter outlines a targeted assessment and problem-solving approach to the management of neurogenic bowel dysfunction. The assessment of the neurogenic bowel is a methodical process, requiring multidisciplinary resources and a small number of investigations. It should take into account environmental and individual aspects. The assessment should identify which parts of bowel function are preserved. A bowel programme should be designed in accordance with patient's disability, impairment, handicap, life goals and expectations.

The acceptability of a bowel program to the patient is crucial to its success. Compliance can be improved by education and reinforcement. Bowel management remains a challenge in rehabilitation. Many methods have been developed, but there is a lack of generalisation of knowledge and techniques between different patients groups. Some methods seem to be confined to SCI, others to spina bifida. There is a need for rigorous evaluation of the many methods that have entered the folklore without being subjected to trial.

References

Addison, R. and Smith, M. (2000) *Digital rectal examination and manual removal of faeces. Guidance for nurses.* London: Royal College of Nursing.

Ashraf, W., Pfeiffer, R.F., Park, F., Lof, J. and Quigley, E.M. (1997) Constipation in Parkinson's disease: objective assessment and response to psyllium. *Movement Disorders* **12**, 6, 946–951.

Astarloa, R., Mena, M.A., Sanchez, V. and de Yebenes, J.G. (1992) Clinical and pharmacokinetic effects of a diet rich in insoluble fiber on Parkinson's disease. *Clinical Neuropharmacology* **15**, 5, 375–380.

Attar, A., Lemann, M., Ferguson, A., Halphen, M., Boutron, M.C., Flourie, B., Alix, E., Salmeron, M., Guillemot, F., Chaussade, S., Menard, A.M., Moreau, J., Naudin, G. and Barthet, M. (1999) Comparison of a low dose polyethylene glycol electrolyte solution with lactulose for treatment of chronic constipation. *Gut* **44**, 2, 226–230.

Awouters, F., Megens, A., Verlinden, M., Schuurkes, J., Niemegeers, C. and Janssen, P.A. (1993) Loperamide. Survey of studies on mechanism of its antidiarrheal activity. *Digestive Diseases and Sciences* **38**, 6, 977–995.

Badiali, D., Bracci, F., Castellano, V., Corazziari, E., Fuoco, U., Habib, F.I. and Scivoletto, G. (1997) Sequential treatment of chronic constipation in paraplegic subjects. *Spinal Cord* **35**, 2, 116–120.

Banwell, J.G., Creasey, G.H., Aggarwal, A.M. and Mortimer, J.T. (1993) Management of the neurogenic bowel in patients with spinal cord injury. *Urologic Clinics of North America* **20**, 3, 517–526.

Bauer, H.J., Firnhaber, W. and Winkler, W. (1965) Prognostic criteria in multiple sclerosis. *Annals of the New York Academy of Sciences* **122**, 542, 551.

Benninga, M.A., van der Hoeven, C., Wijers, O.B., Buller, H.A., Tytgat, G.N., Akkermans, L.M. and Taminiau, J.A. (1994) Treatment of faecal incontinence in a child with sacral agenesis: the use of biofeedback training. *Developmental Medicine and Child Neurology* **36**, 6, 518–527.

Binnie, N.R., Smith, A.N., Creasey, G.H. and Edmond, P. (1991) Constipation associated with chronic spinal cord injury: the effect of pelvic parasympathetic stimulation by the Brindley stimulator. *Paraplegia* **29**, 7, 463–469.

Blair, G.K., Djonlic, K., Fraser, G.C., Arnold, W.D., Murphy, J.J. and Irwin, B. (1992) The bowel management tube: an effective means for controlling fecal incontinence. *Journal of Pediatric Surgery* **27**, 10, 1269–1272.

Briel, J.W., Schouten, W.R., Vlot, E.A., Smits, S. and Van, K.I. (1997) Clinical value of colonic irrigation in patients with continence disturbances. *Diseases of the Colon and Rectum* **40**, 7, 802–805.

Brocklehurst, J.C., Andrews, K., Richards, B. and Laycock, P.J. (1985) Incidence and correlates of incontinence in stroke patients. *Journal of the American Geriatrics Society* **33**, 8, 540–542.

Bruce, R.G., el Galley, R.E., Wells, J. and Galloway, N.T. (1999) Antegrade continence enema for the treatment of fecal incontinence in adults: use of gastric tube for catheterizable access to the descending colon. *Journal of Urology* **161**, 6, 1813–1816.

Cameron, K.J., Nyulasi, I.B., Collier, G.R. and Brown, D.J. (1996) Assessment of the effect of increased dietary fibre intake on bowel function in patients with spinal cord injury. *Spinal Cord* **34**, 5, 277–283.

Caruana, B.J., Wald, A., Hinds, J.P. and Eidelman, B.H. (1991) Anorectal sensory and motor function in neurogenic fecal incontinence. Comparison between multiple sclerosis and diabetes mellitus. *Gastroenterology* **100**, 2, 465–470.

Chia, Y., Fowler, C.J., Kamm, M.A., Henry, M.M., Lemieux, M.C. and Swash, M. (1995) Prevalence of bowel dysfunction in patients with multiple sclerosis and bladder dysfunction. *Journal of Neurology* **242**, 2, 105–108.

Chia, Y.W., Lee, T.K., Kour, N.W., Tung, K.H. and Tan, E.S. (1996) Microchip implants on the anterior sacral roots in patients with spinal trauma: does it improve bowel function? *Diseases of the Colon and Rectum* **39**, 6, 690–694.

Christensen, P., Kvitzau, B., Krogh, K., Buntzen, S. and Laurberg, S. (2000) Neurogenic colorectal dysfunction – use of new antegrade and retrograde colonic wash-out methods. *Spinal Cord* **38**, 4, 255–261.

Clouse, R. and Lustman, P. (1989) Gastrointestinal symptoms in diabetic patients: lack of association with neuropathy. *American Journal of Gastroenterology* **84**, 868, 872.

Corazziari, E., Badiali, D., Bazzocchi, G., Bassotti, G., Roselli, P., Mastropaolo, G., Luca, M.G., Galeazzi, R. and Peruzzi, E. (2000) Long term efficacy, safety, and tolerabilitity of low daily doses of isosmotic polyethylene glycol electrolyte balanced solution (PMF-100) in the treatment of functional chronic constipation. *Gut* **46**, 4, 522–526.

Craven, M.L. and Etchells, J. (1998) A review of the outcome of stoma surgery on spinal cord injured patients. *Journal of Advanced Nursing* **27**, 5, 922–926.

Culbert, P., Gillett, H. and Ferguson, A. (1998) Highly effective new oral therapy for faecal impaction. *British Journal of General Practice* **48**, 434, 1599–1600.

de Kort, L.M., Nesselaar, C.H., van Gool, J.D. and de Jong, T.P. (1997) The influence of colonic enema irrigation on urodynamic findings in patients with neurogenic bladder dysfunction. *British Journal of Urology* **80**, 5, 731–733.

DiPalma, J.A., DeRidder, P.H., Orlando, R.C., Kolts, B.E. and Cleveland, M.B. (2000) A randomised, placebo-controlled, multicenter study of the safety and efficacy of a new polyethylene glycol laxative. *American Journal of Gastroenterology* **95**, 2, 446–450.

Driver, C.P., Barrow, C., Fishwick, J., Gough, D.C., Bianchi, A. and Dickson, A.P. (1998) The Malone antegrade colonic enema procedure: outcome and lessons of 6 years' experience. *Pediatric Surgery International* **13**, 5–6, 370–372.

Dunn, K.L. and Galka, M.L. (1994) A comparison of the effectiveness of Therevac SB and bisacodyl suppositories in SCI patients' bowel programs. *Rehabilitation Nursing* **19**, 6, 334–338.

Edwards, L.L., Quigley, E.M. and Pfeiffer, R.F. (1992) Gastrointestinal dysfunction in Parkinson's disease: frequency and pathophysiology. *Neurology* **42**, 4, 726–732.

Eire, P.F., Cives, R.V. and Gago, M.C. (1998) Faecal incontinence in children with spina bifida: the best conservative treatment. *Spinal Cord* **36**, 11, 774–6.

Emmanuel, A.V. and Kamm, M.A. (1999) Laser Doppler measurement of rectal mucosal blood flow. *Gut* **45**, 64, 69.

Ernst, E. (1999) Abdominal massage therapy for chronic constipation: a systematic review of controlled clinical trials. *Forschung Komplementarmedizin* **6**, 3, 149–151.

Feldman, M. and Schiller, L. (1983) Disorders of gastrointestinal motility associated with diabetes mellitus. *Annals of Internal Medicine* **98**, 378–384.

Ferguson, A., Culbert, P., Gillett, H. and Barras, N. (1999) New polyethylene glycol electrolyte solution for the treatment of constipation and faecal impaction. *Italian Journal of Gastroenterology and Hepatology* **31** (Suppl. 3), S249–S252.

Frisbie, J.H. (1997) Improved bowel care with a polyethylene glycol based bisacodyl suppository. *Journal of Spinal Cord Medicine* **20**, 2, 227–229.

Frisbie, J.H., Tun, C.G. and Nguyen, C.H. (1986) Effect of enterostomy on quality of life in spinal cord injury patients. *Journal of the American Paraplegia Society* **9**, 1–2, 3–5.

Gattuso, J.M. and Kamm, M.A. (1993) Review article: the management of constipation in adults. *Alimentary Pharmacology and Therapeutics* **7**, 5, 487–500.

Gattuso, J.M. and Kamm, M.A. (1994) Adverse effects of drugs used in the management of constipation and diarrhoea. *Drug Safety* **10**, 1, 47–65.

Glickman, S. and Kamm, M.A. (1996) Bowel dysfunction in spinal-cord-injury patients. *Lancet* **347**, 9016, 1651–1653.

Graham, C. and Kunkle, C. (1996) Do rehabilitation patients continue prescribed bowel medications after discharge? *Rehabilitation Nursing* **21**, 6, 298–302.

Hanson, R.W. and Franklin, M.R. (1976) Sexual loss in relation to other functional losses for spinal cord injured males. *Archives of Physical Medicine and Rehabilitation* **57**, 6, 291–293.

Hinds, J.P., Eidelman, B.H. and Wald, A. (1990) Prevalence of bowel dysfunction in multiple sclerosis. A population survey. *Gastroenterology* **98**, 6, 1538–1542.

House, J.G. and Stiens, S.A. (1997) Pharmacologically initiated defaecation for persons with spinal cord injury: effectiveness of three agents. *Archives of Physical Medicine and Rehabilitation* **78**, 10, 1062–1065.

Hurdon, V., Viola, R. and Schroder, C. (2000) How useful is docusate in patients at risk for constipation? A systematic review of the evidence in the chronically ill. *Journal of Pain and Symptoms Management* **19**, 2, 130–136.

Iwama, T., Imajo, M., Yaegashi, K. and Mishima, Y. (1989) Self washout method for defaecational complaints following low anterior rectal resection. *Japanese Journal of Surgery* **19**, 2, 251–253.

Jameson, J.S., Rogers, J., Chia, Y.W., Misiewicz, J.J., Henry, M.M. and Swash, M. (1994) Pelvic floor function in multiple sclerosis. *Gut* **35**, 3, 388–390.

Jeffries, J.S., Killam, P.E. and Varni, J.W. (1982) Behavioral management of fecal incontinence in a child with myelomeningocele. *Pediatric Nursing* **8**, 4, 267–270.

Kamm, M.A. and Lennard-Jones, J.E. (1990) Rectal mucosal electrosensory testing – evidence for a rectal sensory neuropathy in idiopathic constipation. *Diseases of the Colon and Rectum* **33**, 5, 419–423.

Kang, Y.S., Kamm, M.A., Engel, A.F. and Talbot, I.C. (1996) Pathology of the rectal wall in solitary rectal ulcer syndrome and complete rectal prolapse. *Gut* **38**, 4, 587–590.

Kelly, S.R., Shashidharan, M., Borwell, B., Tromans, A.M., Finnis, D. and Grundy, D.J. (1999) The role of intestinal stoma in patients with spinal cord injury. *Spinal Cord* **37**, 3, 211–214.

King, J.C., Currie, D.M. and Wright, E. (1994) Bowel training in spina bifida: importance of education, patient compliance, age, and anal reflexes. *Archives of Physical Medicine and Rehabilitation* **75**, 3, 243–247.

Kirk, P.M., King, R.B., Temple, R., Bourjaily, J. and Thomas, P. (1997) Long-term follow-up of bowel management after spinal cord injury. *Spinal Cord Injury Nursing* **14**, 2, 56–63.

Kokoszka, J., Nelson, R. and Falconio, M. (1994) Treatment of fecal impaction with pulsed irrigation enhanced evacuation. *Diseases of the Colon and Rectum* **37**, 161–164.

Krogh, K. and Laurberg, S. (1998) Malone antegrade continence enema for faecal incontinence and constipation in adults. *British Journal of Surgery* **85**, 7, 974–977.

Krogh, K., Nielsen, J., Djurhuus, J.C., Mosdal, C., Sabroe, S. and Laurberg, S. (1997) Colorectal function in patients with spinal cord lesions. *Diseases of the Colon and Rectum* **40**, 10, 1233–1239.

Levine, A.M., Nash, M.S. and Green, B.A. (1992) An examination of dietary intakes and nutritional status of chronic healthy spinal cord injured individuals. *Paraplegia* **30**, 880–889.

Liebl, B.H., Fischer, M.H., Van Calcar, S.C. and Marlett, J.A. (1990) Dietary fiber and long-term large bowel response in enterally nourished non-ambulatory profoundly retarded youth. *Journal of Parenteral and Enteral Nutrition* **14**, 4, 371–375.

Liptak, G.S. and Revell, G.M. (1992) Management of bowel dysfunction in children with spinal cord disease or injury by means of the enema continence catheter. *Journal of Pediatrics* **120**, 2 (Part 1), 190–194.

MacDonagh, R.P., Sun, W.M., Smallwood, R., Forster, D. and Read, N.W. (1990) Control of defaecation in patients with spinal injuries by stimulation of sacral anterior nerve roots. *British Medical Journal* **300**, 6738, 1494–1497.

Malone, P.S., Ransley, P.G. and Kiely, E.M. (1990) Preliminary report: the antegrade continence enema. *Lancet* **336**, 8725, 1217–1218.

Malouf, A.J., Vaizey, C.J., Nicholls, R.J. and Kamm, M.A. (2000) Permanent sacral nerve stimulation for fecal incontinence. *Annals of Surgery* **232**, 1, 143–148.

Matzel, K.E., Stadelmaier, U., Hohenfellner, M. and Gall, F.P. (1995) Electrical stimulation of sacral spinal nerves for treatment of faecal incontinence. *Lancet* **346**, 8983, 1124–1127.

Minton, P.N. (1983) Video tape instruction: an effective way to learn. *Rehabilitation Nursing* **8**, 3, 15–17.

Munchiando, J.F. and Kendall, K. (1993) Comparison of the effectiveness of two bowel programs for CVA patients. *Rehabilitation Nursing* **18**, 3, 168–172.

Murray, C.D.R. and Emmanuel, A.V. (2002) Medical management of diverticular disease. *Baillière's Best Practice, Research Clinical Gastroenterology*, October, 611–620.

Nakayama, H., Jorgensen, H.S., Pedersen, P.M., Raaschou, H.O. and Olsen, T.S. (1997) Prevalence and risk factors of incontinence after stroke. The Copenhagen Stroke Study. *Stroke* **28**, 1, 58–62.

Nelson, A., Malassigne, P., Amerson, T., Saltzstein, R. and Binard, J. (1993) Descriptive study of bowel care practices and equipment in spinal cord injury. *Spinal Cord Injury Nursing* **10**, 2, 65–67.

Nordenbo, A.M., Andersen, J.R. and Andersen, J.T. (1996) Disturbances of ano-rectal function in multiple sclerosis. *Journal of Neurology* **243**, 6, 445–451.

Puet, T.A., Jackson, H. and Amy, S. (1997) Use of pulsed irrigation evacuation in the management of the neuropathic bowel. *Spinal Cord* **35**, 10, 694–699.

Rothwell, P.M., McDowell, Z., Wong, C.K. and Dorman, P.J. (1997) Doctors and patients don't agree: cross sectional study of patients' and doctors' perceptions and assessments of disability in multiple sclerosis. *British Medical Journal* **314**, 7094, 1580–1583.

Saltzstein, R.J. and Romano, J. (1990) The efficacy of colostomy as a bowel management alternative in selected spinal cord injury patients. *Journal of the American Paraplegia Society* **13**, 2, 9–13.

Schiller, L.R. (1999) Clinical pharmacology and use of laxatives and lavage solutions. *Journal of Clinical Gastroenterology* **28**, 1, 11–18.

Shepherd, K., Hickstein, R. and Shepherd, R. (1983) Neurogenic faecal incontinence in children with spina bifida: rectosphincteric responses and evaluation of a physiological rationale for management, including biofeedback conditioning. *Australian Paediatric Journal* **19**, 2, 97–99.

Stiens, S.A. (1995) Reduction in bowel program duration with polyethylene glycol based bisacodyl suppositories. *Archives of Physical Medicine and Rehabilitation* **76**, 7, 674–677.

Stiens, S.A., Bergman, S.B. and Goetz, L.L. (1997)

Neurogenic bowel dysfunction after spinal cord injury: clinical evaluation and rehabilitative management. *Archives of Physical Medicine and Rehabilitation* **78**, 3 (Suppl.), S86–102.

Stiens, S.A., Luttrel, W. and Binard, J.E. (1998) Polyethylene glycol versus vegetable oil based bisacodyl suppositories to initiate side-lying bowel care: a clinical trial in persons with spinal cord injury. *Spinal Cord* **36**, 11, 777–781.

Stone, J.M., Wolfe, V.A., Nino-Murcia, M. and Perkash, I. (1990) Colostomy as treatment for complications of spinal cord injury. *Archives of Physical Medicine and Rehabilitation* **71**, 7, 514–518.

Subbarao, J.V. (1987) Spinal cord dysfunction in older patients – rehabilitation outcomes. *Journal of the American Paraplegia Society* **10**, 2, 30–35.

Sullivan, S. and Ebers, G. (1983) Gastrointestinal dysfunction in multiple sclerosis. *Gastroenterology* **84**, 1640–1646.

Sun, W.M., Katsinelos, P., Horowitz, M. and Read, N.W. (1996) Disturbances in anorectal function in patients with diabetes mellitus and faecal incontinence. *European Journal of Gastroenterology and Hepatology* **8**, 10, 1007–1012.

Sussman, G.L. and Dorian, W. (1990) Psyllium anaphylaxis. *Allergy Proceedings* **11**, 5, 241–242.

Teichman, J.M., Harris, J.M., Currie, D.M. and Barber, D.B. (1998a) Malone antegrade continence enema for adults with neurogenic bowel disease. *Journal of Urology* **160**, 4, 1278–1281.

Teichman, J.M., Barber, D.B., Rogenes, V.J. and Harris, J.M. (1998b) Malone antegrade continence enemas for autonomic dysreflexia secondary to neurogenic bowel. *Journal of Spinal Cord Medicine* **21**, 3, 245–247.

Uher, E.M. and Swash, M. (1998) Sacral reflexes: physiology and clinical application. *Diseases of the Colon and Rectum* **41**, 1165–1177.

Ungar, A. (2000) Movicol in treatment of constipation and faecal impaction. *Hospital Medicine* **61**, 1, 37–40.

Varma, J.S., Binnie, N., Smith, A.N., Creasey, G.H. and Edmond, P. (1986) Differential effects of sacral anterior root stimulation on anal sphincter and colorectal motility in spinally injured man. *British Journal of Surgery* **73**, 6, 478–482.

Venn, M.R., Taft, L., Carpentier, B. and Applebaugh, G. (1992) The influence of timing and suppository use on efficiency and effectiveness of bowel training after a stroke. *Rehabilitation Nursing* **17**, 3, 116–120.

Wald, A. (1983) Biofeedback for neurogenic fecal incontinence: rectal sensation is a determinant of outcome. *Journal of Pediatric Gastroenterology and Nutrition* **2**, 2, 302–306.

Wald, A. and Tunuguntla, A.K. (1984) Anorectal sensorimotor dysfunction in fecal incontinence and diabetes mellitus. Modification with biofeedback therapy. *New England Journal of Medicine* **310**, 20, 1282–1287.

White, M.J., Rintala, D.H., Hart, K.A. and Fuhrer, M.J. (1993) Sexual activities, concerns and interests of women with spinal cord injury living in the community. *American Journal of Physical Medicine and Rehabilitation* **72**, 6, 372–378.

Whitehead, W.E., Parker, L.H., Masek, B.J., Cataldo, M.F. and Freeman, J.M. (1981) Biofeedback treatment of fecal incontinence in patients with myelomeningocele. *Developmental Medicine and Child Neurology* **23**, 3, 313–322.

Wiesel, P.H., Norton, C., Roy, A.J., Storrie, J.B., Bowers, J. and Kamm, M.A. (2000) Gut-focused behavioural treatment (biofeedback) for constipation and faecal incontinence in multiple sclerosis. *Journal of Neurology, Neurosurgery, and Psychiatry* **69**, 2, 240–243.

Wiesel, P., Norton, C. and Brazzelli, M. (2001) Bowel management for adults with neurological disease or injury. *Cochrane electronic library of systematic reviews* (www.cochrane.org).

Wineman, N.M., Durand, E.J. and Steiner, R.P. (1994) A comparative analysis of coping behaviors in persons with multiple sclerosis or a spinal cord injury. *Research In Nursing and Health* **17**, 3, 185–194.

Yang, C.C. and Stiens, S.A. (2000) Antegrade continence enema for the treatment of neurogenic constipation and fecal incontinence after spinal cord injury. *Archives of Physical Medicine and Rehabilitation* **81**, 5, 683–685.

Younoszai, M.K. (1992) Stooling problems in patients with myelomeningocele. *Southern Medical Journal* **85**, 7, 718–724.

Zigmond, A.S. and Snaith, R.P. (1983) The hospital anxiety and depression scale. *Acta Psychiatrica Scandinavica* **67**, 6, 361–370.

Chapter 18

Bowel Control and Intellectual Disability

Linda Smith and Paul Smith

Encopresis in the field of learning disability

Before reviewing the evidence on prevalence, aetiology and treatment of encopresis in this field, it is important first to clarify the terminology used in this chapter.

Learning disability

Learning disability is the term currently used in the UK to describe people who have a significant developmental intellectual disadvantage or impairment. The term formerly used in the UK was mental handicap. That used by the World Health Organisation, together with the rest of the English-speaking world, is mental retardation, although the latter is regarded in the UK as more stigmatising. Unfortunately, the term learning disability is used in the USA to refer to other, specific developmental disorders such as hyperactivity and attention deficit disorder, autism and dyslexia. If you do not work in the field, this can be confusing. This chapter will use the terms learning disability and intellectual disability interchangeably to equate to mental retardation. Learning disability is distinguished from dementia by its developmental component: learning disability is a failure to acquire abilities, whereas dementia involves a loss of previously-acquired abilities. It should also be remembered that learning disability includes both children and adults.

Encopresis

This chapter briefly overviews the prevalence and aetiology of encopresis, before reviewing treatment studies. The terms faecal incontinence, faecal soiling and encopresis seem to imply a clearer distinction between different types of bowel incontinence than may be easily justifiable. Some distinguish between the trained and untrained bowel, and reserve encopresis to refer to the voiding of faeces in socially unacceptable locations, when the person actually has the ability to be continent. Encopresis is used here more loosely to refer to faecal soiling where an original organic cause is not readily apparent. However, encopresis may often reflect both physiological and psychological factors together, and a simple dichotomy between organic and psychogenic encopresis is difficult to sustain. (See page 217 for a more detailed discussion of the aetiology of faecal incontinence in children.)

Prevalence of encopresis in learning disability

Although a number of surveys have addressed the prevalence of encopresis in the field of learning disability, their quality is variable. Comparison across studies is complicated by methodological differences, including lack of common methods of measurement across studies, differing degrees of intellectual disability, failure to define terms such as constipation, lack of information about the reliability of measures and low response rates in community studies.

Arguably the most informative community survey of prevalence is that of von Wendt et al. (1990) who studied 137 twenty-year-olds with learning disabilities, of whom 105 responded. The only birth cohort of people with learning disabilities living in the community, it provides concurrent figures for bowel control at age 20 and retrospective figures for control at age 7 (Table 18.1).

These results indicate that the prevalence of encopresis in those with mild learning disability is little different from that of the general population; that rates for those with moderate and severe learning disability are similar to each other; and that, notably, prevalence is substantially higher in those with a profound learning disability. Nevertheless, around half of those with a profound disability will acquire bowel control by adulthood.

Dalrymple and Ruble's (1992) survey of 315 people with autism aged from 9 to 39 years is also of interest. Intellectual ability ranged from 'gifted' within the general range of intelligence to profound learning disability. Mean age of accomplishment of bowel training is provided for 86 respondents said to have acquired bowel control (Table 18.2).

These results again support the view that the acquisition of bowel control presents a considerably greater problem for those with the most severe learning disabilities. They must, however, be viewed with caution due to the very low response rate (under one third) and the retrospective nature of reports as to age of attainment. Combined results for severe and profound learning disabilities mean that the acquisition of control cannot be compared across those categories.

Table 18.1

Intellectual Ability Level	*N*	*Encopresis at age 7*	*Encopresis at age 20*
Mild	36	1 (2.8%)	0 (0%)
Moderate	34	11 (32.4%)	6 (17.6%)
Severe	21	8 (38.1%)	6 (18.6%)
Profound	14	12 (85.7%)	8 (57.1%)

Table 18.2

Age Bowel Training Accomplished, N = 86

*Intellectual Level**	*Mean Age*
Gifted	3.5 years
Average	4.0 years
Mild	4.2 years
Moderate	3.8 years
Severe + Profound	7.1 years

*Number of subjects by level of ability not specified.

Prevalence of constipation in learning disability

Constipation is said to be a factor in around 80% of cases of encopresis in the general population (Doleys et al., 1981). There is a widespread belief that chronic constipation and faecal impaction are major problems for high-dependency populations in general (Kobak et al., 1962; Thomas et al., 1984; Agnarsson et al., 1993), although little empirical evidence is available in the field of learning disability. However, it has been suggested that some learning disability syndromes such as Rett's syndrome and Down's syndrome (Leung et al., 1986; Saavedra and Perman, 1990) are associated with constipation and encopresis. These studies are subject to a number of methodological criticisms and have not demonstrated a direct causal relationship between the syndromes concerned and symptoms of constipation and encopresis.

Aetiology

There has been very little study of aetiological factors in encopresis in the field of learning disability. Why this should be so is unclear, but empirical evidence from other high-dependency fields supports the view that encopresis in people with intellectual disabilities is often perceived as 'normal' and the prognosis for treatment is viewed pessimistically. People with severe or profound learning disabilities may be deemed to have failed to reach some prerequisite level of development necessary for the acquisition of bowel control, so that the presence of a learning disability is assumed to be *the* aetiological factor. Investigations of an invasive nature can be difficult to carry out in people with severe learning disabilities. In addition, the inability to consent to investigations for non-emergency medical procedures or for research purposes hampers the investigation of the failure to acquire and breakdown of bowel control in people with severe and profound learning disability.

Studies of children in the general population have associated encopresis with general developmental delay, learning and cognitive deficits, speech and language deficits, hyperactivity, poor neuromuscular co-ordination and general neurological immaturity (Gabel 1981; Stern et al., 1988; Madge et al., 1993). It is clear, however, that their presence is not predictive: most encopretic children are of average intelligence and neurologically intact (Bellman, 1966; Fritz and Armbrust, 1982) and, conversely, most people with intellectual disabilities are not encopretic.

Learning disability

Groves (1982) has asserted that a co-present learning disability is commonly assumed to be *the* causal factor in encopresis. Thus, those with a learning disability who remain encopretic into adulthood are deemed to have failed to reach a prerequisite level of development. The consequence of this assumption is that people with learning disabilities are disadvantaged in terms of investigation and diagnosis, and prognosis for bowel training is viewed pessimistically (Groves, 1982).

That learning disability should not be seen as the sole cause of encopresis is supported by the fact that the prevalence of encopresis in those with a mild learning disability is little different from prevalence in the general population (Smith, 1979; von Wendt et al., 1990; Dalrymple and Ruble, 1992). Furthermore, around one half of those with profound learning disabilities do acquire bowel control (Smith, 1979; von Wendt et al., 1990). On the other hand, that encopresis increases with degree of learning disability supports its role as a factor of some importance (Lohmann et al., 1967; Spencer et al., 1968; Eyman et al., 1970; Smith, 1979; von Wendt et al., 1990; Dalrymple and Ruble, 1992).

In addition to more severe degrees of learning disability, there is evidence that the presence of factors such as hyperactivity and deficits of attention, negativity and other challenging behaviours militate against the acquisition of bowel control.

In a study of 3847 cases of learning disability, 30% of whom were rated as being hyperactive to some degree, Jenkins and Stable (1971) found that severe hyperactivity was significantly associated with enuresis and encopresis.

Dalrymple and Ruble's (1992) survey of encopresis and toileting problems in adults and children with autism identified that 32% of those with encopresis or regression in bowel control had toilet-related phobias. Regression was also commonly associated with change in routine.

In a 5-year follow-up of 3427 institutional residents with learning disabilities, Lohmann et al. (1967) found that regression in bowel and bladder control and the irregular acquisition of control were associated with the presence of behavioural problems. Similarly, in a much smaller sample, Spencer et al. (1968) found that bowel control was significantly associated with negativistic behaviour and lack of social responsiveness. Of note, these were not statistically associated with progress on a subsequent behavioural toilet training programme.

Constipation and impaction

Constipation and impaction are generally regarded as the most predictive factors in encopresis in the general population (Doleys et al., 1981) although definitions of constipation have been somewhat inconsistent (Floch and Wald, 1994).

Suggested physiological causes for severe, idiopathic constipation have included abnormally slow gastrointestinal transit time (Lanfranchi et al., 1984), increased threshold to sensation in the rectum (Meunier et al., 1976;

Lanfranchi et al., 1984; Read et al., 1986), failure of relaxation or paradoxical contraction of the puborectalis or external sphincter (Read et al., 1986; Loening-Baucke and Cruikshank, 1986) or a combination of these factors (Read et al., 1986).

Abnormal physiological responses of the colon, rectum and anus have been found in many sufferers of chronic constipation and faecal impaction (Meunier et al., 1976; Arhan et al., 1983; Molnar et al., 1983; Loening-Baucke and Cruikshank, 1986), with a sizeable proportion having experienced such problems from infancy (Kottmeier and Clatworthy, 1965; Tobon and Schuster, 1974; Arhan et al., 1983). However, the nature of the relationship between abnormal physiological responses, constipation and faecal incontinence appears to be complex. For example, asymptomatic controls have been found to show similar frequencies of abnormalities (Wald and Handen, 1987) and physiological abnormalities have been found to remain despite successful treatment of symptoms (Loening-Baucke, 1984b).

Furthermore, one randomised trial of biofeedback treatment found that some people's symptoms improved with treatment for a physiological response which had not been faulty in the first place; some improved without any treatment at all; and some failed to improve despite biofeedback training which corrected faulty physiological mechanisms (Latimer, 1984). The complex relationship between nervous system abnormalities and bowel symptoms has also been demonstrated in people with cognitive deficits in a study of ano-rectal manometry in children with cerebral palsy, constipation, faecal incontinence and distress on defaecation, most of whom were non-ambulant (Agnarrson et al., 1993). The same aversion to painful defaecation can operate with disabled as with non-disabled children (see Chapter 19).

Although constipation may develop for different reasons at different stages in childhood, one author has asserted that the two most common causes are excessive use of artificial elimination aids and the persistent failure to respond to the urge to defaecate (Schaeffer, 1979). A number of other factors which promote constipation are commonly found in high-dependency fields such as learning disability. These include low fibre or high sugar diet; insufficient fluid intake; poor dentition; impaired mobility or general lack of exercise; anxiety, depression or major mental illness; and the use of many common constipating medications (Resnick, 1985; Wrenn, 1989; Smith and Ross, 1992).

Whatever the initial cause of constipation, possible complications of severe impaction include acute intestinal obstruction (Tobon and Schuster, 1974) and profound shock following its treatment with elimination aids (McGuire et al., 1983). Serious sequelae including fatality, though rare, present a greater threat to institutionalised, non-verbal and cognitively-impaired individuals (Leventhal and Gimmon, 1978).

Groves (1982) has suggested that individual vulnerability to encopresis in the field of learning disability can best be expressed in terms of a *continuum* of predisposing characteristics, of which increasing degree of learning disability might be one. Although it is unclear which additional factors might be important (Spencer et al., 1968), there is evidence to support a role for hyperactivity and deficits of attention as well as 'challenging' behaviours in a variety of forms.

Treatment

It is undeniable that people with severe and profound learning disabilities today enjoy generally higher standards of care in the community than were previously found in large Victorian institutions, with their pervasive smell of urine and faeces. However, although Parker (1984) has expressed the belief that recent years have seen a 'quiet revolution' in the approach taken to incontinence in this field, recent, albeit flawed, prevalence studies in community-dwelling samples seem to offer little support to this assertion. The easy availability of a wider range of aids and appliances for the more effective management of incontinence may simply reduce its obviousness and ameliorate its worst effects.

Protinsky and Dillard (1983) suggest that the important question in relation to treatment concerns whether the child is '... old enough, sane enough and intelligent enough'. Regardless of whether the problem is one of urinary or faecal incontinence, it is not clear how to assess 'readiness' in the field of learning disability. According to Schaeffer (1979), for example, a child is physiologically ready for daytime bowel training when there is regularity in bowel movements and control of the bowels during sleep. However, the current toilet training fashion encourages parents to delay training until the child can understand simple instructions and can communicate the need to eliminate (Dunlap et al., 1985; Smith and Smith, 1987; Howe and Walker, 1992).

The trend to later toilet training does, however, have serious implications for attitudes towards intervention in the field of learning disability, where treatment of encopresis has been obscured by problems of definition and aetiology. Consequently, treatment reports are rare and 'No substantive treatment guidelines exist' (Groves, 1982). Even now, studies tend to involve single cases or small groups of cases, largely confined to secondary (previously clean) rather than to primary (never clean) soiling and to those with milder rather than severe learning disability. Where a child with a learning disability has a co-existing neurological bowel problem it may be necessary to use the methods outlined in Chapter 17 to aid effective evacuation.

Double incontinence

Before moving on to retentive and non-retentive encopresis separately, it is appropriate to look initially at the issue of bowel training in those cases where there has been a failure to acquire control of both bladder and bowel. It might be assumed that the rational continence training approach would be to train for bowel control first, as children commonly acquire bowel control before bladder. However, Smith (1979) noted that during intensive, behavioural bladder training of eight doubly incontinent children with profound learning disabilities, a substantial reduction in bowel accidents occurred simultaneously. Although detailed information is not now available on the presence, or otherwise, of constipation in these children, the data do imply substantial generalisation from bladder to bowel control. The implication is that where there is double incontinence, bladder training carried out first may result in the simultaneous acquisition of bowel control.

Retentive encopresis

Where encopresis is associated with a history of constipation, then this is referred to as retentive encopresis. As with other high dependency fields, treatment of retentive encopresis in the field of learning disability has traditionally involved medical management. Four decades ago, Kobak et al., (1962) described '... administration of enemas two or three times a week when necessary and the use of various laxative agents.' Of concern, some thirty years later, one study of constipated and/or faecally incontinent children with cerebral palsy found elimination aids still in regular use in the majority of cases (Agnarsson et al., 1993). It may be that behavioural methods would be more appropriate for many of these children.

Use of fibre

A number of studies have investigated the effects of increased fibre on the bowel function of constipated or faecally impacted people with learning disabilities. Increased fibre and proprietary bulking agents have been demonstrated to increase the discriminative stimulus (pre-defaecation urge) for toilet sitting in the general population (Houts and Peterson, 1986). However, studies relying solely on the addition of bulk to the diet of those with severe learning and physical disabilities have shown rather more variable results (McCallum et al., 1978; Lupson and Walton, 1981; Fischer et al., 1985; Liebl et al., 1990; Capra and Hannan-Jones, 1992).

There are a number of possible reasons for this. According to Read and Timms (1986), constipated people probably represent a diverse group of disorders with a common symptom. As the above studies make no reference to gastroenterological investigation, constipated participants in the above studies may have had one of a number of underlying causes. Whereas simple constipation due to poor diet or constipating medication may be easily-remedied by the addition of fibre to the diet, constipation in other cases may be caused by a more complex disorder less easily remedied by the addition of fibre over a week or two (see Chapter 21). This, together with differences in the types and quantities of fibre used, may explain the variable results obtained by different studies.

Given the limited available evidence on the aetiology of constipation in the field of learning disability, it is appropriate that constipation in those with severe/profound learning disability or severe physical handicaps should initially address general issues such as fluid intake and dietary fibre. Some authors are, however, unhappy about the routine use of increased fibre in high-dependency, immobile or cognitively less able groups (Donald et al., 1985; Rosenthal and Marshall, 1987). Indeed, the use of increased fibre or bulking agents of any type is not without risk in such populations: phytobezoars, that is compacted lumps of undigested vegetable fibre, though uncommon, have occurred in institutionalised people or those suffering from mental illness (Sroujieh, 1988). Furthermore, the addition of large amounts of uncooked bran to the diet can compromise the uptake of vitamins and minerals (Agnarsson et al,. 1993) in those whose diet may already be less than optimal. By contrast, other authors in such fields recommend routine increases in fibre (de Silva et al., 1992). Though some of the above studies have found benefits in the use of added bulk with severely disabled individuals, there is a clear need for caution to be exercised through careful monitoring, and more 'natural' dietary medication should usually be the first option.

Behavioural treatment

Five reports concern retentive encopresis (Dalrymple and Angrist, 1988; Carpenter, 1989; Piazza et al., 1991; Jansson et al., 1992; Smith et al., 1994). Retentive encopresis has been decreased by using rewards for cleanliness and/or aversive, negative or punitive consequences for soiling such as reprimands or withdrawal of attention, while appropriate evacuation has been increased by rewards for toilet use, these techniques being used either singly or in combination.

Dalrymple and Angrist (1988) describe the successful treatment of encopresis over two years in a 15-year-old girl with autism and profound learning disability. Chronic constipation had previously been treated unsuccessfully using laxatives, suppositories and enemas. Treatment involved daily mineral oil; scheduled (unspecified) toilet trips; rewards of attention, praise and small edibles for appropriate elimination; and 'positive practice' (unspecified, but the term is usually used to refer to an aversive consequence) for soiling. Treatment gains were maintained at one-year follow-up. It is not clear whether elimination aids were phased out.

Jansson et al. (1992) describe the successful treatment of retentive encopresis in an 8-year-old boy with a 'borderline' learning disability, hyperactivity and conduct disorder. Prompted toilet sitting and rewards (both unspecified) were used together with a regimen of enemas, suppositories and laxatives. Although the regimen of elimination aids is clearly specified, the bowel 'retraining' component is not. Although the child was described as defaecating in the toilet after three weeks, no data are provided. It is unclear whether elimination aids were phased out.

Carpenter (1989) treated a 22-year-old male with secondary retentive encopresis, moderate learning disability and challenging behaviours. Treatment consisted of play therapy and 'individual therapy' (both unspecified), rewards (unspecified) for appropriate toileting and training in bottom wiping. Aversive consequences were not used. Length of treatment is not specified – indeed, whether treatment was successful or not is not specified and no data are provided.

Piazza et al. (1991) successfully treated primary retentive encopresis over 14 weeks in a 15-year-old boy and a 5-year-old girl with profound learning disabilities. Regular toilet sits, rewards for appropriate elimination, punishment for inappropriate elimination, increased fibre and the use of elimination aids had been tried unsuccessfully. In order to increase the frequency of elimination, both continent and incontinent stools were rewarded initially, using praise, snacks and preferred objects. It was planned to later use discrimination training to teach elimination in the toilet. However, this stage proved unnecessary as rewards for *incontinent* stools resulted in a significant increase in continent bowel evacuation, improving both constipation and incontinence.

This important multiple-phase study, although limited to two cases, raises questions about the necessity and effectiveness of both artificial elimination aids and punishment procedures, both of which had failed to reduce encopresis or increase continent evacuation, and the latter of which had exacerbated retention. The authors suggest that both punishment techniques and elimination aids may reduce the likelihood of continent stools, the latter because of the individual's reduced control over bowel function and the former because people with profound intellectual disabilities may retain further in an attempt to remain clean.

Smith et al. (1994) describe the treatment of chronic faecal impaction and faecal incontinence in four young people from 13 to 23 years, three of whom had severe or profound learning disabilities. The programme involved supervised, prompted toilet sits after meals with praise and rewards for appropriate elimination. Neither punishments for soiling nor rewards for clean underwear were used, lest these resulted in retention in an effort to keep clean. Artificial elimination aids were replaced with bulk-forming agents such as Normacol or Fybogel, or bran and high-fibre diets. Enemas or suppositories were used only after abdominal examination. Stool size and frequency increased, stool consistency improved, soilings decreased and the use of enemas or suppositories was discontinued in all cases. Improved perception of the need to evacuate was demonstrated by the increased frequency of self-initiated toiletings. Treatment times were, however, long, ranging from 56 to 132 weeks. Results also indicated a continuing, somewhat erratic pattern of bowel function. Smith et al, like Piazza et al, found little evidence to support a major role for artificial elimination aids such as enemas or suppositories in bowel retraining using a behavioural training approach. This view has been supported by Doleys et al. (1981), who has asserted that there is, in fact, no mechanism whereby artificial elimination aids can, by themselves, have a 'training' effect on the bowel.

Non-retentive encopresis

Seven reports have concerned behavioural treatment of non-retentive encopresis in people with learning disabilities. Following the definition of retentive encopresis, non-retentive encopresis correspondingly occurs where there is no association with a history of constipation. As with retentive encopresis, these have involved the use of rewards for clean underwear and appropriate elimination and aversive consequences for soiling, these techniques being used either singly or in combination.

Marshall (1966) used edible rewards for appropriate evacuation and corporal punishment for soiling in the treatment of an 8-year-old, non-verbal, hyperactive, autistic boy with primary non-retentive encopresis. A statistically significant reduction in soiling took place in the first 23 compared to the last 23 of 46 treatment days.

Chopra (1973) successfully treated secondary, non-retentive encopresis using praise and rewards for elimination in the toilet in an 11-year-old boy with Down's syndrome and a mild learning disability. Improvement was seen after six weeks and the child was described as a 'changed boy' 'after five-month follow up'.

Matson (1977) successfully reduced non-retentive encopresis to zero in two weeks in a 16-year-old boy with secondary non-retentive encopresis, autism and an unspecified level of learning disability. The programme involved praise for appropriate toilet use, together with cleanliness training and 'correction' for soiling, involving ten minutes of cleaning up the environment. One accident occurred on Day 1 of training, with only two more during the next two weeks of training and none during the following three months. Results such as these are unmatched even in treatment reports for children within the general population.

Lyon (1984) reduced primary non-retentive encopresis to zero in five weeks in an 8-year-old boy with a mild learning disability, using praise and rewards for cleanliness and appropriate evacuation and 'correction' for soiling. Treatment involved daily underwear checks, praise and stickers for cleanliness and appropriate toilet use, together with 'correction' for soiling, involving assuming responsibility for cleaning and changing himself and washing soiled clothing. Cleanliness checks and rewards were progressively phased out.

Smith (1994) describes the successful treatment of non-retentive, nocturnal encopresis in a 21-year-old, non-ambulant woman with a hemiplegia and a severe learning disability. She had never defaecated continently but was soiled and smeared between four and seven times a week when her mother entered her bedroom in the morning. The client was first wakened at 6.30 a.m. prior to soiling, in an attempt to 'catch' and reward a bowel movement on the toilet. This procedure failed and no stool, continent or incontinent, was passed that day. As this could have led to retention, a suppository was administered before breakfast if she failed to defaecate of her own accord when toileted at 6.30 a.m.. Should she fail to defaecate unaided, the use of a suppository should serve to increase the urge to defaecate and increase the chance of continent evacuation after breakfast. Suppositories were administered for three mornings, after which she began to defaecate continently without their use, sometimes before and sometimes after breakfast. By week 24 she had achieved four consecutive clean weeks. After a further eight weeks, time of waking was gradually shaped back to normal. Punishments for soiling were not used. Rewards included a choice of small edibles from a 'goody' bag.

Smith (1996) used praise and edible rewards for clean underwear and appropriate toilet use in the successful treatment of primary non-retentive encopresis in five males between the ages of 18 and 37 years, four of whom had severe learning disabilities. The participants were prompted to the toilet for ten minutes after each main meal or snack in the hope that an association might develop between eating and toilet use. In addition, underwear was checked at eleven key points throughout the day. Soiled underwear was briefly drawn to the attention of the participants and minimum assistance given for cleaning and changing. Punishments were not used. Large soilings reduced to zero over periods ranging from 44 to 144 weeks. Underwear checks and rewards were gradually phased out. Stainings or very small bowel accidents continued to occur in some cases.

Follow-up on the permanence of effects is an important issue which is often ignored. Huntley and Smith (1999) followed up nine out of ten of the cases reported by Smith (1994), Smith (1996) and Smith et al. (1996). Results showed that treatment effects had largely endured over periods ranging from 5 to 17 years. Six of the nine were free of major soiling accidents, although one continued to have minor stainings in connection with imperfect wiping. Of the three still experiencing major soiling accidents, one had relapsed completely a few weeks prior to follow-up, after remaining continent for 8 years, in association with a major deterioration in physical health; one had one full-sized soiling in 21 consecutive days, but also passed 22 continent stools; one had experienced a partial relapse which had already responded to retraining, and was currently averaging one soiling per two months. Of interest, those whose encopresis had been retentive in nature maintained more successfully than those with previously non-retentive encopresis.

Stimulus control

An important distinction needs to be made at initial assessment of encopresis between lack of skills and alternative explanations for encopresis, such as challenging behaviour. Despite the success of a skills-training approach to encopresis in people with learning disabilities, some children with learning disabilities prove treatment-resistant and persistently refuse to eliminate on the toilet. Such children are often described by parents as 'stubborn' and are diagnosed as autistic or characterised by obsessive-compulsive behaviour. While they may readily eliminate into a nappy or diaper, they withhold elimination and even refuse to sit on the toilet.

Heyward (1988) has interpreted the failure of such children to acquire control as a failure of skills generalisation. Difficulty in generalising skills across settings is well-documented in people with severe and profound learning disability (Dunlap et al., 1985). Luiselli (1996) believes the defining characteristic of such children is that because they have never eliminated on the toilet, the desired behaviour cannot be – and therefore has never been – reinforced. These explanations imply a simple failure to learn the connection between the stimulus (toilet) and response (performance).

The distinction between a straightforward skills deficit and more complex explanations involving anxiety or various forms of 'challenging' behaviour may be important in explaining the failure of some children to acquire control in the normal way. The nature of the problem described in these cases may not be best interpreted as a simple failure to learn, since such children appear to have a substantial degree of control over their eliminatory functions. Children with a mild learning disability understand what is wanted, but either refuse to comply or else learn behaviour patterns which are functional for them. In such cases, the learning disability itself is unlikely to be the aetiological factor: Dalrymple and Ruble (1992) have found similar toileting problems in people with autism, regardless of cognitive ability.

Taylor et al. (1994) have proposed that the nappy/potty/underpants have developed strong stimulus control over the elimination response due to a longstanding pattern of incorrect evacuation. The toilet, with its dissimilar stimulus attributes, thus inhibits evacuation. The commonly-reported rigid, obsessive-compulsive behaviours, described by Smith et al. (2000) and implied in other reports involving both encopresis and urinary incontinence (Heyward, 1988; Dalrymple and Boarman, 1989; Taylor et al., 1994; Luiselli, 1996) may be definitive in these cases. Dalrymple and Boarman (1989) have discussed the use of behavioural techniques such as shaping and desensitisation, commonly used in the treatment of phobic anxiety, for the treatment of toilet-refusal. The aetiology of eliminatory disorders in these cases may have more in common with that of paruresis, where difficulty or inability to urinate in unfamiliar or public toilets is deemed to be anxiety-based (and is thought to be common in the general population).

Two reports have described the use of behavioural techniques such as 'shaping' (change of response), 'fading' (change of stimulus) and reinforcement to transfer stimulus control over defaecation from the inappropriate to the appropriate stimulus, e.g. nappy to toilet. Annell (1992) used stimulus control in the treatment of two encopretic children of unspecified level of cognitive ability. The children were first trained to sit on the toilet wearing disposable nappies which readily elicited the eliminatory response. Nappies were then gradually dismantled over a period of weeks until the children eliminated in the toilet without them. No data are provided.

Smith et al. (2000) have described the treatment of nocturnal encopresis in two 8-year-old, treatment-resistant boys, one with Fragile X syndrome and one with autism, both with a mild learning disability. Both children displayed a rigid adherence to routine and an obsessive dislike of environmental change. Both were continent of urine by day and would stand to pass urine at the toilet, but persistently refused to sit on the toilet, withholding faeces until some time during the night when each would defaecate into his disposable nappy between five and seven times per week. Constipation was not present in either case. The basic framework of the programme to transfer stimulus control of defaecation from nappy to toilet was the same in both cases, although the number of steps taken differed.

First, soiled night nappies were rewarded in the morning with praise, small edibles, stickers or other small rewards. This soon resulted in both children defaecating as soon as they went to bed and reporting it immediately in order to earn the reward. The children were next encouraged at bedtime to sit on a child-sized commode with a hole in it, while wearing the nappy in which to defaecate. The size of the nappies was then gradually diminished. Simultaneously, the chair was gradually moved closer to the toilet. Finally, the child sat on the toilet, stools falling through the remaining nappy until the nappy was completely faded out. Both children resisted changes in toileting procedures throughout, so that treatment, although successful, was prolonged.

Conclusions

With a success rate of 70% or better reported for children within the general population (Young, 1973; Kaplan, 1985; Bosch, 1988; Dawson et al., 1990), behavioural approaches, which focus on the appropriate and inappropriate eliminatory behaviours themselves, appear to represent a low-risk, effective treatment.

Studies involving treatment of encopresis in learning disability are limited to small sample studies often involving a simple phase-change, or 'A-B', design. However, spontaneous remission of encopresis is unlikely after the mid-teens, acquisition of bowel control in older teenagers and adults being likely to require an intensive, structured approach.

The few treatment reports available in the field of learning disability suggest that non-retentive encopresis can be treated effectively using behavioural techniques, within several weeks or months, in younger subjects with learning disabilities or adults with mild learning disabilities. Adults with a profound learning disability may take longer. Retentive encopresis can likewise be treated successfully using a behavioural approach. Treatment in those with faecal impaction or a profound learning disability is, however, likely to be prolonged.

A number of behavioural programmes in the field of learning disability have utilised aversive consequences for soiling, both in the treatment of retentive and non-retentive encopresis. Aversive consequences for soiling are commonly used in the treatment of encopresis in children in the general population. Not only is there a lack of evidence to demonstrate the superior effectiveness of aversive consequences for soiling over rewards for continent evacuation, their use may result in retention in people with a severe or profound learning disability.

The state of knowledge concerning the prevalence, aetiology and treatment of encopresis in learning disability remains unclear. The evidence currently does suggest that encopresis is associated with more severe degrees of intellectual disability, with hyperactivity and deficits of attention, and with behaviour problems. The role of constipation is less certain. At the same time, learning disability alone is not a sufficient explanation for failure to acquire bowel control, given that 50% of those with even the most profound intellectual disabilities will acquire control.

Faecal incontinence remains a major problem in learning disability, but there is empirical evidence to demonstrate that it should not be accepted as intractable. The challenge, in service terms, is to establish more clearly those factors associated with encopresis and to use available treatment strategies to reduce the prevalence significantly.

Finally, although learning disability is not the same as dementia, both are characterised by cognitive impairment, and there is a similarity in some of the issues facing clients, services and carers. The techniques for treating faecal soiling in learning disability may have some application, in principle, to the loss of continence associated with dementia (Smith and Smith, 1993; Woods, 1999).

References

Agnarsson, U., Warde, C., McCarthy, G., Clayden, G.S. and Evans, N. (1993) Anorectal function of children with neurological problems II: Cerebral palsy. *Developmental Medicine and Child Neurology* **35**, 903–908.

Annel, E. (1992) Blojbajsning – en speciell form en enkopresis? *Scandinavian Journal of Behavior Therapy*, **35**, 141–151.

Arhan, P., Devroede, G., Jehannian, B., Faverdin, C., Revillon, Y., Lefevere, D. and Pellerin, D. (1983) Idiopathic disorders of fecal incontinence in children. *Pediatrics* **71**, 774–779.

Bellman, M.M. (1966) Studies on encopresis. *Acta Paediatrica Scandinavica* **56**, 1–151.

Bosch, J.D. (1988) Treating children with encopresis and constipation: an evaluation by means of single case studies. In: Emmelkamp, P., Everaerd, W., Kraimat, F.R. and van Son, M.J.M. (eds), *Advances in theory and practice in behaviour therapy*. Amsterdam: Swets & Zeitlinger.

Capra, S.M. and Hannan-Jones, M. (1992) A controlled dietary trial for improving bowel function in a group of training centre residents with severe or profound intellectual disability. *Australian and New Zealand Journal of Developmental Disabilities* **18**, 111–121.

Carpenter, S. (1989) Development of a young man with Prader-Willi syndrome and secondary functional encopresis. *Canadian Journal of Psychiatry* **34**, 123–127.

Chopra, H.D. (1973) Treatment of encopresis in a mongol with operant conditioning. *Indian Journal of Mental Retardation* **6**, 43–46.

Cohen, I. (1995) Behavioural profiles of autistic and non autistic Fragile X males. *Developmental Brain Dysfunction* **8**, 252–269.

Dalrymple, N.J and Angrist, M.H. (1988) Toilet training a sixteen year old with autism in a natural setting. *British Journal of Mental Subnormality* **34**, 117–129.

Dalrymple, N. and Boarman, M. (1989) *Functional programming for people with autism: toileting.* Bloomington, Indiana: Indiana Resource Center for Autism, Institute for the Study of Developmental Disabilities, Indiana University.

Dalrymple, N.J. and Ruble, L.A. (1992) Toilet training. *Journal of Autism and Developmental Disabilities* **22**, 265–270.

Dawson, P.M., Griffith, K. and Boeke, K.M. (1990) Combined medical and psychological treatment of hospitalised children with encopresis. *Child Psychiatry and Human Development* **20**, 181–190.

De Silva, P., Deb, S., Drummond, R.D. and Rankin, R. (1992) A fatal case of ischaemic colitis following long-term use of neuroleptic medication. *Journal of Intellectual Disability Research* **36**, 371–375.

Doleys, D.M., Schwartz, M.S. and Ciminero, A.R. (1981) Elimination problems: enuresis and encopresis. In: Marsh, E.J. and Terdal, L.G. (eds) *Behavioural assessment of childhood disorders.* New York: Guilford Press.

Donald, I., Smith, R., Cruikshank, J., Elton, R. and Stoddardt, M. (1985) A study of constipation in the elderly living at home. *Gerontology,* **31**, 112–118.

Duckro, P.N., Purcell, M., Gregory, J. and Schulz, K. (1985) Biofeedback for the treatment of anal incontinence in a child with uretersigmoiostomy. *Biofeedback and Self Regulation* **10**, 325–333.

Dunlap, G., Koegel, R.L. and Koegel, L.K. (1985) Continuity of treatment: toilet training in multiple community settings. *Journal of the Association for Persons with Severe Handicaps*, **9**, 134–141.

Eyman, R.K., Tarjan, G. and Cassidy, M. (1970) Natural history of acquisition of basic skills by hospitalised retarded patients. *American Journal of Mental Deficiency* 75, 120–129.

Fischer, M., Adkins, W., Hall, L., Scaman, P., His, S. and Marlett, J. (1985) The effects of dietary fibre in a liquid diet on bowel function of mentally retarded individuals. *Journal of Mental Deficiency Research* **29**, 373–381.

Floch, M.H. and Wald, A. (1994) Clinical evaluation and treatment of constipation. *Gastroenterologist* **2**, 50–60.

Fritz, G.K. and Armbrust, J. (1982) Enuresis and encopresis. *Psychiatric Clinics of North America* **5**, 283–296.

Gabel, S. (1981) Fecal soiling, chronic constipation and encopresis. In: Gabel, S. (ed.), *Behavioral problems in childhood*, 213–228. New York: Grune and Stratton.

Groves, J.A. (1982) Encopresis. In: Hollis, J. and Meyers, C.E. (eds), *Life threatening behavior: analysis and intervention*, Monograph 5. Washington DC: American Association of Mental Deficiency.

Hagerman, R. (1990) The association between autism and fragile X syndrome. *Brain Dysfunction* **3**, 218–227.

Heyward, E. (1988) Generalisation of toileting skills of a mentally handicapped boy. *Behavioural Psychotherapy* **16**, 102–107.

Houts, A.C. and Peterson, J.K. (1986) Treatment of a retentive encopretic child using contingency management and dietary modification with stimulus control. *Journal of Pediatric Psychology* **11**, 375–383.

Howe, A.C and Walker, C.E. (1992) Behavioral management of toilet training, enuresis and encopresis. *Pediatric Clinics of North America* **39**, 413–432.

Huntley, E. and Smith, L. (1999) Long term follow-up of behavioural treatment for primary encopresis in people with intellectual disability in the community. *Journal of Intellectual Disability Research* **43**, 484–488.

Jansson, L.M., Diamond, O. and Demb, H.B. (1992) Encopresis in a multihandicapped child: rapid multidisciplinary treatment. *Journal of Developmental and Physical Disabilities* **4**, 83–90.

Jenkins, R.G. and Stable, G. (1971) Special characteristics of retarded children rated as severely hyperactive. *Child Psychiatry and Human Development* **2**, 26–31.

Kaplan, B.J. (1985) A clinical demonstration of a psychobiological application to childhood encopresis. *Journal of Child Care* **2**, 47–54.

Kobak, M.W., Jacobson, M.A. and Sirca, D.M. (1962) Acquired megacolon in psychiatric patients. *Diseases of the Colon and Rectum* **5**, 373–377.

Kottmeier, P.K. and Clatworthy, H.W. (1965) Aganglionic and functional megacolon in children = a diagnostic dilemma. *Pediatrics* **36**, 572–582.

Lanfranchi, G.A., Bazzocji, G., Brignola, C., Camperi, M. and Labo, G. (1984) Different patterns of intestinal transit time and anorectal motility in painful and painless chronic constipation. *Gut* **25**, 1352–1357.

Latimer, P., Campbell, D. and Kasperki, J. (1984) A components analysis of biofeedback in the treatment of faecal incontinence. *Biofeedback and Self Regulation* 19, 311–324.

Leung, A.K.C., Mui, C.Y. and Lau, J.T. (1986) Hirschsprung's disease and mongolism. *Journal of the National Medical Association* **78**, 443–446.

Leventhal, A. and Gimmon, Z. (1978) Toxic idiopathic megacolon: fatal outcome in a mentally retarded adolescent. *Diseases of the Colon and Rectum* **21**, 383–386.

Liebl, B., Fischer, M., van Calcar, S. and Marlett, J. (1990) Dietary fiber and long-term large bowel response in enterally nourished nonambulatory profoundly retarded youth. *Journal of Parenteral and Enteral Nurtrition* **14**, 371–375.

Loening-Baucke, V.A. (1984a) Sensitivity of sigmoid colon and rectum in children treated for chronic constipation. *Journal of Pediatric Gastroenterology and Nutrition* **3**, 454–459.

Loening-Baucke, V.A. (1984b) Abnormal rectoanal function in children recovered from chronic constipation and encopresis. *Gastroenterology* **87**, 1299–1304.

Loening-Baucke, V.A. (1990) Efficacy of biofeedback training in improving faecal incontinence and anorectal physiologic function. *Gut* **31**, 1395–1402.

Loening-Baucke, V.A. and Cruikshank, B.M. (1986) Abnormal defaecation dynamics in chronically constipated children with encopresis. *Journal of Pediatrics* **108**, 562–566.

Loening-Baucke, V., Desch, L. and Wolraich, M. (1988) Biofeedback training for patients with myelomeningocele and faecal incontinence. *Developmental Medicine and Child Neurology* **30**, 781–790.

Lohmann, W., Eyman, R.K. and Lask, E. (1967) Toilet training. *American Journal of Mental Deficiency* **71**, 551–557.

Luiselli, J.V.K. (1996) A transfer of stimulus control procedure applicable to toilet training programme for children with developmental disabilities. *Child and Family Behavior Therapy* **18**, 29–34.

Lupson, S. and Walton, D. (1981) A trial of bran to relieve constipation in young mentally and physically handicapped patients. *Apex* **9**, 64–66.

Lyon, M.A. (1984) Positive reinforcement and logical consequences in the treatment of classroom encopresis. *School Psychology Review* **13**, 238–243.

McCallun, G., Ballinger, B.R. and Presly, A.S. (1978) A trial of bran and bran biscuits for constipation in mentally handicapped and psychogeriatric patients. *Journal of Human Nutrition* **32**, 369–372.

McGuire, T., Rothenberg, M. and Tyler, D.C. (1983) Profound shock following intervention for chronic untreated stool retention. *Clinical Pediatrics* **23**, 459–461.

MacLeod, J. (1987) Management of anal incontinence by biofeedback. *Gastroenterology* **93**, 291–294.

Madge, N., Diamond, J., Miller, D., Ross, E., McManus, C., Wadsworth, J., Yule, W. and Frost, B. (1993) The National Childhood Encephalopathy Study: a 10-year follow-up. A report on the medical, social, behavioural and educational outcomes after serious, acute, neurological illness in early childhood. *Developmental Medicine and Child Neurology – Supplement* **68**, 1–118.

Marshall, G.R. (1966) Toilet training of an autistic eight-year-old through conditioning therapy: a case report. *Behaviour Research and Therapy* **4**, 242–245.

Matson, J.L. (1977) Simple correction for treating an autistic boy's encopresis. *Psychological Reports* **41**, 802.

Meunier, P., Mollard, P. and Marechal, J.M. (1976) Physiopathology of megarectum: the association of megarectum with encopresis. *Gut* **17**, 224–227.

Molnar, D., Taiz, L.S., Urwin, O.M. and Wales, J.K.H. (1983) Anorectal manometry results in defaecation disorders. *Archives of Diseases in Childhood* **58**, 257–261.

Parker, G. (1984) Training for continence amongst children with severe disabilities. *British Journal of Mental Subnormality* **30**, 38–43.

Piazza, C.C., Fisher, W., Chinn, S. and Bowman, L. (1991) Reinforcement of incontinent stools in the treatment of encopresis. *Clinical Pediatrics* **30**, 28–32.

Protinsky, H.Y. and Dillard, C. (1983) Enuresis: a family therapy model. *Psychotherapy: Theory, Research and Practice* **20**, 81–89.

Read, N.W., Timms, J.M., Barfield, L.J., Donnelly, T.C. and Bannister, J.J. (1986) Impairment of defaecation in young women with severe constipation. *Gastroenterology* **90**, 53–60.

Resnick, B. (1985) Constipation: common but preventable. *Geriatric Nursing,* July/August, 213–215.

Rosenthal, M.J. and Marshall, C.E. (1987) Sigmoid volvolus in association with Parkinsonism: report of four cases. *Journal of the Geriatric Society* **35**, 683–684.

Ryan, R. (1992) Treatment-resistent chronic mental illness: is it Asperger's syndrome. *Hospital and Community Psychiatry* **43**, 807–811.

Saavedra, J.M. and Perman, J. (1990) Constipation in girls with Rett syndrome, pamphlet, pp. 19–20. London: UK Rett Syndrome Association. (www.rettsyndrome.org.uk)

Schaeffer, C.E. (1979) *Childhood enuresis and encopresis: causes and therapy*. New York: Van Nostrand Reinhold Co.

Smith, F. and Ross, F. (1992) Laxatives. *Community Outlook* Nov/Dec, 21–24.

Smith, L.J. (1994) A behavioral approach to the treatment of non-retentive nocturnal encopresis in an adult with a severe learning disability. *Journal of Behavior and Experimental Psychiatry* **25**, 81–86.

Smith, L.J. (1996) A behavioural approach to the treatment of non-retentive encopresis in adults with learning disabilities. *Journal of Intellectual Disability Research* **40**, 130–139.

Smith, L.J. and Smith, P.S. (1993) Psychological aspects of faecal incontinence in the elderly. In: Barrett, J.A. (ed.) *Faecal incontinence in the elderly*. London: Edward Arnold.

Smith, L.J., Franchetti, B., McCoull, K., Pattison, D. and Pickstock, J. (1994) A behavioural approach to retraining bowel function after longstanding constipation and faecal impaction in people with learning disabilities. *Developmental Medicine and Child Neurology* **36**, 49–57.

Smith, L.J., Smith, P.S. and Lee, S.K.Y. (2000) Behavioural treatment of urinary incontinence and encopresis in children with learning disabilities. *Developmental Medicine and Child Neurology* **42**, 276–279.

Smith, P.S. (1979) *The development of urinary continence in the mentally handicapped.* Unpublished PhD thesis: University of Newcastle-upon-Tyne.

Smith, P.S. and Smith, L.J. (1987) *Continence and incontinence: psychological approaches to development and treatment*. London: Croom Helm.

Spencer, R.L., Temerlin, M. and Trousdale, W.W. (1968) Some correlates of bowel control in the profoundly retarded. *American Journal of Mental Deficiency* **72**, 879–882.

Sroujieh, A.S. (1988) Phytobezoars of the whole gastro-intestinal tract: report of a case and review of the literature. *Dirasat* **15**, 103–109.

Stern, H.P., Prince, M.T. and Stroh, S.E. (1988) Encopresis responsive to non-psychiatric interventions. *Clinical Pediatrics* **27**, 400–402.

Taylor, S., Cipani, E. and Clardy, A. (1994) A stimulus control technique for improving the efficacy of an established toilet training program. *Journal of Behavior Therapy and Experimental Psychiatry* **25**, 155–160.

Thomas, T.M., Egan, M., Walgrove, A. and Meade, T.W. (1984) The prevalence of faecal and double incontinence. *Community Medicine* **6**, 216–220.

Tobon, F. and Schuster, M.M. (1974) Megacolon: special diagnostic and therapeutic features. *Johns Hopkins Medical Journal* **135**, 91–105.

von Wendt, L., Simila, S., Niskanen, P. and Jarvelin, M-R. (1990) Development of bowel and bladder control in the mentally retarded. *Developmental Medicine and Child Neurology* **32**, 515–518.

Wald, A. and Handen, B.L. (1987) Behavioural aspects of disorders of defaecation and fecal continence. *Annals of Behavioural Medicine* **9**, 19–23.

Woods, B. (1999) Promoting well-being and independence for people with dementia. *International Journal of Geriatric Psychiatry* **14**, 97–105.

Wrenn, K. (1989) Fecal impaction. *New England Journal of Medicine* **321**, 658–662.

Young, G.C. (1973) The treatment of childhood encopresis by conditioned gastro-ileal reflex training. *Behaviour Research and Therapy* **11**, 499–503.

Chapter 19

Constipation and Faecal Incontinence in Childhood

Graham Clayden and Gillian Hollins

Introduction

The symptoms of constipation and faecal incontinence in childhood are greatly influenced by the stage of development of the child. As occurs in other health problems in children, there is a weave of biological, psychological and social factors that influence the onset, severity and persistence of the symptoms. In this chapter, overflow faecal soiling as a result of faecal retention is the main focus. Other conditions that result in faecal incontinence are also reviewed. Multi-agency working appears to be the most effective way of helping the child and supporting the family. Ways of working together for professionals and the changing partnership with the increasingly competent child during development are discussed.

Causes of faecal incontinence in children

Throughout this chapter the terms used to describe the defaecation disorders are as follows:

- constipation – delay and/or difficulty in defaecation
- soiling – involuntary passage of loose or incomplete stools in the clothing
- encopresis – the passage of normal stools in socially unacceptable places.

In the United Kingdom there is a wide consensus that would agree with these definitions, but in the United States the term encopresis is often used to describe any form of faecal incontinence. This makes the interpretation of the medical and nursing literature confusing. With our convention it is important to appreciate that a child may have a combination of soiling and encopresis over time. (See Chapter 18 for a further discussion of the definitions relating to intellectual disability.)

The causes of faecal incontinence in children are best understood in the light of the normal development of continence and the biological structures that are necessary to support this skill. Babies and infants defaecate intermittently with no voluntary or conscious contribution. They demonstrate the physiological defaecation responses without the moderation of learned or conscious voluntary control. The rectum is usually empty or contains a stool of small size that has not provoked the recto-anal inhibitory reflex. During feeding, the gastro-colic reflex leads to a filling of the rectum as a result of propulsive colonic contractions. This rectal filling provokes rectal contraction and consequent anal sphincter inhibition and the stool is passed, often aided by reflex grunting that raises intra-abdominal pressure. Between the ages of 1 and 2 years most children discover the defaecation-delaying effect of contracting their voluntary sphincters when sensing the urge to defaecate. Between 2 and 3 years, children discover the social benefits of depositing stools in pots and lavatories. This acquisition of the skill of continence depends on having the normal physical structure of the anorectum, pelvic muscles and sensory/motor nerve supply, the ability to integrate sensations and muscle contractions with learning the value of using these muscles, all within an environment that values continence and the efforts made to achieve this. Not surprisingly there are many problems in childhood that interrupt this. These can be grouped and summarised as follows:

Embryological problems

- of the anus: ano-rectal malformations such as imperforate anus, ectopic anus, anal stenosis
- of the intrinsic autonomic gut nerves (myenteric plexus): Hirschsprung's disease
- of the sensory and motor nerves from the spine: neural tube disorders (spina bifida)

Acquired physical problems

- of the anus causing pain: anal fissure, mucosal prolapse, perianal streptococcal infection, lichen sclerosis, food intolerance, Crohn's disease, child abuse
- of the anus causing muscle weakness: trauma including following anal surgery or abuse
- of the capacity of the rectum: chronic faecal retention and megarectum (although often probably originally larger than average, long-term retention will increase capacity)

Developmental problems

- of learning: global developmental delay and learning difficulties
- of muscle coordination: cerebral palsy
- of social awareness: autism

Environmental problems

- of parental interest and motivating response: maternal depression, parental learning difficulties, parental neglect
- of available water supply and clean, private lavatory facilities: many schools, poverty, war

Psychological problems

- of stress responses: stress precipitated defaecation with sudden fear or panic or more chronically in response to emotional trauma
- of refusal to cooperate: fear of pot / lavatory, conflict of wills to eat, drink, take medicine or use pot/lavatory
- of dissociation or denial: response of older children to chronic apparently intractable problems of constipation or soiling
- of behaviour: faecal smearing and some types of encopresis

It is neither wise nor possible to fit individual children into a single category from this list. Many children have a mixture of factors from several of these fields. Many acquire then lose a number of these factors as their problem evolves.

It is helpful in the planning of an individual child's management to keep this grid of possibilities in mind. Many treatment strategies fail because needs from some of these underlying factors are not being met. Chronic constipation with overflow soiling is the most prevalent cause of faecal incontinence in children over three years of age (Baker et al., 1999). Because the physiological and psychological responses to this aggravate the underlying factors that precipitated it, consideration of this problem needs to be detailed. Armed with a clear insight into the pathophysiological features of chronic constipation and the treatment strategies for this, the management of most of the other conditions are more easily understood.

Chronic constipation in childhood

A typical case history should illustrate the way factors often cluster at the onset of the child's problems, and how resolving these factors influences the evolution and eventual resolution of the soiling.

Tom, a 3-year-old boy, was brought to see the paediatrician by his worried mother. Her main complaint was Tom's inability to come out of nappies during the day. This was preventing him from attending his local nursery school. He had difficulty with passing hard, dry stools when weaned from breast to formula feeds at the age of 4 months. By the age of 1 year he often had delays of 3 to 4 days between stools and then finally passing a large, hard stool with great discomfort and occasional bleeding.

Stool softeners were started by the GP after the Health Visitor's advice to give Tom more fluid and fibre had not led to any improvement. Stool softness helped with the regular discomfort and screaming but did not make defaecation more frequent. Following a viral sore throat aged 2 years he passed a very large hard stool, and an anal fissure with posterior skin tag was seen. The intervals between stools became longer and he spent most of the last two days of the week between stools straining and hiding behind furniture. Adding stimulant laxatives to his treatment increased the frequency of defaecation but the passage of each stool was still resisted. For many months he would open his bowels in his nappy just after falling asleep in the evenings. He would stand to pass urine into his pot but refused to sit on it or on the special child-sized lavatory seat. Over the previous three weeks before seeing the paediatrician only loose stools were passed into his nappy throughout the day. He was unwilling to take his medication as he complained it caused pain.

On examination a firm rounded mass extending from the pelvis to above the umbilicus was palpated. The anus was soiled and the posterior skin tag visible. A digital rectal examination was not performed as Tom was distressed even by inspection of his anus. Plans were made for him to be admitted to the local children's ward for an enema but that night he passed a very large stool that blocked the lavatory. An increase in the dosage of his stimulant laxatives established more regular defaecation, but for six months he would only pass stool in his night nappy. By the age of 4 years he was opening his bowels spontaneously every two to three days with no discomfort.

At the age of 6 years he was brought to the paediatrician with a relapse of his faecal soiling. Hardly a day would pass without him returning home from school with loose stool soiling his pants. Stool softeners and stimulant laxatives were restarted, but this led to increased soiling earlier in the day and consequent teasing at school. Higher-intensity laxatives were restricted to weekends and he began to establish a pattern of passing large stools every Saturday morning prior to playing football in the afternoons. Over the next few months the episodes of soiling that occurred on Thursdays and Fridays became less and he often passed stool midweek with no discomfort. He and his parents were reluctant to reduce the amount of medication, as they feared a relapse. By the age of 8 years he had no complaints about defaecation and only occasionally took a laxative.

Unfortunately, at the age of 10 years his family were going through a difficult time that eventually led to Tom's father leaving the home. Over this period Tom became more unreliable with his faecal continence. His mother often found soiled pants that had been hidden in the house. He was secretive about his bowel habit but denied any delays in defaecation. However, a large abdominal mass of faeces was palpated. High-dose laxatives and two enemas (a third was refused) failed to clear the mass, which was eventually disimpacted manually under a general anaesthetic. Following two years of regular laxatives and parallel psychological help, he was opening his bowels successfully with no incontinence. His only complaint at 14 years of age was of his size and development. By 16 years he had caught up with his peers in stature and pubertal development and had no bowel complaints.

Many who have managed children with constipation and soiling will recognise elements of this history. It was given in some detail to allow us to draw from it, after looking in greater depth at the pathophysiology of the megarectum, the pharmacology of the laxatives used in childhood and the psychology related to problem of this type.

Pathophysiology of chronic constipation

Children who are subject to many days of delays between stools often have a high capacity rectum. This can be seen on abdominal X-ray – particularly if radio-opaque gut transit markers have been given in the days leading up to the X-ray being taken (Papadopoulou et al., 1994), on ultrasound (often seen during routine investigation of urinary tract infection to which constipated children are prone), or on ano-rectal manometry (although this test is not performed routinely).

The large rectum is often incompletely emptied, or stools can be withheld more easily when the rectum is large.

When the rectum is loaded, regular contractions occur that are associated with short episodes of internal sphincter relaxation (recto-anal inhibitory reflex). Those not accustomed to a permanently loaded rectum experience an urge to defaecate as the faecal mass descends onto the very sensitive upper anal canal, but those with persistent loading appear to lose this urge sensation. This leads to faecal soiling, as there is no sensation of the anal canal relaxing that leads most of us to a rapid contraction of the voluntary external sphincter and pelvic floor muscles, as we urgently search for a lavatory. The loaded rectum, in common with other obstructed hollow organs (e.g. stomach, bladder or heart), increases in size and wall thickness, which in itself increases the risk of faecal retention or makes it much easier for the child who has learned to be afraid of defaecation to postpone the painful event. It can be debated whether the increased thickness of the sphincter muscle prevents the descent of the stool into the anal canal and is a major factor in the reduced sensation during rectal contractions.

It is uncertain whether children are born with a megarectum or whether it develops. It is probably a combination. A child who has a larger-capacity rectum than average is more likely to form a hard dry stool if his fluid intake is poor. If he is then able to delay defaecation as a result of this liberal rectal capacity, he is more likely to eventually pass a large hard stool and confirm his belief that defaecation should be avoided. Even small babies will contract their muscles as a result of local discomfort. If this happens with the external sphincter, those with high-capacity rectums will retain the stool whereas those with normal capacity will pass the stool, even though uncomfortably. In this way the normal high-capacity rectum can develop into one much more capacious than normal, although the precise definition of megarectum has yet to be agreed. This reasoning supports the view that even those prone to constipation may be prevented from developing a megarectum by early attention to their fluid and fibre intake and no reluctance to start laxatives. Perhaps this view of a normal tendency to constipation in those who have larger than average rectums explains the frequent familial tendency to constipation. In previous generations where gastroenteritis was a major factor in childhood mortality, having a large capacity rectum and a final chance to reabsorb vital fluid may have favoured these ancestors. The relatively recent reduction in gastroenteritis, except in less developed parts of the world, might explain the apparently increasing prevalence of the problem of childhood constipation in affluent societies. Once established, a megarectum can persist into adult life (see Chapter 21).

The use and pharmacology of laxatives

For a child who has a megarectum with overflow faecal incontinence, the problem is not whether laxatives are necessary but rather in which order they should be used. When a large faecal mass is palpable on abdominal examination there is little chance that this can be cleared with a large dose of stimulant laxative, which is likely to produce only abdominal pain and increase the overflow soiling. A useful stratagem is to first attempt to soften the residual stool with a surface-wetting agent, such as docusate, which may allow complete emptying to occur naturally or will make evacuant methods more likely to succeed. These evacuant methods include purging doses of stimulant laxatives such as senna or sodium picosulphate, or a volume of polyethylene glycol (Kleanprep or Movicol) that will flush the softened stool from the rectum, having taken the medicine by mouth.

A more direct route for evacuating the rectum is by enema (micro-enema or phosphate enema) or suppository (glycerine or bisacodyl) but for a child who is already terrified of anal pain this route is likely to intensify the fear and withholding. If evacuation would entail forcibly passing a nasogastric tube to administer an effective dose of polyethylene glycol, or sedation does not allow giving an enema without distress and the faecal mass is so large that it is unlikely to be passed spontaneously, a manual disimpaction under general anaesthesia may be indicated. Similarly, if the child is in severe pain, is vomiting, is in urinary retention or even respiratory difficulties due to abdominal distension reducing diaphragm movement, evacuation of the faecal mass obstructing the pelvis justifies the small risk to health from general anaesthesia.

As the evacuation phase is always fraught with the risk of distress and even potential danger, it is essential that, once the rectum is clear, regular and effective maintenance laxatives be used. This is where the stimulant laxatives (senna, picosulphate or magnesium salts) play the key role. Although there are some useful statements of consensus about the laxatives (*Drug and Therapeutics Bulletin*, 2000; Baker et al., 1999 & 2000), there are few clinical trials to provide evidence of the most effective regime. Most clinicians rely on following a protocol and modifying it to suit the severity of the original symptoms, the response to mild treatments, and the particular likes and dislikes of the child. Here is a typical cascade of intensity of treatments where it is hoped only a minority of children will require the more powerful methods:

- ensure adequate fluid and fibre intake
- add stool softener such as lactulose or docusate
- add stimulant laxative such as senna or picosulphate
- use bulking agent such as methyl cellulose or lubricant such as mineral oil (instead of stool softener)
- use high dose senna or picosulphate or polyethylene glycol orally
- use nasogastric polyethylene glycol or sedated enema
- consider manual evacuation under general anaesthesia.

Some points on these medications

- Lactulose helps to retain water in the stool and increases stool bulk by encouraging growth of the normal colonic bacteria
- Docusate has detergent qualities that help to break up the surface of old hard retained stools
- Senna is a traditional herbal laxative known since ancient Egypt and even quoted by Shakespeare in Macbeth. It is now used as standardised sennosides with a reasonably predictable effect. With most children a single daily dose will provoke defaecation in 18–24 hours. This may allow a degree of timing for the most likely defaecation time and so help with reducing soiling or faecal accidents at school. Senna is not activated until it passes into the colon, and so there is little chance of reducing nutrition by hurry through the small intestine. Abdominal colic can be caused if too high doses are used, and superficial blistering may occur if the soiling is left in contact with the skin.
- Sodium picosulphate has a softening and stimulating effect; it is rather more rapid in its action than senna as it does not need to be activated in the gut. It may cause more discomfort than senna, but is likely to evacuate moderate stools where senna may have only produced more overflow soiling. Children may tolerate picosulphate as a regular daily laxative when they do not cope with senna, and vice versa. Many children seem to manage better with their evening senna regime when given boosting doses of picosulphate every 4–7 days.
- Polyethylene glycol was designed to be used as Kleanprep or Golytely as a pre-operative bowel preparation but has been found to be useful in flushing out the residual stools in children with severe constipation. Large volumes may be required, and this is where the nasogastric route has been used. Smaller doses are more easily tolerated and available as Movicol. These are either used as weekend booster medications similar to that use of picosulphate, or as evacuants at the first sign of relapse when being maintained by the stimulant laxatives.
- Bisacodyl can be used in tablet form as an alternative to senna, and in its suppository form for those who tolerate this. Some

teenagers find this the most effective as it is much more instant than the oral laxatives and helps them to fit their pattern of defaecation into their increasingly complicated social life.

- Mineral oil can lubricate the stool to assist defaecation and resist withholding of faeces. Many paediatricians have been anxious about its potential for reducing the absorption of the fat-soluble vitamins such as vitamin A, D and K, but there is little evidence for this. More of a worry is the potential for lipid aspiration pneumonia, and so it is best avoided in reluctant toddlers and under-threes who might choke on it, or with parents who might be tempted to hold their noses and pour it in. The symptom that leads to most distress in older children is that the mineral oil is likely to increase the penetration of the soiling through the clothing and make washing greasy clothes, and possibly furnishing, more difficult.

Although there are relatively few laxatives, their use is often confusing and if used in an incorrect order they are likely to aggravate rather than relieve the symptoms. Without the help of an easily accessible nurse, many parents will flounder and lose their confidence in the medicines. A child cannot be expected to cooperate with rather unpleasant or annoying treatment regimes unless they fully understand the function of the treatments. They can only do this if time is spent listening to their questions about their bowels and their queries about medication. Explanations to them regarding the reasons for the medicines, and how these fit in with the other routines, will have a beneficial effect. This is another key role of the nurse.

Useful routines

The total management regime is dependent on the working together of all of these strategies:

- eating
- drinking
- liaison with the school
- exercise
- self-massage
- toileting and bowel training, and
- laxatives.

Each of these requires parents to establish regular routines and to encourage beneficial habits – a consistent pattern of behaviour with which the child can become familiar, confident and at ease.

Eating

It is important to establish regular eating habits and to avoid continuous picking between meals. This allows the gastric-colic reflex to give encouraging signals to prompt the child of the need to defaecate. A healthy appetite at mealtimes is advantageous. Three meals a day are very important for healthy bowel function. Adults often forget that children have to learn to like good food, in the same way that they learn to wash and dress themselves. When communal mealtimes are the norm, children eat better. The presence of an adult, who can gently prompt the child into eating what is on offer, can make a big difference to how much they eat.

A healthy diet includes fibre, such as fruit, fresh, frozen or dried; vegetables, cooked or raw; wholemeal bread; pasta and brown rice. However, considerable ingenuity is needed to persuade many children to eat 'wholefood' options. Cereals such as Weetabix, Allbran, Branflakes and Shredded Wheat can be eaten without milk or mixed with other cereals for a more popular breakfast. Pulses – for example, baked beans and kidney beans – are a good source of fibre, too. Fibre helps to keep the stools soft, though too much fibre can cause a lot of wind and exacerbate symptoms. Adequate fluid intake is important with fibre supplements. Parenting skills and persuasion strategies may be needed to coax children into eating different foods (Blythman, 1999).

A simple approach to encouraging a more positive way of eating is to involve the child, if old enough, by persuading him or her to make a good food list and a hate food list, and allowing the child to make reasonable food preferences. Breakfast is an essential start to the day. A good breakfast is not only warming and energy-boosting but will prevent picking during the day, and can help activate the bowel effectively before the child goes to school. Breakast does not necessarily mean eating a bowl of cereal. There are many alternatives and some practical guides (Karmel, 1991).

Drinking

A well-organised fluid intake is useful for good health and regular bowel movements. A structured drink pattern in toddlers will help to keep stools soft, which in turn helps avoid problems such as anal fissure. Some laxatives work by retaining water in the stools, so fluids help the laxative to have a maximum effect. Without water, dietary fibres in the bowel can become dry, which can make it stick in the bowel. As well as being detrimental to bowel function, a poor fluid intake can result in headache (Singh et al., 2000).

Learning to take fluids at regular times every day is the first step towards a healthy drinking routine. Clinical experience also suggests it is more helpful to bowel function to have a cupful of water or juice all at once rather than sipping the same drink over a period of time, as it is more likely to stimulate colonic activity. So an effective regime would be: one mug full of water or juice before going to school, another mid-morning, the same at lunchtime, yet again mid-afternoon and a further cupful at tea-time. Some children drink a great deal of milk, which has a constipating effect on the bowel. It is preferable to limit the total dairy intake to about one pint a day. This allows for milk at breakfast time and a drink of milk at bedtime.

Once the routine is established pre-school, it is easier to apply it to the school day. However, children have a tendency to drink less fluid during the school day than at weekends (Rugg-Gunn et al, 1987). Some schools discourage the taking of drinks onto the premises and there is often no ready access to supplies of drinking water (Haines and Rogers 2000). A recently launched campaign, 'Water is Cool in School' (ERIC 2001) seeks to overcome these barriers and aims:

- to increase awareness of the health benefits of drinking good levels of water during the school day
- to improve the provision of drinking facilities in schools and pupil access to these
- to obtain a government review of the regulations relating to drinking facilities in schools.

Liaison with the school

Parents often like to have the support of the school nurse as well as the teacher. It is helpful to tell the school nurse if there is a child with constipation problems in one of their schools. Once this has been agreed with the parent, the nurse can alert the school teacher that the child will bring in drinks to school for break-times. Allowing the child immediate access to the lavatory is also essential, as 'holding back' or storing faeces exacerbates constipation. If there is a particular problem with the school lavatory, e.g. lack of privacy or no toilet roll, again, the school nurse can talk to the teacher. It is with continuing support from schoolteachers in allowing these things to happen that independence skills can learned by the child. A specialist nurse can provide an excellent link between clinical services and the school and parents.

Exercise

Holistic, regular exercise is vital for good bowel activity; a lack of exercise tends to lead to a sluggish bowel. Getting children to walk more, say to and from school, should not be overlooked. Some parents report improved bowel routines after the child has taken up swimming, football, or gym classes after school. Exercise and socialising increase self-awareness and self-esteem – this in turn will help the child feel more confident.

Two specifically focused exercise strategies are:

- a short period of exercise before going to the lavatory, and

- self-massage, either on the lavatory or during or after a warm bath.

Self-massage

This involves massaging up the ascending colon of the large bowel across the transverse section, moving from right to left, and then down the descending colon (Figure 19.1). This technique helps to promote peristalsis and so move more stool into the rectum and relieve flatulence. Firm pressure can be applied locally and more general pressure in the direction of stool movement.

An earlier version of this treatment, around the time of the Battle of Waterloo, involved a 7 lb cannonball which should be 'rolled over the abdominal wall following the direction of the colon' (*Sunday Telegraph*, 1999). More recently, there have been articles on abdominal massage (Richards, 1998) and trials (Forschende, 1999), but good quality evidence is lacking.

Toileting or bowel training

This requires the child's co-operation and, in chronic constipation, the motivation to change. Some key points in a successful training programme are summarised as follows:

- *Environment*
  The child must be warm to help relax muscles. They must be comfortable, be able to get the bottom lower than the hips in the lavatory, and have their feet resting on a solid surface using a step or footstool if necessary. Also, the use of a child's toilet seat can help ensure a feeling of security.
- *Timing*
  The best time to try to empty the bowel is either after a meal or after a warm bath at bedtime. Children prefer to use their own lavatories at home, and they generally avoid using those at school. During the school day they often hold back and store the faeces, so it can be a good idea to try after school too. With an inadequate fluid intake, the faeces can dry up and be difficult to pass. The more a child learns to store the faeces, for whatever reason, the larger the rectum becomes to accommodate it, resulting in diminished sensation and eventually overflow soiling. Ignoring the messages to empty the bowel can become a habit, so in chronic constipation laxatives are used to help give the

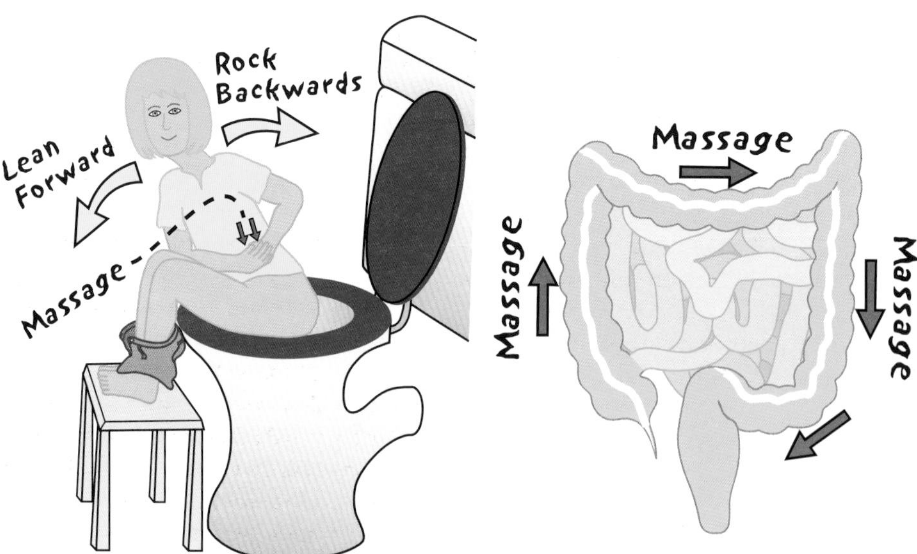

Figure 19.1 (Drawn by Catherine Arter RGN, RSCN).

sensation to 'go' and encourage regular emptying. This results in the child feeling hungrier and healthier, and improves the shape of the lower bowel. On the basis that the time it takes to empty is variable, it is best to give the 'trying' time 5–10 minutes after breakfast, after tea, or after a warm bath and at bedtime.

It is important that toilet training does not become a battle between parent and child. Support, encouragement and a relaxed attitude are important.

- *Trying*
  Boys in general are unlikely to sit down on the lavatory unless they have the feeling to defaecate. As our bowels vary in shape and size, the feelings that tell us we want to empty also differ. Therefore, a sit on the lavatory, twice a day to 'try' is helpful both for boys and girls.
- Sitting on the lavatory with the bottom lower than the hips helps to accommodate the 80° ano-rectal angle, and makes it easier to empty. To rest, lean forward on the left hand, allowing the wrist to be in the area of the left groin. The right hand can be placed over the top of the left, as this is quite a comfortable posture. This helps to encourage more stool to move down in to the rectum and can trigger a sensation to go, because the stool is nearer to the ano-rectal angle. 'Trying' means to rock back to ease the passageway for the stool, and then to try to pass wind through the bottom. The same should then be repeated, rocking forward again with the lower part of the left hand, by the wrist, in the left groin and the right hand over the top, rocking back again and trying to pass wind through the bottom. Alternate at intervals between resting and trying.
- *Specific strategies*
  Immediate response to the signal to empty the bowel.

  Emptying the bladder first if necessary, can make it easier to defaecate.

  It is important to teach the child to clean his/her own bottom and wash the hands after using the lavatory.

  The use of star or sticker charts can be motivating for some children. 'Black marks' for incontinence or no defaecation should be avoided.

Laxatives

Some children have a problem taking the laxatives prescribed. For young children, they can be mixed with a favourite food or a small drink. It is important to know that some laxatives come in different preparations, e.g. senna in liquid, tablet, or granule forms. An older child should be more informed about laxatives to encourage compliance.

Not all people empty their bowels every day, but it is essential to put in the effort on a daily basis as a way of organising this perfectly natural function and of avoiding accidents. A planned management routine helps to develop regular bowel habits, but the child must co-operate and, most of all, be motivated to change.

Psychological aspects

The major psychological factors involved in children with chronic constipation revolve around the symptoms that most distress them and the way this affects their position in the family.

Distressing symptoms include:

- Pain with defaecation – this conditions the child to avoid the noxious stimulus by contracting every muscle that is likely to prevent the pain of the stool passing through the anal canal. Children usually find the posture that best prevents defaecation for them. There is the classical 'banana' posture, so called because of the extended spine straight and often crossed legs mimicking that fruit. Children often hide and resist human contact, probably as they fear distraction, since that might lead to a moment of relaxation and the subsequent passage of the stool. Parents find this straining to avoid defaecation both distressing and confusing. They often assume that all the effort is into trying to pass the stool – rather than that the child is actually straining with his/her voluntary muscles to hold back the advancing stool pushed on by the involuntary smooth muscle of the rectum. Desperate parents holding the child forcibly over the lavatory intensify vicious circles of fear.

- Fear of pots and lavatories – if the child has experienced painful defaecation or angry parents in relation to the pot or lavatory, the fear is inevitably increased. Poorly-fitting lavatory seats that might slip or nip the skin of the thighs add to the fear. Noisy cisterns and lavatory flushes can make even happily defaecating children anxious, and there are reports of television advertisements that show the hazards of lavatories too graphically, leading to minor epidemics of constipation.
- Embarrassment about soiling and passing very large lavatory-blocking stools. If this is associated with teasing or bullying it can progress from embarrassment to social isolation, loss of self-esteem and helplessness.
- Denial and dissociation can be the coping method for older children who see no end to their distressing problems. This leads to an apparent lack of interest in their symptoms that increases the anger and distress of their parents. This complicates their management because of resistance to continuing lavatory routines, not dealing with episodes of soiling quickly before it is noticed by peers or seeps further through clothing, and non-compliance with medication. The 'belle indifference' that they may show makes engagement for psychological help difficult and slow. If they begin to feel supported then they are more likely to take more interest, and therefore control, over their symptoms and treatment regimes.
- Emotional immaturity may be a consequence of being more closely observed and helped in intimate ways than is usual for a particular age. This close tie with parents may be mutually beneficial or even maintained by the child as a way of holding fragmented families together.
- Secondary gains may occur where the persistence of treatment provides a benefit. As described above it may allow a child to remain more dependent, which might benefit the parent who dreads the gradual loss of their 'baby' and the fears of their child's teenage years. Symptoms may provide a way out of school where bullying by other children or pressure from teachers can be avoided. This may be a major factor where subtle learning or communication difficulties have isolated the child, even without the problem of soiling coming to the notice of their peers. For some families, allowances paid to help them cope with the incontinence may delay the resolution of the problems.
- Abuse which might be emotional, physical or sexual is a possibility, either as a cause of the bowel symptoms (where Munchausen by proxy must be considered) or as a consequence of the above psychological factors.

Practical psychological strategies are graded in intensity in a similar cascade to the treatment ones. Every child with faecal incontinence requires psychological help, even though many need only a boost in their confidence and reassurance that they will overcome the problems and that they are as loveable as children who do not have these symptoms.

The cascade of psychological help is shown below and is a strong argument for the team approach for this problem:

- Explanation, demystification and education (frequent contacts, booklets, games)
- Boosting confidence and co-operation (progress and incentive charts, rewards)
- Family discussions on key areas of conflict/confusion (levels of guilt and innocence related to the symptoms of lavatory avoidance and dealing with soiled clothing)
- Family therapy (addressing the power of the symptoms in the family dynamics)

- Individual therapy (aiding expression and taking on the problem)
- In-patient unit admission (for intensive therapy)
- Alternative family placement.

This last stage would be seen as an exceptional step but there are more intensive medical and surgical treatments that are sometimes used in children and adolescents with very severe symptoms and very large megarectums, such as antegrade colonic enemas via appendix stomas and even resections of parts of the colon.

Team working

It is vital that good multi-agency communication and team working is used, especially for those children where the usual treatments seem to be having little beneficial effect. As with most health problems in childhood, early focused intervention is likely to prevent the development of both the physical vicious circle of the megarectum and the psychological vicious circle of the loss of self-esteem and hope. Each member of the team must know his or her areas of skill and limitations so that advice and referral are seamless and easily understood by the family. Liaison psychiatry, with nurses becoming expert in forming the interface with the families, is the way forward.

Other conditions

Spina bifida and other causes of neuropathic bowel

The problems of soiling are compounded because of the lack of motor and sensory nerve input. This leads to problems with emptying the rectum because of pelvic floor weakness and descent preventing the stool from actually leaving the rectum. The soiling is aggravated by rapid and unopposed recto-anal inhibition and lack of sensation. Early care to avoid faecal retention can prevent the development of megarectum. Enemas may be painlessly given but often flood back due to the open inhibited anus. Enema tubes with a flange or balloon (e.g. Shandling catheter, see Chapter 17) may prevent this, and many children benefit from antegrade continence enemas to allow washout fluids to be administered directly to the colon via an appendix stoma as they progress through childhood (ACE operation, see Chapter 17).

Cerebral palsy

Children with increased tone in their legs and often pelvic floor may find defaecation very difficult. Their associated feeding problems in infancy, and the need for orthopaedic operations with the immobility, analgesia and anaesthesia with oral fluid restriction, increase the chance of faecal impaction.

Conclusions

The balance of factors alters with age throughout childhood and into adolescence. The typical case history of Tom can be linked with the range of managements described. His was a classic case, including the couple of years of pubertal delay. However, he was fortunate to have all the facilities and resources available to him when he and his family needed them. These life-spoiling conditions may significantly impede the development of the child unless treatment is started early and focused on the child's particular set of needs.

The team approach to management of cases like Tom's is not only more personal and supportive for children but also efficient in the flexible deployment of professional staff. Individual children have a very personal cocktail of needs, and individual professionals have their unique collection of skills and innate gifts. The ideal team inevitably works best when these needs and skills are matched. Team management and efficient communication is the key to these complex and distressing conditions that have a very good chance of resolution, despite the hopeless view that the child and family have on many occasions through the problem. Without the team support, individual professionals may become as despondent as their patients. Within the team, a large enough throughput and workload will inevitably encourage those struggling during their patients' low points by providing plenty of stories with happy endings.

References

Baker, S.S., Liptak, G.S., Colletti, R.B., Croffie, J.M., Di Lorenzo, C., Ector, W. and Nurko, S. (1999) Constipation in infants and children: evaluation and treatment. A medical position statement of the North American Society for Pediatric Gastroenterology and Nutrition. *Journal of Pediatric Gastroenterology and Nutrition* **29**, 5, 612–626. [Erratum published in *Journal of Pediatric Gastroenterology and Nutrition* **30**, 1, 109.]

Blythman, J. (1999) *Food our children eat*. London: Fourth Estate (division of HarperCollins).

Drugs and Therapeutics Bulletin (2000) Managing Constipation in Children **38**, 8, 57–60

Enuresis Resource Information Centre ('ERIC'), (2001) Water is Cool in School campaign. (Address: see Appendix II).

Forschende, E. (1999) Abdominal massage therapy for chronic constipation: a systematic review of clinical trials. *Komplementarmedizin* **6**, 3, 149–151.

Haines, L. and Rogers, J. (2000) Fluid intake in schools. *Nursing Times* **96**, 40, 2–4.

Karmel, A. (1991) *The complete baby and toddler meal planner*. London: Ebury Press. (www.cookingforchildren.co.uk)

Papadopoulou, A., Clayden, G.S. and Booth, I.W. (1994) The clinical value of solid marker transit studies in childhood constipation and soiling. *European Journal of Pediatrics* **153**, 560–564.

Richards, A. (1998) Hands on help. *Nursing Times* **94**, 32, 69–75.

Rugg-Gunn, A.J. (1987) The water intake of 405 Northumberland adolescents aged 12–14. *British Dental Journal* **162**, 9, 335–340.

Singh, K., Symon, D.N.L. and McLain, B. (2000) Constipation headache. North Tees and Hartlepool NHS Trust. *Paediatrics Today* **8**, 1.

Chapter 20

Practical Management of Faecal Incontinence

Sonya Chelvanayagam and Christine Norton

Patients with faecal incontinence often benefit from practical advice on managing their symptoms (Norton and Kamm, 1999). Indeed, in a recent randomised trial, practical advice alone was found to be as effective in improving symptoms as advice combined with exercises, or exercises plus biofeedback (Norton, 2001).

Emotional support

Emotional support is difficult to quantify or evaluate, but often patients express gratitude for being given the time and space to discuss their problem with someone who knows what they are talking about. It is common for patients to comment on how good it feels to know that they are not alone, that others have the same problem and that help is possible. Many express relief at finally being able to share what experiencing faecal incontinence really feels like.

Many patients will say they feel very alone with this problem, which they see as taboo. Some cry at the first and subsequent appointments. Feelings of guilt, embarrassment, unattractiveness, comparisons with a baby and the difficulties of hiding the problem all the time are frequently expressed (Chelvanayagam and Norton, 2000). It seems that many see the clinic as a safe environment, in which they can be open and honest about their symptoms without feeling that they will produce a shocked reaction. Patients value being allowed adequate time to explore emotional aspects of their side of the problem, and express appreciation if they do not feel the consultation is rushed (Norton, 2001).

Diet and fluids

Many people find that what they eat influences their bowel function, and diet is therefore reviewed with each patient. It is not easy to offer definitive advice on diet as the influence seems to vary from person to person, and there is very little research on which foods can make incontinence better or worse. What will make life a nightmare for one person seems to have no effect at all on someone else. Eating and drinking should be a pleasure, not just to maintain life, so it would be a great pity to make life a misery by needing to constantly worry about what is eaten.

It is worth experimenting a little to see if each individual can find anything that upsets bowel control. Food rich in fibre is the most common contributor to poor bowel control in individuals who are not constipated (clinical experience). Fibre supplements have been found to contribute to faecal incontinence in frail immobile people (Ardron and Main, 1990; Barrett, 1993). Softer stool is more difficult to hold during an urge to defaecate and is also more likely to passively leak. There are no trials on the effect of fibre reduction on faecal continence, but clinically a lot of patients derive benefit from moderating their fibre intake (Norton and Kamm, 1999). Fibre reduction must of course be done sensibly and with awareness of the benefits of fibre to general health. Table 20.1 (overleaf) shows the advice sheet commonly used with patients who are assessed as probably needing to reduce fibre intake.

Conversely, some patients with mild constipation or with very loose stool may find an increase in fibre helpful (Bliss et al., 1997). Very spicy or hot food can upset some people. Other foods to consider include milk products and chocolate, which some people find make their stools looser or upsets an irritable bowel (Ellard, 1996). A few people find that artificial

Table 20.1: Moderating your fibre intake

Fibre is one of the waste products from your food that your body cannot digest and use. Generally, in Western countries, our diet does not contain as much fibre as it should for good health, and we are often told that fibre is good for you and that you should eat more. However, we know that for people with bowel control problems, this can make matters worse. Fibre will make your bowel motions softer, and so more likely to leak. Fibre also helps to stimulate the bowel, and so can make you pass a motion more often and with greater urgency.

We are not suggesting that you eat an unhealthy diet, but that it may be worth experimenting a little to see which foods make your control better or worse. This is very individual; our bodies do not all react the same and it is a case of trial and error to see which foods, if any, cause problems for you. You should always eat some fruit and vegetables each day – do not cut these out completely. But start by avoiding deliberately high fibre foods (such as bran cereal) and the fruit and vegetables that have a particularly high fibre content.

FOODS RICH IN FIBRE

Wholemeal bread
Wholegrain cereals (e.g. Shredded Wheat, Weetabix, branflakes, porridge, muesli)
Wholemeal pasta
Brown rice
Beans (including baked beans)
Peas
Lentils
Sweetcorn
Wholemeal biscuits (e.g. digestive, rye crispbread, oatcakes)
Fruit (especially if eaten with skin or pips)
Vegetables (especially if eaten with skin or seeds, e.g. jacket potatoes)
Nuts, seeds and dried fruit (e.g. sultanas, raisins, dried apricots)

sweeteners, especially sorbitol (in many low-calorie foods, drinks and chewing gum), have a tendency to make their stools looser. If the patient thinks that there may be a link with what they eat, keeping a diary of diet and bowel frequency may reveal if there is a pattern. A course of antibiotics can upset the bowel, and live natural yoghurt or probiotics such as lactobaccilus (e.g. 'Yakult') can help to restore a more regular habit.

Some foods help to make stools firmer and therefore easier to control for some people. Arrowroot as biscuits or as a flour substitute in sauces or soups, marshmallow sweets and very ripe bananas each help some people. A high fat intake can slow down the speed with which food travels through the bowel, but this is obviously not healthy for other reasons and so cannot be recommended! Some patients have difficulty with fat digestion after cholecystectomy, with this leading to loose fatty stools. Some of these patients will benefit from a reduced fat diet, or use of cholestyramine ('Questran') to aid bile salt metabolism.

The type of fluid intake can make a difference to some people, and again this is individual and it is worth experimenting. Caffeine reduction is almost always worth trying for people with faecal incontinence. Some people have a bowel that seems to be very sensitive to caffeine, which is present in coffee, tea, cola drinks and expensive chocolate. Caffeine is a known gut stimulant (Brown et al., 1990) and many patients find that it will exacerbate urgency. It seems to stimulate the bowel, and so makes the stools move through faster. This means that less fluid is taken from the stools, which are then looser and more urgent. The patient with urgency, frequency or loose stool can try to spend at least a week without any caffeine to see if this helps. A high caffeine intake should not be stopped suddenly, as headaches can result.

Alcohol seems to cause the bowels to be loose and urgent for some people, but less so for others. Different types of alcoholic drink can affect people in different ways. Some find that beer is better than wine, or that white wine is better than red, or vice-versa.

Lifestyle modification and medication

Nicotine is thought to slow upper gut motility and increase total transit time (Scott et al., 1992), but it seems that it can speed recto-sigmoid transit (Rausch et al., 1998); this fits with many people reporting clinically that smoking a cigarette facilitates initiation of defaecation. Smoking cessation has been found useful clinically in some patients with urgency.

Anti-diarrhoeal medication is offered to people with frequent or loose stools. Patients who experience urge incontinence of faeces associated with loose stool, or who have a passive anal seepage of soft stool, may benefit from low-dose constipating medication (Kamm, 1998). Often patients are given insufficient information at the time of prescription to enable optimum drug usage. The variation in individual response to medication is large, and so the dose needs to be carefully titrated to the individual's needs. Timing is also important, as taking medication before meals will help to dampen any gastro-colic response. The nurse can therefore help the patient to adjust timing and dose of medication within the medically prescribed range to maximise effectiveness. Drug treatment is covered in detail in Chapter 16.

General health and fitness advice is offered to patients as appropriate. For some patients it seems as though the decision to take positive action about bowel control is part of a broader decision to regain control of their body fitness and weight, and tackle low self-esteem.

Products for managing faecal incontinence

There are no perfect answers to the problem of coping with leakage from the bowel. It is very difficult to find anything that reliably disguises bowel leakage and smell, and very few products have been designed specifically for faecal leakage. The nurse should be aware of the range of products available to help people with faecal incontinence, such as the anal plug, which may help, as well as pads, skin care, odour control and practical coping strategies (clean-up kits and disposal) (Norton and Kamm, 1999). It is surprising how many people with faecal incontinence seem to have failed to develop practical coping strategies and are repeatedly caught out without any change of clothes or way of cleaning up. It is almost as if some are in denial, not being able to cope with the idea that it might happen, so each episode is experienced as a disaster. This same vagueness and lack of coherent strategies in people who have not verbalised their problem, and so have not developed constructs for explaining or coping with it, has been described in women with urinary incontinence (Ashworth and Hagan, 1993).

For those individuals who have residual faecal incontinence despite either surgical or medical interventions, practical advice in managing their bowel leakage is essential. Such information enables individuals to manage their symptoms and therefore hopefully have less impact on their quality of life. Promocon is a national resource centre for information on continence products. There is a display in Manchester and some other sites around the UK, and a series of fact sheets. For more information contact the address in Appendix II.

It is important to encourage patients to try different products, as it cannot be predicted as to what benefits whom. Some patients will adamantly refuse to wear pads – they view this as a sign that they 'have given in' and therefore have to accept their symptoms. Other patients will use large incontinence pads 'just in case', although episodes of incontinence are rare (see Chapter 5). Many are reluctant to use anal plugs as they find the concept difficult to accept, but are keen to examine them and will consider using them for certain occasions.

Anal plug

An alternative to using a pad is to occlude the escape of faeces from the anus. Some patients with minor leakage of mucus or stool from the anus find that a small piece of cotton wool, rolled between the fingers and then gently inserted just inside the anus, will stop the problem, with the use of Vaseline to aid insertion if required.

Alternatively, a manufactured anal plug (Conveen anal plug) comes wrapped up in a water-soluble film and should be covered with Vaseline so that it is easy to insert – avoid the use of water-based gels such as K-Y as these will dissolve the film and make insertion difficult. The film dissolves once inside the rectum, and the plug opens into a cup shape, with a string for removal in the anus. It comes in two sizes, small and large (see Figure 20.1). It can be left in place for up to twelve hours and removed by pulling the attached cord.

This is a useful device for individuals with passive soiling who can use it on a daily basis or when they wish to do sports activities. It is not really suitable for patients with frequency of defaecation as it would need to be removed each time. The advantage of this device is that it usually stops soiling. However, many patients report that it is uncomfortable to wear and the majority cannot tolerate it (Norton and Kamm, 2001; Christiansen and Roed-Petersen, 1993). For this reason patients with neurological impairments such as a spinal injury or spina bifida benefit from its use, as they frequently lack sensory function in the anal canal. Once they have used their appropriate bowel regime (see Chapter 17) they insert the plug to prevent any further soiling until another bowel action is stimulated.

The plug cannot be flushed down the toilet, and so must be wrapped in paper or a disposal bag and put in the rubbish bin. The manufacturers, Coloplast Ltd, will send samples on request (see addresses in Appendix II) so that patients can see if the plug is suitable for them. It is available on prescription in the UK.

Pads and pants

There are very few products designed specifically for managing faecal incontinence. Most of the disposable pads used for urinary incontinence can be used for containment, but some

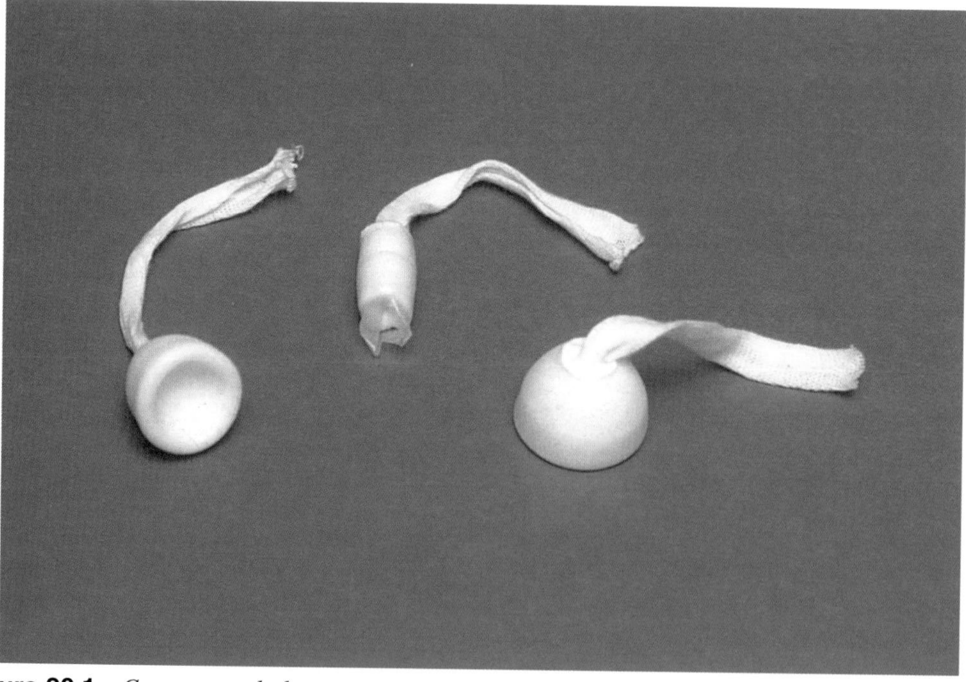

Figure 20.1 *Conveen anal plug.*

patients find them unnecessarily thick and bulky, and not the right shape or length to contain soiling from the anal canal.

The simplest pad for minor leakage is a panty liner, available in supermarkets and chemists. Unfortunately, if used inside the pants, the perianal area often becomes sore as the stool leaks onto the skin initially before reaching the pad. Some patients have found that folding a panty liner between the buttocks and holding it in place with a close-fitting 'G-string', helps to contain soiling and prevent soreness or excoriation (see Figure 20.2). Some panty liners have a soft cover, which seems to be softer than a 'stay dry' cover.

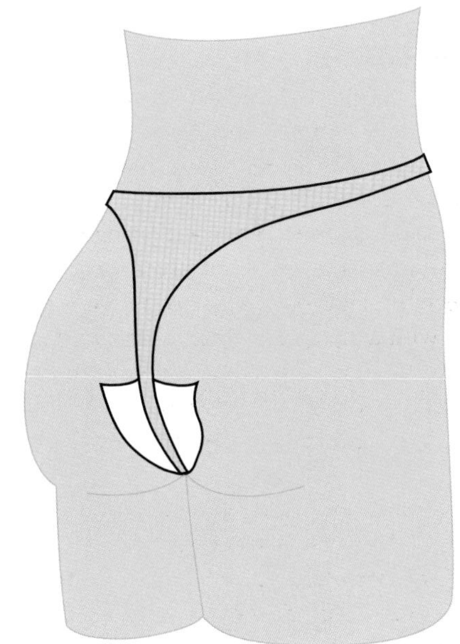

Figure 20.2 *'G-string' pants.*

For individuals who report passive soiling of liquid stool or mucus which occurs infrequently, it may be reassuring to wear pants with a built-in waterproof gusset (see Figure 20.3), especially if they will be away from the toilet for a long period of time. These should stop any leaks from staining clothes; however, they have been developed for urinary incontinence so may be stained by stool. Shiloh have developed their range in black with a black gusset particularly for this reason. They lengthened the gusset to include the anal area.

More major incontinence will require larger pads. These come in all shapes and sizes (see

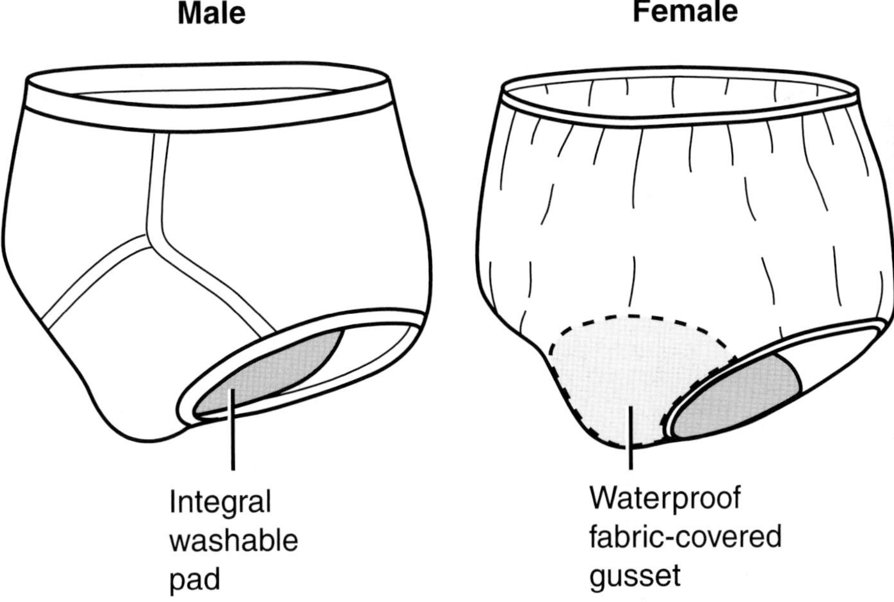

Figure 20.3 *Pants with integral pad.*

Figure 20.4). Many are available free of charge on the National Health Service via the District Nurse or local Continence Adviser if the symptoms are persistent and severe. The Continence Foundation Helpline (see Appendix II) has a directory of continence services to find the patient's local contact.

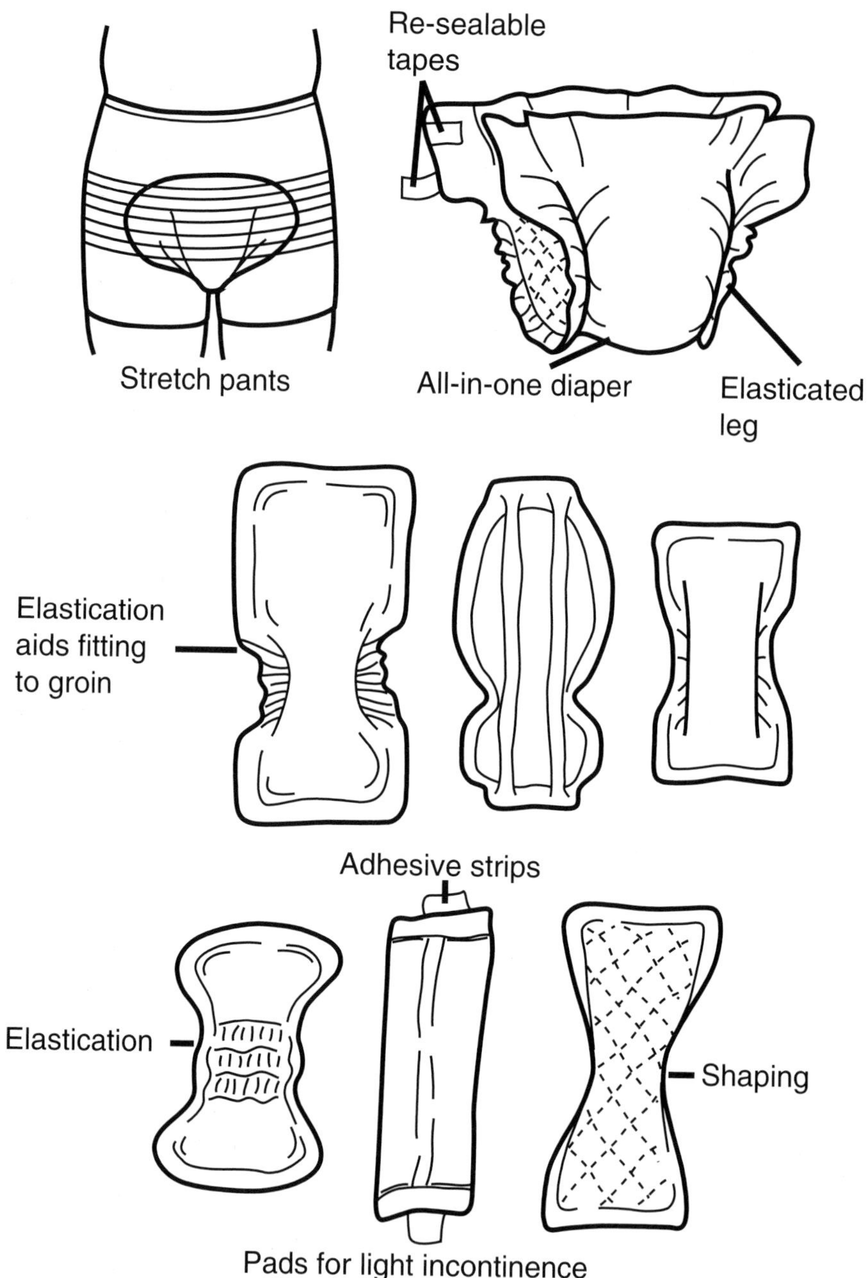

Figure 20.4 *Types of incontinence pad.*

Washing and odours

Patients are very aware of the embarrassment caused by an episode of faecal incontinence and therefore frequently plan their journeys by 'toilet stops'. This helps to alleviate some of their anxiety. Many carry their 'spare kit', and can be advised as to items to include in this bag to help them clean up after incontinence has occurred.

Public toilets seldom have a wash basin in the cubicle, and trying to get clean with dry toilet tissue is difficult and can be painful for those with sore or excoriated skin. Wet wipes are therefore preferable (Andrex Moist have produced a pocket-sized rigid plastic case). Some wipes have alcohol in them and can sting if skin is excoriated. Alternatively, a small plastic bottle can be filled with warm water to take into the toilet to wash. Clothes pegs are useful to keep clean clothes out of the way. Companies which produce stoma appliances have a custom-made peg so that patients are able to clip their clothes out of the way in order to change their appliance. A small pocket mirror is useful to check the perineal area is clean and that there are no apparent stains on clothing before leaving the toilet.

There are a variety of sanitary towel or nappy sacks for sale which are useful for disposal of pads or to carry home soiled clothes. Many are slightly scented, which helps to disguise the smell of the contents. Odours from flatus or stool can be disguised by a small neutraliser or spray perfume – again, stoma companies produce a range which can be used whilst changing in a toilet before or after exposing bowel contents.

Skin care

Anyone who has frequent bowel motions, diarrhoea or faecal incontinence may get sore skin around the anus from time to time. This can be very uncomfortable and distressing. Occasionally, the skin may become so inflamed that it breaks into open sores, which are then difficult to heal. Taking good care of the skin around the anus can help to prevent these problems from developing, and patients frequently seek advice for this problem.

The skin can become sore due to a variety of reasons. Chemicals contained in the bacteria of the stool and digestive enzymes are skin irritants. If there is diarrhoea, there is likely to be a higher content of digestive enzymes as there will have been less time to re-absorb these. If both urinary and faecal incontinence are present, this seems to exacerbate the tendency to soreness (Buckingham and Berg, 1986). Frequency of defaecation leads to repeated wiping, which can damage the sensitive skin of the anus. Wiping with dry paper seems to be more traumatic than using a wet wipe.

Some anal conditions such as skin tags, scars or external haemorrhoids make it very difficult to wipe effectively. Any stool remaining causes irritation, and scratching the area will cause soreness. This can lead to infection, or sometimes infestation may be a problem.

Poor nutrition, inadequate hydration and immobility may exacerbate skin problems.

Table 20.2 (overleaf) gives patient information on preventing soreness.

Patients who are already sore are advised to follow all the advice above on prevention. In addition, damp cotton wool may be found to be the most comfortable to use for wiping. A barrier cream or ointment such as Sudocrem or a small amount of Metanium may suffice. If drying the skin after washing is difficult or uncomfortable, a hairdryer on a low setting may be used, but with great care. The patient is advised not to scratch the anal area, however much they are tempted, as this will make things worse. If the patient scratches the area during sleep at night, wearing cotton gloves in bed (available from a chemist) may help. It is important to allow the air to get to the anal area for at least part of every day. For very sore skin, Chiron Cream (Smiths Industries) or Cavilon spray or cream (3M Healthcare) may be clinically useful, although research is lacking.

Table 20.2: Tips to prevent soreness

With careful personal hygiene it is often possible to prevent soreness, even if you have a bowel problem.

- After a bowel action, always wipe GENTLY with soft toilet paper, or ideally the newer moist toilet paper (available from larger pharmacies and some supermarkets). Discard each piece of paper after one wipe, so that you are not re-contaminating the area you have just wiped.
- Whenever possible, wash around the anus after a bowel action. A bidet is ideal (portable versions are also available). If this is not possible, you may be able to use a shower attachment with your bottom over the edge of the bath. Or use a soft disposable cloth with warm water. Avoid flannels and sponges, as they can be rough and are difficult to keep clean. Sometimes a little ingenuity is needed, especially if you are away from home. Some people find that a small plant spray, watering can or jug filled with warm water makes washing easy on the toilet or over the edge of the bath.
- Do not be tempted to use disinfectants or antiseptics in the washing water – these can sting and many people are sensitive to the chemicals in them. Just plain warm water is best.
- AVOID using products with a strong perfume such as scented soap, talcum powder or deodorants on your bottom. Choose a non-scented soap (e.g. 'Simple'). Many baby wipes contain alcohol and are best avoided.
- When drying the area BE VERY GENTLE. Pat gently with soft toilet paper or a soft towel. Do not rub. Treat the whole area as you would a newborn baby's skin. If you are very sore, a hairdryer on a low setting may be most comfortable (use carefully!).
- Wear cotton underwear to allow the skin to breathe. Avoid tight jeans and other clothes that might rub the area. Women are usually best to avoid tights and to use stockings or crotchless tights instead. Use non-biological washing powder and avoid fabric softener for underwear and towels.
- Avoid using any creams or lotions on the area, unless advised to do so. A few people who are prone to sore skin do find that regular use of a cream helps to prevent this. If you do use a barrier cream, choose a simple one (such as zinc and castor oil), use just a small amount and gently rub it in. Large amounts stop the skin from breathing and can make the area sweaty and uncomfortable. Make sure that the old layer of cream is washed off before applying more. Some people are allergic to lanolin, and creams containing this should be avoided.
- Your doctor or nurse may suggest using a barrier wipe which forms a protective film over the skin, especially if you have diarrhoea and are opening your bowels very frequently (available on prescription).
- If you need to wear a pad because of incontinence, try to make sure that no plastic comes into contact with your skin and that you use a pad with a soft surface. The Continence Nurse can advise you on which pads are best.
- Whenever possible, unless you have been advised not to for other reasons, eat a healthy, balanced diet, drink plenty and take as much exercise as you can. Some people find that certain food or drink makes them more prone to soreness, especially citrus fruit such as oranges. It may be worth cutting these out on a trial basis, and more permanently if this helps.

Note: Women are advised always to wipe front to back, i.e. AWAY from the bladder and vaginal openings – bacteria from the bowel can infect the bladder and vagina if you wipe from back to front.

Conclusions

Patients frequently report that it is often simple advice that makes all the difference. Much of the advice they are given will have been provided by previous patients who have discovered methods of managing their symptoms to minimise the effect of being faecally incontinent on their quality of life .

References

Ardron, M.E. and Main, A.N.H. (1990) Management of constipation. *British Medical Journal* **300**, 1400.

Ashworth, P.D. and Hagan, M.T. (1993) The meaning of incontinence: a qualitative study of non-geriatric urinary incontinence sufferers. *Journal of Advanced Nursing* **18**, 1415–1423.

Barrett, J.A. (1993) *Faecal incontinence and related problems in the older adult.* London: Edward Arnold.

Bliss, D.Z., Jung, H., Savik, K., Lowry, A.C., LeMoine, M., Jensen, L., and Werner, C. and Shaffer, K. (2001) Supplementation with dietary fiber improves fecal incontinence. *Nursing Research* **50**, 203–213.

Brown, S.R., Cann, P.A. and Read, N.W. (1990) Effect of coffee on distal colon function. *Gut* **31**, 450–453.

Buckingham, K.W. and Berg, R.W. (1986) Etiologic factors in diaper dermatitis: the role of feces. *Pediatric Dermatology*, **3**, 2, 107–112.

Chelvanayagam, S. and Norton, C. (2000) Quality of life with faecal continence problems. *Nursing Times* **96** (Suppl.), 15–17.

Christiansen, J. and Roed-Petersen, K. (1993) Clinical assessment of the anal continence plug. *Diseases of the Colon and Rectum* **36**, 740–742.

Ellard, K. (1996) *Irritable bowel syndrome.* East Dereham: Neen Health Books.

Kamm, M.A. (1998) Faecal incontinence: clinical review. *British Medical Journal* **316**, 528–532.

Norton, C. and Kamm, M.A. (1999) *Bowel control – information and practical advice.* Beaconsfield: Beaconsfield Publishers.

Norton, C. and Kamm, M.A. (2001) Anal plug for faecal incontinence. *Colorectal Disease* **3**, 323–327.

Norton, C.S. (2001) Biofeedback and nursing management for adults with faecal incontinence. Unpublished PhD thesis: Kings College, London.

Rausch, T., Beglinger, C., Alam, N. and Meier, R. (1998) Effect of transdermal application of nicotine on colonic transit in healthy nonsmoking volunteers. *Neurogastroenterology and Motility* **10**, 263–270.

Scott, A.M., Kellow, J.E., Eckersley, G.M., Nolan, J.M. and Jones, M.P. (1992) Cigarette smoking and nicotine delay postprandial mouth–cecum transit time. *Digestive Diseases & Sciences* **37**, 1544–1547.

Chapter 21

Constipation

Anton Emmanuel

Introduction

Constipation is merely a symptom – not a disease – and reflects either slowed colonic transit and/or impairment of rectal emptying (Thompson et al., 1999). Its severity may vary from the slight, causing no disruption of life, to the severe, when the patient's social and personal functioning is grossly disrupted. Only a minority of people with constipation present to their general practitioners, and a minority of those are referred to hospital. Typically, such patients tend to be those with more severe impairment of quality of life and for whom trials of dietary fibre supplementation will have failed.

There are two main syndromes of constipation – slow colonic transit and evacuation difficulties. The two can co-exist in the same patient. Patients with slow colonic transit tend to report a reduced frequency of the urge to defaecate, and occasionally the total absence of urge if laxatives are not consumed. Patients with difficulty evacuating and inco-ordination of the rectum, anus and pelvic floor present with symptoms of straining, incomplete rectal evacuation and sometimes the need for anal or vaginal digitation (i.e., inserting a finger into the anal canal or vagina to assist defaecation).

Variables such as stool frequency and consistency are easy to quantify in the history, but there is no generally accepted normal range, and furthermore these variables differ according to race, personality, emotional state and gender. Nonetheless a working definition of 'normal' bowel function is of bowel opening between three times a week to three times a day, and needing to strain on less than 25% of occasions to achieve emptying (Thompson et al., 1999).

Clinical sub-types of constipation

The types of constipation that can be generated by the colon and pelvic floor is limited to either infrequent or difficult defaecation, so it is important to identify discrete clinical sub-types that may have a common aetiology. Patients may have a variety of subjective views of the term 'constipation', and it is essential to understand the patients' symptoms and classify them in a meaningful clinical pattern. The following is a clinically based classification:

Idiopathic (simple) constipation: is often mild. It is commonest in the elderly, and is often ascribable to reduced mental and physical function, a low residue diet or a drug side effect.

Secondary to co-existing systemic illness: is much rarer. A variety of metabolic, endocrine and neuro-muscular disorders may need to be excluded according to the clinical picture (Table 21.1).

Secondary to a colonic cause: Recent onset symptoms or the presence of suspicious symptoms such as bleeding, weight loss and/or abdominal pain should raise the need to exclude tumours or stenotic lesions of the colon by radiology or endoscopy (Table 21.1, see also Chapter 7).

Irritable bowel syndrome: The key features of the irritable bowel syndrome are abdominal pain in the presence of disturbed bowel function. The diagnosis should be entertained in patients complaining of constipation with abdominal pain and bloating with no underlying pathology.

Severe constipation with gut dilatation: is due to either:

(i) idiopathic megarectum or megacolon (see opposite);

(ii) Hirschsprung's disease (see page 248); or

(iii) chronic idiopathic intestinal pseudo-obstruction: this extremely rare condition should be suspected in the presence of a dilated upper intestine.

Severe constipation with a normal diameter colon: is a chronic disorder, affecting predominantly women of child-bearing years (Preston and Lennard-Jones, 1986). Patients in this group are amongst the most commonly referred for hospital management of constipation.

Clinical features

The development of symptoms is frequently insidious. There is often a decades-long 'lag period' between onset of symptoms and first consultation. Occasionally patients describe a clear precipitant to their symptoms, most commonly abdominal or pelvic surgery, childbirth or emotional trauma; this should not alter management. In addition to the already described symptoms of infrequent and incomplete defaecation, patients presenting to hospital with constipation often report abdominal pain, distension and nausea (Preston and Lennard-Jones, 1986). There is often a history of heavy laxative consumption. Malaise and lethargy are almost invariable; headaches, mood swings and poor concentration are frequently reported. There are often non-specific urinary and gynaecological complaints. Faecal soiling and a history of faecal impaction in a young patient should raise the suspicion of a megarectum.

Studies estimate that up to 50% of women who present to hospital with functional gastrointestinal disorders are victims of sexual or physical abuse in childhood (Drossman et al., 1990). An important aspect of the consultation in a constipated patient is to create the atmosphere which allows the patient to discuss such matters, since it is known that dramatic relief of constipation can be brought about synchronous with the release of emotions relating to the abuse (Devroede et al., 1989). However, care needs to be exercised: a patient revealing a history of past abuse will usually

Table 21.1: Causes of constipation

Idiopathic
- *no obvious cause*

Endocrine
- *hypothyroidism*
- *glucagonoma* (a hormone-secreting tumour of the pancreas)
- *diabetes mellitus*

Metabolic
- *hypercalcaemia*
- *uraemia*
- *hypokalaemia*
- *porphyria*
- *amyloidosis*
- *lead poisoning*

Neurological
- *cortical lesions (tumour, infarction)*
- *spinal cord lesions (injury, infarction)*
- *peripheral lesions (autonomic neuropathy e.g diabetes mellitus)*

Neuromuscular disorders
- *systemic sclerosis*
- *dermatomyositis*
- *dystrophia myotonica*

Psychological
- *anorexia nervosa, bulimia nervosa*
- *affective disorder (e.g. depression)*
- *dementia or learning difficulty (inappropriate response to gut signals)*

Physiological
- *pregnancy*
- *old age*

Colonic
- *neuromuscular disorder (Hirschsprung's, megabowel, chronic intestinal pseudo-obstruction)*
- *stricture (tumour, ischaemia, diverticular disease)*

Anal
- *fissure*
- *polyp, tumour*

Functional bowel disorders
- *irritable bowel syndrome*

need considerable skilled psychological help in dealing with the consequences of such a revelation. Constipated patients, especially those with slow whole gut transit tend to have specific psychological profiles, with exaggerated levels of somatisation, anxiety, depression and paranoid ideation (Wald et al., 1989; Devroede et al., 1989).

Examination is usually unremarkable, but the presence of gross abdominal bloating and a faecal mass rising out of the pelvis should raise the suspicion of Hirschsprung's disease or megarectum. Rigid sigmoidoscopy may show the changes of melanosis coli (patches of discolouration within the gut mucosa relating to chronic laxative use) or a megarectum.

Primary care management

Most people who present with simple constipation can be managed successfully in primary care. It is important to decide whether urgent tests are required. Indications for such tests would be when an individual reports new symptoms of constipation, passing of fresh or occult blood, weight loss and or abdominal pain (see Chapter 7), especially in patients over 45 years of age.

Having decided that the patient has simple constipation, the first step is to offer honest reassurance that there is no sinister underlying pathology to explain the symptoms. Discussion should be held regarding the role of dietary fibre, fluids and exercise (see later for details). Patients frequently respond positively to explanations given regarding normal bowel habit and optimal posture to aid defaecation. Short-term use of mild laxatives may be helpful to assist in regaining a regular bowel habit, but prolonged use should be avoided. Simple practical advice on ensuring adequate time and privacy for defaecation and timing attempts to empty the bowel to coincide with meals (the gastro-colic response) and on waking, rather than repeated delays and ignoring the call to stool because of a busy lifestyle will help to resolve mild constipation in many instances.

Investigation of constipation

Special investigations are only indicated for those patients in whom adequate fibre supplementation has failed to help and who have been referred from the primary care setting. Careful selection of investigations can give helpful information on which to base subsequent management.

Colonoscopy or barium enema examination are helpful in excluding a primary colonic cause for constipation. There is no pathophysiological significance to the frequent observation of a long colon in these patients. Blood testing of thyroid function and calcium is routine practice to exclude a secondary cause (Table 21.1)

Radio-opaque marker study of whole gut transit

As well as being the most useful measure of generalised intestinal motor function, this form of investigation has the advantage of being simple, relatively non-invasive and easy to interpret. A well-validated technique involves ingestion of three sets of radio-opaque markers at 24-hour intervals on three consecutive days while laxatives are not permitted; a single plain abdominal X-ray is obtained 5 days (120 hours) after ingestion of the first set of markers. There is a reproducible normal range allowing patients to be classed as having slow transit if there is retention of more than the normal for any one of the three sets of markers (Evans et al., 1992). No stool collection is required and a measure of whole gut transit can be easily obtained. Such a method also has the advantage of identifying patient compliance and accuracy of reporting. For instance, if the patient reports passing only tiny quantities of stool in the five days of the study and yet most of the markers have been passed, it is possible to encourage the patient that in those small quantities sufficient colonic clearance was being achieved (Figures 21.1 and 21.2, overleaf).

Recto-anal inhibitory reflex

Testing for this reflex is indicated in patients with suspected Hirschsprung's disease, since its presence excludes the condition without the need for surgical biopsy of the distal rectum. A distensible balloon is inserted into the rectum and inflated to 50 ml while simultaneous recording of anal sphincter pressure is undertaken. The normal reflex is for relaxation of the sphincter in response to rectal filling, whereas patients with Hirschsprung's disease demonstrate no change in sphincter pressure, even with large rectal distension volumes (see Chapter 8, page 74 and Figure 8.6)

Evacuation proctography

Evacuation proctography, or defaecography, is a technique to study ano-rectal morphology and dynamics during defaecation. Semi-solid barium paste is inserted into the rectum via a rectal catheter and the patient seated on a commode-like receptacle; the patient is encouraged to empty the rectum whilst video-radiography is performed. Evacuation proctography may be indicated if the history is suggestive of an evacuation disorder. Functional abnormalities of rectal emptying such as intussusception or frank rectal mucosal prolpase, rectocoele (protrusion of the anterior rectal wall into the back of the vagina) or solitary rectal ulcer syndrome, excessive pelvic floor descent or puborectalis dyskinesis (failure of the puborectalis sling to relax on evacuation) can be readily identified by proctography (Figure 21.3, page 244).

Ano-rectal sensory testing

Rectal balloon distension volumes tend to be higher in constipated patients than healthy controls, although distension testing is not sufficiently sensitive to be diagnostic. Ano-rectal mucosal electrosensitivity testing is a specific test of the degree of any damage to the nerve supply of the hindgut (lower bowel). Thus constipation complicating neurological diseases (such as multiple sclerosis, spinal cord injury, Parkinson's disease, diabetic neuropathy) can be differentiated from constipation co-incident with neurological disease. If the constipation is a complication of the neurological disease, the nerve supply is unlikely to be normal; if constipation is simply a coincidence in someone who happens to also have a neurological disease, the nerve responses should be normal (see Chapters 8 and 17 for further detail).

Treatment

A major limitation of almost all studies into the management of constipation is that they fail to take into account the natural history of the condition, and furthermore the natural progression of symptoms with time is uncertain. It is not known what proportion of patients stop presenting with intestinal complaints or displace symptoms to another system, and this factor will undoubtedly affect 'success rates' of various treatments. Another factor to bear in mind when reviewing the literature on the treatment of constipation is that, as is common with most functional problems, the longer the period of follow-up after treatment, the worse the outcome (Gattuso and Kamm, 1994).

General measures

Any drugs which may be contributing to the patient's symptoms should be considered (Table 21.2). Once imaging has been performed, where appropriate, to exclude a mechanical cause of the symptoms, many patients simply need reassurance as to what the range of 'normal' bowel frequency and stool consistency is amongst the general population. Establishing good rapport with the patient is obvious, but essential. Many hospital-referred patients have seen a variety of other medical professionals and may have been left with the impression that their problems are trivial or purely psychological. Time spent in understanding how the symptoms impact on the patient's life often gives an insight into what is their main concern. There is no evidence that constipated patients drink less fluid or take less exercise than healthy subjects (Klauser et al., 1992), and it is important to stress the need for a balanced and non-obsessive approach to their lifestyle.

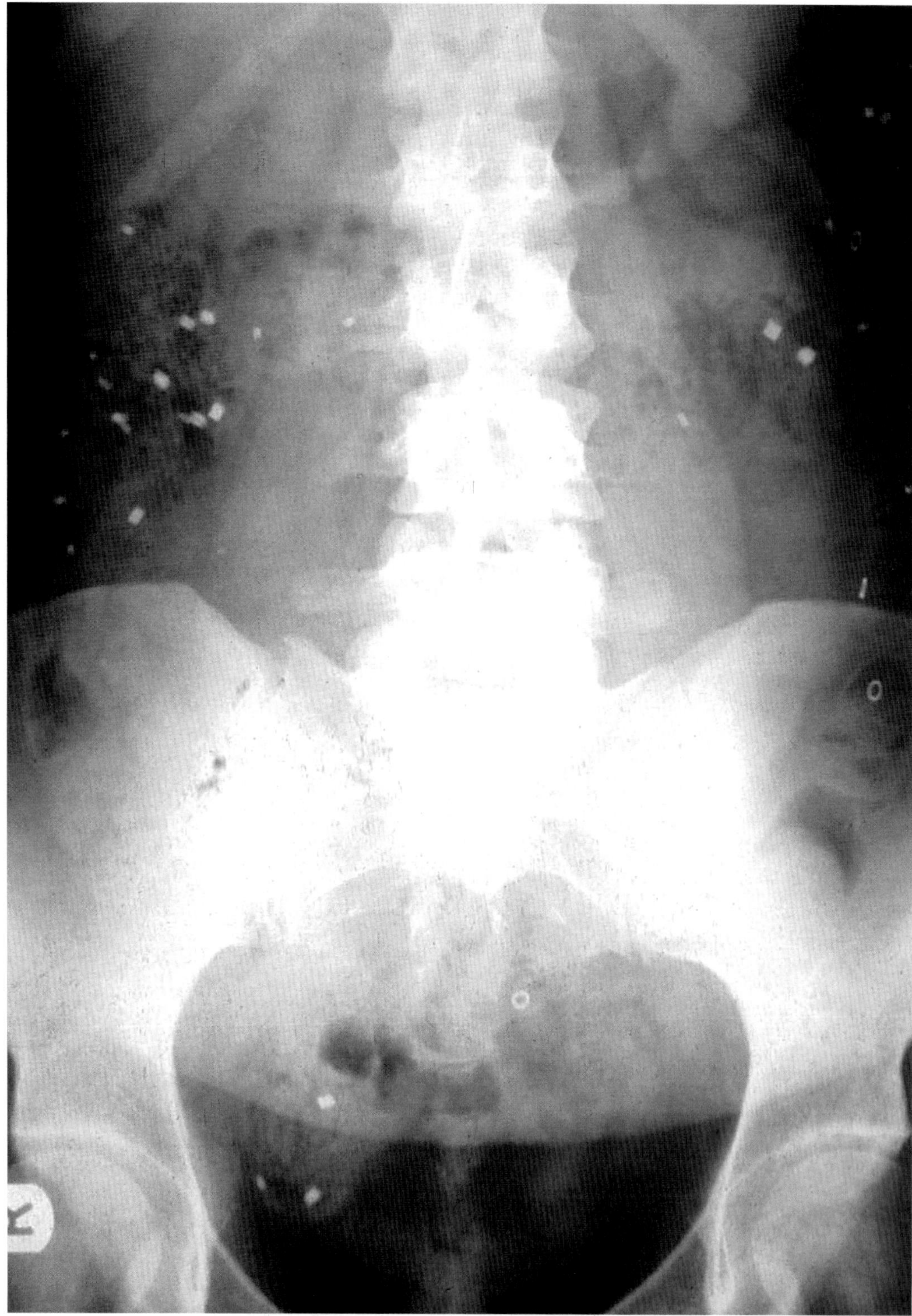

Figure 21.1 *Transit study showing slow transit constipation.*

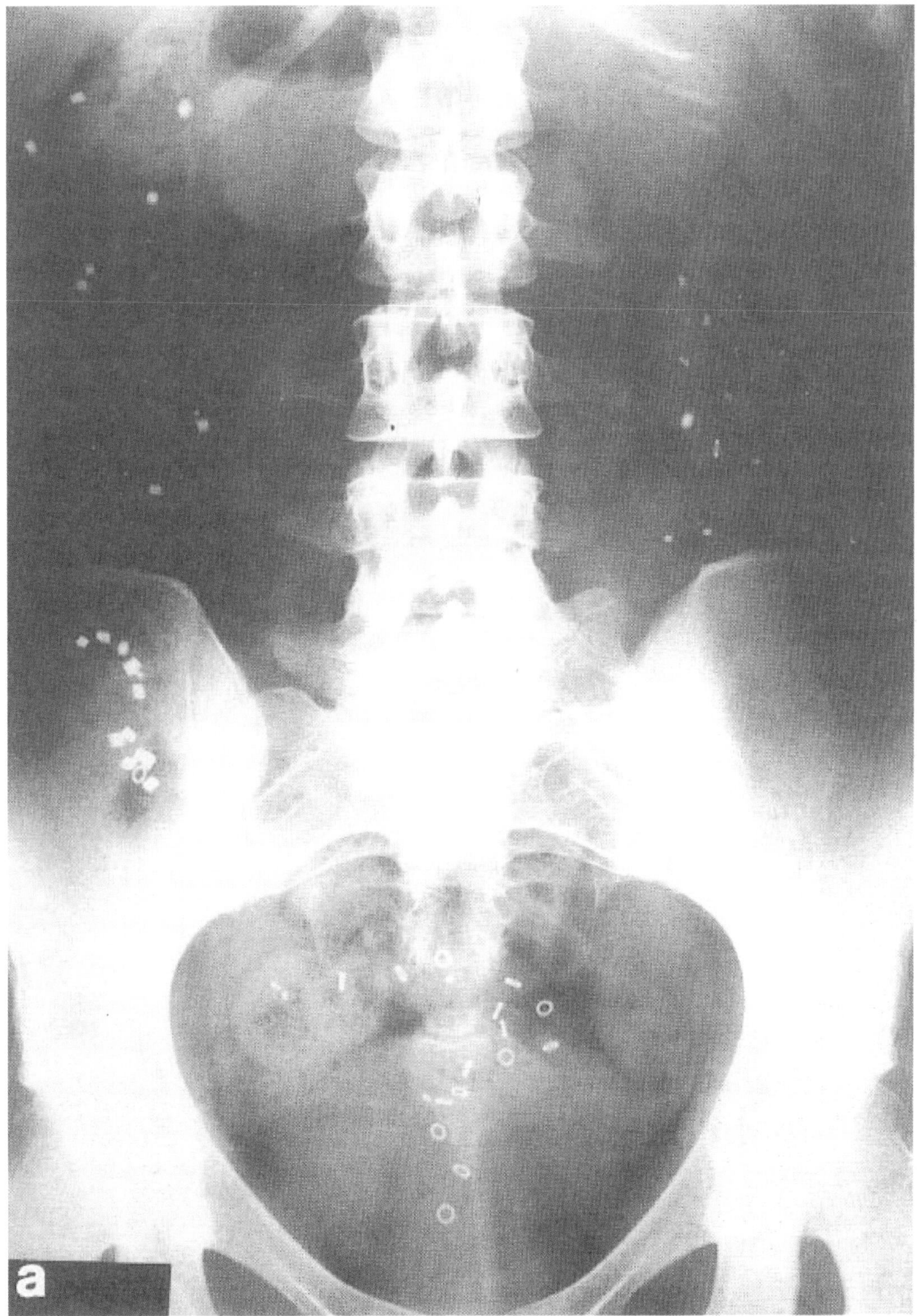

Figure 21.2 *Transit study showing rectal outlet delay.*

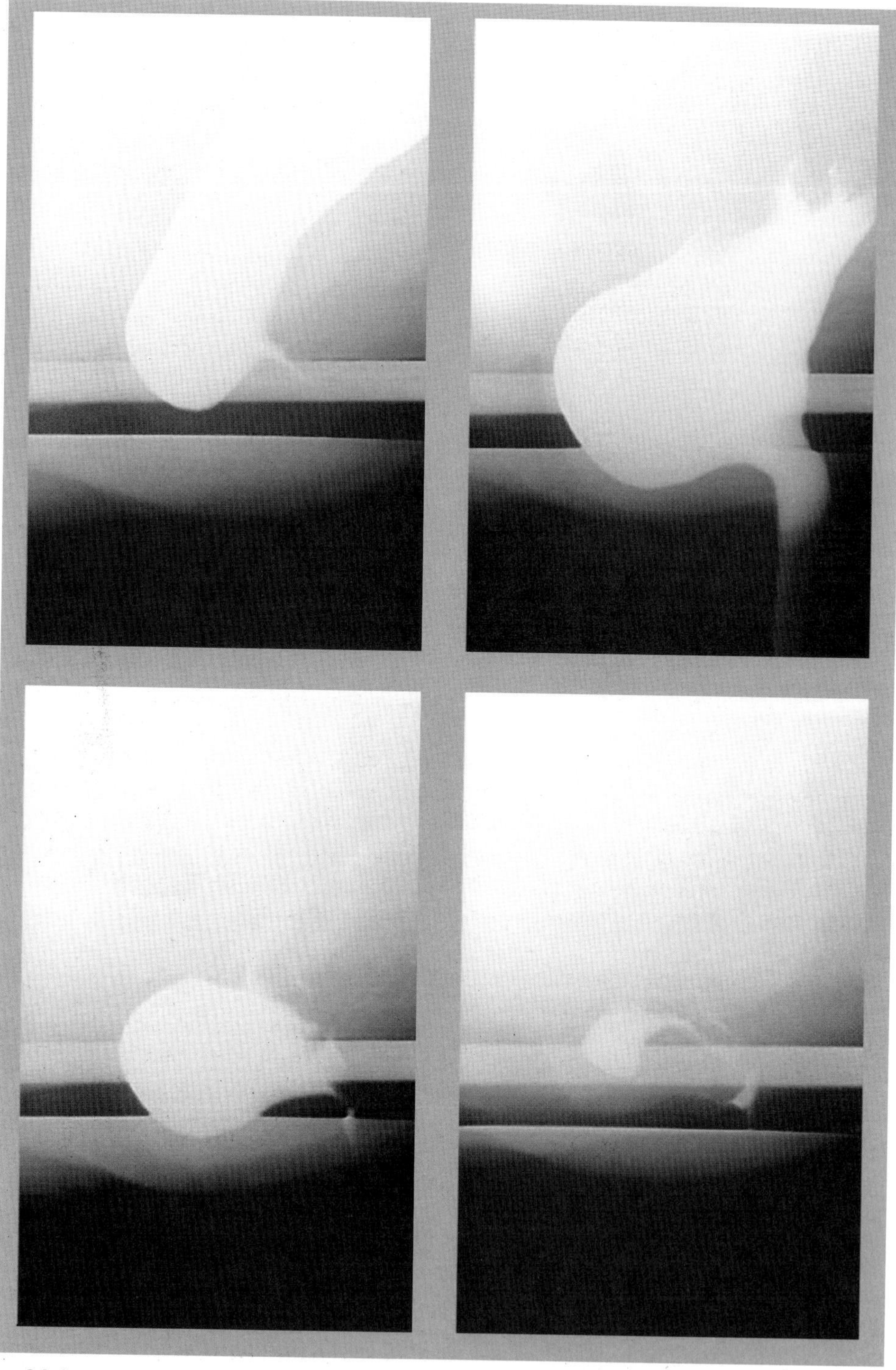

Figure 21.3 *Proctogram showing anterior rectocoele with trapping of contrast. The lower right image shows emptying of rectocoele after vaginal digitation.*

Table 21.2: Common drugs that induce constipation

Tricyclic antidepressants
MAO inhibitors
Anti-psychotics
Opiates
Anticonvulsants
Anti-parkinsonian agents
Antacids (aluminium- and calcium-containing ones)
Beta-blockers
Calcium channel antagonists
Diuretics
Iron

A psychogenic component to the patient's symptoms should be borne in mind. Some patients have been the victims of significant childhood physical and sexual abuse, and many find themselves in occupational or domestic circumstances which are a source of considerable anxiety and stress (Drossman et al., 1990). The association between stress and gastrointestinal motility is well established (Stam et al., 1997), and there is evidence that demonstrating to the patient the relationship between environmental triggers and subsequent development of symptoms can significantly aid management.

Diet

Dietary fibre is not usually effective in the management of severely constipated patients referred to hospital. Nevertheless, increasing dietary fibre to 30 gm (14.4 gm of crude fibre) is the simplest and cheapest preventive measure and should be used as the first-line treatment of chronic constipation in primary care. (Chaussade et al., 1989). To be most effective, it is probably best done by formal dietary advice and encouraging the patient to keep a bowel diary for a full month of treatment. However, 30 gm of fibre per day can prove difficult for some patients to consume – it amounts to four bowls of bran cereal or ten slices of wholemeal bread or twenty apples! Another problem is that dietary fibre only increases stool weight in proportion to the starting weight, and so the more severely constipated the patient the less effective the fibre will be. Furthermore, other variables – such as personality and vegetarianism – affect stool output as much as fibre, and so the role of dietary fibre remains questionable (Devroede et al., 1989).

A further limitation of augmenting dietary fibre is that it may provoke abdominal distension and flatulence in patients with slow transit constipation (Preston and Lennard-Jones, 1986) and incontinence in those with a megacolon.

Pharmacological options

There are many 'combination compounds' available to treat constipation, but for clarity a brief outline of the main classes of laxative is given here, classified by mode of action. Laxatives are 'contact' agents whose action depends upon exposure of the drug to the gut mucosa. They are, accordingly, unpredictable in their mode of action and tend to lose their effect with the passage of time.

Bulk-forming laxatives – e.g. ispaghula, methylcellulose, sterculia

This class comprises naturally-based compounds which are helpful only for those patients with mild symptoms who cannot obtain adequate dietary fibre. Their role is limited for the same reasons as described in the section on dietary fibre. In general, their place in the management of the chronic patient is restricted to improvement of bowel frequency rather than changes in stool consistency or the need to strain.

Stimulant laxatives – e.g. bisacodyl, senna, sodium picosulphate

This class of drugs are more suited to the management of chronic constipation, because their action is more predictable. The drugs enhance colonic motility and improve stool frequency and consistency (Marlett et al., 1987). Although there is no evidence of significant colonic histological or unwanted motility changes with chronic usage (i.e. a sluggish colon), it is usual to attempt to minimise usage to alternate days or every third day.

Faecal softeners – e.g. docusate sodium, liquid paraffin, arachis oil enema
These compounds can be taken either orally or rectally, but are of limited efficacy from the available clinical trials. Nevertheless, they are widely used and can cause side effects related to their detergent or organic chemical composition.

Osmotic laxatives – e.g. lactulose, magnesium sulphate, phosphate enema
Lactulose is a syrup derived from lactose, and acts as a laxative by lowering colonic pH through the generation of fatty acids and fermentation products (Florent et al., 1985). Achieving a clinically significant effect often requires large doses (of what is an expensive agent) and at least two or three days of treatment. Other frequently reported problems include the sweet taste, abdominal distension and flatulence.

Magnesium salts are more potent osmotic laxatives and have the attraction of being able to be taken in a titrated fashion, the intention being to obtain a semi-solid stool without urgency. The salts have an unpleasant taste and it can be hard to achieve the balance between insufficient dose and watery stool.

Prokinetic agents – e.g. erythromycin, and newer agents
Although erythromycin is a potent *upper intestinal* prokinetic (motility stimulant), the motilin analogue effects are not clinically relevant in enhancing *colonic* motility. Specific prokinetic drugs (such as prucalopride and tegaserod, which act via serotonin receptors) are in advanced stages of development as novel, specific and consistent enhancers of colonic motility. Previously, cisapride (another agent which acted on serotonin receptors) was used by some specialists as a prokinetic agent in those patients whose constipation failed to respond to laxatives. However, the drug has been withdrawn from clinical availability due to its potential to cause cardiac dysrhythmias.

Biofeedback

Details of the techniques and results of this behavioural therapy in chronic constipation are given in Chapter 22.

Surgical management

Constipation, as has already been made clear, is a complex disorder affecting the brain, spinal nerves, upper intestine, colon, enteric nerves and intestinal smooth muscle – it is not feasible that a one-off surgical intervention could significantly improve symptoms in a permanent fashion. Surgery for chronic constipation has traditionally been reserved for the most intractable cases, often with significant psychological distress, who have failed to respond to conventional management, and the poor success rates seen may in part reflect this fact. Case selection is therefore a crucial element in the selection of possible candidates for surgery. Colectomy has always been restricted to those patients with documented slow transit – no other physiological or radiological variable has proved accurate as a prognostic indicator.

Perianal procedures
Ano-rectal myectomy and puborectalis division have a success rate no greater than 25% in long-term follow-up studies. Slightly greater success is seen in selected patients undergoing repair of a rectocoele, in whom up to 50% experience some improvement of perineal symptoms.

Colectomy
Segmental resections, based on removal of the regions of the colon with greatest hold-up of radio-opaque markers on a transit study, has not proven to be any more effective than resecting any other 'normal' segment. The more com-

monly performed procedure is a subtotal colectomy and ileo-rectal anastomosis. Results of the long-term follow-up studies indicate a poor success rate of less than 50% (Kamm et al., 1988) with persisting constipation, abdominal pain and bloating. In addition to the high failure rate, there is a high frequency of complications – in particular diarrhoea, faecal incontinence, recurrent obstructive episodes and pelvic sepsis. Critical factors for success after colectomy appear to be the presence of slow transit and the absence of psychological morbidity and defaecatory inco-ordination.

Stoma formation

When a stoma is formed as a primary procedure for constipation, or in patients with neurological disease, the outcome can be excellent (van der Sijp et al., 1992). However, if the stoma is constructed as a salvage procedure after failed previous surgery, it is generally unhelpful. A stoma is not without its own possible complications (see Chapter 15).

Specific conditions

Megacolon is defined clinically as colonic dilatation in the absence of mechanical obstruction. Megacolon can be classified as either congenital (Hirschsprung's disease) or acquired (**acute** – Ogilvie's syndrome; **neurological** – Chaga's disease, chronic intestinal pseudo-obstruction; **myopathic** – scleroderma, amyloidosis). The term 'megabowel' implies dilatation of rectum and colon, whereas megacolon describes dilatation of only the abdominal colon. The frequent elongation of the colon seen in chronic constipation is **not** megacolon.

Idiopathic megabowel

This is an uncommon but important condition to consider in patients presenting with constipation, because the aim of management is quite distinct. It occurs equally in men and women and presentation is typically either in early childhood or early adult life (Kamm, 1993). Both groups present with intractable constipation, but in childhood the symptoms are typically of faecal impaction and soiling, whereas in young adults abdominal pain and no soiling are the norm. The soiling results from overflow due to impacted stool in the rectum, and the resulting fluid is able to leak out through a permanently open anal sphincter.

Anal sphincter dilatation may be evident on examination, in addition to the frequently palpable abdominal mass of a faecal bolus rising out of the pelvis. Investigation by enema contrast study may display (i) faecal loading, (ii) dilatation of the colon at the pelvic brim on X-ray (diameter >6.5 cm), (iii) absence of a 'narrowed segment' (see below) on lateral view, thereby excluding Hirschsprung's disease. Idiopathic megacolon can present as recurrent episodes of an acute abdomen due to a sigmoid volvulus (twisting of the sigmoid colon), and an instant contrast enema is invaluable in demonstrating this. Almost all cases of sigmoid volvulus occur in the context of a megabowel, but not all cases of megabowel present as volvulus. Unresolved volvulus is a surgical emergency.

Management of idiopathic megabowel commences with getting the colon empty (manual disimpaction may be required, but should be avoided if at all possible in view of the potential damage to what may already be a weakened anal sphincter). Thereafter a combination of osmotic laxatives (usually magnesium salts such as Epsom Salts titrated to obtain a 'porridgy' stool), habit training (to encourage regular attempts at bowel opening, usually after meals) and biofeedback (to ease defaecatory inco-ordination) should be strictly adhered to. Stimulant laxatives should be avoided, and patients should be encouraged to maintain a liquid intake of at least 2.5 litres per day. Occasionally suppositories or enemas may be needed if biofeedback has failed to correct an associated difficulty with evacuation. The patient needs to understand that the condition is lifelong and that successful management rests in their own hands.

For those patients in whom strict medical management fails, surgery remains an option. The goal, once again, is to obtain a 'porridgy' stool, and this may be achieved successfully by colectomy and ileo-rectal or ileoanal anastomosis or ileostomy. Other possible surgical procedures depend on the specific anatomy of the patient – a megarectum and normal colonic diameter involves resection of the rectum; for megacolon with normal rectal diameter an ileo-rectostomy is the operation of choice. With medical, and when necessary, surgical management, the outcome of megabowel is usually excellent, with over 90% of patients having normal bowel frequency.

Hirschsprung's disease

This is a congenital megacolon resulting from absence of intramural enteric nerve plexuses, or aganglionosis, affecting the distal colon. This absence of neural relaxation results in a narrow (non-relaxing) segment of the bowel, which is typically in the rectum or sigmoid colon. Stool is unable to cross the narrowed segment (Figure 21.4) and there is consequent dilatation of the colon proximally.

Hirschsprung's disease is a familial condition affecting 1 in 5,000 births, and affecting predominantly males (five times more often than females) (Passarge, 1967). There is an association with Down's syndrome and a variety of congenital anomalies. Presentation is usually as a neonate (with abdominal distension and absolute constipation), but rarely some may not come to medical attention until adult life. Presentation in childhood may be with malnutrition or anaemia, and in the older age group faecal impaction is the commonest symptom. The presence of overflow incontinence in a severely constipated patient should raise the possibility of idiopathic megabowel, as incontinence almost never occurs in Hirschsprung's. Abdominal examination reveals gross distension, and rigid sigmoidoscopy confirms an empty rectum.

Contrast studies are helpful in showing the hallmark narrow bowel segment in Hirschsprung's disease. Ano-rectal physiological testing for the presence of the recto-anal inhibitory reflex can obviate the need for full-thickness biopsy of the rectum. Inflation of a balloon in the rectum causes a reflex relaxation of the internal anal sphincter; this reflex is absent in Hirschsprung's patients due to the aganglionosis. If the reflex is equivocal, then biopsy of the rectum is required. Suction biopsy may not give sufficient depth of tissue to stain the neural plexuses, in which case full-thickness biopsy under anaesthetic is required. Some cases remain uncertain despite these investigations, in which case immunohistochemical techniques and expert pathological input may clarify the situation. Treatment is surgical, the principle being to excise or bypass the narrowed segment, for which there are a variety of techniques. Although the outcome is usually excellent, parents need to be advised that long-term soiling occurs in about 10% of patients (Kamm and Lennard-Jones, 1994).

References

Chaussade, S., Khyari, A., Roche, H., Garret, M., Gaudric, A., Couturier, D. and Guerre, J. (1989) Determination of total and segmental colonic transit time in constipated patients: results in 91 patients with a new simplified method. *Digestive Diseases and Sciences* **34**, 1168–1174.

Devroede, G., Bouchoucha, M. and Girard, G. (1989) Constipation, anxiety and personality: what comes first? In: Bueno, L., Collins, S. and Junior, J.L. (eds) *Stress and digestive motility*, pp. 55–60. London: John Libbey Eurotext.

Drossman, D.A., Leserman, J., Nachman, G., Li, Z.M., Gluck, H., Toomy, T.C. and Mitchell, C.M. (1990) Sexual and physical abuse in women with functional or organic gastrointestinal disorders *Annals of Internal Medicine* **113**, 828–833.

Evans, R.C., Kamm, M.A., Hinton, J.M. and Lennard-Jones, J.E. (1992) The normal range and a simple diagram for recording whole gut transit time. *International Journal of Colorectal Diseases* **7**, 15–17.

Florent, C., Flourie, B., Leblond, A., Rautureau, M., Bernier, J.J. and Rambaud, J.C. (1985) Influence of chronic lactulose ingestion on colonic metabolism of lactulose in man. *Journal of Clinical Investigation* **75**, 608–613.

Gattuso, J.M. and Kamm, M.A. (1994) Adverse effects of drugs used in the management of constipation and diarrhoea. *Drug Safety* 1994, **10**, 47–65.

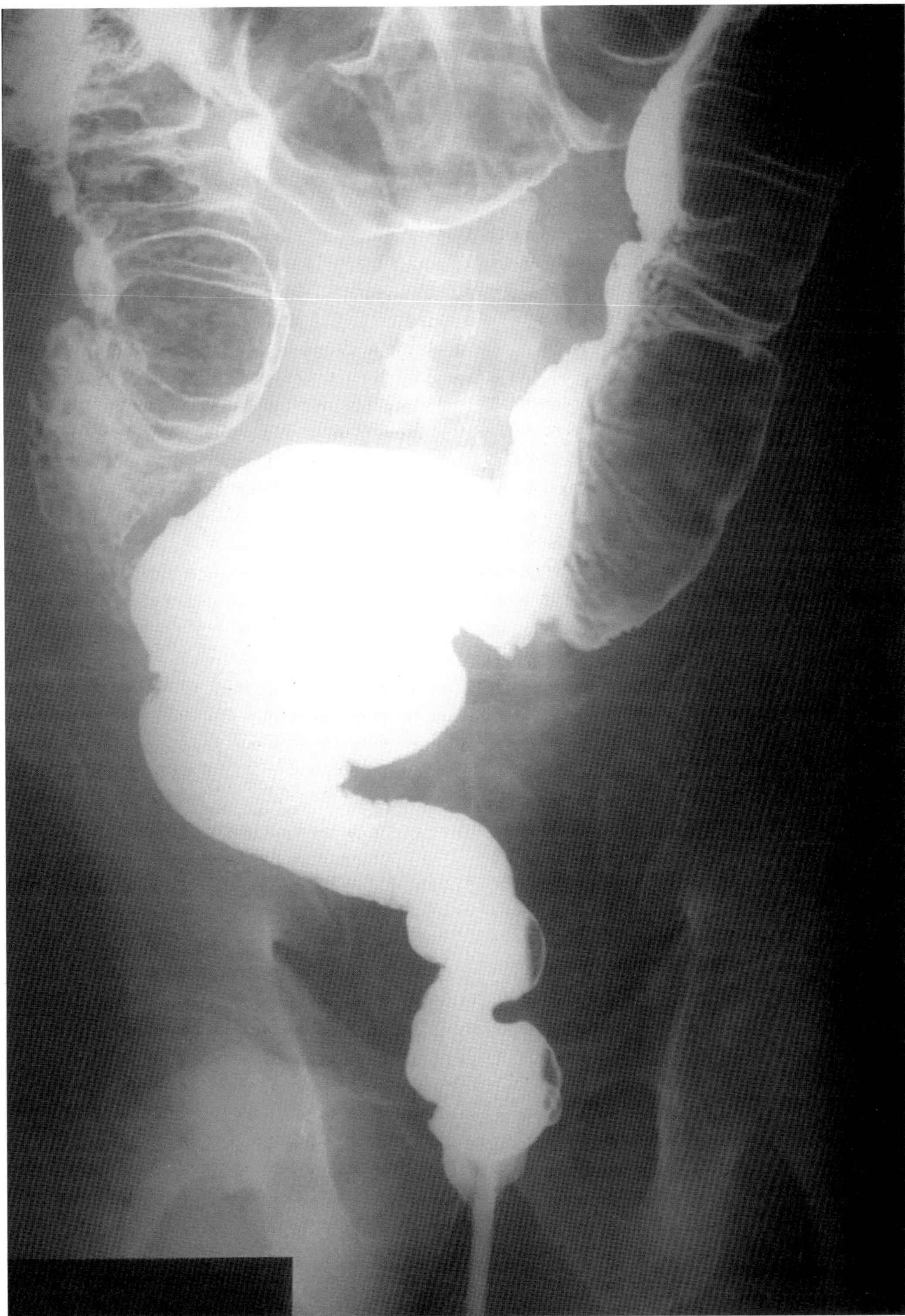

Figure 21.4 *Hirschsprung's disease with megacolon.*

Kamm, M.A. (1993) Investigation and management of megarectum and megacolon. *Hospital Update* **19**, 5, 280–286.

Kamm, M.A. and Lennard-Jones, J.E. (1994) *Constipation*. Petersfield: Wrightson Biomedical Publishing Ltd.

Kamm, M.A., Hawley, P.R. and Lennard-Jones, J.E. (1988) Outcome of colectomy for severe idiopathic constipation. *Gut* **29**, 969–973.

Klauser, A.G., Peyerl, C., Schinbleck, N.E. and Muller-Lissner, S.A. (1992) Nutrition and physical activity in chronic constipation. *European Journal of Gastroenterology and Hepatology* **4**, 227–233.

Marlett, J.A., Li, B.U.K., Patrow, C.J. et al. (1987) Comparative laxation of psyllium with and without senna in an ambulatory constipated population. *American Journal of Gastroenterology* **82**, 333–341.

Passarge, E. (1967) The genetics of Hirschsprung's disease. Evidence for heterogenous etiology and a study of sixty-three families. *New England Journal of Medicine* **276**, 138–141.

Preston, D.M. and Lennard-Jones, J.E. (1986) Severe chronic constipation of young women: 'idiopathic slow transit constipation'. *Gut* **27**, 41–48.

Stam, R., Akkermans, L.M.A. and Wiegant, V.M. (1997) Trauma and the gut: interactions between stressful experience and intestinal function. *Gut* **40**, 704–709.

Thompson, W.G., Longstreth, G.F., Drossman, D.A., Heaton, K.W., Irvine, E.J. and Muller-Lissner, S.A. (1999) Functional bowel disorders and functional abdominal pain. *Gut* **45** (Suppl. II); 43–47.

van der Sijp, J.R.M., Kamm, M.A., Evans, R.C. and Lennard-Jones, J.E. (1992) The results of stoma formation in severe idiopathic constipation. *European Journal of Gastroenterology and Hepatology* **4**, 137–140.

Wald, A, Hinds, J.P. and Camana, B.J. (1989) Psychological and physiological characteristics of patients with severe constipation. *Gastroenterology* **97**, 932–937.

Chapter 22

Behavioural and Biofeedback Therapy for Evacuation Disorders

Nicky Horton

Introduction

The term 'evacuation disorders' relates to a range of symptoms and conditions which cause difficulties with defaecation (Table 22.1). Normal defaecation is a complex process that requires ordered intestinal and colonic transit, normal ano-rectal sensation, and coordination of the ano-rectal reflexes with the anal sphincters. The external anal sphincter is voluntarily contracted to hold faeces until there is an appropriate time for defaecation. For evacuation, the external and internal anal sphincters relax in combination with increased intra-abdominal pressure caused by abdominal muscle contraction (Rieger et al, 1997).

Biofeedback is a re-education tool or a learning strategy, in which information concerning a normally subconscious physiological function is relayed to the patient in real time. The patient may therefore learn to bring about a change in this function. The theoretical basis for biofeedback is 'learning through reinforcement' (Miller, 1968). Behavioural therapy may be a more appropriate name for this treatment.

Table 22.1: Conditions treated by evacuation biofeedback

Idiopathic constipation
Constipation-predominant irritable bowel syndrome
Rectal prolapse
Rectocele
Megarectum / megacolon
Solitary rectal ulcer syndrome
Evacuation difficulties with an ileoanal pouch

Idiopathic constipation is the most frequent reason for referral for evacuation biofeedback therapy and is described as an infrequent or incomplete evacuation not caused by disease or medication (see Chapter 21 for further information). For many patients with constipation, normal bowel emptying has been disrupted and the defaecatory muscles no longer coordinate in the correct way to allow a 'normal' bowel action to occur.

Treatment options for many of these patients are limited. Biofeedback therapy is often recommended in those patients who have become resistant to laxatives and require increasingly larger doses with decreasing effect. The results of surgery for idiopathic constipation are variable. A study by Kamm et al. (1988) reviewed 44 patients following colectomy performed to treat the symptoms of intractable constipation. The results showed that following colectomy 22 patients had a normal bowel frequency but 17 patients now suffered from diarrhoea and 5 patients had persistent or recurrent constipation. Two thirds of patients still experienced abdominal pain, and some still required laxatives. As a result, biofeedback has become a first-line treatment for severe idiopathic constipation in the author's hospital (Storrie, 1997). About two thirds of patients benefit from biofeedback therapy, and this is largely maintained on medium-term follow-up (Chiotakakou-Faliakou et al, 1998).

No studies of evacuation biofeedback have described the methods used in detail. This chapter describes the treatment protocols used in a tertiary referral centre which sees approximately 700 new patients for biofeedback each year.

Aims of treatment

The aims of evacuation biofeedback therapy are to improve coordination of the defaecatory muscles and improve defaecatory control without the use of laxatives, suppositories and enemas. The objective is that patients report an improvement in their bowel symptoms. The frequency of bowel actions is not important, but rather whether the patient feels that their symptoms are improved. It is important that the patient feels comfortable after each bowel action and that this comfort is maintained until the next bowel action. The patient has to take responsibility for their treatment and realise that to improve their symptoms they need to do the defaecatory exercises as instructed. The therapist can give advice and information, but it is up to the patient to take responsibility for their treatment and change their current functioning.

Prior to biofeedback therapy commencing, most patients will have an abdominal transit study (Evans et al., 1992). All laxatives, suppositories and enemas are stopped during this test. There is no difference to the outcome of the biofeedback therapy between patients with slow or normal colonic transit (Emmanuel et al., 2001).

Patterns of presentation

A diverse group of patients present to the evacuation biofeedback clinic at St Mark's Hospital. Many patients have no identifiable precursors to their constipation. They are predominantly women. Approximately 10% of patients are men.

Some patients have been raped or sexually abused in the past, which may have precipitated their bowel disorder (Drossman et al., 1990). These people disassociate from the pelvic area; they cut themselves off from their muscles from the waist down and therefore have problems with opening their bowels.

Patients with eating disorders may present in gastrointestinal clinics with constipation. This group of patients, whether they are anorexic or bulimic, do not do well with this type of therapy because the psychopathology underlying the bowel problem needs to be addressed before any other treatment is tried.

Some people are very tense and find it hard to relax to open their bowels, others are too busy to go to the toilet and defer defaecation so frequently that they 'lose' this urge. There is a group of patients who have a dislike of the toilet. This may be from a childhood experience or because it is always a struggle to open their bowels. Some people are very particular about their bowel habits and spend far too much time in the toilet. There may be additional obsessional personality traits. However, with some individuals their regular bowel habit has altered, for example following childbirth or surgery, and there appears to be no abnormal psychopathology.

Idiopathic constipation and constipation-predominant irritable bowel syndrome

Patients who suffer from constipation will report a number of symptoms, such as less frequent bowel actions, incomplete evacuation, straining at stool, abdominal distension and pain. Irritable bowel syndrome can cause alternating constipation and diarrhoea. It is important to inform the patient that biofeedback treatment is aimed at improving their defaecatory function and unfortunately will not eradicate their irritable bowel syndrome, although it may improve some of their symptoms.

Rectal prolapse

A rectal prolapse may be caused or exacerbated by excessive straining. A rectal prolapse can either refer to prolapse of the rectal lining (mucosa) or a complete prolapse of the rectum. Biofeedback can teach these patients to evacuate effectively without straining, and for some this will stop the prolapse from occurring. Others will need surgery, but even these patients can benefit from the training, since if straining continues there is an increased risk of the prolapse recurring after surgery.

Rectocoele

A rectocoele is a weakness of the anterior rectal wall. The rectal wall herniates into the vagina. This herniation is like a 'pocket' which can bulge into the vagina. A rectocoele can cause difficulty with effective rectal emptying because stools can become trapped in this 'pocket'. Common symptoms include difficult defaecation, incomplete evacuation, and vaginal discomfort. Such symptoms can lead to numerous attempts to defaecate. The sensation of incomplete evacuation means increased straining, which can exacerbate the rectocoele and therefore worsen the problem. Often these women have to digitate vaginally or rectally or both, or apply pressure on the perineum or around the anus, to aid evacuation. Biofeedback therapy can help reduce the severity of these symptoms in some women (Mimura et al., 2000).

Surgery may be required to repair a rectocoele, especially if it is large and fails to empty completely. Biofeedback therapy is a good way of re-educating the patient on how to use their defaecatory muscles properly, which should help avoid renewed straining after surgery.

Megarectum and megacolon

A megarectum is a grossly dilated rectum. The colon, however, is usually of normal diameter. The condition often begins in childhood or adolescence. Symptoms of a megarectum include a delay in feeling rectal contents, which can lead to faecal impaction, loss of normal reflexes causing soiling, and diarrhoea due to the liquid stool passing around the hard stool in the rectum.

These patients require disimpaction before any treatment can commence. This may be as an inpatient, and normally involves using phosphate enemas until the rectum is empty, although occasionally disimpaction under anaesthetic is needed. To avoid further impaction the patient should be prescribed a powerful osmotic laxative such as magnesium sulphate. The dose can be titrated so that the patient has two or three loose bowel actions each day. Some patients can achieve spontaneous and satisfactory bowel actions without laxatives following biofeedback therapy (Mimura et al., unpublished data).

A megacolon is wider than a normal colon. The passage of waste through the megacolon will be slower than through a normal colon. The condition often begins in adulthood. Symptoms of a megacolon include abdominal pain and bloating, heartburn, and no 'urge' to open bowels.

Solitary rectal ulcer syndrome

Solitary rectal ulcer syndrome is a condition where there is a benign ulceration of the rectum. It is a relatively uncommon condition. The cause is unknown, but these patients seem to have a behavioural disorder (Vaizey et al., 1997). Excessive straining, prolonged periods of time spent in the toilet, digitating per rectum to extract stool, and constipation may be contributory factors.

Patients commonly experience a frequent urge to defaecate and make repeated attempts to open their bowels. Often the evacuation feels incomplete so they strain excessively and digitate to aid evacuation. The more attempts that are made to defaecate, the more the ulcer is aggravated. Blood and mucus are often passed with stool, or on their own with excessive straining. The ulcer gives a 'false' urge, and sensation of incomplete evacuation. This is a vicious circle which is hard to stop. Biofeedback therapy can reduce the attempts at defaecation and improve symptoms (Vaizey et al., 1997), although the benefit deteriorates with time (Malouf et al., 2001).

Evacuation difficulties with an ileoanal pouch

People with ulcerative colitis or other bowel disease may undergo surgical construction of an internal ileoanal pouch. Some patients experience difficulties with pouch emptying. This may be due to inability to utilise the correct defaecatory muscles, especially as prior to the pouch some patients have had a stoma or severe diarrhoea and have therefore 'forgotten' how to use these muscles. They may report incomplete evacuation, pain in the pouch and abdomen, and trapped wind in the pouch. Also, patients with a pouch frequently report frequency of defaecation, which may be related to a loose stool consistency but also because the pouch is not emptying effectively. Some patients have severe emptying problems and therefore need to use a Medina rectal catheter to aid evacuation. The catheter is a rigid plastic tube inserted into the pouch by the patient. The liquid stool then drains from the pouch via the catheter. Sometimes the stool is too thick to pass through the catheter. The patient may need to irrigate the pouch with water through the catheter, which will make it easier to pass.

Table 22.2: Bowel evacuation assessment questions

- When did the bowel problems start?
- What is the main bowel problem at the present time?
- Does the patient ever feel an urge to have bowels open?
- How often do they pass a motion?
- What is the consistency of the stool?
- Does the patient pass blood or mucus?
- Does the patient digitate per rectum / vagina or both to help aid defaecation?
- Does the patient feel that evacuation is incomplete?
- Does the patient strain?
- Does the patient experience bloating?
- Does the patient use laxatives, e.g. enemas / suppositories. How much, how often?
- What is the patient's diet like i.e. types of fibre / regular meals?
- Previous surgery, medical problems?
- Medication?
- Their relationship status: married / in relationship / single. Does the bowel problem affect this relationship?
- Pregnancies: history of miscarriage / termination, any problems at birth i.e. episiotomies / forceps / known tear?
- Is the patient working: their occupation. If not working is this due to bowel difficulties?
- How does the patient perceive their bowel problem in relation to everyday life?
- Does the patient feel that stress affects / contributes to their bowel problem?

The biofeedback session

A course of biofeedback therapy consists of a total of five appointments, usually at four-weekly intervals. The patient sees the same therapist at each visit. The components of a biofeedback therapy session include taking a detailed bowel assessment (see Table 22.2), health education, defaecatory muscle exercises, and psychosocial support. There is a large behavioural element to this therapy. The biofeedback programme is very strict and patients have to adhere to it or they may be discharged. The emphasis of this therapy is for the patient to take control of their bowel function again, without relying on medication to make the bowel work.

Assessment

When did the bowel problems start?
It is important to identify whether this problem is lifelong or recent, and how their life has altered to accommodate their symptoms. If recent, did anything precede this change in bowel habit? An unexplained change in bowel habit needs medical investigation (see Chapter 7).

What is the main bowel problem at the present time?

The therapist needs to ascertain what is the patient's greatest concern. Some patients may identify pain and bloating but others may dislike taking laxatives and therefore have sought help.

Do you ever feel an urge to open your bowels? If you do feel an urge, do you feel it in your tummy or back passage?
The therapist needs to identify if the patient has an urge to defaecate and what occurs if they respond. Some patients may have a bowel action in a response to an urge to defaecate, whereas others may sit on the toilet and be unsuccessful. Other patients report no urge to defaecate unless they take laxatives. If patients respond to an abdominal urge to defaecate, their attempt may be unsuccessful. However, an urge felt in the rectum is more likely to lead to a successful bowel action. This question provides the therapist with an insight into the patient's perception of bowel function.

How often do you pass a motion? What has been the longest number of days you've passed nothing?
The therapist needs to ascertain the patient's present bowel routine. Do they pass a stool spontaneously or only after taking laxatives, or both? Some patients report no bowel actions for several weeks, although on closer questioning it is elicited that they have in fact passed a small amount of stool. They discount these bowel actions because they only pass a small amount of stool and the evacuation feels unsatisfactory.

What is the consistency of the stool? Are the stools hard or soft?
Patients with slow transit constipation or incomplete evacuation may pass hard small stools. Patients who report frequency of bowel actions may pass softer, unformed stools because they are continuously straining, which can increase colonic transit time.

Do you pass blood or mucus? If blood is passed is it bright or dark? Is it mixed in with the stool, does it drip into the toilet, or on the paper when wiping? Is mucus passed with motions, or on its own?
A patient may pass bright red blood if they have a fissure, haemorrhoid or solitary rectal ulcer syndrome. Dark blood mixed with stool may indicate the presence of a carcinoma and require further investigation (see Chapter 7). Patients with solitary rectal ulcer syndrome, rectal prolapse and frequency may report passing excessive mucus and passive mucoid soiling.

Do you feel that you've emptied your bowel properly? Do you put a finger in your back passage or vagina, or both, to help you empty your bowels? Do you do this to start your bowel action, complete your bowel action or both?
The patient may report the sensation of incomplete evacuation of stool because they still feel distended abdominally. This sensation does not necessarily mean the patient has not emptied their bowel effectively, and therefore further straining to defaecate should be avoided. Patients with solitary rectal ulcer syndrome, rectal prolapse or rectocoele may have a continuous sensation of incomplete evacuation of stool in their rectum. Further attempts to defaecate will exacerbate this symptom.

The therapist needs to identify whether patients are digitating vaginally or rectally to assist defaecation. Some patients press on the perineum or around the anus to aid defaecation. Some women with a rectocoele digitate vaginally to aid evacuation. Patients should be reassured this will not weaken or damage their muscles. Patients that digitate rectally may irritate the lining of the rectum and should be advised to avoid this behaviour.

Do you strain? How long do you sit on the toilet? Does straining help?
Straining normally indicates difficulty passing stool, which may relate to poor propulsive force and/or paradoxical contraction. Many patients strain repeatedly throughout the day, and/or spend too long sitting on the toilet in an attempt to defaecate. Straining can lead to conditions such as haemorrhoids, solitary rectal ulcer syndrome and rectal prolapse. Patients should be advised to limit the time they spend attempting to defaecate to no more than ten minutes.

Do you have pain? Is it constant or intermittent? What triggers the pain? Does anything help ease the pain?
Many patients will experience pain associated with their bowel problem. It is important to identify where the pain occurs, and whether the pain is intermittent or constant. The therapist should ask if anything triggers their pain. There could be more than one factor that may trigger or intensify a patient's pain, and the therapist may be able to advise on how to avoid these triggers. Some patients may report pain prior to opening their bowels and gain relief following a bowel action. Some may report pain after eating and therefore try to eat less. It is important for the therapist to explain that the pain they experience after eating may be an indication of peristalsis. The therapist must identify what the patient does to try to relieve their pain, and whether this is affective. The patient may take analgesics to try to ease their pain, which may be exacerbating their bowel problem. The therapist will need to discuss reducing or stopping constipating analgesics if possible.

Do you have bloating? Does anything trigger this?
Bloating is a common symptom for patients with bowel dysfunction. The therapist should identify with the patient possible causes for this symptom and suggest ways for them to avoid these. Some patients report certain foods or stress as a trigger for their bloating. It may be possible for the patient to avoid such foods, and avoid certain stress triggers. Some patients report abdominal distension that requires several different clothes sizes to accommodate their expanding waistline. Other patients feel 'full' and uncomfortable constantly, and report a decrease in appetite because of this.

Do you use laxatives/enemas/suppositories? How much, how often?
Identify how the patient uses their medication and the effectiveness of their regimen. The therapist should ask if they take their medication regularly or after a certain period of time, or as a 'rescue' remedy. Some patients may take a combination of laxatives, enemas and suppositories, including over-the-counter or 'herbal' remedies (many of which contain powerful laxatives such as senna). If patients don't take anything, the therapist should ask whether they have used anything in the past, and with what effect.

What is your diet like, e.g. types of fibre/regular meals? Are you following a special diet?
It is important to ascertain whether the patient eats regularly. Regular eating is important for a healthy digestive system and vital for general wellbeing. Some patients avoid eating because they feel the more they eat the more they need to defaecate. The therapist should reassure the patient that this is normal and that eating stimulates peristalsis. The therapist should elicit if the patient eats a balanced diet, with a combination of different sources of fibre. Some patients may be eating a special diet and the therapist needs to identify if this is due to their bowel complaint or for another reason.

Previous surgery, medical problems, current medications
Identify any other general health problems. The therapist should identify if the patient is taking any regular medication and whether this may affect the patient's bowel complaint. The therapist may be able to advise alternative medications that do not affect the bowel. The patient may have an ongoing medical condition, such as a gynaecological problem, that may be exacerbating their bowel complaint. Some patients may have a history of previous abdominal or rectal surgery. The therapist should identify whether this was performed because of the bowel condition or whether this preceded, or exacerbated, their bowel condition.

Relationship status: married/in relationship/single. Does the bowel problem affect this relationship?
The therapist should ascertain if the patient is in a relationship and whether the partner is aware of the bowel difficulties, and how sympathetic and supportive he or she may be. Some patients report that their bowel symptoms affect their sex life. Some patients may find sex painful, or avoid sex because of their bowel condition.

Patients sometimes find it difficult to discuss such matters and will not volunteer this information. It is important for the therapist to broach the subject.

Pregnancies: history of miscarriage, termination, any problems at birth e.g.. episiotomies / forceps / known tear
It is important for the therapist to identify if the patient has had any difficulties in this area, and whether any of the above caused or affected the bowel complaint.

Are you working? Occupation. If not working is this due to bowel difficulties?
Identify if the patient works outside the house, whether this employment is full or part time, and whether it is regular hours or shift work. Some patients find it hard to establish a good bowel routine if they are working irregular hours. The therapist should ascertain if the patient enjoys their work, and whether it is stressful. Some patients report an increase in their bowel symptoms due to a dislike of their job and stress at work. Some patients may not be in employment and the therapist should identify if this is due to their bowel complaint, or for other reasons.

How does the patient perceive their bowel problem in relation to everyday life?
The therapist should identify what life is like for the patient. Some patients feel their bowel complaint prevents them pursuing certain activities and feel very restricted because of this. However, other patients 'get on with life' and don't allow their bowel complaint to restrict their enjoyment.

Does the patient feel that stress affects / contributes to their bowel problem?
The therapist should identify any areas of stress in the patient's life, and whether this stress causes or contributes to their bowel complaint. Some patients can identify a direct link with stress and their bowel symptoms, whereas other patients do not associate their bowel complaint with stress. The therapist may be able to identify stress factors and begin to make links with the possible broader psychological issues that may be at the root of the patient's bowel complaint.

Health education

The basic function of the digestive tract is explained using simple diagrams (Figures 22.1 a, b and c, overleaf). Few patients actually understand what happens to food when it enters the body, and how stools are formed. Test results can be explained at this point. If a patient has slow gut transit it is important to stress that the movement in the bowel is 'slow', not that the bowel does not function at all. Patients must also understand that they will not necessarily have a bowel action each day. They may only pass small, hard pellets once every 1–2 weeks, or less. An explanation is given as to why pellet-shaped stools occur, using the analogy of the transition of a grape to a raisin. A grape is soft and plump because it is full of water; the longer that stools stay in the colon the more that the water in them is absorbed, so they become smaller, harder and drier like a raisin that is dehydrated and smaller due to its lack of water. Therefore patients who have infrequent bowel actions will generally pass less stool. Patients need to understand why this occurs so that they are less likely to become concerned.

Many patients will have been told to increase their fibre intake as a way of improving their bowel condition. This may work in some cases, but rarely works well for those with severe chronic constipation. If a patient has slow gut transit, increased fibre intake merely adds bulk which exacerbates the problem, and excessive gases will increase abdominal distension. Decreasing dietary fibre may help relieve symptoms of abdominal distension and abdominal pain. Patients are advised to avoid wholemeals / wholegrains, dried fruit and nuts, muesli, bran, porridge, sprouts, broccoli and cabbage. To maintain a balance, fibre can be found from other sources such as fresh fruits and other vegetables. Patients should be advised to eat regularly, since they frequently reduce their food intake in the hope of reducing abdominal distension. Some find it helpful to eat little and often rather than one large meal per day. Although dietary advice is helpful it is a small component of this therapy.

Medication

All patients are required to stop taking all laxatives at the start of treatment. If patients continue to take laxatives it is more difficult to retrain the defaecatory muscles. The aim is for the patient to be able to achieve a satisfactory bowel action without the use of any medication. Patients may be apprehensive about stopping laxatives, but should be reassured that the situation is being monitored over the course of the biofeedback therapy. They can use glycerin suppositories as a 'rescue' if they haven't passed anything for four or five days. Even if only one small pellet is passed, this counts as a bowel action and no suppositories are allowed. It is important for patients to understand that initially they will pass less than they did when they were taking laxatives, but however small the stool is, the colon is working. Realistically they may feel

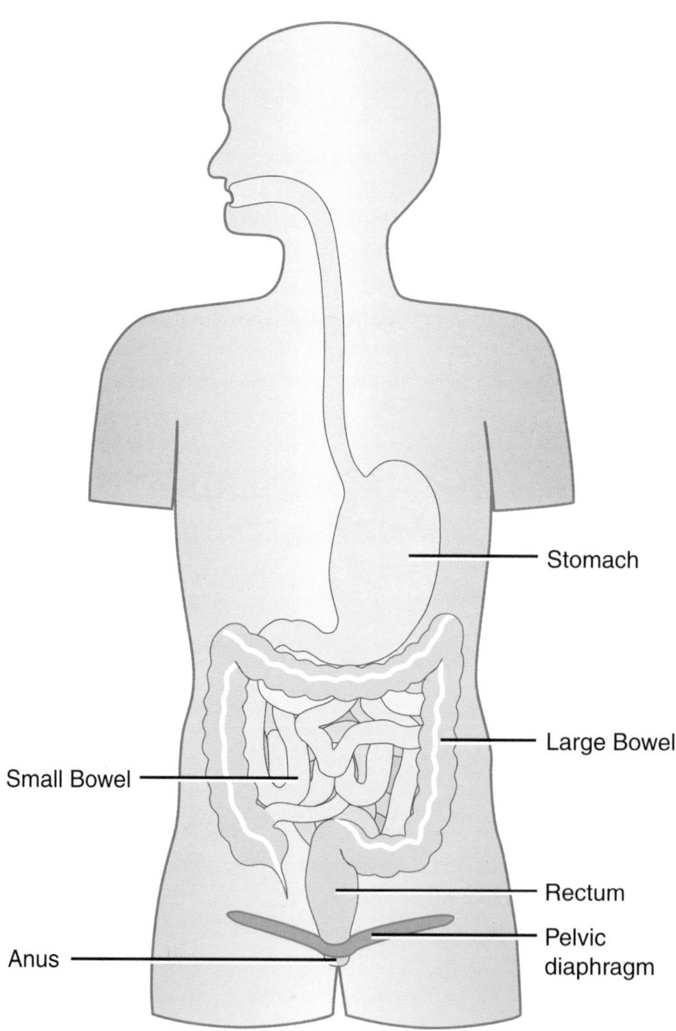

Figure 22.1a *Patient-teaching diagrams.*

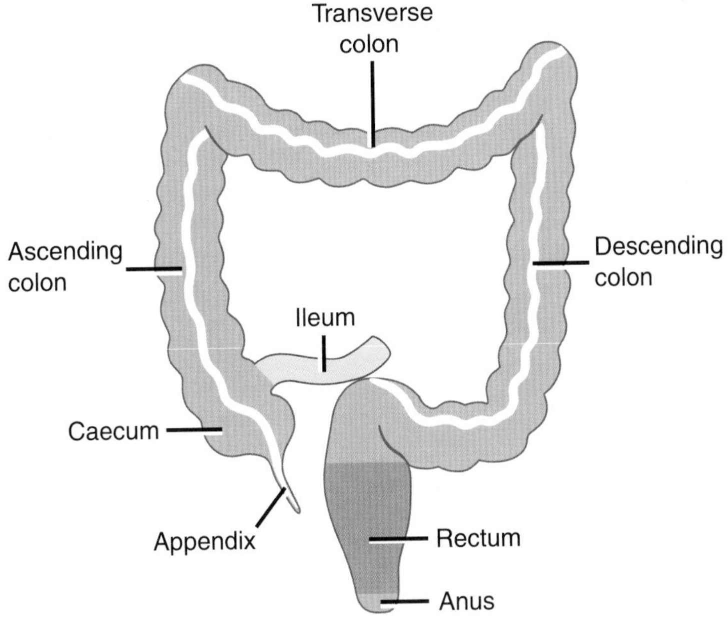

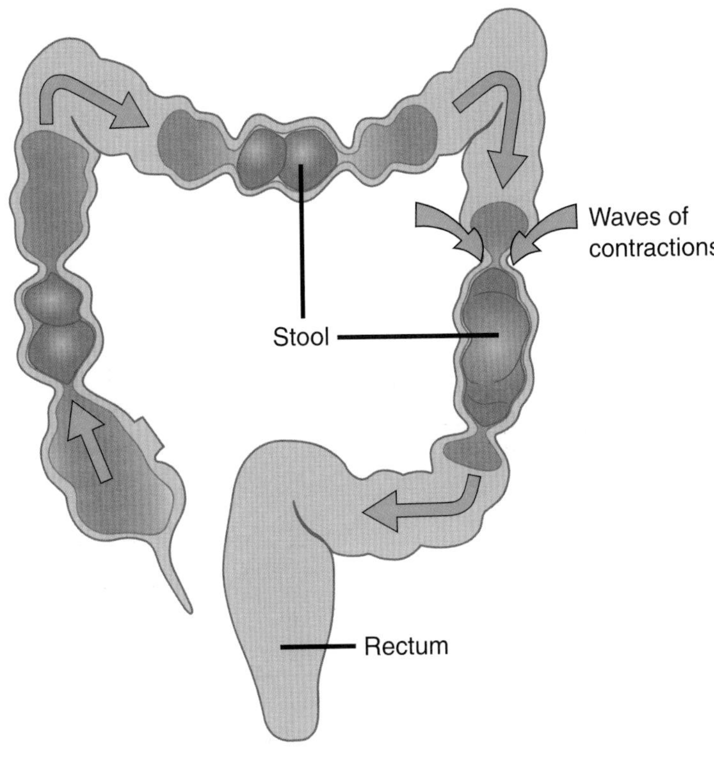

Figures 22.1 b,c

worse before any benefit is felt – they should be informed of this as they may discontinue treatment, thinking their condition is deteriorating.

Some patients may need to continue using suppositories after treatment. Suppositories are acceptable because they work locally in the rectum and aid evacuation by softening, lubricating and slightly stimulating the rectal mucosa. Patients with a megarectum may still require magnesium sulphate to maintain a porridgey type stool.

Defaecatory muscle exercises

Prior to starting the exercises a patient is asked how they sit on the toilet to defaecate. Patients often try a range of positions, including lying in the bath, to assist defaecation. They are taught to lean forwards with their arms on their lap and shoulders relaxed (Figure 22.2). Some patients find it helpful to raise their feet on a block or stool.

When the patient is examined they lie on a couch in the left or right lateral position, facing the therapist. They are covered with a sheet to maintain dignity. Once informed consent is given, a balloon is inserted into the rectum and inflated with 50 ml of air (Figure 8.5, page 75). This simulates a stool in the rectum and the urge to defaecate, so the patient has something to work with. The therapist can manually assess what the patient can and cannot do with their muscles, by holding on to the end of the balloon. Initially the patient is asked to contract the external anal sphincter as if they were 'holding on' or deferring defaecation. This demonstrates to the patient and the therapist that he or she can control the muscles. Then they are asked to expel the balloon. The majority of patients demonstrate inco-ordination of their defaecatory muscles. Specifically they may demonstrate the following:

Poor propulsion: The patient holds their breath and strains, often tensing head, neck and shoulders. This straining may result in a bowel action but the patient is unlikely to evacuate completely, and straining can lead to other anorectal problems such as haemorrhoids.

Paradoxical contraction: The patient contracts the external anal sphincter when trying to expel the balloon, instead of relaxing it. This makes it more difficult to evacuate stools on the toilet, and may lead to retrograde peristalsis and slower transit (Klauser et al., 1990).

The patient may demonstrate one or both of these problems. At this point in the initial assessment the patient may ask why they are demonstrating inco-ordination of their defaecatory muscles. This may occur following abdominal or perineal or anal surgery (e.g. gynaecological or colorectal procedures), when patients may develop bad habits during defaecation. Initially it may be painful to have a bowel action, and the patient may tense the external sphincter instead of relaxing it. Some may compromise the way in which they push, to protect their surgical incision. This inco-ordination may continue once the patient has recovered. However, it may also occur following childbirth. They may feel pain in the abdominal and/or perineal area, irrespective of the mode of delivery. This pain may cause inco-ordination, which again continues after the pain has eased.

For other patients there is a psychological reason for lack of defaecatory co-ordination. As already mentioned, patients with a history of abuse can completely cut themselves off from their pelvic region, and as a result may demonstrate inco-ordination of their defaecatory muscles. They are no longer able to associate themselves with these muscles. These patients tend to demonstrate paradoxical contraction.

In many clinics biofeedback therapy normally involves using electromyography (EMG) as a visual aid to retrain the patient's muscles. The patient has electrodes placed around the anus or intra-anally and these convey muscle activity to a computer screen. The patient is then able to change how they use their muscles by watching the screen. The EMG machine only records what the external anal sphincter is doing, i.e. whether it is relaxing appropriately when the patient attempts to expel the balloon. If patients demonstrate poor propulsion but relax their external anal sphincter correctly, the EMG

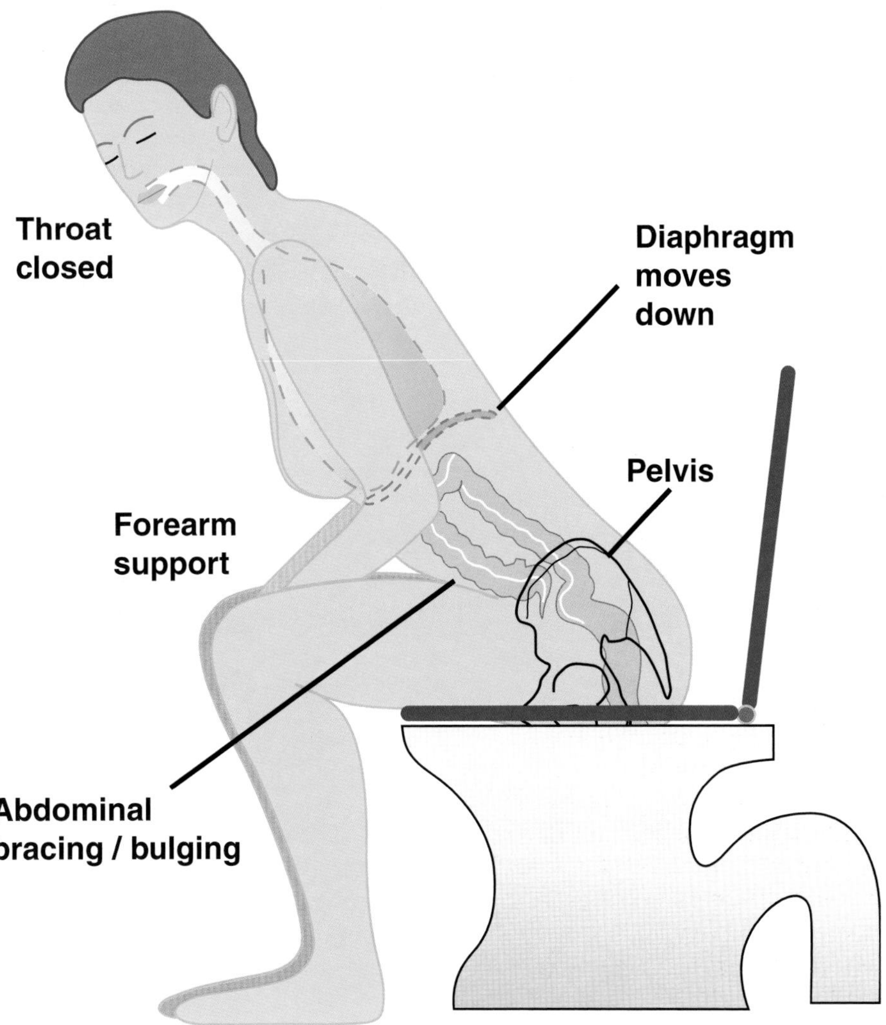

Figure 22.2

machine will not demonstrate any abnormality, and so is of no use to this group. Because of the variety of evacuation disorders treated with biofeedback, less than a third of our patients demonstrate paradoxical contraction at initial assessment. This has meant that the treatment has evolved and we no longer find the EMG machine helpful in our practice. Use of EMG with a visual display has been found not to make a difference to the outcome of biofeedback (Koutsomanis et al., 1995).

Teaching the exercises

The patient is advised to sit correctly on the toilet and relax their shoulders, arms and legs. They should breath normally, and not hold their breath.

The following two exercises can be taught.

The 'Brace'

An effective way for the patient to locate the abdominal oblique muscles needed to brace, is to place their hands either side of their waist and cough. Their waist should widen and become barrel-shaped.

They are then instructed to slowly brace outwards (widen the waist, without coughing) and when fully braced, push/propel from the waist backwards and downwards into the back passage at an angle as if 'skiing' on a toilet. This should avoid pushing into the vagina. They then relax for one second, very slightly (i.e. maintain the level of pressure with the brace muscles but do not push with them) and brace outwards and push downwards again. This should be repeated several times. They should then relax completely. Then repeat the above.

The 'Lift' (Table 22.3)
First the patient should imagine they are going to have an accident in a public place and so have to defer defaecation by telling them to 'hold on'. At this the patient will tighten their external anal sphincter. This exercise is taught using the analogy of a lift. When relaxed, the external anal sphincter is the equivalent of a lift resting on the first floor. In tightening the external sphincter, this is the equivalent of the lift moving upwards. This is a good way of demonstrating to the patient which muscle to focus on. The patient is advised that during defaecation they should use their anal sphincter muscles in the opposite way, i.e. relax and take the lift down to the ground floor and then to the basement. Once the patient understands which muscle to use, they need to focus on relaxing this muscle.

Table 22.3: The lift exercise

1) Imagine your back passage is a lift, resting on the first floor.
2) Slowly push the lift down to ground floor, down to basement, down to cellar.
3) Take the lift down as far as it will go.
4) If you relax for a second do not allow your lift to rise.
5) When the lift has come down as far as possible push your waist out wide and channel the strength from your waist down to your back passage.

The exercises teach the patient to correctly co-ordinate their defaecatory muscles. This enables them to achieve an effective bowel action and therefore relieve any symptoms. It is in effect 'going to the toilet correctly' and should not be viewed as something separate to this. The aim of the exercise routine is to teach the patient to:

1) Make time to go to the toilet every day
2) Sit correctly on the toilet
3) Relax before opening bowels
4) 'Brace' or widen the waist for effective propulsion
5) Relax the external anal sphincter instead of squeezing it.

An individual routine is devised which is to be followed until the next appointment. The exercise is given in written form to reinforce what was learnt at the first session. A common starting point is five to ten minutes twice a day.

Biofeedback protocols

The exercises and routine are modified slightly for patients with different evacuation disorders. The routines for the main syndromes are outlined here.

Idiopathic constipation, constipation-predominant irritable bowel syndrome, megarectum / megacolon

The focus is to increase the frequency of bowel actions, improve evacuation, and establish a good bowel routine.

- Patients must practice their exercise each day at a similar time. This will help establish a routine. Many patients with constipation will only attempt to open their bowels after taking laxatives or when they get the urge, so this may mean that attempts are infrequent.
- The patient should sit on the toilet about 30 minutes after breakfast (or evening meal). Eating will stimulate peristalsis via the gastro-colic response, which may lead to an urge to defaecate. Regardless of an urge being present, or whether anything is passed, it is important for patients to keep to this routine.

The patient is advised to sit on the toilet for about 10 minutes in total. During this time the patient will 'practice' the coordination exercise the therapist has given them. The exercise should teach the patient to avoid straining and holding their breath whilst opening their bowels. This time allows the patient to focus and establish a routine, so that they get used to sitting on the toilet at a similar time each day.

- Regular practising should also stimulate the bowel to work more effectively and may lead to improved colonic transit (Emmanuel et al., 2001). It also enables the patient to improve the coordination of their defaecatory muscles, which will help them evacuate more effectively.

Case history: constipation

Tina, aged 31, was referred from a consultant physician with longstanding constipation. She had been constipated since childhood, but her symptoms had been more severe eighteen months prior to referral. She felt this was due to stress at work. A transit study showed slow colonic transit. She said her main bowel problems were the pain and bloating she experienced. She was planning on getting married and wanted to be well for her wedding.

Bowel assessment

- Tina opened her bowels 3 to 4 times daily
- Stools were soft and porridgey
- She passed mucus with her stools
- She digitated per rectum to aid evacuation
- She had a sensation of incomplete evacuation
- She had lower abdominal pain and bloating
- She took 50 senna tablets each night
- She was eating a high-fibre diet.

Tina demonstrated no propulsion at initial examination.

Programme set

1) Practice 'brace/pump' exercise daily on the toilet
2) Stop laxatives, use glycerin suppositories if bowels not opened for 3–4 days
3) Eat 'little and often', and reduce fibre intake.

After five appointments, at monthly intervals.

- She opened her bowels once every 3 days
- She passed soft, formed stools
- She no longer digitated per rectum
- She experienced much less pain and bloating
- She did not take any laxatives, but occasionally used glycerin suppositories.

Tina was discharged two years ago, has since got married and has remained well.

Solitary rectal ulcer syndrome, rectocoele, rectal prolapse, frequency

The main focus is to reduce the number of attempts to defaecate, to reduce the pressure exerted on the pelvic floor through excessive straining, and establish a better bowel routine.

Patients must not strain when opening their bowels.

Patients are advised not to digitate rectally to aid evacuation. This can exacerbate a solitary rectal ulcer.

Patients with solitary rectal ulcer syndrome, rectocoele, rectal prolapse and frequency are advised to only attempt defaecation a maximum of 3 times daily. This should be after mealtimes. This reduction on attempts should lessen the pressure in the rectum and vagina. Ultimately the aim is for patients to have a bowel action 1–2 times daily. Patients with an ileoanal pouch are advised to attempt to empty between 4–6 times in 24 hours.

- The patient may need to find distractions to prevent more frequent attempts in the toilet, e.g. go for a walk or make a telephone call.
- Time spent at each attempt in the toilet should be a maximum of 10 minutes.
- To help to reduce the feeling of pressure in the rectum and/or vagina, the patient is instructed to pull the muscles of the rectum and vagina inwards and upwards and hold for 10 seconds. This is particularly useful before lifting an object, or coughing and sneezing.
- Some women find if they support their perineum during defaecation it helps. It may

also help to digitate per vagina. This will assist emptying of the rectocoele. Patients should be informed that further damage will not be caused by doing this.

Case history: Solitary rectal ulcer syndrome and rectal prolapse

John, aged 21, was referred from a consultant surgeon with solitary rectal ulcer syndrome and rectal prolapse. This had been confirmed histologically. John had ano-rectal physiological tests which were normal. John said his main problem was he had to open his bowels 15 times daily, and his rectal prolapse occurred during defaecation and on exercise which was interfering with his job as a soldier. He had been taken off active duty.

Bowel assessment

- John experienced a constant urge to defaecate
- He opened his bowels 15 times each day
- Blood was passed with each bowel action
- Mucus was passed with each bowel action, and also when his rectum prolapsed at other times
- He had a sensation of incomplete evacuation after each bowel action
- He strained at each attempt to defaecate.

John demonstrated inco-ordination of his defaecatory muscles at initial examination.

Programme set

1) Only attempt to have a bowel action 3 times daily at the most
2) No longer than 10 minutes each attempt
3) No straining, use the 'brace' technique.

After three appointments, at monthly intervals:

- John experienced an urge to defaecate prior to opening his bowel
- He opened his bowels once each day
- No blood was passed
- No mucus was passed
- No sensation of incomplete evacuation
- He didn't strain, but pushed effectively
- His rectum did not prolapse any more
- He returned to normal duty.

John was discharged 18 months ago and has remained well.

A solitary rectal ulcer can take a long time to heal, so patients are usually reviewed in the Outpatient department to allow the ulcer to be monitored. Some patients can relapse with time and revert back to disordered defaecation. A group of patients were reviewed up to 36 months following discharge from the biofeedback clinic. Twelve patients were available for review from the original thirteen. Eight patients had previously felt 'cured' or 'improved'. At review, only half the patients felt this improvement had been maintained. The conclusions drawn from this study are all patients with a solitary rectal ulcer may benefit from having a 'refresher session' to maintain benefit (Malouf et al., 2001).

Follow-up appointments

It is important that the patient attends regularly so that the therapist can monitor the progress made. At each appointment the same questions are asked to monitor symptom improvement, and the co-ordination of the defaecatory muscles is assessed by using balloon expulsion. Patients can contact the therapist by telephone between scheduled appointments should they have any concerns. Symptoms may initially become worse, especially if patients have been accustomed to high-dose laxatives, and patients need encouragement to persevere with the therapy.

Psychological issues

If patients have experienced any type of abuse they may cite this as the cause of their problem. Some people may wish to discuss this immediately with the therapist, others may bring the subject up at a future session. There are some who may never feel able to discuss such events. It is essential that psychological referrals can be made should the need arise. If patients disclose for the first time that they have been raped or abused, it is important to be able to offer them professional help should they need it. If referrals can not be made it is perhaps not prudent to offer biofeedback therapy.

If psychological support is required this can sometimes run concurrently with the biofeedback therapy. Patients can have the practical treatment for their physical problem, and also take active steps to tackle their psychological problems. Sometimes the biofeedback therapy will need to be suspended, depending on the severity or nature of the psychological problem.

It is worth noting that other psychosocial issues, e.g. a bereavement, may also be a relevant factor to the patient's bowel problem and may also need addressing through counselling or psychotherapy.

Discharge

When patients are discharged it is important that they continue with the biofeedback exercise programme and do not return to their former dysfunctional evacuation behaviour. It can take up to twelve months for patients to gain maximum benefit from this treatment. Sometimes patients need 'refresher sessions' to remind them what to do.

If the biofeedback therapy fails, patients can be offered an appointment for review in the Outpatient department. These patients usually need conservative management of their residual symptoms. What they have learnt with biofeedback therapy is insight into their condition, and a better ability to cope with their symptoms.

Efficacy of feedback for evacuation disorders

When the condition of paradoxical puborectalis contraction or 'anismus' during defaecation was first recognised (Preston and Lennard-Jones, 1985), biofeedback to teach the patient to relax instead of contract was seen as a promising method of treatment (Enck, 1993; Lancet, 1992; Turnbull and Ritvo, 1962). There has since been a large number of studies reported, mostly with positive results whatever method of 'biofeedback' was used (Glia et al., 1997; Karlbom et al., 1997; Ko et al., 1997; Patankar et al., 1997). However, a few have reported that it did not help the majority of patients (Keck et al., 1994; Rieger et al., 1997). There have been almost no studies with a genuine control group. One controlled study in children found that biofeedback gave no added benefit when compared with well-monitored conventional treatment (van der Plas et al., 1996), and one study in adults found no benefit from using a visual display to teach exercise over verbal instruction alone (Koutsomanis et al., 1995).

Conclusions

Behavioural retraining and/or 'biofeedback' has been found to be of at least some benefit in the majority of reports to date. However, good controlled trials are needed to determine whether it is the feedback, the exercises, or general information and support that is the most important in determining the outcome.

References

Chiotakakou-Faliakou, E., Kamm, M.A., Roy, A.J., Storrie, J.B. and Turner, I.C. (1998) Biofeedback provides long term benefit for patients with intractable, slow and normal transit constipation. *Gut* **42**, 517–521.

Drossman, D.A., Leserman, J., Nachman, G., Li, Z.M., Ghuck, H., Toomy, T.C. and Mitchell, C.M. (1990) Sexual and physical abuse in women with functional or organic gastrointestinal disorders. *Annals of Internal Medicine* **113**, 828–833.

Emmanuel, A.V. and Kamm, M.A. (2001) Response to a behavioural treatment, biofeedback in constipated patients is associated with improved gut transit and autonomic innervation. *Gut* **49**, 2, 214–219.

Enck, P. (1993) Biofeedback training in disordered defaecation. A critical review. *Digestive Diseases and Sciences* **38**, 11, 1953–1960.

Evans, R.C., Kamm, M.A., Hinton, J.M. and Lennard-Jones, J.E. (1992) The normal range and a simple diagram for recording whole gut transit time. *International Journal of Colorectal Diseases* **7**, 15–17.

Glia, A., Gylin, M., Gullberg, K. and Lindberg, G. (1997) Biofeedback retraining in patients with functional constipation and paradoxical puborectalis contraction. *Diseases of the Colon and Rectum* **40** 889–895.

Kamm, M.A., Hawley, P.R. and Lennard-Jones, J.E. (1988) The outcome of colectomy for severe idiopathic constipation. *Gut* **29**, 969–973.

Karlbom, U., Hallden, M., Eeg-Olofsson, K.E. Pahlman, L. and Graf, W. (1997) Results of biofeedback in constipated patients. *Diseases of the Colon and Rectum* **40** 1149–1155.

Keck, J.O., Staniunas, R.J., Coller, J.A., Barrett, R.C., Oster, M.E., Schoetz, D.J., Roberts, P.L., Murray, J.J. and Veidenheimer, M.C. (1994) Biofeedback training is useful in faecal incontinence but disappointing in constipation. *Diseases of the Colon and Rectum* **37** 1271–1276

Klauser, A.G., Voderholzer, W.A., Heinrich, C.A., Schindlebech, N.E. and Muller-Lissner, S.A. (1990) Behavioural modification of colonic function. *Digestive Diseases and Sciences* **35**, 1271–1276.

Ko, C.Y., Tong, J., Lehman, R.E., Shelton, A.A., Schrock, T.R. and Welton, M.L. (1997) Biofeedback is effective therapy for fecal incontinence and constipation. *Archives of Surgery* **132** 8, 829–833.

Koutsomanis, D., Lennard-Jones, J.E., Roy, A.J. and Kamm, M.A. (1995) Controlled randomised trial of visual biofeedback versus muscle training without a visual display for intractable constipation. *Gut* **37**, 95–99.

Lancet (1992) Editorial: anismus and biofeedback. *Lancet* **339** 217–218.

Malouf, A.J., Vaizey, C.J. and Kamm, M.A. (2001) Results of behavioural treatment (biofeedback) for solitary rectal ulcer syndrome. *Diseases of the Colon and Rectum* **44**, 72–76.

Miller, N.E. and DiCara, L.V. (1968) Instrumental learning of heart rate changes in curarised rats: shaping and specificity to discriminate stimulus. *Journal of Comparative and Physiological Psychology* **63**, 12–19.

Mimura, T., Roy, A.J., Storrie, J.B. and Kamm, M.A. (2000) Treatment of impaired defaecation associated with rectocoele by behavioural retraining (biofeedback). *Diseases of the Colon and Rectum* **43**, 9, 1267–72.

Mimura, T., Nicholls, T., Storrie, J.B. and Kamm, M.A. Treatment of constipation in adults associated with idiopathic megarectum by behavioural retaining (biofeedback). (Unpublished data, St Mark's Hospital)

Patankar, S.K., Ferrara, A., Levy, J.R., Larach, S.W., Williamson, P.R. and Perozo, S.E. (1997) Biofeedback in colorectal practice: a multicenter, statewide, three-year experience. *Diseases of the Colon and Rectum* **40**, 7, 827–831.

Preston, D.M. and Lennard-Jones, J.E. (1985) Anismus in chronic constipation. *Digestive Diseases and Sciences* **30**, 5, 413–418.

Rieger, N.A., Wattchow, D.A., Sarre, R.G., Saccone, G.T.P., Rich, C.A., Cooper, S.J., Marshall, V.R. and McCall, J.L. (1997) Prospective study of biofeedback for treatment of constipation. *Diseases of the Colon and Rectum* **40**, 1143–1148.

Storrie, J.B. (1997) Biofeedback: a first-line treatment for idiopathic constipation. *British Journal of Nursing* **6**, 152–158.

Turnbull, G.K. and Ritvo, P.G. (1992) Anal sphincter biofeedback relaxation treatment for women with intractable constipation symptoms. *Diseases of the Colon and Rectum*, **35**, 530–536.

Vaizey, C.J., Roy, A.J. and Kamm, M.A. (1997) Prospective evaluation of the treatment of solitary rectal ulcer syndrome with biofeedback. *Gut* **41**, 817–820.

van der Plas, R.N., Benninga, M.A., Buller, H.A., Bossuyt, P.M.. Akkermans, L.M., Redekop, W.K. and Taminiau, J.A. (1996) Biofeedback training in treatment of childhood constipation: a randomised controlled study. *Lancet* **348**, 9030, 776–780.

Wiesel, P.H., Norton, C., Roy, A.J., Storrie, J.B., Bowers, J. and Kamm, M.A. (2000) Gut focused behavioural treatment (biofeedback) for constipation and faecal incontinence in multiple sclerosis. *Journal of Neurology, Neurosurgery and Psychiatry* **69**, 2, 240–243.

Chapter 23

Making Toilets More Accessible for Individuals with a Disability

Helen White

Introduction

Faecal incontinence is common in disabled people of all ages. People with functional impairment and problems with dexterity, balance or mobility, and who may also have a neuropathic bowel (Chapter 17), may be at special risk, but incontinence is not inevitable. An assessment of the functional and psychosocial needs of the individual by a skilled occupational therapist working with the continence nurse, together with the provision of appropriate advice or equipment, can greatly minimise this risk. Care pathways to encourage this multiprofessional approach are being developed nationally (Cowley, 2001).

This chapter describes good practice for accessible toilet facilities and explores the range of equipment and resources available for disabled people to achieve optimum independence and bowel control.

Environmental issues and continence

The consequences of faecal incontinence and their effects on quality of life have been well described in Chapter 5. Environmental factors often trigger faecal incontinence in people who normally have complete bowel control. Inaccessible and unacceptable lavatories are major problems. Poor sign-posting, ambiguous toilet signs, a flight of steep stairs, a doorway too narrow to admit a walking aid or wheelchair, or an inward-opening door in a cubicle toilet which is too small to admit a disabled person with a carer, are obvious barriers to easy access. Essential journeys to the shops, visits to friends, outings to the pub or an evening at the theatre all have to be carefully planned around accessible toilet facilities. Holidays at home or abroad can be a nightmare for even the most stalwart traveller, and many disabled people avoid them altogether. Airlines and rail companies continue to lag behind in providing appropriate toilet facilities for able as well as disabled travellers.

Problems are not confined to public places. Access to lavatories in hospital, residential and home settings can prove impossible for people with poor mobility or balance problems, and for those confined to a wheelchair. Hospitals are major offenders. Travers et al. (1992) found toilet facilities in one teaching hospital to be woefully inadequate, the worst toilets being on a ward for elderly people. As none were suitable for disabled patients, commodes had been substituted. Unpublished surveys in other areas have reached similar conclusions. Practice will have to change with the implementation of the Disability Discrimination Act (1995). The risk of falling is a real fear in older people, to the extent that they may be reluctant of get out of chair to walk to the toilet or sit correctly on the toilet (Downton 1993).

The taboos and inhibitions connected with bowels and toileting in our multicultural society must be addressed, and provision made for religious and cultural needs. Douching facilities are necessary for Muslims, who cleanse with water instead of paper after a bowel movement, and generally a wash basin within a toilet cubicle is essential for individuals who suffer from incontinence. Access to a unisex toilet is needed by disabled people accompanied by a carer of the opposite sex, and appropriate changing facilities for children and adults. Disposal units in all male and female toilets need to be standard practice.

The British Toilet Association (see Appendix II) is vigorously campaigning for accessible lavatories and changing facilities for disabled people and their carers. The implementation of the Human Rights Act 1998 will help to strengthen these peoples' rights.

Improvements in toilet facilities in public places, at school and in the home are being made. Since 2000, all new dwellings, public and private, must be wheelchair accessible. The Department of the Environment, Transport and Regions in their Building Regulations 2000 give guidance on toilet design for disabled people. The British Standards Institute has revised Part 2 of BS 6465 (1996), which covers the provision of sanitary facilities in public buildings, and recommends at least one unisex facility in a range of public amenities. The Centre for Accessible Environment's (1988) guidelines on design for lavatories remain applicable today. Anybody installing a public toilet for disabled people may subscribe to The National Key Scheme (NKS) administered by the Royal Association for Disability (RADAR; see Appendix II). This system provides nationwide access to disabled toilets – individuals subscribe for a key as these toilets are kept locked as a protection against vandalism. RADAR also publishes a location guide to accessible toilets (RADAR 2001).

Funding is available from the Department of Education and Employment Service to adapt existing premises for people working or about to work, and in 2002 this will be extended to all education premises under the Disability Discrimination Act (1995). In certain circumstances, people living at home can apply for a Disabled Facilities Grant from the local authority to build a new bathroom where existing facilities are inaccessible.

Public and private toilets – a guide to good practice

Lavatories concern us all, and for disabled people and those who spend a long time opening their bowels, they can be the focal point in their life. Faeces or soiled tissue which does not flush away is embarrassing. A brightly lit, warm toilet with good ventilation, an effective easy-to-flush system and privacy are fundamental requirements for all.

The following are points of good practice:

- Clear sign-posting with easily recognisable symbols are helpful for people with visual or cognitive or any communication impairment.
- A level or ramped approach makes for easy wheelchair access. If there are stairs, handrails should be provided, and in some situations installing a lift may be a cheaper than building a new toilet.
- Easy-to-open doors which will stay open at 90 degrees with a clear wall space on the side of the opening allows for manoeuvrability. Handles, locks and rails should be large enough to grab easily, light to use with minimal strength, and low enough to reach easily from a wheelchair. Lever handles are easier to operate than knob handles.
- Non-slip, easily cleaned floor coverings give confidence for people with balance problems and those using walking frames or wheelchairs.
- Comfortable temperature encourages regular toileting. Low-energy bulbs and lights with an integral heater provides warmth and light. An overheated toilet can be as uncomfortable as a cold one.
- Natural or mechanical ventilation minimises lingering odours. Aerosol air fresheners mask rather than remove smells and can be as unpleasant as the smell you wish to remove.
- Grab rails within reach when on the toilet give extra confidence to people with balance and spatial awareness problems, and can aid getting on and off the toilet.
- Shaped, padded toilet seats fitted correctly provide extra stability for transfers. The moulding of ergonomically shaped seats can be extremely uncomfortable and cause pressure for people who can only transfer askew onto the seat.

- Flushing systems with an easy handle at a height between 900 mm and 1050 mm are acceptable. Button push or pull handles or the narrow standard lever handles can be difficult for people with impaired dexterity. Spatulate lever handles which can be depressed by either the hand or elbow are easier to manage for people with weakened wrists; as is a foot action flushing mechanism for some people in wheelchairs.
- Toilet-paper holders need to be positioned within easy reach when sitting on the toilet and not on the back of the toilet door.
- Hand-washing facilities with lever taps or foot mechanisms are easier for people with limited hand movement. Mixer taps with premixed water are safer for frail people. Hand dryers can be problematical as an alternative to roller or paper towels in communal settings.
- Supplies of cleaning implements and materials should be readily available at all times and in all settings, as people with balance or mobility problems may accidentally soil the toilet area.

Accessible toilets – designs and recommendations

Figures 23.1 and 23.2 (overleaf) show a cubicle layout to accommodate wheelchair and ambulant users. Unless the cubicle space is large, the door should open outwards or slide, because an inward-opening door takes up too much space. Handles, locks and rails should be large enough to grasp easily, light enough to use with minimal strength, and low enough to use easily from a wheelchair. A cubicle of at least 1.5 m x 2 m should allow transfer from a wheelchair either from in front or from the side. Some people can stand and turn with the chair either from the front or from the side. Some people can stand and turn with the wheelchair in front of the toilet; others prefer to remove one arm from the chair and transfer sideways. A few people, such as those with a double-amputation, transfer sideways or at a 90° angle using a wide transfer board. Wheelchair users require the height of the seat to be 475 mm from the floor to the top of the seat.

Alternatives to the toilet

At present there is no neat receptacle for faeces comparable to a hand-held urinal. A light-weight simple plastic potty is useful for able-bodied users but is not suitable for people with functional impairment. A person sitting in a wheelchair can use a pan-type container by inserting it from behind. Some people improvise with a bucket placed under a toilet frame. Commodes can provide an immediate solution for an inaccessible toilet. Chemical toilets and commodes may be a quicker and cheaper alternative to adapting an existing, or building a new, toilet. However, these alternatives are not always acceptable. Naylor and Mulley (1993) found that some people disliked the idea of a commode in the living area or bedroom, especially if there were other people around.

Commodes and chemical toilets

The potential benefits of a commode or chemical toilet to an immobile user with urgent and frequent bowel movements may outweigh the embarrassment of having to depend on a carer to empty it. The style of commode will depend on personal needs, the location in which it will be used, and where it will be stored when not in use (Table 23.1, overleaf). The commode-type chemi-loo with an extra large bucket only needs emptying once or twice a week. Wooden or fabric-covered commodes may be more acceptable at home than the fully adjustable, easily stackable type for communal use in hospital and residential settings. Mobile commodes and sanichairs (Figure 23.3, page 272) can also be used for bathing, but may be cumbersome in smaller, private accommodation. Brakes fitted to the castors provide maximum safety. A chemical commode, as used in camping, may be more acceptable for people with bowel problems, but can be difficult to operate by a user with poor hand function. The

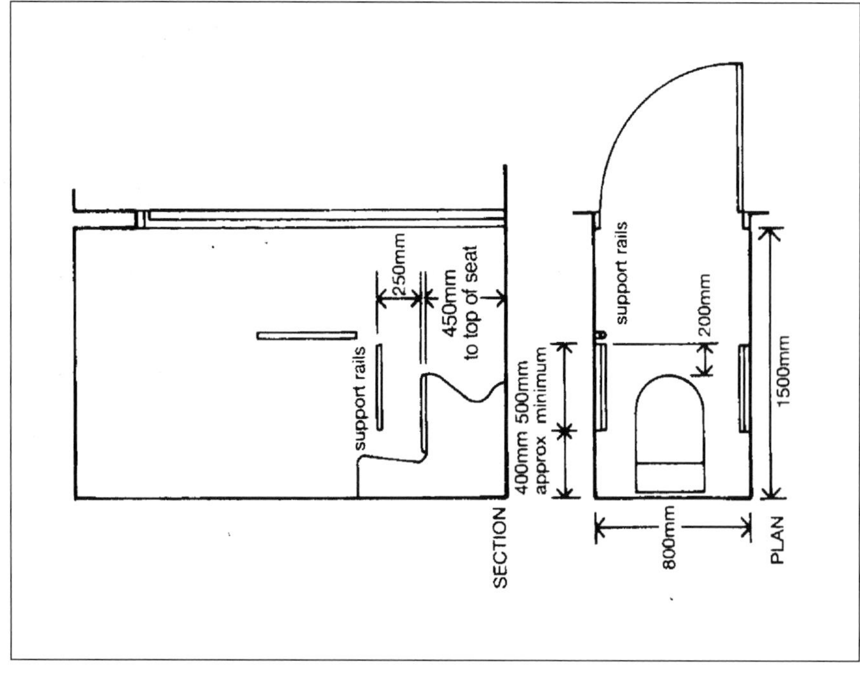

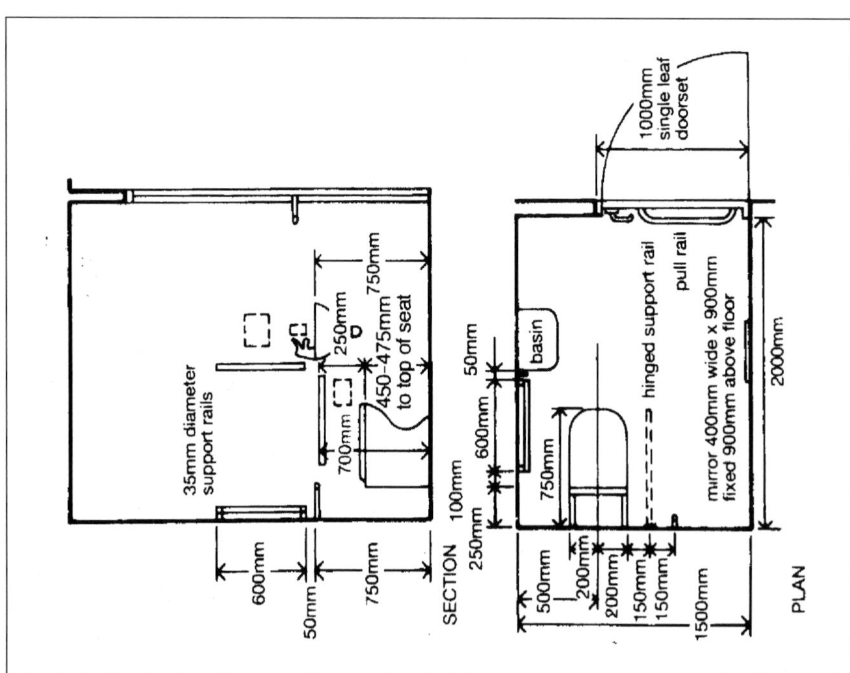

Figures 23.1 and 23.2 *Toilet design from DoE.* (Crown copyright material is reproduced with the permission of the Controller of HMSO and the Queen's Printer for Scotland.)

Table 23.1: Requirements and specifications for commode use

Users' Requirements	Specifications
Height and weight	Very short / tall people or those over 20 stone (127 kg) in weight may require specialised / modified equipment.
Mobility, stability and dexterity	Maintain independence for sitting, standing and cleaning whilst transferring from and to whilst transferring from and to the chair / bed. Removable or adjustable arms: essential for users who transfer sideways. Splayed legs and the back of the commode placed against a wall give extra stability. Some commodes can be fixed to a bed. A cut-away seat is easier for cleansing or performing manual evacuation. Sturdy brakes.
Posture, comfort and degree of muscular control	Cushions may help to position the user, but if in doubt never leave a user unattended. Comfort of seat back and arm rests. Straps and harnesses are no longer encouraged.
Emptying and cleaning of commode	Difficult for users with impaired dexterity or frail carers – it is advisable to check who will have this responsibility. Seat aperture: compatible with the container to minimise risks of soiling commode or carpet. Container: oval-shaped, plastic containers with two handles. Easy to remove, clean and replace.

Portapotty is available with a frame for extra support and can be dismantled for travelling. The final decision on the model should be made by the user, as a disliked product might not be used.

Accessories for the toilet

The range of equipment is extensive, and communally used lavatories will require equipment which is adjustable to allow for people's individual needs. At home the size of the toilet, and space to store these accessories whilst other people are using the facilities, both need to be considered.

Illustrations and details of the various types are given in Equipment for Disabled People Personal Care (1996) and the Disabled Living Foundation (DLF) Hamilton Index Part 3 Section 14, Toilet Equipment and Accessories (2001) (see Appendix II).

Toilet seats and supports

Specialised toilet seats are available with a range of specialised features, and some are supplied in a variety of colours. The Ergosit toilet seat is designed to support all sizes as well as stimulate bowel movement. The Commode bath hoist cushion fits on both toilet and commode seats and has straps for extra security. The Readywarm is an electrically heated seat with a lid providing a warm backrest when raised.

Raised seats attached to the toilet bowl are helpful for people with painful or stiff joints, where a grab rail is not sufficient. It is important that an accompanying foot support to raise the knees and support the feet in the correct position is provided. Seats vary between 450–550 mm, depending on the height of the user. Frailer people will require styles which can be easily secured for stability. Wobbly seats are unnerving and can be dangerous. The Ashby and Derby seats are available with a bidet. The Taunton has a longer aperture than most seats, making it easier for personal cleansing.

Self-raising seats suit people who have limited movement. Extra care is needed with light and frail users. The Looeez is manually-operated and the Solo Toilet Lift is power-operated.

Frames to fit over the toilet may be free-standing or fixed to the floor for stability. The choice will depend on the weight and balance of the user. The Stirling Frame is available in a variety of heights, extra width for the larger user, and with drop-down arms for easier transfer and stability. Many frames are also suitable for commodes.

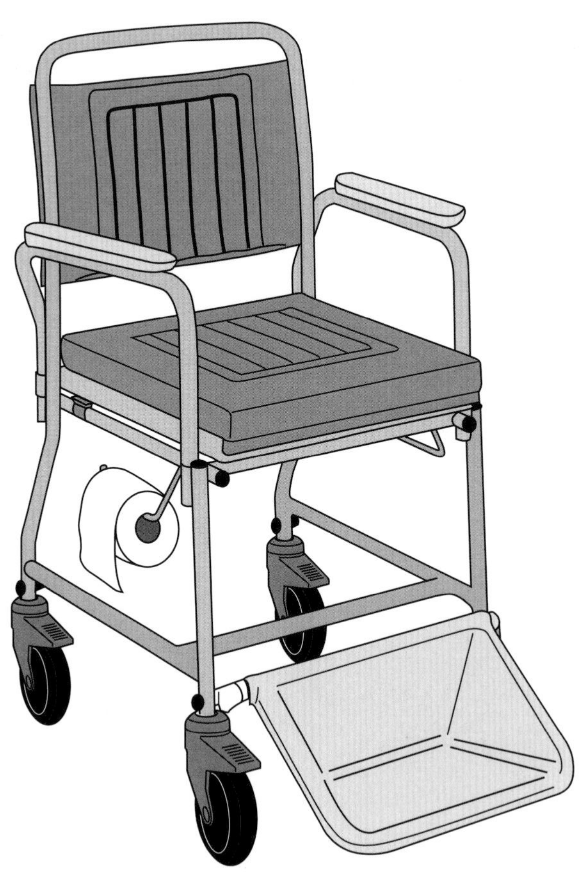

Figure 23.3 *Sanichair.*

Hygiene appliances

Cleansing after a bowel movement can be problematic for any person with a functional impairment. Depending on the degree of impairment and personal preference, equipment ranges from a simple hand-held bottom wiper to a sophisticated toilet with an automatic washing and drying system. Toilet tissue paper holders are handy for people with limited reach and hand function. It is important to check it is positioned on the appropriate side of the toilet.

Bottom wipers are easier to use sitting on an open or cut-front toilet seat. Single sheets of toilet paper or large three-ply tissues or moist, alcohol-free wipes are fitted on to or wrapped around the bottom-wiper (women cleaning from front to back) (Figure 23.4). A wall bracket is available for storage.

Portable bidets provide a relatively quick, easy and cheap solution. The lightweight plastic oval bowl fits over a standard toilet pan. Models vary from a simple bowl which is filled with warm water, placed over the pan, with the water tipped into the toilet pan after cleansing, to more complicated models with attachments to a separate water system and a drain away. Bidets are not suitable for people unable to part their legs. Special models with higher seats for ambulant people to get on and off easily, are available. Wheelchair users will require the height of the bidet to be the same as the wheelchair for easy transfer.

A combined bidet and toilet with a douche is available. Warm water automatically washes and warm air dries the anal area. The water and drying spray requires positioning to the user's anal area. The system may be operated by a flush handle, hand- or foot-operated switches or a back bar, depending on the needs of the individual. Models are available mounted on the floor or wall. A separate wash / dry system can be added to an existing toilet but must conform to the local water bylaw. Again, the height of the bidet is important for wheelchair users.

Disposal units, or a large airtight container such as the Sangenic Easiseal system for soiled disposable incontinence products, should be provided as necessary.

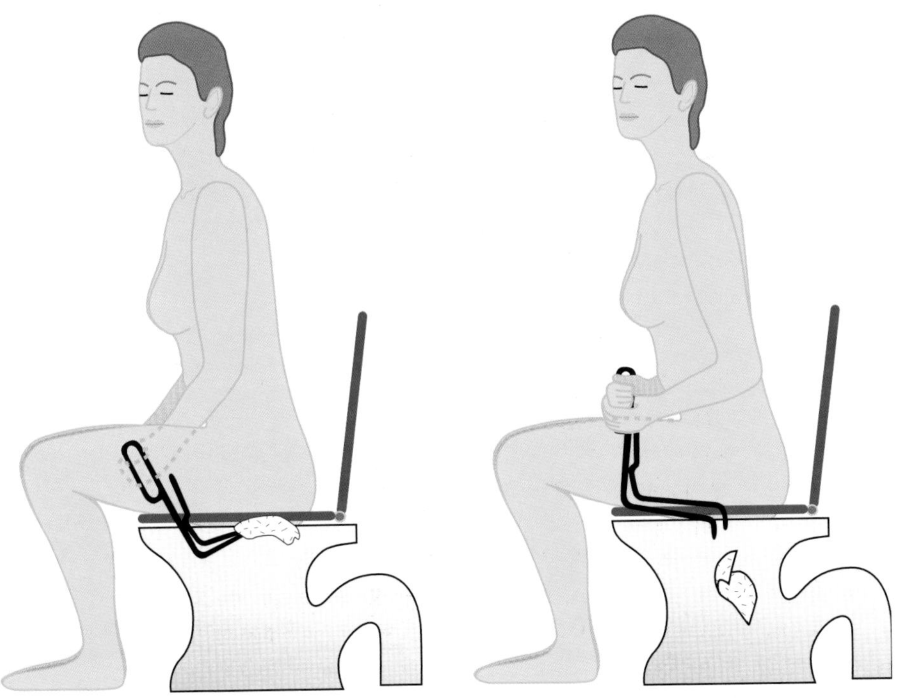

Figure 23.4 *Bottom wiper.*

Obtaining and supplying equipment

Finding appropriate equipment is time consuming, and purchasing the wrong equipment can be a costly mistake. In hospital the Occupational Therapy Department can assess and advise both for hospital and home needs. People living at home can contact their local Social Services Department for an assessment by an Occupational Therapist. Selected items of equipment may be provided free of charge depending on the local policy, but many services offer a restricted range with a long waiting list. Clarification on instructions, maintenance and the overall responsibility of the care of the product is particularly important for disabled users. Inappropriate equipment, unauthorised modifications and poor maintenance are causes for litigation. The Provision and Use of Work Equipment Regulations (1998) give guidelines on good practice.

Increasingly, people are choosing to purchase their own equipment. Price is not an indication of performance. Personal purchasers should be encouraged to 'try before they buy'. Disabled Living Centres (DLCs) – alternatively known as Independent Living Centres or Disability Resource Centres – provide impartial and free information and advice on equipment and products for easier living. The DLCs carry displays of up-to-date equipment which disabled people and their carers can try. There are over 40 centres in the UK and many display core products for continence management (address from DLCC, see Appendix II). Staff liaise with the local health and social service and in some cases may be able to arrange a home visit.

In some instances where the disability may be so profound that appropriate equipment is not available, Remap – (Technical Equipment for Disabled People – Appendix II) a voluntary national organisation of engineers, medical and paramedical professionals who specialise in designing, making or adapting existing products, will modify or make individualised equipment.

Conclusions

Loss of bowel control has devastating consequences on the lives of disabled and elderly frail people, their family and friends. Opportunities to reduce the incidence of bowel problems, constipation in particular, and to improve the quality of care and life for these people are immense. This chapter has described some of the environmental factors and equipment required to improved access to toilet facilities and the relevant professional and government agencies who can help. Implementing change to bring about these improvements may be daunting to the busy nurse. Collaborative working with colleagues from other professions can improve our quality of care and be rewarding to our patients and to ourselves.

References

British Standards Institution (1996) *BS 6465 Part 2*. London: BSI.

Centre for Accessible Environments (1988) *Good Loo Guide*. London: CAE.

Cowley, T.A. (in preparation) *Education and Integration*. Manchester: PromoCon.

Department of Education and Employment (1998) *Access to work through adaptations*. Department of Education and Employment Services. London: HMSO.

Department of Environment, Transport and Regions (1999) *Approved Document M – access and facilities for disabled people*. London: HMSO.

Department of Environment, Transport and Regions (2000) *Building regulations* (2000 SI 2531). London: DoE.

Department of Environment, Transport and Regions (2002) *Disabled facilities grant*. London: DoE.

Disability Discrimination Act (1995) *Part 3: disabled people's rights of access to goods and services*. London: HMSO.

Disabled Living Foundation (2000) *All dressed up*. London: DLF.

Downton, J.H. (1993) *Falls in the elderly*. London: Edward Arnold.

Equipment for Disabled People (1996) *Personal care* (7th edn). Mary Marlborough Centre, Nuffield Orthopaedic Centre, Oxford OX3 7LD.

Health and Safety Commission (1992) *Provision and use of work equipment regulations L22*. London: HMSO.

Home Office (1998) *The Human Rights Act*. London: HMSO.

Naylor, J.R. and Mulley, G.P. (1993) Commodes: inconvenient conveniences. *British Medical Journal* **307**, 1258–1260.

Provision and Use of Work Equipment Regulations (PUWER) (1998) *HSE books – safe use of work equipment – approved code of practice and guidance.* PO Box 1999, Sudbury, Suffolk, CO10 6FS. (www.hse.gov.uk)

Royal Association for Disability and Rehabilitation (2001) *National Key Scheme Guide*. London: RADAR.

Travers, A.F., Burns, E., Penn, N.D., Mitchell, S.C. and Mulley, G.P. (1992) A survey of hospital toilet facilities. *British Medical Journal* **304**, 878–879.

Appendix I

Shaw's model of the nurse's effectiveness in continence care (Shaw, C., Williams, K.S. and Assassa, R.P. (2000) Patients' views of a new nurse-led continence service. *Journal of Clinical Nursing*, **9**, 574–584.) See page 5 for discussion.

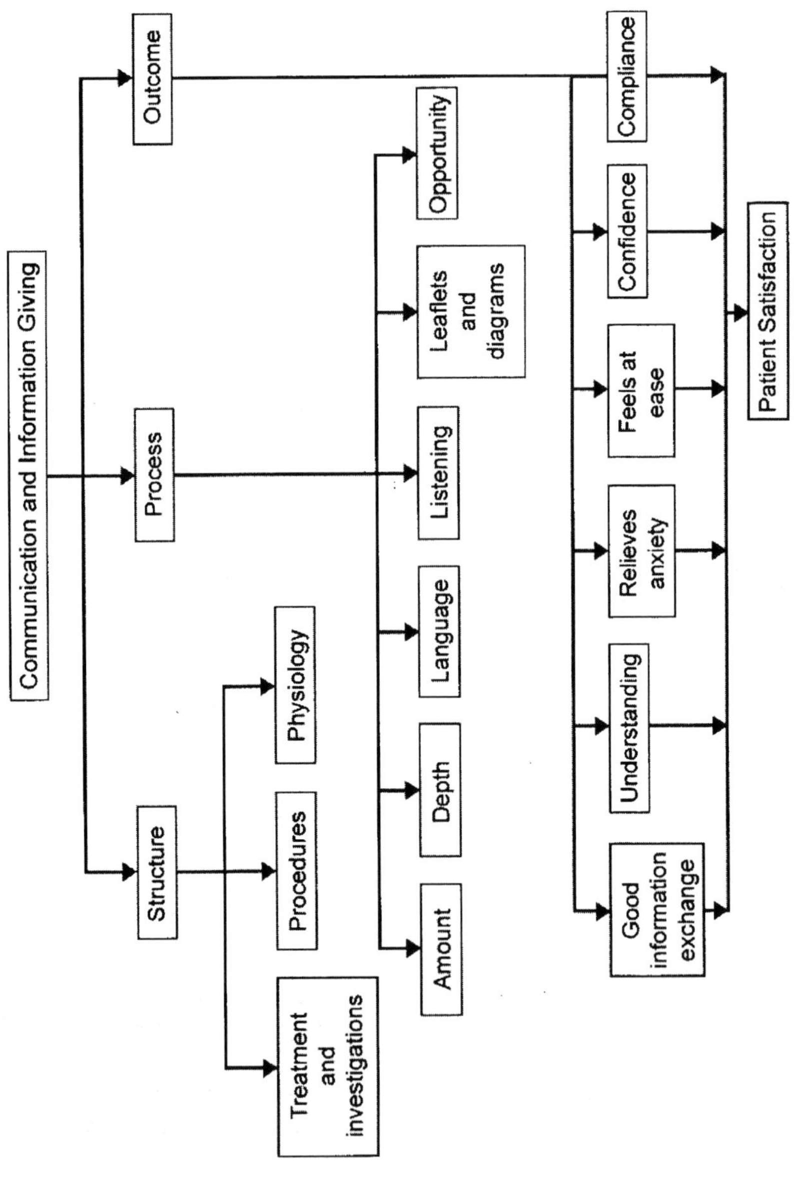

Appendix II

Useful UK Addresses

Adam, Rouilly Ltd
Crown Quay Lane
Sittingbourne ME10 3JG
Tel: 01795 471378. Fax: 01795 479787
(Anatomical models for patient teaching)

Alzheimers Disease Society
Gordon House, 10 Greencoat Place
London SW1P 1PH
Tel: 020 7306 0606
Fax: 020 7306 0808
Helpline: 0845300 0336
Email: infor@alzheimers.org.uk
Website: www.alzheimers.org.uk

Association for Continence Advice (ACA)
102a Astra House, Arklow Road
London SE14 6EB
Tel: 020 8692 4680
Fax: 020 8692 6217
Email: info@aca.uk.com
Website: www.aca.uk.com

Association of Coloproctology
of Great Britain & Ireland
c/o Association of Surgeons,
Royal College of Surgeons
Lincoln's Inn Fields, London WC2A 3PE
Tel: 020 7973 0307
Fax: 020 7430 9235
Email: acpgbi@asgbi.org.uk
Website: www.acpgbi.org.uk
(Nurses are entitled to join as Associate Members. Annual scientific meeting and regional group meetings)

Association to aid the sexual and personal relationships of the disabled (SPOD)
286 Camden Road, London N7 0BJ

Association for Spina Bifida and Hydrocephalus (ASBAH)
ASBAH House, 42 Park Road,
Peterborough PE1 2UQ
Tel: 01733 555988
Fax: 01733 555985
Email: gillw@asbah.org
Website: www.asbah.org

Beating Bowel Cancer
Email: info@beatingbowelcancer.org
Website: www.advocacyonline.net/bbc

Bowel Control
Website: www.bowelcontrol.org.uk
(St Mark's Hospital website for people with faecal incontinence)

B. Braun Medical Ltd
Thorncliffe Park, Sheffield S35 2PW
Tel: 0114 225 9000
Fax: 0114 225 9123
Email: opmhomecare.bbmuk@bbraun.com
Website: www.bbraun.com

British Colostomy Association (BCA)
15 Station Road
Reading RG1 1LG
Tel: 0118 9391537
Website: www.bcass.org.uk

British Toilet Association
P.O. Box 17, Winchester SO23 9WL
Tel: 01962 850277
Fax: 01962 870220
Email: enquiries@britloos.co.uk
Website: www.britloos.co.uk

City University (St Bartholomew School of Nursing)
20 Bartholomew Close, London EC1A 7QN
Tel: 020 7040 5828
Fax: 020 7040 5717
Email: Nurseweb@city.ac.uk
Website: www.city.ac.uk/barts

Coeliac UK
P.O. Box 220
High Wycombe HP11 2HY
Tel: 01494 437278
Fax: 01494 474349
Helpline: 0870 444 8804
Email: chiefexec@coeliac.co.uk
Website: www.coeliac.co.uk

Coloplast Ltd
Peterborough Business Park
Peterborough PE2 0FX
Tel: 01733 392000
Fax: 01733 233348
Website: www.coloplast.com
(Anal plug)

Continence Foundation
307 Hatton Square, 16 Baldwins Gardens
London EC1N 7RJ
Helpline: 0207 831 9831 (Monday-Friday 9am–5pm; talk in confidence to a specialist nurse)
Email: continence.foundation@dial.pipex.com
Website: www.continence-foundation.org.uk

Continence Worldwide Website
www.continenceworldwide.org
(Links to national continence organisations in many different countries around the world)

Digestive Disorders Foundation
3 St. Andrew's Place, London NW1 4LB
Tel: 020 7486 0341
Fax: 020 7224 2012
Email: ddf@digestivedisorders.org.uk
Website: www.digestivedisorders.org.uk
(A range of information leaflets on common bowel disorders)

Disabled Living Foundation
380 – 384 Harrow Road
London W9 2HU
Tel: 0845 130 9177
Email: info@dlf.org.uk
Website: www.dlf.org.uk
(Information on equipment and resources for people with disabilities. Includes toilet aid, adaptations and alternatives)

Disabled Living Centres Council (DLCC)
Redbank House, St Chad's Street
Manchester M8 8QA
Tel: 0161 834 1044
Fax: 0161 839 0802
Email: dlcc@dlcc.co.uk
Website: www.dlcc.co.uk

ERIC (Enuresis Resource & Information Centre)
Old School House, Britannia Road
Kingswood, Bristol
BS15 8DB
Tel: 0117 960 3060
Fax: 0117 960 0401
Email: info@eric.org.uk
Website: enuresis.org.uk
(Information for children and parents with childhood soiling; helpline)

Hollister Ltd
Rectory Court, 42 Broad Street
Wokingham RG40 1AB
Tel: 0800 521 377
Email: samples.uk@hollister.com
Website: www.hollister.com

*IN*CONTACT
United House, North Road
London NW1 9DP
Tel: 020 7700 7035
Email: info@incontact.org
Website: www.incontact.demon.co.uk

IBS Network
Northern General Hospital
Sheffield S5 7AU
Website: www.uel.ac.uk/pers/C.P.Dancey/ibs.html
(Organisation for people with irritable bowel syndrome)

The Ileostomy and Internal Pouch Group
P.O. Box 132
Scunthorpe DN15 9YW
Tel: 01724 720150
www.ileostomypouch.demon.co.uk

International Foundation for Functional Gastrointestinal Disorders
IFFGD P.O. Box 17864
Milwaukee WI 53217-8076, USA
Tel: (USA) 001 414 964 1799
Fax: 001 414 964 7176
Email: iffgd@iffgd.org
Website: www.aboutincontinence.org

Multiple Sclerosis Society
23 Effie Road, Fulham
London SW6 1EE
Tel: 020 8438 0700
Helpline: 0808 800 8000
Website: wwwmssociety.org.uk

National Association for Colitis & Crohn's Disease (NACC)
PO Box 205, St. Albans AL1 1AB
Tel: 01727 844296
Fax: 01727 862550
Email: nacc@nacc.org.uk
Website:www.nacc.org.uk

Norgine Ltd
Chaplin House, Widewater Place
Moorhall Rd, Harefield UB9 6NS
Tel: 01895 826600
Fax: 01895 825865
Website: www.norgine.com
(Range of information on IBS and constipation; Bristol stool form chart)

Parkinson's Disease Society
United Scientific House
215 Vauxhall Bridge Road
London SW1V 1EJ
Tel: 020 7931 8080
Fax: 020 7233 9908
Helpline: 0808 800 0303
Email: enquiries@parkinsons.org.uk
Website: www.parkinsons.org.uk
(Understanding your bladder and bowel in Parkinson's disease)

Promocon (continence product information sheets and display)
Redbank House, St. Chad's Street
Cheetham, Manchester M8 8QA
Tel: 0161 832 3678
Fax: 0161 214 5961
Email: promocon2001@disabledliving.co.uk
Website: www.promocon2001.co.uk
REMAP
National Organiser
Igtham, Sevenoaks TN15 9AD
Tel: 01732 883818

Royal College of Nursing: Continence Forum and Gastroenterology and Stoma Care Forum
20 Cavendish Square
London W1G 0RN
Tel: 020 7409 3333
Fax: 020 7647 3458
Website: www.rcn.org.uk

Spinal Injuries Association
76 St James Lane
London N10 3DF
Tel: 0208 444 2121
Website for management of spinal bowel:
www.spinal.co.uk/help/bowl.htm (sic)

Index